How Do Predators Find Their Prey?

Biology for Kids
Children's Biology Books

BABY PROFESSOR

EDUCATION KIDS

Speedy Publishing LLC
40 E. Main St. #1156
Newark, DE 19711
www.speedypublishing.com

Oh my! The fearsome snarling of teeth and the slashing claws! Predators are hunting their prey!

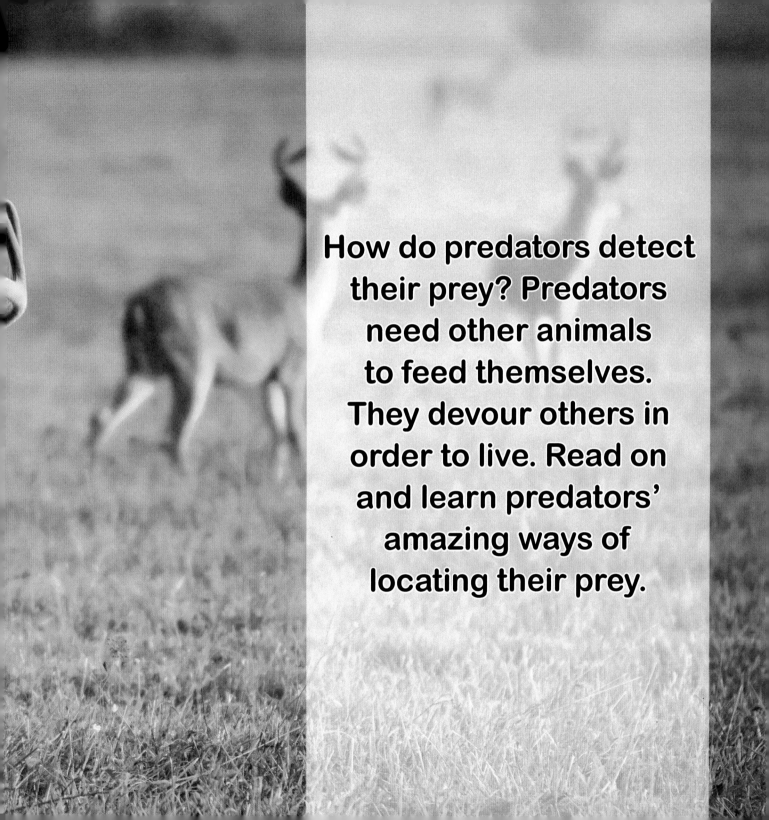

How do predators detect their prey? Predators need other animals to feed themselves. They devour others in order to live. Read on and learn predators' amazing ways of locating their prey.

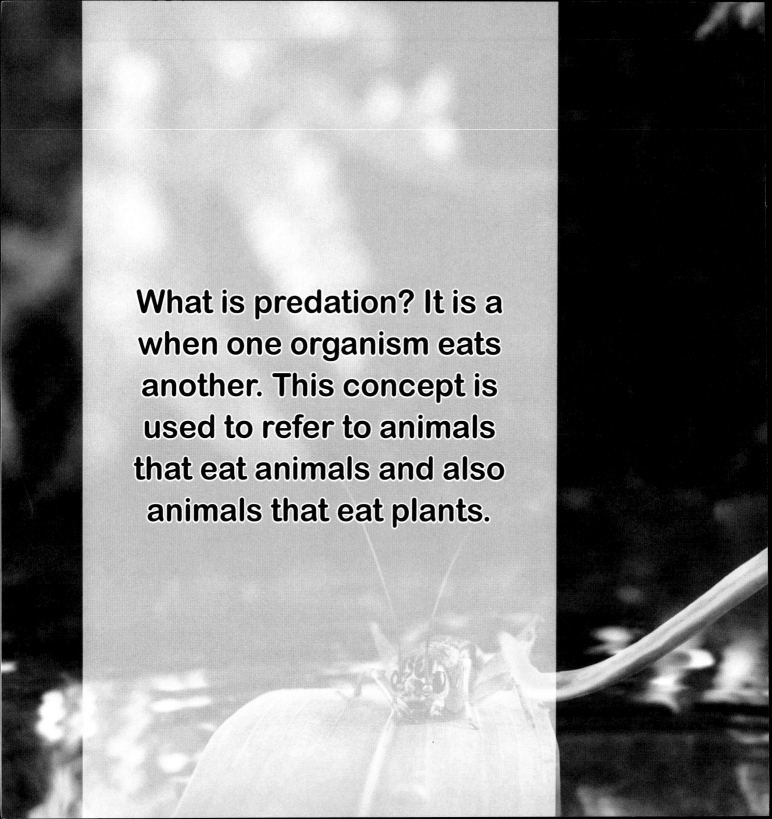

What is predation? It is a when one organism eats another. This concept is used to refer to animals that eat animals and also animals that eat plants.

What is a predator? It is an animal that devours or eats another organism of inferior strength. The prey is the helpless organism eaten by the predator.

They are able to locate their prey through sensory signals. Examples of predator-prey relationships are hawk and rodents.

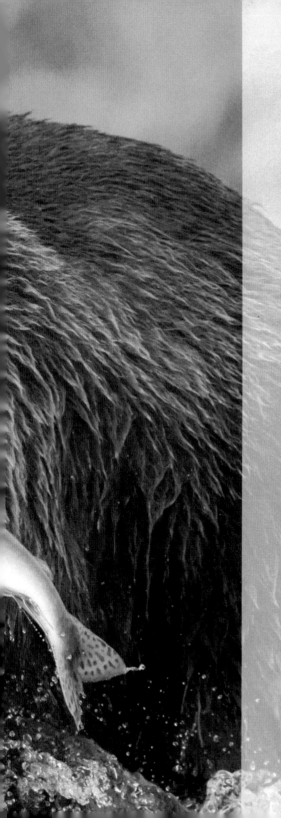

Animals who eat other animals are fierce and wild. They hunt for their meals. Examples of these wild predators are wolves, weasels, grizzly bears, and lions.

Most predators are carnivores. They feed on meat. Some are omnivores, which means they eat both plants and animals. Animals who eat only plants are also predators, but they don't have to be fierce like lions to get their dinner.

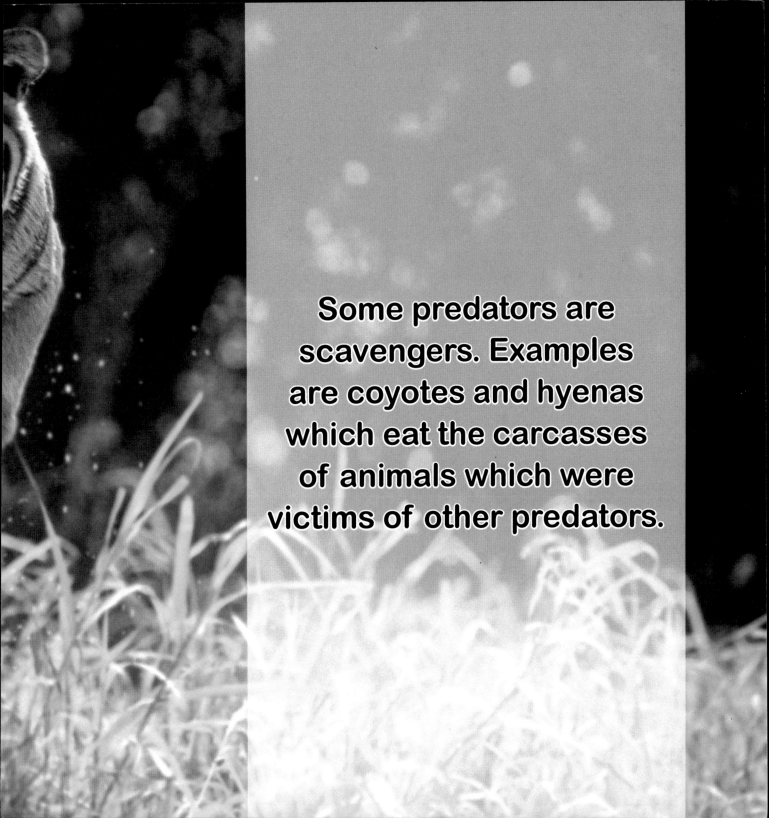

Some predators are scavengers. Examples are coyotes and hyenas which eat the carcasses of animals which were victims of other predators.

Predators have amazing hunting strategies to catch their prey. Hawks, for example, chase their prey to catch them.

Some predators stalk their prey. Examples are the herons. They stalk fish for their meals and catch their prey through their long, sharp beaks.

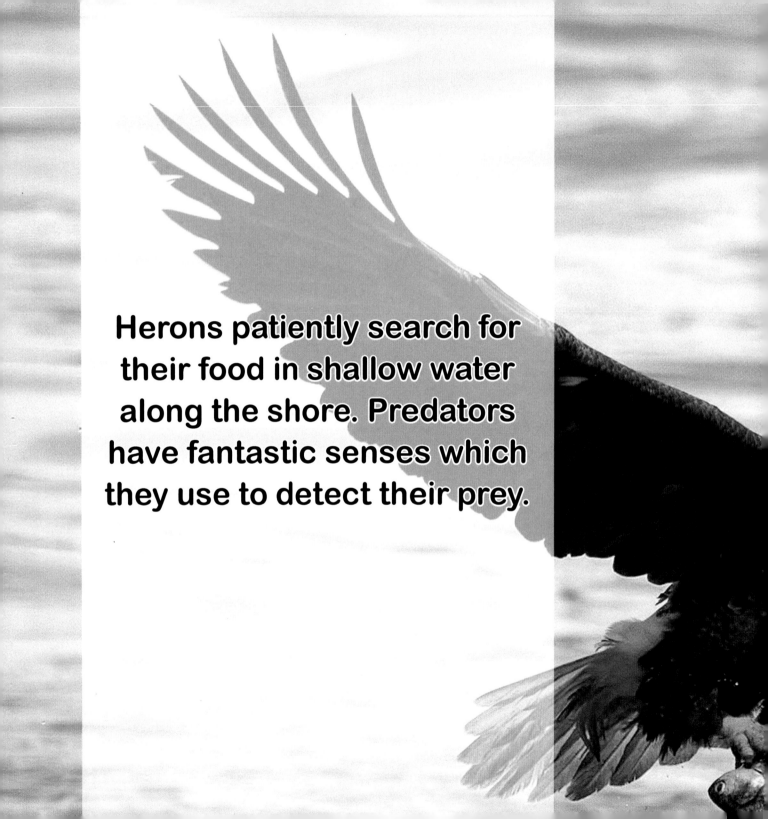

Herons patiently search for their food in shallow water along the shore. Predators have fantastic senses which they use to detect their prey.

VISION. This is the most significant sense for most predators. Predators have binocular-type vision. Their eyes are located in front of their head, facing forward. These animals are able to know how far away their prey is, and how fast it is moving.

Take for example the bird of prey's vision. It's like a telescope and is amazingly stronger than ours.

Other predators such as spiders and scorpions can easily spot their prey because they have six to eight sets of eyes. However, the spider, in spite of its eight eyes, can only see its prey if it's less than one foot away.

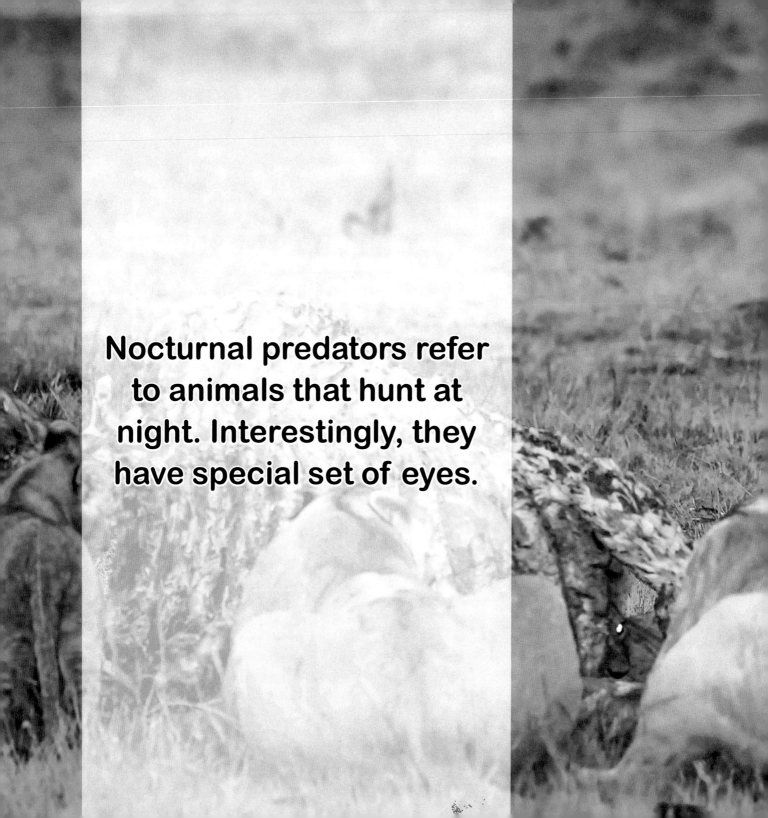

Nocturnal predators refer to animals that hunt at night. Interestingly, they have special set of eyes.

At the back of their eyes are structures which are like mirrors. These structures help them see in the dark. These structures are also found in deep sea animals.

HEARING. Predators can have an impressive sense of hearing. They find it easy to locate their prey by just locating where the sound comes from.

Mammals usually have external ear flaps. They move them forward and backward to locate the direction of the sound they want to hear.

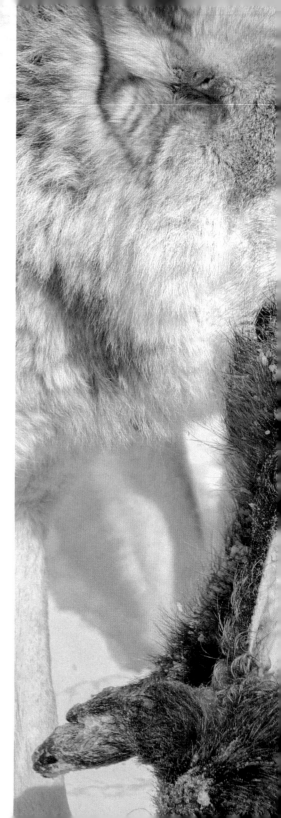

Other examples are the bats. Their ears have unusual shapes. Birds also have a very good sense of hearing. In fact, the owls have the most outstanding sense of hearing. This is because of their ear structures. One of the ears is higher than the other, which helps them know the direction of a sound.

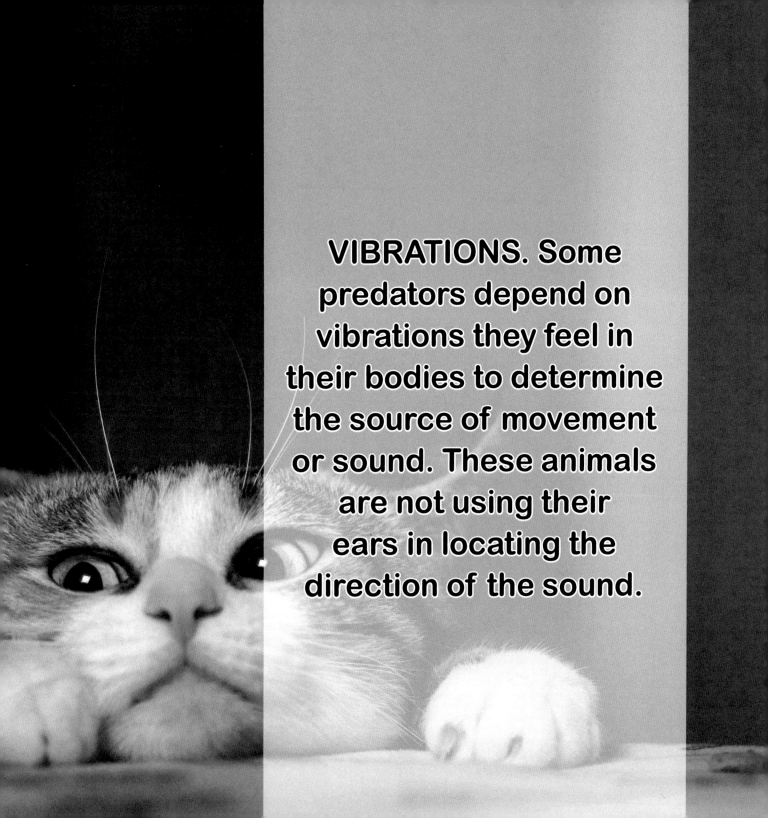

VIBRATIONS. Some predators depend on vibrations they feel in their bodies to determine the source of movement or sound. These animals are not using their ears in locating the direction of the sound.

Moving prey on the ground make vibrations. Salamanders and snakes are able to feel these vibrations.

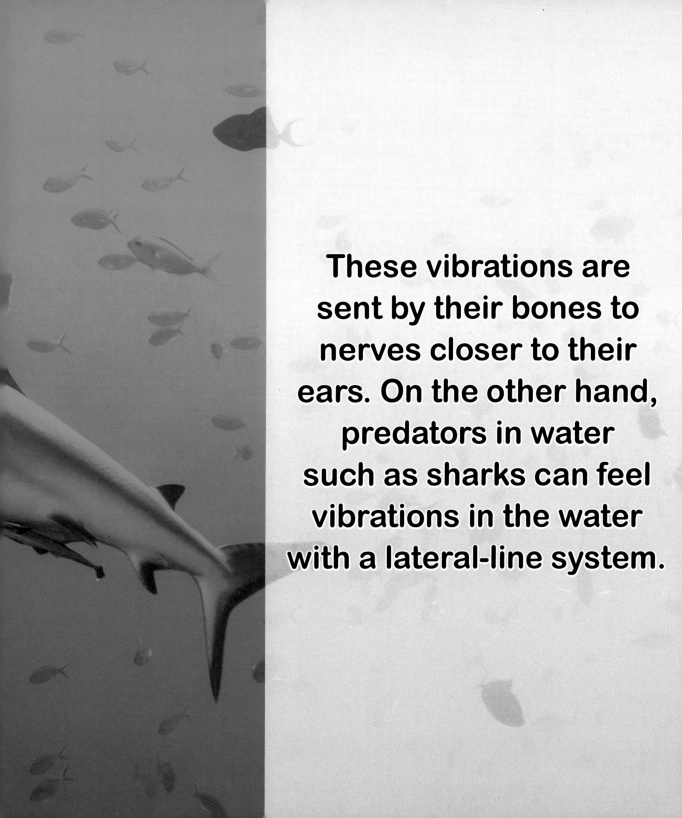

These vibrations are sent by their bones to nerves closer to their ears. On the other hand, predators in water such as sharks can feel vibrations in the water with a lateral-line system.

Beneath the skin of the shark's body are canals filled with small pores and fluid. When vibrations strike the open pores, the shark learns where its prey is. These canals are located along the sides of its head and body.

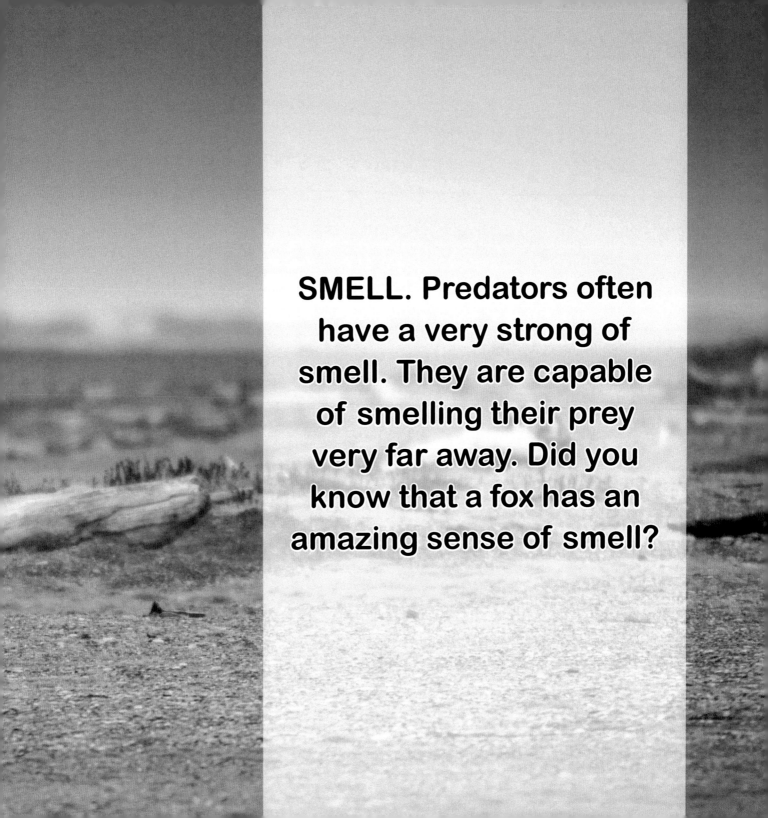

SMELL. Predators often have a very strong of smell. They are capable of smelling their prey very far away. Did you know that a fox has an amazing sense of smell?

Its sense of smell can even reach to food which is buried two feet in the ground.

Snakes also have amazing sense of smell. Do you know why snakes flick their tongues? Amazingly, they use their tongues to smell.

A snake uses its tongue to smell the air and it picks up dust particles. The mouth of the snake has detectors to taste these dust particles. It is in this manner that a snake is able to determine what meals are near.

Did you know that sharks have amazing smell ability? Yes, a shark is capable of smelling prey which is two miles away.

They use their nostrils for smelling. These predators are able to smell the water that flows in and out of the nostrils.

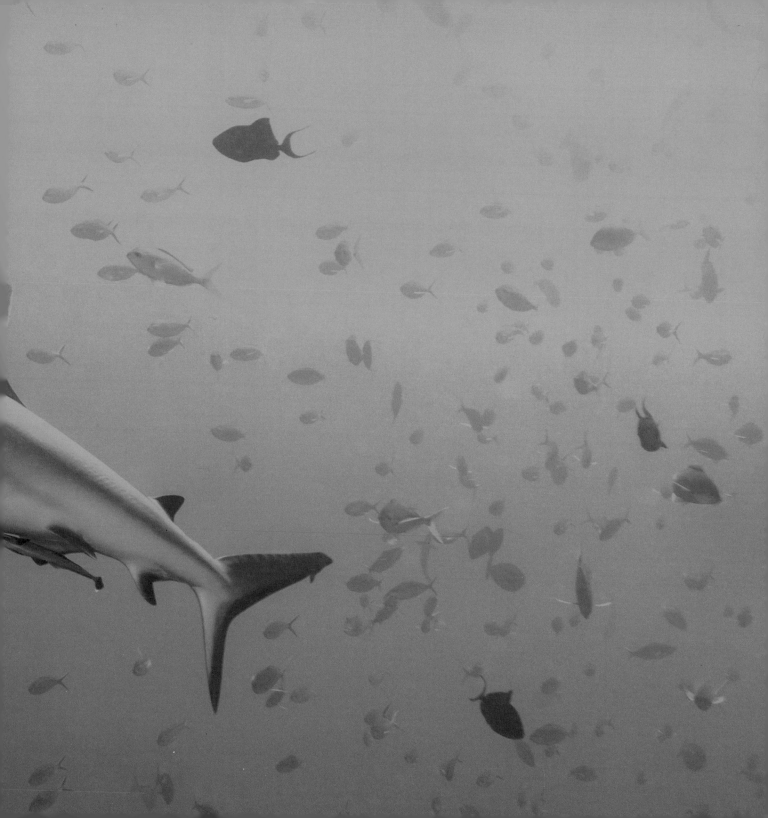

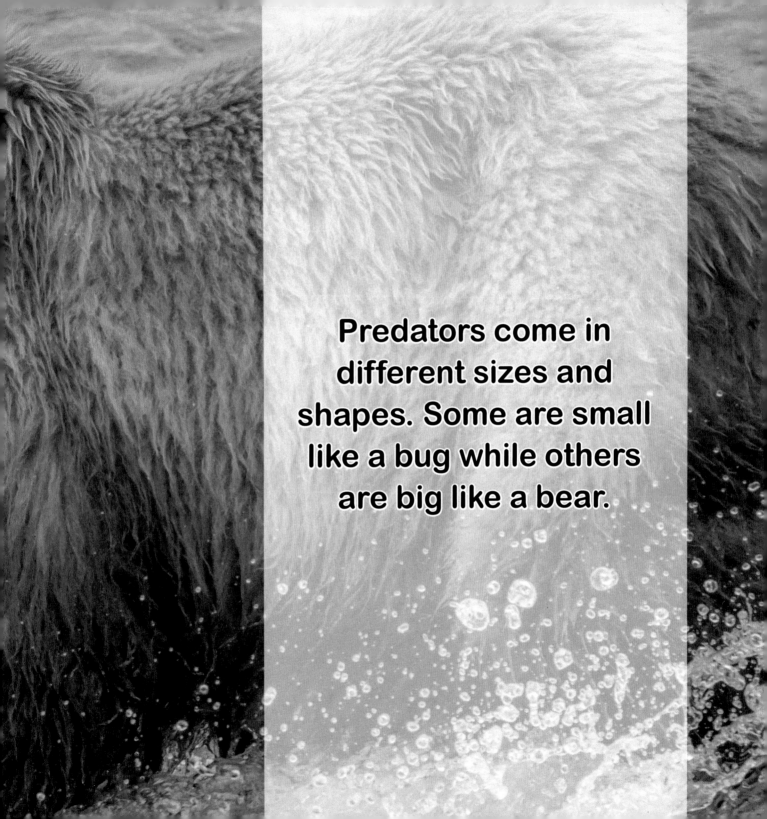

Predators come in different sizes and shapes. Some are small like a bug while others are big like a bear.

Predators are not bad guys. It is their nature to eat other animals in order to survive. They get hungry just like you and me.

Made in the USA
Middletown, DE
01 December 2020

All I've Wanted
All I've Needed

A.E. VALDEZ

Thank You

Thank you for being on this journey with me. Harlow and Acyn were living in my head for almost a year before I wrote their story. My only hope is, and always will be, that others love my characters and their stories as much as I do. You've given me that. The five-year-old me who was always lost in different worlds in her head is so proud.

Sunshine + Ace truly are my beginning of forever. I'm living my dream and wouldn't be here without each of you.

1

Harlow

I should've known something was up when a race red Ferrari pulled up to my house. Hendrix has always been flashy, from his material items to his personality. He commands the spaces he occupies. Hendrix is a man used to going after, and getting, anything and anyone he wants.

Except me. I'm the girl to tell him, "No."

My response stuns him, and he asks, "It's a no then?"

Slowly, he rises from the kneeling position he adopted mere seconds ago to ask me this life changing question.

"You deserve better than me," I say as tears sting my eyes. I'm aware people are staring now. I thought we were in for an intimate night, sitting at a candle-lit table scattered with rose petals, tucked away at the back of the restaurant. But there's nothing intimate about prying eyes focused on us, watching me refuse my boyfriend's proposal.

He sits back down in his seat and reaches across the table for my hand. "You're my beginning and end, Harlow. All I want is you."

I can't bring myself to meet his gaze. Staring into his honey brown eyes will only make this harder.

He watches me in silence, probably trying to figure out why I would say no to his proposal. We've been together for two years and things were going great. We're often the couple people describe as "relationship goals." But despite seeming picture perfect, I can't shake the feeling that this isn't lasting love.

"Don't you ever feel like we're just settling, Hendrix? As though we're together because we're comfortable, not because we're in love with one another?" My eyes still haven't met his. I didn't want to have to sift through this with him tonight. I hadn't expected him to propose to me. I for damn sure didn't expect him to do it in a public place.

Still not letting go of my hand, he asks, "Are you saying you're no longer in love with me?"

"I love you, I do, but I can't say yes to your proposal knowing that I feel like something is missing from our relationship. I feel like we're together because it's what's expected of us, and not because we want to be together. You're my best friend and..."

He grabs both of my hands and looks into my eyes as if the version of me he fell in love with will reappear. "We can hold off on the engagement if that's what you want but please, please don't ruin us."

A tear rolls down my cheek. He gently brushes it away. There's nothing wrong with Hendrix; he's an amazing boyfriend. But we've always felt more like friends than a couple. I'm unsure if he feels it too and doesn't want to let go of the comfort, or if he truly is oblivious. Or perhaps, he really is in love with me, and I never fell for him.

I hadn't considered that until this moment. *Maybe I am the bad guy here.*

It was the morning after he arrived home from college when he placed the kiss on my lips that intertwined our lives for the past two years. At that time, all I knew was that he wanted me, and I wanted him. The kiss turned into countless dates, laughter, and a deepening of our connection. We were discovering each other in a new light. When our circle of friends found out we were a couple they told us, they knew we would end up together. It seemed to be inevitable for us. Best friends turned to lovers. He pulls me back to the present moment. "Harls, say something, please. We can wait if engagement isn't a step that you're ready to take right now."

I exhale a shaky breath. "Hendrix, I don't want to marry you. I love you but I can't say yes to this proposal." Tears stream down my face as he holds my hand. "I-I didn't mean for this to happen. I thought I loved you in that way but – "

He drops my hands as if I slapped him across the face. Pulling away from me, he sighs and eases back into his seat with his eyes locked on mine. His usually warm eyes have no light in them. For a moment, I'm worried he's going to yell at me. I wouldn't blame him. I'd want to scream bloody murder if the person I had spent the past two years with admitted they didn't love me like I loved them.

Silence falls between us for what feels like an eternity. The people around us returned to their conversations and meals when we didn't erupt into a fight worthy of going viral. He sits there, examining the black velvet ring box in his hands as if it is a magic eight ball. As if it could tell him an answer that would make more sense than mine.

He isn't crying, but the pain I caused him is clearly etched on his face. "What have we been doing for the past two years? Did you ever love me?" He stares at me, waiting for me to answer.

I look away from him. "I do love you."

He scoffs and nods his head. "Right, as what? A friend who knows you inside and out, literally?"

Closing my eyes I turn away from him. I deserved that. "Hendrix, I'm sorry. I really am. I love you. I know I keep saying that and you probably don't believe it but I do care about you. I can't say yes when I know that I'm not all in."

He continues staring at the ring box in his hands and then looks up at me. "I'm sorry to lose us," he whispers.

Hendrix's chair slides across the floor, cutting the near-silence of our little bubble. He stands without saying another word and presses a kiss to my forehead. I momentarily melt into the familiarity of him, then miss his warmth as he pulls away. He sets the ring box next to me as he whispers, "I love you and this will always belong to you."

And then he leaves.

I break into sobs because it didn't occur to me that I would be losing my best friend by saying no.

2

Harlow

Stepping into my house, I catch a glimpse of myself in the entryway mirror. My reflection is unrecognizable. Another wave of grief hits me as I lean against the door, then slide down it until I'm a heap on the floor.

I'm not sure I made the right choice tonight. Maybe I just fucked up my entire life just so that I could "find myself" and figure out what I want. I don't know if I just broke his fucking heart for no good reason.

My dad hears me crying and comes to find me.

"Hey, hey, what's wrong?" he asks in a soothing tone, crouching down in front of me.

I doubt he'll understand any words that come out of my mouth, but I try to choke the words out. "Hendrix and I ... broke up." I don't look at him, trying to hide from the judgment I'm sure will come.

My dad pulls me into a hug. Somehow, he helps me up off the floor and guides me to the couch. He leaves me for a few minutes and comes back carrying cups of steaming chai tea. He hands me a cup and I hug it in between my hands, staring into it as if it can tell me everything will be okay.

"Do you want to talk about it?" my dad asks me sympathetically. I don't want to talk about it, but at the same time, I know my dad can offer the wisdom I don't have.

I continue to stare at my cup of chai and then I tell him everything: how I've felt like Hendrix and I were together because we were comfortable, how Hendrix expected me to revolve my life around him because he's the next big major league baseball player, how I felt like I was suffocating. I tell him about how I really want to do things for myself and not because I feel it's what others expect of me. I tell him how Charlotte, Hendrix's mom, always tells me what my mom would have wanted for me, as if she knows. I let it all out.

He grabs my hand after I'm done spilling my guts. "I'm sorry you've felt that way for so long, kiddo. I had no idea. I can tell you right now that the only thing your mother would ever want for you is to be happy. Whether that's with Hendrix, alone, or with someone else."

I look at him and he offers me a smile. "Do you really mean that?" I ask him between sniffles.

"Yes, I truly mean that. Whatever makes you happy, I am going to support you... even if it isn't a college degree," he says, and I laugh. It feels so good to laugh when all I want to do is fall apart.

"Will you ever let that college degree go?"

"I support whatever makes you happy, but that doesn't mean I'm not going to bring it up from time to time," he says with a grin.

"Fair enough." I chuckle.

"It will take time for you to feel better, Harlow. You and Hendrix have been an integral part of one another for so long. Don't be so hard on yourself." He rubs my back as he reassures me.

I let out a sigh. "I didn't want to break up with him, but I feel like we're being pulled in opposite directions right now, with him going off to spring training and me being completely unsure of what I want."

"You're doing what is best for you. Don't feel bad. If you two are truly meant to be, you'll find your way back to each other. I think it's good that you want to find yourself outside of him. I love Hendrix too, but I wouldn't want you to feel like you've devoted your life solely to him."

My dad's reassuring words ease my anxiety. "Thank you, Dad." I hug him. "I love you."

He hugs me back. "I love you, too, kiddo."

I pull away from him and finish the rest of my chai tea. "I think I'm going to go to bed."

"Alright, I'll be here if you need me," he says as he reaches for the remote and settles into his recliner.

I smile at him and make my way upstairs to my room. After kicking off my shoes and stripping out of my clothes, I crawl into bed. I check my phone and for the first time in a long time, there are no texts from Hendrix.

The past few days have been a blur. There have been moments when I thought I would be okay and moments when I miss Hendrix terribly. I still haven't heard from him. It's funny how things change so quickly. He's even been silent on social media. I checked his Instagram and all the photos he took of us and me are still on there. Maybe he doesn't totally hate me... *yet.*

I sigh and toss my phone to the side. I've considered texting him, but I don't know if he even wants to hear from me. I know he made it back to spring training safely because I heard Will, Hendrix's dad, telling my dad that Hendrix is doing good. I was grateful when my dad didn't say anything about the breakup. Instead, he changed the subject.

I'm sitting in bed with a pile of half-eaten snacks, searching Netflix for something to watch when my door flies open. "Where the hell have you been?"

I bolt upright in bed as my eyes focus on my best friend, Marisa.

"Marisa, how did you –" when I peer over her shoulder, I see my dad grinning at me.

"Thought you could use some company." He continues smiling at me and closes the door.

"I didn't expect to have to hunt you down. What is going on?" she asks as she stares around at all the clutter that is in my room and then studies me, waiting for me to answer.

Looking down at my can of Pringles I murmur, "Hendrix and I broke up... a few days ago."

She covers her mouth and gasps. "Oh babe, I'm so sorry. If you would've talked to me, I would have been here for you."

I nod. "I know. I just needed a few days to," I sigh and shrug, "wallow, I guess."

She pulls me into a hug and I try to remember if I showered today. Pretty sure I haven't brushed my teeth yet and it's nine at night. I guess I'm just a walking biohazard now.

"I'm sorry," Marisa rocks back and forth as she holds me. "How are you feeling now?"

"Not great. I feel stupid for being bothered that I haven't heard from him." I blink back tears because I refuse to shed any more. "Every single thing in my room, my house, the street, my car... it all reminds me of him. Everything. Everything is him."

She doesn't say anything, and I continue. "I thought for the longest time that this is what I wanted... but now I'm second guessing myself. I've had to stop myself from calling him to tell him that I want to be with him. My dad said this will pass, but it hurts. And I know Hendrix can take the pain away."

"At what cost?" she asks me as she cradles me.

"What do you mean?"

"Meaning, is he worth losing your sense of self over?"

I sit there in silence, and she rubs my back as she continues to hold me. That's the thing about Marisa, she will ask you hard questions in a simple way. "It isn't, and that's why I'm in this predicament now."

"Have you showered today?" she asks me and begins picking up all the empty food wrappers and containers. She closes my laptop and sets it on my desk. Then, she starts cleaning and I stare as if I've never seen someone clean before. She looks at me again as she continues tidying up my room. "If you haven't showered, go shower. Maybe you'll feel better. Then we can talk more if you want. I'll clean up."

The only people who have ever cared for me in this way are my mom, my dad, and now Marisa. I don't know why she decided to show up now, but I'm glad she did. I climb off my bed and glance at her before I close my bathroom door. "Thank you," I say, and I hope she knows how truly grateful I am. All she does is smile and continue making my room presentable.

When I come out of the shower, I do feel better. My room is clean, much cleaner than I would have been able to get it, and she has even lit a candle. It smells like lavender and chamomile. When she comes back in my room, she is carrying tea for the both of us. "How do you feel?" she asks as she sets the tray with the tea on the nightstand.

"Better." I smile. "Thank you for coming over."

"Of course. When you weren't at class on Sunday and then again today, I knew something was up. You haven't missed any classes in the two years I've known you. I also wanted to talk to you about something. And after hearing what you're going through, this may be the perfect thing."

Sitting cross-legged on my bed, I wait for her to continue.

"Would you be interested in attending a yoga teacher training with Quinn and I?" Quinn is our other best friend. We all met because of yoga. Marisa is the co-owner of a popular studio here on Galveston Island. As soon as it opened, two years ago, I signed up. I met Quinn in a class, we became regulars in Marisa's classes, and then the three of us bonded over green smoothies and fruit bowls.

"Me?" I place a hand on my chest, a little shocked. "Doesn't Quinn have school?"

"Yes, you." She chuckles. "Quinn does have school, but she has a month-long break at the same time as the training."

"Oh, I've just never considered becoming a yoga teacher before. The thought of leading an entire class of people makes me nervous."

"I personally think you would be great at it. Plus, just because you complete the training doesn't mean that you need to become a teacher. If anything, it's a nice way to deepen your practice and get away."

I raise my eyebrows, my interest piqued. "It wouldn't be here?"

"No, it's in Bali."

My heart instantly yearns to go. I haven't traveled since I went to Australia two years ago. With Hendrix's training schedule it was hard to find time to get away. Even when there was time, it wasn't like he wanted to go anyway. "How long is the training?"

"Twenty-two days. The price of the training covers accommodations and food."

My eyes light up for the first time in a long time. "Twenty-two days? In Bali?"

"Yep, the session we're planning to attend is in a month. That gives you plenty of time to think about whether you want to go or not."

"Are you kidding me?" I almost yell. "Of course I want to go!" My whole body is vibrating with excitement. It almost feels foreign.

She smiles at me. "I didn't think you would say no. It's been a while since you've traveled. I'll e-mail you all the information when I get home later. I've got to go pick up my brother. Are you going to be okay?"

I shrug. "I will be... eventually."

"You will be." She gives me a hug. "Give yourself some grace. It's okay to not be okay. Plus, you have two amazing best friends to help you along the way."

I let out a sigh, noticing I feel a little lighter after spending some time with her. "I do." I squeeze her back. "You better go before –"

Her phone starts to ring, and we both start to laugh. "Before I'm late to pick up my brother as I always am?" she asks.

"Yes. Thanks for checking on me, babe."

I walk her to the door and wave goodbye as she pulls out of the driveway. I'm not sure what I would have done without Marisa and Quinn over the past two years. I slowly started to feel isolated after Hendrix and I started dating. Everything became about him. The two of them helped me keep a little bit of myself. It wasn't totally terrible being with Hendrix, but I had erased a lot of myself to be with him.

Traveling became my life after graduating high school. While my peers sent applications to colleges, I planned trips around the world. At first it was just hopeful planning, adding pretty locations to my Pinterest boards. Then my dad surprised me with paying for my travels as a graduation gift.

I spend the rest of the evening reading up on the yoga teacher training program and Bali, which looks gorgeous. I can't wait to go. Even though everything feels like it's falling apart, I can't help but to also feel like everything is falling into place.

The next morning, I find my dad in his office typing away on his computer. His work never quite seems to be done. He's the president of the university here on the island. Even through loads of paperwork, meetings, and events, he has somehow always managed to make time for me.

I plop down onto a chair and pull one of my favorite pictures off his desk. It's a candid shot of me, my mom, and my dad. I'm sitting between them, smiling at the camera, as my parents look at each other, laughing. Even though it's been eleven years since my mom passed away, it still feels like yesterday.

My dad pulls me from my thoughts. "You seem more upbeat today. Did Marisa's visit help?"

I grin at him. "Yes, it did. Thank you for letting her in even if I was a mess."

He smiles. "What did you do today?"

"Paid for my yoga teacher training, booked a trip to Bali, and listened to depressing music. You?"

He leans back in his chair, crosses his arms, and chuckles. "Back to traveling?"

I grin. "You know me, Dad."

"Were you able to pay for it all?"

"Yep, I've had nothing to do but save since Hendrix paid for everything and," I shift uncomfortably in my seat, "I haven't spent a dime of mom's life insurance money." I let out a sigh and look at him. "I'm sure she would want me to use it for something I love. Yoga is something I love."

His eyes are glistening with unshed tears. "She would, kiddo." He bows his head. "She would." There's a moment of silence. "When do you leave?" he asks as he clears his throat.

"Next week."

"You know that I'm proud of you, right?"

A wide smile spreads across my face. "Yes, I do." I get up to leave. "Don't work too hard, Dad."

3

Harlow

I collapse onto the bed and exhale. We've finally made it to Bali and are settling into the suite we'll be calling home for the next three weeks. I melt into the plush bed, happy to finally be on solid ground. Quinn and Marisa crash onto their beds too.

My exhaustion starts to overcome me. I feel my eyes growing heavy. As much as I want to get out of this bed and explore, I know my body needs rest. I kick off my shoes, crawl under the covers, and drift off to sleep.

I awake with a jolt hours later. I'm disoriented because it takes my brain a few seconds to realize I'm not home. The noise that awoke me is my phone ringing. I clamber out of my bed and frantically dig through my bag to find it before it wakes up Quinn and Marisa. My hand lands on it and I pull it out. Hendrix's face is on my screen. My phone almost slips from my fingertips. It stops ringing seconds later.

My heart rate starts to slow back down, and I relax back onto the pillows. Why the hell is he calling me now after weeks of silence?

I start to drift off to sleep again, but then my phone chimes with a text.

Hendrix: I miss you, Harls.

I re-read the text over and over as I chew on my thumbnail, unsure of what to say or if I even want to respond. After a few moments pass without any texts, I power off my phone. I don't want to be tempted to engage in a conversation with him right now. Although I hate to admit it, a part of me still thinks about getting back together with him. I can't let that part of me win.

I am wide awake now, despite it being three a.m. here in Bali and decide to go sit by the pool. Once I'm outside in the balmy night air, I feel like I can breathe. Everywhere my eyes look is lush and green. I feel like I've stepped into another world. Sitting on the edge of the pool, I dip my feet in. The cool water wrapping around my legs relaxes me.

The past two years with Hendrix weren't irredeemable. We have so many good memories together. Not just from our time together, but even before that. Since our parents are best friends, we were practically raised together. We were born only twenty-four hours and one second apart. When my mom was alive and I asked her if it was planned, she swore up and down that it wasn't.

I can't lie and say that I don't miss him, but a growing part of me has felt at peace since the breakup. I've felt guilty for it because I don't usually say no to people, especially Hendrix. But we all get to a point where we decide we want more, don't we? Even if we are seemingly happy and content. I know there is more out there for me, and I want to find out what it is.

I must have been sitting out here lost in my thoughts for a while, because I see the first hints of the sunrise on the horizon. It starts off subtle and then orange starts to slowly bloom across the sky. Hints of yellow start to intermix with the orange as the sun continues to rise. I stare in wonder at the picture being painted in front of me. I smile at the sun as a sense of hope warms my body with the sun's rays.

"You've changed since you've been here," Marisa says to me over breakfast one morning. We've been here for twenty out of the twenty-two days. It's true what they say, time flies when you're having fun.

Quinn smiles at me. "Yes, you're looking very iridescent."

I smile and bite into my mango and juice dribbles onto my hand. I have never eaten this good in my life. The food is all organic and plant-based. It is confirmation that food is indeed a love language. I wipe the juice from my hand. "Is this a start of an intervention?" I ask with a piqued eyebrow as I stare at them both.

They erupt into a fit of laughter which causes me to laugh right along with them. "No, no you just seem more...vibrant here," Marisa reassures me.

"You're more relaxed," Quinn adds.

I shrug. "It's peaceful here. Plus, I feel like I can be myself... enjoy myself and not have to worry about anyone else." I do feel more vibrant and relaxed, but I think our days being filled with yoga, meditation, learning, and relaxation contribute to that greatly.

Marisa sips her green juice and continues staring at me. "Have you talked to Hendrix since the breakup?" she asks.

Quinn sucks her teeth. "Please, she isn't worried about that man."

I snort with laughter because Quinn is always the straight shooter. "He tried to Facetime me the first night we got here. When I didn't answer, he texted me that he missed me."

"Do you miss him?" Marisa asks.

"Yes and no," I reply honestly. "I miss him, but I also feel relieved to not have to attend practices, events, meetings, and whatever else it is he does for his career."

"Girl," Quinn scoffs. "You were doing way too much for him. More like a manager than a girlfriend. I know he thinks he's hot shit now after signing that multi-million-dollar contract with the Houston Astros. I am proud of you for saying no when you knew in your heart he wasn't your forever."

"If he hadn't of asked me to marry him," I look away from them, "I think I would still be with him," I admit.

"Sometimes we are forced to make changes," Marisa says.

I quirk an eyebrow. "What are you? A therapist?"

Quinn and I fall into a fit of laughter.

"I should start charging you bitches then," Marisa says as we continue to laugh.

"We'd be lost without you." Quinn nudges her shoulder with a grin.

I look between the two of them. "I think we'd all be lost without each other."

"Amen to that, sis," they say in unison.

It is our last day before graduation. We just wrapped up our final session while here. I'm proud of the growth I've experienced in our short time here. The past few weeks haven't been easy, but they have commanded me to bring out a different version of myself. I'm wiping the sweat off my face with a washcloth when Marisa grabs my arm.

"I want you to meet someone," she says.

"Now?" I ask as I try to tame my unruly curls. She ignores me and pulls me toward a woman with her back to us.

"Now or never." She clears her throat and places her hand on the woman's back. "Celeste, this is my best friend, Harlow. I told you about her a few weeks ago. Harlow, this is my dear friend, Celeste. She owns a yoga studio in LA but is opening up another one in Seattle in a week."

I smile politely although I am confused as to why I needed to meet her friend when I look a mess.

Celeste extends her hand out to me, "Pleasure to meet you. Have you been to Seattle?"

"Uh..." I side eye Marisa. "No, I haven't. I know my dad's brother lives there but I haven't seen him since I was twelve. Do you like it there?" This conversation is off to an awkward start.

"Let me cut to the chase," Celeste grins. "I've been talking to Marisa, trying to find instructors for my new studio opening next week."

I nod and smile, unsure of where this is going. Maybe Marisa is moving and this is her weird way of telling me.

Celeste continues, "Marisa thinks that you would be a good fit. I pay generously," she gives me a pearly white smile. "You would be teaching a mix of both group classes and private lessons."

"Oh I –" I stare at Marisa with wide eyes. "Why me?" are the only words that come out of my mouth.

"I've seen you grow leaps and bounds in the short time you've been here. I'd love to work alongside you at my new studio in Seattle."

Celeste is a woman about her business. This is a lot to take in. Quinn joins the conversation while I stand, staring at Celeste in stunned silence.

"Honestly, Harls," Quinn says, then takes a sip of her water. "What do you have to lose?"

I look outside at the swaying palm trees. Quinn is right. I don't have anything to lose. My mind is racing with how I can make this work, even though the thought terrifies me. I would be leaving my dad behind but it's not like I couldn't visit him. Really, I think the most important piece is finding a place to live in less than a week. I could ask my dad to reach out to my uncle and see if he knows anyone who has a place to rent.

Celeste chimes in, as if reading my mind. "If housing will be a problem for you, please let me know and I would be happy to help."

I get the notion that she can and will make a lot happen for me. "I... would love to work with you." I smile. It's a quick decision but there isn't anything to think about. Maybe this is how I find myself. I am so comfortable with familiarity that I've lost myself in it. A change of scenery would be nice.

"Great," Celeste claps her hands together. "We can talk in a few hours after dinner and go over all the details and your start date. I look forward to working with you, Harlow."

I watch her leave. As soon as she is out of sight Marisa and Quinn squeal as they hug me.

"This will be so good for you," Marisa assures me. "Don't overthink it."

"You are going to knock this out of the ballpark, babe," Quinn says and then cringes. "Wait, fuck Hendrix. You're going to make this next chapter of your life the best one yet."

I snort with laughter. "You two set me up, didn't you?"

"Sometimes we are forced to make changes," Marisa says with a smirk.

We all start laughing.

"I guess I'm moving to Seattle," I say out loud so that it sinks in. "*Holy shit*, I'm moving to Seattle."

It's Marisa and Quinn's turn to laugh at me.

I hold up my certificate of completion, grinning when my dad answers my video call.

"I did it!" I squeal while I bounce up and down in my seat with excitement. The past few weeks have been the most fulfilling of my life. "I am officially a yoga instructor!"

He beams at me with tears in his eyes. "You look so happy, and I am so proud of you!" I am surprised he woke up to talk to me given the difference in time. But that's my dad. He wouldn't miss an opportunity to ever see me shine.

"Thank you, Dad!" My cheeks hurt from smiling so much. "I am proud of myself."

"What are you three doing to celebrate your last day in Bali?"

"Exploring, celebrating my new job, and see where the day takes us."

"That's gre –" His brow furrows. "Wait, new job?"

"Dad, I got offered to teach at a yoga studio in Seattle. I took it. I mean, what do I have to lose? And it's not like I can't come visit you. Plus doesn't Uncle West live there?"

It's hard to read his reaction because whatever he initially felt only flitted across his face for a moment.

"Congratulations, kiddo," he says, beaming. "I am so proud of you and all that you're doing for yourself. You're right. Uncle West does live in Seattle with his wife, Ava. I'm assuming you'll need a place to stay. When do you have to be there?"

"I do, but Celeste says she could help me if it's difficult to find a place." I cringe. "I have to be there in a week. I know it's short notice, but I don't have much to pack. Having a place to stay is the most important."

"Let me call West and see what he says. I want to make sure you're in a good area."

"You're the best, Dad. I really am so excited to have a fresh start."

"I know, kiddo. I'm excited and happy for you too. Let me let you go so that I can get things in motion with West," he says as he rifles around his desk.

"Alright Dad, love you." I grin at him and wave.

"Love you too and I am so proud of you. By the time you're home tomorrow, I should hopefully have everything sorted out. Enjoy your last day." He smiles and ends the Facetime call.

Marisa twirls into the room. "Are you ready for our final day in Bali?"

A giggle escapes me. "Yes, you look great." She has her bikini on with a bohemian, macrame-style beach sarong tied around her hips. Quinn appears behind her moments later with a matching sarong in a different color and tosses something my way.

When I catch it I realize it is the same one but in yellow, my favorite color. I smile at her. "Didn't think we'd leave you hangin' did you?" Quinn says with a smirk.

"Never." I grin. "Give me ten minutes to get ready."

After a full day of breathtaking views, delicious food, and amazing conversation, we're walking back to our place as the sun sets.

"Guys, we should get tattoos!" Quinn squeals. My eyes go wide as I look around for what gave her this wild idea. I am all for living a little, but I am incredibly indecisive and the thought of picking out a tattoo on the spot gives me anxiety. My eyes land on the little tattoo shop coming into view as the light from the shop spills onto the street. Music becomes louder as we get closer.

"Um, are you sure about this?" I ask wearily. We are only steps away now and Marisa looks as skeptical as I do.

Quinn turns around to face us. "Oh, c'mon guys. It will be a good memory."

"You're tipsier than I thought," Marisa says as she stands firmly next to me. "Guys, have we not had an amazing time together?" Quinn asks.

When I quiet my anxiety, the thought that this has been the best time I've had in a long time settles in. I nod and so does Marisa.

"Okay, so why not commemorate it with a small little tattoo?" Quinn asks hopefully with her brows raised.

She has a point. It would be nice to have something with—well, on—me, that always reminds me of how free I felt here. To remind me that what I desire matters.

"I'm down," I say. Marisa's eyes snap to mine, and she smiles when she sees my resolve.

"Let's do this!" she replies.

Minutes later, I chew my thumbnail as I flip through the book of possible tattoo options. Midway through the book, my eyes land on a simple yet beautiful butterfly tattoo. "I want this one," I say without hesitation. Quinn and Marisa stop flipping through their books and come to see what I'm looking at.

"That's cute!" Quinn exclaims.

"Let's get that!" Marisa adds.

I look at both of them, shocked that they're letting me choose what they want tattooed on their body. "You guys can get whatever you want I just –"

"It's cute, Harlow, and it works for our trio perfectly," Marisa reassures me as she beams with excitement glittering in her eyes. "I feel all three of us are constantly changing, growing, and leveling up. Like a butterfly. I'm proud of us."

I smile at them because I don't know what we would have done without one another.

"Are we getting it somewhere inconspicuous?" Quinn asks.

"I was thinking my hip..." I say.

"Oooh, sexy!" Marisa says while winking at us. It makes me laugh and relax a bit. "So a butterfly on our hips?"

"I'm down for whatever," Quinn says with a smirk.

Not long after our agreement, I am sitting in the tattoo chair. I'm nervous, but an excited nervous. I haven't made a spur of the moment decision since I stopped traveling two years ago. The tattoo artist places the stencil on my skin. No backing out now.

"Ready?" she asks with a smile.

"As I'll ever be." I laugh nervously. Seconds later, the first prick of the gun connects with my skin. It isn't comfortable but it isn't excruciating pain like I anticipated it being. It's ...exhilarating. I don't see myself covered in ink anytime soon, but I can easily see why people get addicted. It doesn't take her long to finish and I grin at myself in the mirror when she's done. It's perfect.

Bali has been healing for my heart. I've been able to find myself again. Fall in love with myself again. I am ready for the next chapter of my life. This tattoo is a representation of all that I hope and dream. A representation of my journey for *more*.

4

Harlow

As soon as I arrive home from Bali, I begin packing my things for Seattle. My uncle and aunt have a guest house that they're generous enough to let me rent. Now all I have to do is pack my things.

I rummage around my room, realizing I have more clothes and clutter then I anticipated. The overwhelming load of all I have to do before I move to Seattle creeps in. I am doing my best to keep all the anxious thoughts out of my head. But then I pull Hendrix's sweater from the pile. It's the one he had on the last time he was here.

My shoulders sag as I hold it and rub the buttery soft fabric between my fingers. It's his favorite one. I bring it to my nose, inhale, and close my eyes. The comforting, musky scents of cedarwood and sandalwood greet me. A sadness settles in my chest. I stare at the sweater wondering if we'll talk again or if the last time I saw him was truly the last time.

I don't have much time to be in my feelings because my dad interrupts my thoughts.

"Are you ready?" he asks as he settles on the edge of my bed.

"Yep," I grin, "I only have a few boxes to pack and then they can be sent."

"Ol' Blue is getting picked up tomorrow and will be there after you arrive," my dad says.

Ol' Blue is my baby blue 1971 Ford Bronco that my dad and I restored together my senior year. She means the absolute world to me, and I treat her like she is my baby.

"I can't wait to take her to all those amazing trails in Washington." I grin. I've been obsessively looking at things to do near Seattle and there are a plethora of outdoor activities. I'm looking forward to exploring.

"You'll have no problem getting around with her." He looks around my room. "It's going to be weird," he bows his head, looking at his hands, "with you being gone. I know you were gone for a year but that was different." He looks at me and lets out a sigh as his shoulders sag. "I knew then that you were coming back every so often. But now, you're moving. This is all I've hoped for you, but I am sure going to miss you, kiddo."

I get up and wrap him in a tight hug. "I'm moving but nothing can keep me away from you. I know it's hard because it's just us." I told myself I wasn't going to cry until we were at the airport but it's too late for that now. "I love you, Dad. This isn't goodbye. I'll be back once I get settled in there. I promise."

"I know you will." He hugs me back.

My feet are propped on the dashboard of my dad's car as we make our way to the airport. I am scrolling through my phone while he is on a call to his office. He had to take the day off work so that he could drop me off. Marisa offered but my dad wasn't going to let anyone else take me to the airport. Over the past two weeks, he and I have spent a lot of quality time together. I haven't spent time like that with him in years and it felt good to be in each other's company.

I decide to post to my Instagram with my Dr. Marten's on the dashboard and a caption that says, "Seattle bound." I've never posted as much as Hendrix does, but people still follow me because I *was* his girlfriend. It feels weird for me to think of us in a past tense. I haven't heard from him since the text, and I haven't tried to reach out to him either.

My phone lights up with notifications and I check the picture I just posted. It's already received hundreds of likes. Part of the reason I stopped posting is because I felt weird about the "insta-fame" that I had from being Hendrix's girlfriend. Celeste asked me if I had any social media accounts and if I would be willing to use them to promote the studio. She looked like she saw gold when I showed her that my account had almost a million followers. I left out the part that it was thanks to my ex-boyfriend who is a rising pro-athlete. Speak of the devil; my heart stops when I see Hendrix has liked my post. I have to remind myself to breathe when I see he shares it to his story.

I drop my phone into my bag as if it's on fire and decide not to think too much into it. I must admit that when I posted, a small part of me hoped that he would see it. Okay, a large part of me. But that all fades away when the signs to the airport become visible. We're almost there. The excitement makes me feel like my body is vibrating. I can't believe that I'm leaving Texas.

Once in the airport and checked in, my dad walks me as far as security and then embraces me.

"I am going to miss you so much, Harlow." His voice cracks. "Know that all your mother and I ever want for you is to be happy. I am always here if you ever need anything, even if I'm not living there."

I cling to him and tears well in my eyes. "Thank you. For everything. I'll be back to see you before you know it."

"I hope so, kiddo. I love you. Call me when you land and give West and Ava a hug for me," he says with tears in his eyes as he releases me.

"I will, Dad. I love you." I give him one last hug and then walk towards security. I glance over my shoulder at him as he waves, and I wave back. I turn quickly back around as the tears start to fall. I may have traveled, but there is a different feeling when you know you are traveling to a new place to call home. I am leaving behind my entire life in the hopes that I can create a new one. Even though sadness grips me right now, I know that I am making the best choice for myself. I hold onto the excitement that hasn't left me for the past week and look forward to new beginnings.

As I approach the baggage claim, my stomach is in knots. I haven't seen my Uncle West since I was twelve. His wife Ava and I have talked on the phone a few times over the past week to ensure that everything goes as smoothly as possible. I'm looking forward to getting to know her more. Once I'm closer to baggage claim, I see two people holding a sign that says, "Welcome to Seattle, Harlow Shaw." My face lights up as I see the man and woman holding it.

My uncle resembles my dad except that his eyes are a lighter brown, and his hair is more... trendy. He has faded sides and corn rows up top, which are pulled into a man bun. I wasn't expecting this, but my dad did say that his brother was a "free spirit." His wife looks like she just left her glam team because she is perfect from head to toe. There is not a curl out of place on her head and her outfit is immaculate.

She starts waving and bouncing up and down when she sees me. I beam at them both and all the uneasiness I was feeling melts away. Once I reach them, they embrace me in a hug.

"Welcome to Seattle!" Ava says enthusiastically.

"How was your flight?" West asks.

"It was great. It all went well. Thank you so much for having me."

Ava waves her hand in the air. "Don't mention it, it was the least we could do. When West told me that you wanted to come live in Seattle, I couldn't say no. When I started the renovations on the guest house a few months ago, he told me I was crazy, but I just had a feeling we would need it soon. And here you come!"

West looks at Ava like she is the most beautiful and rare creature in the world. "Ava will make you feel right at home, Harlow," he says, beaming at her. They are so in love. It's beautiful to see. He turns his attention to me. "You know, you look just like Evie."

I smile. "I get that a lot actually. Thank you. It's always nice to hear."

"You'll have to show me pictures of your mama, Harlow." Ava smiles at me and intertwines her arm in mine as she steers us closer to the baggage carousel. She has a southern twang to her voice that is more apparent with some words then others.

"Are you from Seattle?" I ask her.

Splaying a hand across her chest, Ava gives me a surprised look. "Me? Oh, no honey, I'm from Tennessee. I moved out here for West," she says as she looks back at him and winks. "I've lived here for ten years but the accent will be with me for the rest of my life." Turning her attention to West, she grins. "Let West know what bag is yours, and he can do all the heavy lifting while we sit back and look pretty." I let out a snort of laughter as West shakes his head at Ava and rolls his eyes.

Ava is captivating. She has a head full of golden-brown curls that are cascading down her back. Gold bangles wrap around both her wrists, offsetting her rich copper skin. Her honey-colored eyes are wide and warm, immediately making me feel welcome. I've only been around her for a few minutes and I can already see why West married her.

I slide into the backseat of West's car. Ava turns around as she buckles her seatbelt. "You'll have to let me know what you think of your apartment. If you want to change anything, let me know."

"I doubt I will. It looks perfect in the pictures you sent me."

"And we have a personal chef," Ava says.

I try to hide the shock on my face, but she picks up on it.

"West and I have done well for ourselves." She grins. "But the chef can make anything you want if you just let him know what you like."

"That sounds amazing." My mouth starts to water as I start building a menu in my head.

I haven't stopped grinning since I got off the plane. It feels so good to finally be here in Seattle. I trust that whatever Ava has done to the place will be far better than what I could imagine. While Ava and West are talking, I send a text to my dad.

Harlow: Made it safe and sound. Ava and West are amazing. I'll call you when I'm settled in.

He responds a few minutes later.

Dad: Miss you already, kiddo! Can't wait to hear your voice.

Ava wasn't kidding when they said they had done well for themselves. As I step out of the car, I take in the views of their house. It is magnificent and stark white with a sprawling, lush green lawn. A forest surrounds their entire home, and I can't wait to see the backyard because I bet it's gorgeous, too. On the drive here, Ava told me that she owns an interior design company, and that West owns two coffee shops with a third location opening in the next few weeks. He also owns a marijuana dispensary. I now understand what my dad meant by free spirit.

We get inside and the look of awe hasn't left my face.

Ava smiles at me. "I love what I do."

"Love in an understatement. This is art," I say.

She tosses her head back and laughs. Taking my arm, she guides me through the house to give me a tour. It is modern yet cozy, and windows are everywhere, letting in lots of natural light. We step into the living room where there are large plush couches, a fireplace, a bookcase, and a TV. The living room seems like the place they spend most of their time, since it's the one area that looks lived in. Everything else is pretty much immaculate, like Ava. I hope she doesn't think I'm a slob with my organized chaos. I can't help but ask her, "Do you clean all of this yourself?"

"Goodness, no! If there is someone that can do something for me, I will hire them." She grins. "Why stress about something when I don't have to?" She shrugs. I can't argue with her because if I could hire someone to do stuff for me that I didn't want to, I would.

She continues. "It's big, but hopefully one day West and I can have a few kids of our own." Ava doesn't look at me as she says this. I sense the sadness in her tone, but I don't pry because if she wanted to tell me, she would. I'm sure she and West will be amazing parents when the time comes.

We make it through the house and step out into the backyard. I was right. The backyard is fabulous. There is a pool, a jacuzzi, and a small courtyard with a firepit and a garden off to the side. I am grateful that summer is right around the corner because I can't wait to spend my days out here. I was worried that I was going to miss being near the ocean, but I think I can get use to the lushness of the Pacific Northwest.

As we move through the backyard, I see a small little cottage with lights on, and it takes everything in me not to skip down the path towards it.

As we near it, Ava looks over her shoulder and smiles at me. "This is your home. Of course, you're always welcome to come in the house and hang out with me and West, but this also has everything you need."

I am speechless as I step inside. The living room is light and cozy, much like the interior of the main house, with cream-colored walls and harlequin-painted hardwood floors. There is a whimsical, antique chandelier hanging from the ceiling over a plush oversized white sofa that looks ready to be sunk into with a good book.

"Is there anything you'd like to change?" Ava asks me.

I look at her like she is crazy, and she laughs at me.

"Ava, what could I possibly change about this? You must not know that I'm coming from my childhood bedroom to a guest house. I am over the moon happy right now."

"Great!" She smiles. "I had hoped you'd love it."

We make our way into the kitchen, which is all white with black and white marble countertops. I can't wait to cook my first meal here. There is also a small dining space that will be nice to host people when they visit. I think of Marisa, Quinn, and my dad. Hopefully, I make new friends here, but I try not to get ahead of myself.

There is also a loft above the living room that Ava turned into a yoga space for me. I am overwhelmed with gratitude, and I hug her. She made this space specifically with me in mind. "This is perfect, Ava."

Hugging me back, she says, "We're family. I know this isn't Texas, but I sure hope it feels like home."

It does feel like home. I miss my dad, but my heart knows that this is now home. She shows me the bedroom last, which has a blue accent wall behind the white, plush bed. Mirrors sit on both sides of the bed and there's even a little nook with a vanity where I can do my hair and makeup. Everything is perfect. I'm not sure how to thank West and Ava for even allowing me to stay here. I am pretty sure if they rented this space out, they could get a lot of money for it. Then again, money doesn't seem to be a problem for them.

Ava clasps her hands together. "Okay, I am going to leave you to it. West already set your bags in your room and the boxes that were sent are in the living room. If you need anything at all, let us know."

"Thank you," is all I can muster to say. Ava turns to leave and then she stops.

"Oh, West and I usually have breakfast at seven-thirty. Text me some foods you like, and we can be sure to have them for you," she says with a smile.

Once the door closes behind her, I sigh and look around. I let out a squeal because I cannot believe that this is real life right now. I have been running on exhilaration and adrenaline all day. Now that I'm finally here, I want to relax. I dig through my suitcase and pull-out Hendrix's sweater because it's comfortable... and I miss him. I kick off my boots and strip down to my panties and slip it on. I find some socks and put those on too. It is a little bit cooler here, but Ava said it will start to warm up soon.

I flop down on my bed and put some Sabrina Claudio on the Bluetooth speaker. I considered doing a tour of my new place for Instagram, but I figure it will look better in the morning with the light filtering through all the windows. Instead, I post a picture of myself in the mirror sitting cross legged on the floor smiling with the caption that says, "Home" and put my location in Seattle, WA. I silence my IG notifications because I don't really want to chat with anyone. I toss my phone on the end of the bed and go rummage through the fridge. Ava has it fully stocked. I have never met a person who is as prepared as she is.

I grab a bottle of water, some grapes, and cheese. Sitting back down on my bed, I consider calling my dad. My phone chimes and I expect to see my dad's name but instead, it's Hendrix.

5

Harlow

My heart starts to race, and my palms feel clammy. It's been weeks since he last texted me.

Hendrix: How's Seattle?

I stare at my screen, annoyed with myself that I am so happy to finally get a text from him. He must be staring at his screen, too, and saw that I read his text because he sends another one.

Hendrix: I would have texted you sooner, but I was trying to give you space.

Chewing on my thumbnail I am trying to decide what to say. Instead, I press the camera button to start a video chat. He picks up almost immediately. At first, all I can see are his inky black curls and then he centers the camera on his face. I smile like a fool as soon as he appears.

"Fuck, I've missed your face," he says. "Harlow Shaw up and moved all the way to fucking Seattle."

I tell my face to stop smiling but it won't listen to me. Unfortunately, he is still one of my favorite people on the planet and the past couple of months without him haven't been easy. "I did," I say.

He chuckles and my heart constricts. I've missed that sound. "You look so happy. Do you have your own place? I ran into your dad when I was visiting my parents and he didn't say much... just that you're happy."

I get off my bed and flip my camera around and slowly turn so he can see my room. "I am. I officially have my own place. Well, it's on my Uncle West's property but... it's mine." I go out to the kitchen and living area to show him those spaces, too. "West and Ava are... perfect." I flip the camera back around so it's on my face and sink into the plush cushions of the couch.

"That's amazing, baby. I'm so happy for you. When do you start your new job?"

"In a couple of days. Celeste wanted to give me time to get settled in. How's spring training?"

He yawns. "Tiring, but you know baseball has always been my first love." A grin tugs at his lips.

I nod, knowing all too well. "Can I ask you something?"

"Anything," he says with his eyes trained on me.

"Why did you propose?" It is a question that has been on my mind since the night it happened. We had previously talked about eventually getting married and starting a family. That was after we first started dating, but we hadn't talked about it since. The proposal felt like a rushed decision on his part.

He lets out a sigh as his jaw flexes, "You're going to think it's childish." His eyes are focused somewhere else as he tries not to look at me.

"Try me," I shrug and smile, despite the unsettling feeling in my stomach.

"Alright," he sits up on his bed and he finally looks into the camera. "After I signed with the Astros, and I asked you to come with me to Palm Beach for spring training, you said no."

This isn't what I was expecting. Right after he signed, he asked me to go stay with him for spring training and then move in with him. I didn't directly say no but I did say that I'd think about it. An *I'll think about it* to Hendrix Moore is saying no to him because he doesn't instantly get what he wants.

"Wait," I cradle my face in my hands. "You proposed because I told you I'd think about it?" I furrow my brows. "Not because of love?" I've been thinking our breakup was all my fault when he is clearly as guilty as I am. I admitted to Quinn and Marisa that I would still be with him if he hadn't proposed. I guess Marisa was right. Sometimes we are forced to make changes.

"Harls, babe, listen... please." He rakes his fingers through his curls. "I noticed that you were pulling away from me after I signed."

He switched up and became a different person after he signed. Hendrix has always had a charmed life. His parents made sure that he got everything he wanted. After he signed his multi-million-dollar contract with the Astros, his sense of entitlement was suddenly on steroids.

He looks at me. "I felt like I was losing you and I thought the proposal would help us. I can count on one hand the times you've said no. Look, I know this sounds awful and I know I fucked up by proposing, but I thought if you said yes that –"

"Let me get this straight," I interrupt him. "You didn't propose because of love?"

He bows his head as his shoulders sag. "Harls, I know I fucked up."

He is still avoiding my question. That is all the answer I need. "I thought I was crazy for feeling the way that I felt. As if saying no to you was a major fuck up... but it turns out it was the right thing. You're not ready to be married or settle down with me either."

"But... I love you, Harls."

"You can love me, but that doesn't mean that we're meant to be together, Hendrix."

"Is it so bad that I want you in my life?"

I scoff. "It is when you try to force me to be on your terms."

Silence falls between us. I feel his eyes on me.

"I'm sorry... I really am," he says and then lets out a sigh. "Is there any possibility..." He rakes his hands through his hair again. "That we can still be friends and then maybe see where that takes us?" he asks with a grin.

"Friends," I scoff. "Do you really think we can be friends?"

"We've been friends our whole lives. Why not?" he asks.

"Yeah, that was before... I don't think we can be just friends." I don't see us being able to go back to where we were before we got together.

"Tell me this," he says. "Would you consider getting back with me?"

My heart rate quickens. I've thought about this countless times. Getting back together with him would be easy. Too easy. I look away from him. "No, not right now." I'm unsure if my answer will ever change. I'm also unsure if I am ready to not have him in my life. Even if it is just as a friend.

"I just royally fucked this up... *us* up," he says with regret in his tone.

I don't say anything for a few beats as he looks at me expectantly. "We both did," I shrug. "I don't mind trying being friends. I stress *trying*. I can't promise that it will take us back to where we were or even somewhere new. I am going to admit now that me agreeing to be friends is for purely selfish reasons. I've missed you." Letting go is a lot harder than it seems.

He tosses his head back and laughs. "I'm okay with that. I really did try to give you space but then you posted that picture of you in my sweater and I said fuck space."

I can't help but smile. "Funny how you get space and then don't want it."

He smiles. "You mean you haven't found a boyfriend yet?"

I scoff. "Oh yeah, I have three boyfriends now. I bounced right back." I roll my eyes with a grin on my face. "In all seriousness, I am going to focus on getting settled here and not worry about relationships for a while. Any new girls for you?"

"Fuck no," he answers abruptly. "It's only you. Even though we aren't together. I only see myself with you."

Looking away from the camera, I pick at my sock. "If you find some pretty girl to change your life, don't stop on my account."

"Nah, I'm looking at her right now. Plus, I don't have time, nor do I care to chase after girls right now. My only focus is baseball... and you. As it's always been," he says seriously.

So much for a clean break up.

"What are the odds of me getting that sweater back?" he asks with a piqued eyebrow and a grin.

I start laughing. "Never," I reply.

Nodding, he says, "That's fair enough." Hendrix and I talk for hours. It's as though we didn't break up at all and it comforts yet terrifies me at the same time. Neither of us are making it easy to move on from the other. I wonder if there will ever be a point where we feel like we can live without one another. Right now, I feel as though we may never reach that point. Instead of degrading myself for still loving and wanting him in my life, I accept that this is where I am. Things can change at any given moment.

Sitting outside wrapped up in anxiety and a blanket, I sip my latte. It's 6:00 a.m. and today will be my first day adulting at my job. I have a private yoga session at nine a.m. and, of course, I couldn't sleep because I thought of everything that could possibly go wrong. When I did fall asleep, I dreamt that I was late. Celeste assured me that everything will go smoothly and that I am an amazing teacher. Yesterday, she had me guide her through a session and she said I did amazing. I'll take her word for it because Celeste doesn't seem like someone who says things just to be nice. She says them because she means them.

After finishing my latte and aimlessly scrolling through social media for an hour, I decide to join West and Ava for breakfast. I haven't felt out of place since I've been here. They do everything they can to make me feel comfortable. I'm not the most talkative person but Ava could strike up a conversation with a tree if she wanted to.

"Good morning," she says in a sing-song tone as I enter the kitchen.

"Morning."

"West had to leave early this morning to oversee some last minute things at the new shop. So, it's just us girls this morning." She smiles and sits down next to me at the kitchen island.

"Is the new shop far from here?" I ask as I grab a chocolate croissant from the tray in front of me.

"It's in downtown Seattle. About a thirty-minute drive from us if traffic isn't terrible." She takes a sip of her coffee. "Are you ready for today?" she asks.

I sigh and put my croissant down on my plate. Suddenly I'm not hungry anymore. "I guess I am." I shrug. "I've thought of everything that could possibly go wrong."

"Now you've got to think of everything that could possibly go right," she quips and winks at me.

I blink at her, not having even considered that anything could go right. "I suppose I could." I smile.

"Believe in yourself, babe! You are exactly where you need to be. You wouldn't be sitting here with me right now if you weren't." She gets up and puts her dishes in the sink.

Ava is right. I do spend a lot of time doubting myself and thinking about how there are people more deserving than I am. If I am going to be teaching others though, I need to find some confidence.

"I saw your Instagram, by the way," she adds as she looks through her phone. "Did you take photography classes in high school or something?"

"No, why?"

"You have an eye for it. Your feed is gorgeous. I also saw all the pictures you put up in the apartment." She glances up from her phone. "Maybe you should take some classes," she suggests.

I study her. "Did my dad put you up to this?" I ask suspiciously.

Ava cackles. "No," she says, putting her hands up in front of her. "I promise he didn't. This is my suggestion."

"I never thought of it, to be completely honest. I just like to take pictures of things."

Even before Hendrix and I were a thing, I had a large following due to my travels and random posts of myself. I am not an influencer by any means, but I do enjoy being able to share my pictures with others. But photography classes have never crossed my mind.

"Think about it. I've got to go. Remember, you've got this, and you deserve to be here." Giving my arm a reassuring squeeze, Ava smiles at me, and then grabs her bag as she heads out the door.

Glancing at my watch, I decide to head to the studio early so I can do a warmup flow by myself before my client arrives. I dig deep to find my confidence because Ava is right, I do deserve to be here.

I arrive at the studio an hour early and warm up. It isn't very far from my place. I still smile every time I say or think "my place." It feels good to be on my own.

Sitting at the front desk, I check my phone because the woman who is supposed to be here for the private session is running ten minutes late. Glancing up from my phone, I see a black Tesla SUV zip into the parking lot. Seconds later a woman frantically gets out and comes running for the doors. I'm worried she may slam into them at the speed she is coming in.

She in fact does slam into them and drops her bag. I hear her scream, "Fuck!"

I decide I better help her because she looks like she's had a hell of a morning. Jogging over to the door, I open it for her. She finishes gathering the contents spilled from her bag, blows her bangs out of her face with a huff, and gives me an apologetic smile.

"Hi, I'm Sevyn. Sorry I'm late!" She extends her hand out to me.

I shake it with a smile. "Welcome, I'm Harlow."

"My twins thought it would be hilarious to hide my keys this morning. Then once I found my keys, they had hidden my purse and it... it really was just a mess," she admits, covering her face. "I understand if you don't have time to squeeze me in," she says in a rush.

All I can do is smile at her authenticity. Most people wouldn't admit to having a shit morning. They would pretend that everything is fine. "We have time. Don't worry about it."

"Really?"

"I'm positive. Plus, you look like you could use some relaxation."

She scoffs. "You have no idea."

My session with Sevyn goes perfectly. Afterwards we end up talking for a while and she tells me about her twins who are only two and a half. They sound like they keep her busy, but I can tell that they are her whole entire world. I tried to offer to babysit, and she told me she wouldn't bring that hell into my life.

6

Harlow

"How are things going, kiddo?" my dad asks me as a we video chat.

I shrug and sigh. "They're okay. I miss you but I guess I'm settling in alright."

"You haven't even been there a month yet. It will take some getting used to," he reassures me with an encouraging smile.

"I have no friends here, Dad. Don't get me wrong, Ava and West have made me feel welcomed but it's not like we can hang out and be besties."

He chuckles. "You have to leave the house to make friends. Have you done that?"

I roll my eyes and grin. "No, I'm too –"

"Too stubborn to venture outside your comfort zone?"

I suck my teeth and laugh because he is right. "No, I just..." I try to come up with an excuse and can't think of one. "Fine, I guess you're right. But, in my defense, I've been going through a lot of changes lately."

He nods. "You have, and I'm proud of you. But you're going to have to push yourself to make friends. Work and home is a boring life to live."

"Oh, so I'm boring now?" I quirk an eyebrow.

He laughs. "You know what I mean."

"I do," I chuckle. "I'll get out there eventually."

My dad's phone chimes. "Will's here to pick me up for golf. We'll catch up later?"

I smile. "Yeah Dad, love you. Have fun golfing."

"Love you, kiddo." He ends the call.

"Wow, my dad has more of life then I do," I mutter to myself. He's right, as much as I hate to admit it. I haven't been here long but not having friends here makes me homesick. I didn't realize how much time I spent with Marisa and Quinn until now. I'm not even sure where to go to make friends here. Do I even know how to make friends?

My phone chimes with a text and I'm shocked to see Kyrell's name pop up on my screen. I met Kyrell in sixth grade, shortly after I lost my mom, when he became friends with Hendrix. He is just as close to me because before I met Marisa and Quinn, I was always with Hendrix and Kyrell.

Kyrell*:* Hey Harls, I'm in Seattle for some business. Do you wanna link up?

I haven't seen Kyrell in almost a year. He moved out to California shortly after he and Hendrix got back from Louisiana State University. He visited Texas frequently after he first moved and then he stopped. From what Hendrix has told me, and from what I see on his social media, he is doing well for himself. He's working on opening his own dispensary.

Harlow*:* I'd love to! Let me know when and I'll be there.
Kyrell: I'm a gentleman. I'll pick you up! Text me the address.
Harlow: Sure you are! What time will you be here?

I text him the address and he promptly texts me back.

Kyrell: 7 because I gotta make myself look presentable. Can't have you outshine me.

I snort with laughter and leap off my bed. I'm excited to hang out with Kyrell because he knows how to have a good time and makes me laugh. Maybe he will be able to help me get over this homesick feeling that has had a grip on me the past few days.

He arrives at exactly seven p.m. looking dapper in a simple white t-shirt, skinny jeans, and some Yeezy's on his feet. Flowers are in his hand and a smile is on his face. He hugs me and hands me the flowers.

"Why the hell did you bring me flowers?" I ask with a raised eyebrow and a smile as I let him in.

"Why not? You're a girl. Don't you like flowers?" He enters and looks around my apartment, inspecting it.

I make my way to the kitchen to look for a vase while he settles on flipping through my record collection.

"That's presumptuous of you to think I like flowers just because I'm a girl."

Grinning, he asks, "Do you like them?"

"I love them," I admit as I set the vase now filled with roses on the center of my table.

"Then accept them as a gift and nothing more. Plus, I haven't seen you in a while," he says and starts looking at my pictures on the wall. "You know you're pretty good with the camera."

I grin as I go to my room to find my shoes. "You're the second person to say that this week. It's just something I enjoy. Nothing serious." I shrug as I slip some flats on.

"It could be." His eyes roam over me. "You look great, by the way."

"Thank you." I grin.

"I was serious about what I said all those years ago. I am willing to get caught in an entanglement situation with you whenever you're ready." He winks.

I start cracking up. "Shut the hell up, Kyrell."

Kyrell loves to joke with me. After Hendrix and I got together, he told me the exact same thing after I tried to convince Hendrix that Kyrell isn't attracted to me. He had to make it known that he was in fact attracted to me. A fight broke out between them over the comment.

He grins at me. "You do look great, though. Are you ready?"

I smile at his compliment and glance in the mirror. My kinky coils are pulled up into a half top knot bun and I'm wearing a tight white long sleeve crop top, with high waisted skinny jeans and flats. I would wear heels, but I have no clue what Kyrell will get us into tonight, so I felt flats were the safest option.

"Yeah, I'm ready. Where are we going anyway?"

He shrugs and puts his arm out for me to hold. "No clue, but the night is young."

Kyrell takes me to a gorgeous rooftop bar that overlooks Elliot Bay in downtown Seattle.

"It's gorgeous here." I say. "Views like this make it hard for me to miss Texas."

"You miss that place?" he asks with a smirk.

I shrug. "It's where I was born and raised... hard not to miss it."

"Do you miss Texas or do you miss Hendrix?"

"Both," I reply without hesitation. He doesn't say anything so I continue on. "I feel guilty for leaving my dad. I miss Quinn and Marisa. Weekly video chats aren't the same as spending physical time with them. And Hendrix... he annoys the hell out of me. He's arrogant and selfish but for some stupid reason I am still in love with him. I miss the familiarity of him. I'm just... homesick. I don't know. Maybe moving out here wasn't a good idea."

Kyrell leans toward me. "Aren't you curious as to how your life will turn out here? It would be easy to go back home, back to him... back to all you've ever known. Sometimes comfort is what kills us. You said you wanted more, right? Maybe this move is your more. Stop doubting yourself."

"I do want more, but after the breakup, everything seemed at an all-time low for a few weeks. Then I went to Bali, got offered a new job, and then moved here. It was a series of highs. I was distracted from anything but the good. But now, I'm here alone and I'm not sure I want to be alone."

"So... face your shit."

My eyes snap to his. "Excuse me?"

"Face your shit. You can't run from good thing to good thing hoping it will erase the bad shit that happened. It happened. You're sitting at this table with me *because* it happened. Why would you want to go back to it?"

I let out a puff of air. "Damnit... you're right." I want to argue with him but there isn't anything I can say in protest. Going back home would be easy. "I guess I need to focus on my life here instead of focusing on what used to be."

"Exactly!" he exclaims. "Let yourself enjoy life here and more importantly, let yourself enjoy the night with me."

"I can drink to that." I say as I raise my glass in the air to meet his.

After a fun night out with Kyrell that included eating, drinking, dancing, and sharing some joints, he drops me off at two a.m. I'm surprised to see that the lights in the main house are still on. I know West and Ava stay up late but this is late for them. I was going to make a trip through the kitchen to grab some snacks and food but now I'm contemplating whether I should. I don't know what they're doing up this late and I'm not sure that I want to know.

My stomach grumbles and I decide that I better go through the kitchen after all. I open the door and tip-toe through the house. As I near the kitchen I hear them arguing in the living room.

"You can't take on more right now. I'm not willing to risk it," West says with a finality in his tone.

Ava scoffs. "Then tell me, what the hell are you going to do? You have no one to help you at the coffee shop now that Jewel decided she wanted to run off with her boyfriend."

"I'll figure it out!"

"How, please tell me how you will figure it out?" Ava demands. "I already see you so little now and that stresses me out just as much as helping out as the coffee shop would. If you're working there, the other two locations, and the dispensary, please tell me when the hell am I going to see you?"

"Ava," West says with regret in his tone. "I know. I'm sorry. I just don't see how else this will work out if we're going to open on time."

I sneeze. I tried like hell to hold it in, but it escapes me. Their heads snap in my direction, and I look back at them like a deer in headlights.

I chuckle nervously. "Hi." I wave.

Ava smiles at me as if they weren't just in the middle of an argument. "Hey, girl! You look like you had fun." She smiles.

I know that I look a mess. I spilled a drink on myself and am now wearing Kyrell's shirt that is too big, my eyeliner is smudged, and my hair is poofy from sweating on the dance floor. But, I did have a lot of fun.

"I did. Thanks," I say sheepishly. "Sorry to interrupt. I was just going to grab some snacks and get out of your way."

"No need to apologize," West assures me with a smile. "I get the muchies, too."

I cover my mouth and let out a snort. "Is it that obvious? Oh God, please don't tell my dad!" A laugh escapes me and doesn't stop.

West and Ava both laugh along with me. "Yeah, it's very obvious," they say together.

"Your secret is safe with me, but your dad does know I own a dispensary. He pretends that I don't but..." West shrugs. "Maybe one day he'll learn to loosen his collar a bit."

I scoff. "Good luck with that! You guys aren't usually up this late," I say as I make my way to the kitchen to grab my snacks.

"West and I ran into a snag with the new coffee shop," Ava says as she plops onto the couch.

"I know, I heard," I say as I take a bite of a cupcake. Then my eyes go wide. "Not that I was eavesdropping, I just –"

West puts up his hand with a smile. "Chill, Harlow, you're fine."

I swallow the piece of chocolate cupcake. "You know." I lick the frosting off my finger. "I could help."

"No, no. You need to focus on yourself right now," Ava interjects.

"Oh please, it's the least I could do. That way you and West can spend more time together." I look at them both hoping I haven't crossed a line.

"Ava's pregnant," West blurts out.

I blink and stare between Ava and West, not sure what to say. When she mentioned kids a few weeks ago after I arrived, there was a sense of longing and sadness in her voice. I can only assume that they just found out.

Ava is beaming. "We just found out today. I wasn't feeling well and..." She shrugs. "Well anyway, I am not that far along, and this is a dream come true for us both because it's been hard to conceive but... West is right, I really don't need the added stress right now."

"Then let me help. I mean, I don't know how to make coffee, but I am capable of learning," I assure them.

"Are you sure?" West asks.

"I wouldn't offer if I wasn't," I say with a smile.

West's shoulders fall and it looks like a huge weight has been lifted off his shoulders. "You are a lifesaver, Harlow. I need to step back and focus on Ava but it's hard to do that when my employees decide to run off to Vegas with a biker named Big Joe."

I cackle. "Big Joe?"

West shakes his head. "I know, I know, but she's gone now. Anyway, if you want to help, I would appreciate it. It would only be temporary until I can find someone. Of course, I will pay you, but I am just so relieved that this worked out."

Ava gets up and hugs me. "Thank you. You have no idea how big of a help this is for us."

I hug her back. "No problem guys." She releases me from the hug, and I pick up all my snacks. "I'm going to let you two be. Good night!"

"Thanks again, Harlow," West says as I walk out the door.

I wave a hand to let him know I heard and make my way to my apartment.

When I get inside, I collapse on my couch and open a bag of Cheetos. I pull out my phone and see that Kyrell has tagged me in some pictures. As I scroll through them, I see a steady progression of our night unfolding. The last one is of a shirtless Kyrell and me in his shirt with the caption: *wild night with the best*. I smile because Kyrell expects nothing from me other than to be myself. I believe that is why we always have a good time together.

He asked me about Hendrix tonight and I told him everything. His reply to it all was that I deserve to be 100 percent happy, whether that is with or without him and to not hold myself back for his sake. Kyrell knows how Hendrix can be and admitted to it being part of the reason they are not as close as they once were. Of course, when Hendrix saw that Kyrell and I were together, he texted Kyrell multiple times. Kyrell decided to ignore him. It wasn't even about making him jealous. It was more of a celebration of us no longer being in his shadow.

7

Harlow

Talking with Sevyn after class, I glance at my watch and mumble, "Shit."

She gives me a puzzled look and asks, "Are you okay?"

"Yes, I am going to be late to my other job though!" I start to roll up my mat.

"You have another job?" she asks.

"Yeah, I help my uncle out at his coffee shop part-time."

Sevyn groans. "I would love a coffee right now. Would you mind if I stop by later? The kids will be spending the weekend with Zane's parents." She tosses her head back dramatically and puts her hand over her heart. "Thank God!"

Snorting with laughter, I say, "You have the weekend alone with Zane and you want to come see me at a coffee shop?"

"Of course! Besides, Zane won't be home until later this evening, and he made plans for us. Until then, I am free to do as I please. What's the name of the shop you work at?"

"Holy Shot, it's downtown."

"Oh, I know where that is! It just opened, didn't it?"

"It did. Just last week. It's worth stopping in. The vibe is warm and cozy," I mention as I get ready to head into the showers.

"Alright, I'll let you get ready and then see you in a few hours!" She slings her mat over her shoulder and waves.

The coffee shop has only been open for two weeks and it's already insanely busy. I quickly understood why West and Ava needed help. His coffee houses are not only known for their coffee, but the entertainment they bring. Each evening, they have local artists come and perform music, comedy, poetry, or plays. It really is hard for me to call it a job when I enjoy it so much. I didn't think I would ever be a barista but it turns out I'm a damn good one.

The afternoon lunch rush just died down and I am wiping down tables. Who knew that there would be a lunch rush for coffee? One thing that I've learned since starting here is that people fucking love their coffee. If there was an IV drip available for it, people would buy it.

I make my way back to the counter and hear the door open as someone enters. When I glance up, I see that it's Sevyn and she looks like she just stepped off the runway. She is dressed in a black jumpsuit with a Gucci belt cinched around her waist, her deep red curls frame her face, and she carries a black clutch in her hand. She waves when she sees me. "I was worried I would miss you! I took a little longer than I anticipated to get ready." She twirls on the spot.

"You look drop dead gorgeous. Zane is going to eat you up!" I say.

"You weren't lying, this shop is a whole vibe," she remarks as she looks around.

The coffee shop has an industrial design with warm, rich colors throughout. There is a stage for performances, coffee tables in the center of the shop, and then plush chairs are scattered throughout. One of the walls has a floor-to-ceiling bookshelf that is stacked with a variety of books. Ava and West did a good job creating a space where you can relax and socialize.

"It really is. Did you want me to make you something?" I ask as I walk behind the counter and wash my hands.

Sevyn scrunches up her face as she studies the menu behind me. "Mmm... let me get the house blend, please."

"Alright, coming right up." I busy myself with making the shots. I'm listening to Sevyn talk when I look up and the air is stolen from my lungs. A guy strides in and every inch of his rich copper brown skin that I can see is adorned with tattoos. My eyes slowly rake up his hands and arms emblazoned with the most intricate ink. I imagine tracing each one with my fingertips. Ink covers the piece of chest exposed at the V-neck of his shirt that is pulled tautly over his broad shoulders. They continue to coil around his neck and abruptly stop at his sharp jawline. There are no tattoos on his face and his lips are plump. They look soft enough to kiss. Our eyes lock onto one another; his are pensive and remind me of embers in a fire.

Sevyn continues talking to me, but I don't hear her. All noise is drowned out as we continue to look into one another's eyes. I tear my gaze away when the shot of coffee I am holding spills over the sides of the shot glass and onto my finger. "Shit," I hiss pulling my hand away.

"Are you okay?" Sevyn asks.

"I'm alright," I say while observing my fingers that are now beginning to turn red. "Just got a little distracted is all." The guy who is the source of my distraction chuckles and heat creeps up my neck.

Sevyn turns her attention to him. "Well, well, well, nice of you to finally arrive."

I try not to stare between them, but he is hard not to look at. I wonder if they're related. His gaze moves to Sev, and I feel ridiculous for being disappointed his eyes are no longer on me.

"You act like you didn't just see me this past weekend." His voice is smooth and deep.

"Is it a crime for me to want to see my brother often?" Sevyn asks him. She never mentioned she had a brother.

"Why do you want to meet up at some hipster ass coffee shop anyway? All this bullshit tastes the same," he says.

Figures, he fits the whole asshole vibe. I may be taking more offense then necessary because it's my uncle's coffee shop. But I think this guy is probably just an asshole.

Sevyn raises her hand towards me like she is presenting me on a game show. "Harlow works here."

His brow furrows as his eyes rake over me. "And why does this matter?"

My eyes narrow and I glare at him. I am a *this to him*, not even a *she*. Well, fuck you too, then. If I hadn't blinked, I would have sworn I saw a smirk tugging at the corner of his lips.

"It matters because she is fucking amazing," Sevyn says matter-of-factly. I hand her order to her, and she takes a sip and closes her eyes. "Harlow, this is so good." She takes another sip and side-eyes her brother.

"This, regrettably, is my brother Acyn. He owns a tattoo shop a few blocks from here." She looks at me and beams. "Acyn, this is Harlow. She's my yoga instructor but she works here to help out her uncle, so I thought I would come see her. And I'm glad that I did because this coffee is fucking delicious." She hugs her cup between her hands.

I give him a half-smile because he behaves more pretentiously than the hipsters that frequent this shop. But I still try to practice good customer service. "Nice to meet you. Can I get you anything?"

"Eight-ounce Americano." It comes out of his mouth like a demand.

"Coming up." I force a smile, but it fades as soon as I turn around. I roll my eyes because he was a pleasure to look at... until he opened his mouth. He and Sevyn walk off and settle into armchairs near the window. The sun is just starting to set and it's almost time for me to go home. I don't mind helping my uncle, but I feel exhausted on days I work both jobs.

I walk over to them and hand Acyn his coffee. He takes the coffee and observes it for a moment then puts the cup to his lips. As he sips, his ember eyes peer at me from over the rim of the cup.

"It's good, right?" Sevyn asks.

He takes another sip and then sets the cup back down on the saucer. "It tastes burned."

I cover my mouth with my hand and then reach for his cup. "I'm so sorry. I can-"

He puts his tattooed hand over mine to stop me from taking his cup and I bite my lip because his touch feels electric.

"You're fine, I'll choke it down somehow," he says with a smirk.

I immediately remove my hand as though he burned me and glare at him. I'm two seconds away from calling him an asshole when Sevyn beats me to it.

"You're such an asshole, Acyn. Don't listen to him, Harlow." She gives me an apologetic smile. "He has a permanent dick stuck up his ass."

I try not to laugh but it bubbles up in my throat and escapes me. His eyes narrow at me, but I see the glimmer in them.

"On that note, I am going home. I'll see you next week, Sev. Acyn, if you ever want another burned cup of coffee, you know where to find me." I wave to Sevyn who is now in a fit of laughter. I flip my hair over my shoulder, turn on my heel, and walk away. I'll be damned if I let this guy ruin my day.

When I walk back through the shop to leave, I can feel his gaze on me, but I don't bother looking at him. He can choke on my burned coffee for all I care.

ACYN

I watch her walk out the door and round the corner. I smile into my cup of coffee as I finish it off.

"How long have you known her?" I try to sound casual because I don't want to give my sister any indication that I'm interested.

She puts a finger on her chin and her eyes look up to the ceiling as she thinks. "Only a few weeks now. Do you think she's pretty?" She presses me with a smirk on her lips.

I have to watch what I say, or my sister will be setting up a date.

I keep a straight face and shrug. "She's alright." I'm fucking lying. I couldn't take my eyes off of her. She couldn't keep her eyes off of me either... until I opened my mouth. I tend to have that effect on women. Some, the really thirsty ones, can look past it if they are looking for a quick fuck. If my judgement is correct, Harlow doesn't seem like she would be down for a quick fuck. She seems more like the type that wants to know what your sign is to see if your compatibility is written in the stars.

"Uh huh, I know you're a rolling stone but, it wouldn't hurt to make friends," Sevyn says. "She's new here anyway."

"Where is she from?"

"Texas. She just got her first apartment and—" she looks at me and then narrows her eyes. "Wait, why do you even care?"

"I don't... you just seemed obsessed with her, so I thought I'd ask. Is it a crime to ask questions?"

"No, but you were a bit of a dick to her. Clearly that coffee didn't taste bad, or you wouldn't have finished it."

"Or I just don't want to throw money away..."

She scoffs. "Like you have to worry about fucking money."

Sevyn is right, I don't have to worry about money. I own two tattoo shops and am considering opening up a third. I started when I was eighteen and gave every ounce of energy I had to my art. Now at twenty-five, the hard work is finally paying off. I am more successful than what I could have ever imagined being. I've been booked all year for the past three years and have just started seeing celebrity clients. So no, a four-dollar cup of coffee is the least of my worries.

"Don't you have somewhere to be? I see you put on something other than yoga pants for once." I grin and wait for her to smack me.

She punches my arm. "You try having kids instead of freely dipping your dick into whatever flavor you feel like. Then we'll see how put together you are, asshole."

"I don't freely dip my dick... anymore. That was just a phase. I don't have time for that shit now," I admit while rubbing my arm. That lifestyle used to be exciting for me, but a warm body can only do so much for you. After a while you want more. Not that I am actively looking. I am fine with my own company.

Her phone chimes with a text and she glances at it. "Zane is here. Are you coming by on Sunday for dinner?"

"Do I have a choice?"

With a sarcastic smile, she knocks my foot off the table it is resting on as she walks past.

"No, you don't." She starts walking away when she turns back around. "Be nice to Harlow, okay? I actually think you two could get along. Plus, she has no friends."

"Damn, I'm sure she really appreciates you putting her business out there like that. And if you're her only friend... she's really fucked." I smirk and she flicks me off as she leaves to meet Zane.

8

Harlow

The afternoon sun filters through the trees as Ava and I walk through the forest behind the house.

"How are you settling in here?" Ava asks.

"It's starting to feel like home." I smile.

"Good! Are you making friends? I know it's hard to move from a place you've lived your whole life and start new somewhere else."

"Yeah, it is, but I think I'm doing alright. I've made some friends through teaching classes at the studio. We've hung out a few times and I've enjoyed myself." Aside from Ava, I have met a few other people who have invited me out to do things. I was wrapped up in Hendrix for so long that I forgot what it's like to go out and have friends of my own.

"See, and you were worried about making friends." She nudges my arm, smiling.

"I've never kept a lot of friends anyway. I kind of made my boyfriend my life for two years and I am just rediscovering what friends are."

"I take it you're not dating anyone, then? I thought that maybe you and that boy you were with the other day were seeing each other."

I shake my head. "No, no Kyrell and I are just friends. I am honestly not even interested in dating right now. Things are still complicated between my ex and I." I let out a sigh. "I want to focus on myself. I'm okay with being single."

Ava wraps her arm around me. "There is nothing wrong with being committed to yourself. When you're not focused on love, that's when it sweeps you up."

I tip my face up toward the sun rays and let them warm my skin as we walk home. Love is the furthest thing from my mind. I am not ready for another relationship. Hendrix and I still talk. After our phone call the first night I was here, we talked a lot. Then as we fell into our new routines, the talks became less frequent. I tried to tell myself that I was talking to him because I missed him but honestly, he is also my security blanket. He has been there my whole life and I can't deny that he knows me well. The problem with comfort is that it makes it easier to slip into routines. It makes it easier for us to become stagnant. I don't want to be stagnant and that's what I felt like with him. That I wasn't growing and exploring.

I want to be able to know myself outside of being with someone. I want to fall in love with myself.

No, I *need* to fall in love with myself.

Walking into the yoga studio classroom, I start the music, and then carefully weave my way through the students to the front of the class. Once I reach my mat, I sit cross-legged and rest my palms on my legs. Taking a few deep breaths, I begin the class.

"All you'll need for the next hour is yourself. Give thanks to yourself for being here today. Not only for making it to your mat but, more importantly, for showing up for yourself every single day. Starting each day anew even when you may not feel like it. The most important relationship we will ever cultivate is the one that we have with ourselves."

I look around the classroom and guide everyone to close their eyes. "Whenever you are feeling overwhelmed, whether it be here on your mat or out there in the world, remember you can come back to yourself." After guiding them, and myself, through a few rounds of breath, I begin the class.

I have been working at Celeste's studio, Eunoia Yoga, for almost two months now. I remember being so nervous to start teaching classes because being in front of people, guiding them, makes me nervous. After the first few classes I told Celeste that I wasn't sure if I was a good fit for a yoga instructor. She sucked her teeth and showed me the reviews that had been posted since the studio's opening:

"I took a class with Harlow. Her voice is soothing, and she makes every level of yogi feel welcomed."

"Harlow needs to record herself doing meditations. It was the most relaxing experience I've had."

"I feel like I actually belong to this studio. The instructor is so welcoming."

I can't help but grin because I didn't feel like I was doing a good job. Celeste tells me that I need to stop doubting myself and trust that I know what I'm doing. She teases me that people only come here for me. I always brush off that remark but it's hard to deny when my classes are fully booked as soon as the schedule is posted for the week. The proof is in the pudding, she says.

I am gaining confidence in myself as a teacher. The reviews and Celeste's encouragement help but I still have to find the confidence within myself. People can tell you what you are all day, but you really have to believe it yourself for you to be able to embody it. I am getting there.

For the next hour, I guide my students through their practice. I watch their stress, worries, and anxieties melt down onto their mat with their sweat. I am grateful that I can play a small part in helping someone find peace. Even if it is only for a little while.

Once the class is over, I sit outside waiting for my students as they trickle out of the class to offer them words of encouragement.

Sevyn comes walking through the door, her face flushed, wearing a grin. "Way to kick our asses in there."

The corners of my mouth turn up. "You must enjoy it if you're taking private and group lessons," I tease.

Her brow furrows with contemplation. "When you put it that way, I do sound a little crazy, don't I?"

I let out a laugh. "We all have a little crazy in us."

"Speaking of crazy, would you want to come over to my house today and meet my kids and husband?"

I am both elated and let down that she invited me to her house. "I would love too but, I already committed to helping out at the coffee shop this afternoon." My shoulders sag. "I'm sorry."

"Don't be sorry. You're a busy woman. Trust me, there will be plenty of opportunities for you to come over." She slings her bag over her shoulder.

I grin. "Thanks. I'll see you later!" She waves as she heads towards the front doors. I would much rather spend the day with her then work at the coffee shop. West asked me this morning if I could help out. Well, he practically begged me to help out because another employee called in sick. Since my only plans for the day were to chill at home and sleep, I agreed.

I inhale deeply as I enter the coffee shop. I don't know that I will ever tire of the smell of freshly brewed coffee and warmed pastries. A guitarist is strumming away on stage and his smooth voice carries throughout the shop. Despite there being a line that nearly reaches the doors, the energy is calm and inviting.

Uncle West is behind the counter making drinks and talking to customers. He is in his element. I can tell he really enjoys being here. When he sees me walking in, he smiles. "Hey! Thanks again for coming to help out."

I wave him off and smile. "Not a problem. What can I do to help?"

"We got a delivery order in from a shop a couple of blocks from here. Would you mind making the drinks and delivering them?"

It's a nice spring day so the chance to walk outside sounds perfect. "Yeah, let me set my things down and I'll get on it."

I wrap an apron around my waist and read over the delivery order that came in. There are a total of eight drinks, so I busy myself with making them because the order came in nearly half an hour ago. Once

I finish making them all and secure them in a drink carrier, I tell West that I'm leaving and make my way to the address on the delivery receipt. I am grateful the shop isn't too far because I'm already running late.

As I approach the shop, I stare up at the sign to make sure that I have the right address and then read the shop's name: Crown Ink. It's a sleek, modern tattoo shop. Definitely not what I envision a tattoo shop to be when someone mentions one. I think of seedy locations with neon signs, kind of like the one in Bali, but this shop is none of that.

I enter and walk into the reception area. There is a girl with electric blue hair and black, thick-rimmed glasses sitting behind the counter. "Hi, welcome. Who do you have an appointment with?"

I am too busy staring around the shop and don't immediately respond to her. "Do you have an appointment or are you wanting a consultation?" She smiles.

"Oh no I'm—" but before I can state why my eyes fall on a familiar face.

ACYN

I just finished up with my afternoon client and glance out my shop's windows. I have to double-take because I realize that the girl my sister introduced me to is standing out there staring at the sign. She has the coffees I ordered— I glance at the clock on the wall— almost an hour ago in her hands. Not that I give a fuck about how long it took her to get here. I'm actually glad it took her longer because it would have gone cold while I finished up with my client. That doesn't stop me from wanting to give her shit about it. A smile pulls at my lips as I make my way to the lobby.

I hear her talking to Riley. Well, more so, Riley talking to her, because Harlow is too busy looking around the shop with curiosity to listen to what she has to say. I enjoy the view of her. She has a willowy frame with legs for days, a nice ass. Her skin is a rich, velvety golden brown, and she has light brown kinky curly hair that is piled on top of her head in a bun, Her bright brown almond shaped eyes look like sunshine shining through a glass of whiskey. Okay, so I may have studied her a little harder than what I let onto my sister. Fucking sue me. It would be a sin to not appreciate a nice view.

She starts to respond to Riley. "Oh, no I'm—" but when she turns around to examine the rest of the shop her gaze falls on me and she stops mid-sentence.

"Late," I finish her sentence for her.

She stands there with her lips slightly parted as if she isn't sure what to say.

Her full lips curve into a smile and she starts looking around the shop again as she talks. "Yeah, sorry, it's busy at the shop and I shouldn't even be working today, but my uncle needed me so I decided to work so..." Her voice trails off and she holds out the cup holder to me. "They should be hot..."

I don't immediately take them, I just let her stand there for a few seconds holding them out to me while I continue to stare at her. She raises an eyebrow, still with a smile on her face, and I take them. Does she always smile this much?

"Is it burned?" I ask and try my best to keep the smile off of my face.

Her eyes narrow and she crosses her arms over her chest. "I don't know, why don't you taste it and tell me since you're such a coffee connoisseur."

I can't help the smile that pulls at my lips. I look for my cup of Americano and grab it. I turn my attention towards Riley. "Can you take these back for the rest of the crew?" Riley gets up and looks between Harlow and I, clearly confused. I rarely make small talk with people. Especially someone who is delivering coffee.

Harlow's eyes follow Riley as she leaves. Her smile is back on her face. "She's nice."

"That's because I pay her to be."

"Yeah, imagine customers having to deal with you first? Tragic." Her voice sounds like honey laced with venom.

This time, I give her a genuine smile and she rolls her eyes.

"Well, I better get back to the shop. It's really busy right now."

I pique an eyebrow. "Aren't you curious as to whether the coffee is burned or not?"

She rests her hands on her hips. "I know it isn't, Acyn." I'm shocked she remembered my name and that she calls me Acyn instead of Ace. Only family and a few close friends call me Acyn. To everyone else I'm Ace, the tattoo guy.

"You can call me Ace."

She blinks at me and snorts with laughter.

"What's so funny?" I ask.

"Nothing... Ace," she says my nickname with a sarcastic tone and then chuckles. "I'll call you Acyn. It sounds better anyway."

I study her for a moment as she stands there, and she shifts her weight to her other foot, waiting for me to say something back. Instead, I take a sip of the coffee she brought me and peer over the cup at her. When I am done with my sip, which was fucking good, she raises her eyebrows waiting for me to say something.

"It still tastes burned. Who—" but before I can finish my sentence, she closes the gap between us and reaches for my cup of coffee. She snatches it from my hand, and I brace to have hot coffee thrown on me. Instead, she raises the cup to her lips and takes a drink. She takes another drink and smacks her lips loudly at me.

"What the hell are you doing?" I ask her, confused because, one: she doesn't know me and she just drank from my cup, and two: she is smacking her lips at me like she's lost her fucking marbles.

She scrunches up her face as she continues to taste my coffee. "I'm just trying to see if I accidentally put a shot of asshole in there and I think I fucking did."

I raise my brows in disbelief and then let out a rumble of laughter.

She smiles and hands me back my cup of coffee. "Enjoy your burned coffee, asshole." Before I can think of a comeback, she is heading out the door. Once outside, she looks over her shoulder at me with a smile.

Harlow

I hustle back to the shop knowing I took too long talking shit with Acyn. Who the hell does he think he is anyway? That coffee wasn't burned in the slightest. It's almost as if it pains him to be a decent human being towards me. But maybe he's just like that with everyone. I don't know, but what I do know is that he isn't going to talk to me any type of way. I may be quiet but that doesn't mean I'm not willing to stand my ground.

Thankfully when I re-enter the shop the crowd that was in earlier has died down. I find West behind the counter again.

"Did you find the shop okay?" he asks.

"Yeah, I did," I say with a smile and leave out the part that the owner of the shop is an asshole.

"Good." He smiles. "I'm going to head out then unless you wanted me to stay, and you can go since you've been working all day?"

"No, go home to Ava. I'll be fine, just don't ask me for shit tomorrow."

He lets out a bark of laughter. "Fair enough. Thanks for coming in."

"Yeah, yeah. See ya later." I wave him away.

Since the crowd has now died down, I decide to pull out my laptop and research photography courses. It is something that has been in the back of my mind since Ava mentioned it to me weeks ago. There is an abundance of courses available, so it really comes down to me choosing one. That's another reason why I haven't said no to any extra hours here at the shop; I want to be able to pay for the photography courses. Although I know that if I asked my dad, he wouldn't hesitate to help me.

But this is something that I want to do for myself. Since I've been "adulting" I've learned that things mean more to you when you're the one who has to invest in them. I'll tell my dad once I've enrolled in a few classes. That way he can't try and pay for them. For the next few hours, I switch between my laptop and the counter, helping customers. The live entertainment that was here earlier has now gone and there is a steady trickle of people placing orders.

I glance at the clock and realize it's nine p.m. I wait for the last few customers to leave and then lock the door behind them. I turn up the music a little louder and start cleaning. It doesn't take me long because West, that work-a-holic, took care of most of it before he left.

I am in the middle of wiping down the counter when I see someone walk past the front of the shop. When I glance up again, I see it's Acyn. He goes to try the door and I stand there staring at him with a smile on my face. He points to the handle signaling for me to open it. I hold up a finger to tell him to wait a second. I quickly find a piece of paper and scribble on it. "We're fresh out of burned coffee."

I make my way around the counter and head towards the door. He has a smile on his face. Once I reach the door, I place the paper against the window so he can read it. I must admit that I find so much fucking joy as he leans down to read the paper and as he registers what it says. I then press my middle finger to the glass and give him a smile.

He tosses his head back and erupts with laughter. I laugh along with him. Once he catches his breath, he looks at me, raises his hands, and says, "Fair enough. I'll see you around Harlow." He gives me a two-finger salute and walks off into the night.

I watch him go and smile as he does.

9

Harlow

Sevyn and I sit out on the trampoline while her kids bounce around us. I was going to stay in bed all day since it's Sunday and I have a full day off, but she said she had food and mimosas. Who am I to pass that up? Plus, I enjoy her company.

"Let me know if they're bothering you and I can send them inside with Zane."

I suck my teeth. "Girl, please, they're fine. Look at how happy they are." Her twins Eli and Emery zip around the trampoline in circles, giggling and chasing each other.

"When we first had Eli and Emery, Zane and I lost a lot of our friends. We were nineteen and most of them were into the party lifestyle. He and I weren't. Well, we couldn't be because I got pregnant. We became focused on our family and education," Sevyn says. "You know that I work as a healthcare claim specialist and Zane works in software development. We've created a nice life for ourselves and our kids... but I would be lying if I said I don't miss having real friends and being like most twenty-four year-olds. So, when I met you and we clicked, I hoped you wouldn't be a bitch about me being so young and having kids."

I tilt my head to the side. "So you're telling me that people you grew up with jumped ship once you started building a life?"

She nods.

"That's low of them, but... people who fade in and out of your life... they don't matter. The ones who do matter will stand by your side regardless of what you got going on."

She lets out a sigh. "You're right, but it's still difficult to make friends."

"I think making friends doesn't come as naturally as everyone makes it out to seem. Or maybe it does because we're friends now." I smile.

"Yeah, you're stuck with me," she says. We both laugh. "Are you sure you don't want to stay for dinner? Zane is making BBQ," she asks.

"Thank you for offering, but my aunt and uncle are expecting me. Besides, doesn't your whole family come over on Sunday?"

"They do and now that I think of it, they are all running late per usual."

I laugh at her look of annoyance and hop off the trampoline. "Maybe another time then. Thanks for having me over. It was a lot of fun." She hops down off trampoline and gives me a hug.

"Tell Harlow goodbye, you two," she says to the twins.

"Byeeee," they say in unison. I give them a wave and they giggle in response.

"I'll see you in class." Carrying my shoes in my hand, I let my toes sink into the lush green grass as I head to my car. I had a nice afternoon with her adorable family. Sevyn and I are a year apart, but she is wise beyond her years. I wish I had my shit together like her. I don't think she realizes how badass she is. Not many people could create the life she has while raising two kids. She definitely needs to give herself more credit.

When I reach my car a sleek, matte black Mercedes G-Wagon pulls up next to mine. The window rolls down and a familiar smooth, deep voice calls my attention.

"Are you stalking me?"

Amused, I peer through the opened window at Acyn. "Don't flatter yourself. You're not that exciting."

He chuckles and gets out of his car. "I see you're not busy subjecting anyone to your terrible coffee making skills." He teases with a grin on his face.

"Hahaha... you're hilarious," I say with a roll of my eyes as I climb into my car.

"Nice car. Did you restore it?" he says, referring to my 1971 baby blue Ford Bronco.

I smile at him. "Thank you. My dad and I did."

He gives me a curious look as I start my car. "You're not staying for dinner?"

I slide my shades on. "No, I just came to see Sev and the kids. I'll see you around."

He nods. "Yeah, see you around. Maybe I'll stop by for another cup of shitty coffee."

I snort with laughter. "Go to hell." I put my car in reverse. "Watch your toes, I would hate to run them over."

He takes a few steps back with a grin on his face.

Between teaching group and private classes at the yoga studio and shifts at the coffee shop, I am beat. I just finished my shift at the coffee shop and instead of going home, I decide to a do a little more research on photography classes. I'm a naturally indecisive person who likes external validation, and that carries over into all areas of my life. I have read each class's description at least a hundred times. But I've yet to pull the trigger on enrolling in one. After the week I've had, the thought of adding one more thing to my already busy schedule makes me question my sanity.

Before I can even take a class, I need to buy an actual camera. I've only ever used my phone and if I want to be professional, I can't pull out my phone and expect people to pay me. If people already like my photos, the thought of what I could do with a real camera makes me excited.

I am hunched over staring at my computer screen, when the sound of a chair being dragged across the floor and someone clearing their throat interrupts my thoughts. When I look up, Acyn plops down on the seat in front of me. He has a smile on his face and cup of coffee in his hand.

"Uh, hi." I scan the room to see if maybe all the other tables are full, they aren't. "Why are you sitting here?"

"Why not?" he asks with a shrug of his shoulders.

I straighten up from being hunched over my computer screen. "I mean, I guess... I just... never mind." I don't understand why he is sitting with me when there are plenty of seats around me available.

"What are you working on?" he asks as he takes a sip of his coffee.

I sit back in my chair and cross my arms. "Are you really interested in what I'm doing or are you just here to be annoying?"

Usually, if I'm working, Acyn will stop in for a drink and then proceed to tell me how terrible it tastes. I know he's full of shit but that doesn't stop him from telling me all the improvements that could be made. Next time he does that, I am going to tell him to get behind the counter and make it.

"Both," he says with a piqued brow. Then he reaches for my laptop and spins it around to face him before I can close it.

"Excuse you." I reach for it, and he moves it off the table out of my reach. I don't have the energy to get up and snatch it back, so I sit back in my seat and wait for him to finish being nosy.

He scrolls for a good minute. "Are you into photography?"

"I mean... kind of. It's something I want to try and get better at. My aunt suggested I try it since my Instagram does so well."

He smirks. "Are you an influencer?"

"No, I just enjoy traveling, food, and an occasional picture of myself if the lighting is good. I've built up a decent following."

He nods and goes back to looking at the cameras. "Maybe you can come and take pictures at the studio. I've been wanting to up our social media presence and update our website." I scoff and his eyes snap to mine. "What's so funny?" he asks.

I set my elbow on the table and rest my chin on my hand. "Why, when you don't even like me? All you do is give me a hard time."

"I don't." He shrugs. "But that doesn't mean that I couldn't hire you to take nice pictures." He sets my laptop back on the table and I snap it close.

"I don't get you, but if you're going to give me money to take pictures of your shitty tattoos, why not?"

He lets out a bark of laughter and I try to suppress a smile.

"Why be nice to you when giving you shit is so much more fun?" he asks.

"So fun," I say sarcastically. My phone starts ringing where it's sitting on the table. I see Hendrix's photo on my screen. I ignore it. I don't want to talk to him right now.

"You're not gonna answer that?" he asks.

I shake my head and silence my phone when it rings again. He's already calling me back. "Not when I am engaged in this riveting conversation with you."

"Take a picture of me," he suggests, straightening up in his chair. He gives me a lopsided grin waiting for me to take a picture.

A giggle escapes me. "What the hell is that?"

His smile fades. "What?"

"Is this supposed to be your," I form air quotes with my hands, "sexy look?"

He scoffs. "You can't handle a sexy look from me," he says giving me an up and down look.

"You're so confident in yourself. I've seen better." I'm lying through my fucking teeth. Acyn is a fine specimen of a man, but I will give no indication that I find him attractive. Instead, I start to take pictures of him as he laughs at my remark. He is mid-laugh, the light is filtering in through the windows, really making his tattoos stand out against his rich copper skin.

I slide my phone across the table when I'm satisfied with the pictures I've taken. "Don't swipe too far," I say with a wink.

"What the hell do you have on your phone?" he asks curiously. I shrug and wait for him to look at the pictures while I start packing up my things. I haven't taken any risqué pictures in a while, so if he scrolls all he will see are food and scenery pictures. But the look on his face is hilarious.

He scrolls cautiously and then a smile appears on his lips as he looks at the pictures I took of him. "You're surprisingly good at capturing people."

I snort. "Gee, thanks for the backhanded compliment." I snatch my phone out of his hand as I stand to leave.

"I didn't mean it –" He looks at my bag on my forearm. "You're leaving?"

"Yeah, it's been a long week and I'm looking forward to becoming one with my bed."

He chuckles. "Alright, well can I have your Instagram? I was serious about you taking pictures for the shop."

I'm caught off guard. "Oh, yeah, okay. Ummm... if you give me your phone I can just type it into your Instagram search." He leans back in his chair, slides his phone out of his pocket, and hands it to me. I type in my handle and hand it back to him. "Enjoy being a stalker. I'll see you around."

He laughs and gives me a two-finger salute. "See you around."

On my way back to my car, I contemplate uploading the picture of Acyn. It's a great picture. It also helps that he is good-looking. If I upload it though, Hendrix is going to have a shit fit. I have to constantly remind him that we aren't together, and we are both free to do as we please. Even though I'm not doing anything. I've told him a million times I am not interested in a relationship right now with anyone, not just him.

I decide to upload the picture. What good is it being thousands of miles away from him if I still take him into consideration? It's not as though I've strung him along. I have been blatantly clear about where I am right now, and he still thinks we're together. I chew on my thumbnail as my other thumb hovers over the check mark to upload. I say fuck it and press it because I am proud of the picture. I'm exhausted from taking Hendrix's feelings into consideration when we aren't even together. I leave my phone on silent because I know he is going to blow up my phone and I don't want to hear it.

ACYN

I step into my boxers and let the towel that was around my waist fall to the floor. It was a long day and all I wanted was a hot shower and to fall in my bed. But, when I saw Harlow sitting at the coffee shop, I stopped in to talk to her. She doesn't give me the same attention that most women do. Not to be an arrogant son of a bitch, but I don't have to do much when it comes to women. They see the tattoos, the muscles, the nice clothes, the car, and it's a wrap. Not her, though; she's been annoyed with me since the moment she met me.

I find it entertaining and refreshing. I flop onto my bed and decide to finally look at her Instagram. Even though she thought I was joking about taking pictures for the shop, I wasn't. Nowadays you have to have a presence on social media in order to thrive. I've seen businesses miss out on potential customers because their social media presence was lacking. I navigate to her page and mumble, "Holy shit." When she said decent following, I was thinking she meant a few thousand followers... not almost a million followers.

Shit, maybe I can learn something from her. I also can't deny that she really does know how to take pictures. I wonder what she could do if she had a real camera and not just her phone. When I snatched her laptop from her, she was looking at cameras, so I assume that she doesn't have one. I scroll back to the top of her page and sit up when I see someone that looks familiar.

I click on it and it's a picture of me with the caption: *annoying*. It really is a good picture but the fact that she called me annoying has me cracking up. I am even more surprised to see that the photo already has thousands of likes. The comments are "Who is he," "#thristtrap" and lots of people asking if I am a tattoo artist. The entrepreneur in me sees this as an opportunity to boost my business. Even though I'm not looking for clients, the other artists in my shop are just as good as me. I am serious about my business and helping other artists.

I follow her and send her a DM.

Acyn: Hey it's me, annoying.

I scroll through her pictures and see she has photos with friends. There are a few photos that she has a with a guy that looks like a fuck boy. Judging from the comments they were together at some point. I check the date and their last photo together she posted was a few months ago. I do what any sane person does and follow the tag to his page. All his pictures are of Harlow, baseball, himself, and flashy cars. Scrolling past countless pictures of Harlow, I realize he is a professional baseball play for the Houston Astros.

He seems to be... obsessed with her. Clearly Harlow doesn't feel the same way about him as he does her. Reading the captions and his replies to comments it's almost like he has a sense of entitlement to her. Exactly as I said... he's a fuck boy. I switch back to Harlow's page and start to scroll again when I get a DM from her:

Harlow: LMAO I was wondering if you would really check out my page or not.

Acyn: Why wouldn't I?

Harlow: Because you're you...

Acyn: To live up to my name, your pictures are alright. The best one is of me.

Harlow: I knew I just had to wait for the arrogance to drop in.

Acyn: LOL shouldn't you be one with your bed?

She sends me a picture of herself wrapped up like a fucking burrito in her bed. I decide since she responds in pictures I will too. I send her a picture of me laying in my bed with my cat.

Harlow: Your picture would be perfect if you were out of it, and it was just your cat.

Her text causes me to laugh out loud and my cat leaps off the bed. I can't remember the last time I genuinely laughed with a girl who isn't my sister.

Acyn: LOL You talk about me but you're no better.

Harlow: I got to keep up with you and your onslaught of insults.

Acyn: I can't help it. It's a knee jerk reaction when it comes to you.

Harlow: Yeah, yeah... so really... what do you think of my page?

Acyn: I think you do have talent. I'm still serious about working with you.

Harlow: You should comment and tag your business page so I can pin it.

Acyn: Alright.

Maybe Sevyn was right... she and I could be friends. Not because of what she can do for me business-wise, but because I actually enjoy talking to her. I can't tolerate talking to a lot of women because they want one thing usually... but her... she's different.

10

Harlow

I was right. Hendrix lost his shit. I blocked all his calls and messages last night because I already knew the tantrum that was coming my way. After eating breakfast and waking up, I decide to answer his twentieth video call. I wish I were lying, but he really did call me twenty times.

"You're a hard person to reach." His jaw is tense; he looks like he's trying so hard not to fly off the handle.

"Yeah, I came home after work last night and went to sleep." I leave out the part where Acyn and I spent a few hours texting each other.

"Who's your friend with the tattoos?" He wastes no time getting to the root of his distress.

I can't help but roll my eyes. "Oh for fucks sake, is this why you're on my Facetime? Not even to see how I'm doing?"

"You seem to be doing alright if you're posting pictures of guys who look like they belong in prison."

"I didn't realize tattoos were a requirement for prison," I quip.

He shakes his head and rakes his fingers through his curls. "Are you fucking him?"

I erupt with laughter. "Are you fucking kidding me right now? First of all, he would never want to fuck me and last time I checked, I am single and can be friends with whoever I damn well please."

"Is he gay?"

I scoff. "So, the only way he could not want to have sex with me is if he's gay?"

"You act like you're ugly, Harlow."

"You know what, when I see him next, I'll ask him if he wants to fuck me and let you know how it plays out."

His jaw flexes and I can tell he is trying his best to not flip out on me. "Think of how this looks, Harlow. I mean people know Kyrell, but this guy... who the fuck is he?"

"I don't care how it looks, Hendrix, because I know how it is and it isn't how you're making it seem."

He rakes his hands through his curls again and sighs. I don't say anything because there isn't anything left to say. After a moment he finally asks, "Would you tell me if you were seeing someone else?"

"I thought that you and I were friends, but you keep making me think that we would be better off not talking at all," I say. Maybe it was naïve of me to think that he and I could remain friends after being together for so long. I think that maybe there will always be a piece of me that wants him in my life even though I know that we would probably be better off parting ways.

"No, no, baby, don't say that," he begs.

"Look, I've got to go. I'm helping West at the coffee shop. I'll catch up with you when I can." I hang up on him and block his calls and messages... *again*.

Stepping onto my mat, I exhale, feeling as though it is the first time I have breathed all morning. The conversation with Hendrix did nothing for my mood. I am grateful that I have some time on my mat this morning before heading into work. It has become rare for me to be a student here at the studio because I spend so much of my time teaching. While I do enjoy teaching, I miss being a student. When I'm teaching, I have to be mindful of everyone in my class and I can't really focus on poses unless I'm just demonstrating for them to follow along.

By the end of the class, I do feel lighter. I'm still contemplating whether having Hendrix in my life is a good thing or not. We were friends before we ever had a relationship, but I think we've reached the point of no return for that now. I don't know why I can't simply let him go. It isn't as easy as people make it seem. Letting go takes a lot of time, indecisiveness, and fuck ups before you can officially walk away and feel done. I am not there yet, and I guess that's okay, even though I am wishing that I were.

Kyrell is in town and wants to meet up for lunch. Since I'm working, I asked him to come see me during my lunch break. He knows West and Ava now because he and I have become best friends again since I've moved here. When he walks into the shop, West greets him like they have been lifelong friends. It makes me smile because I don't think there is a person that I've met that doesn't like Kyrell.

I shrug out of my apron, hang it up in the back, and go out front to meet him. "Hey." I give him a hug. "It's good to see you. We should eat outside."

"Yeah, sure, whatever you want, Harls." He turns his attention back to West. "We'll have to set up a time to talk more about the dispensary."

"Yes, definitely!" West agrees. "Enjoy your break."

We step outside and I pick a table that is in direct sunlight.

"You know, you would think growing up in humid ass Texas that you would be tired of the sun," Kyrell says with a grin on his face.

I turn my face towards the sun, squint my eyes closed, and smile. "Never will I ever tire of the sun. There's not enough of it here. And you have some nerve living in California."

"Are you happy here despite the lack of sun?"

I chuckle. "Yeah, I am, actually. How about you? Are you enjoying California living?"

He gives me a huge grin. "I love it. Probably the best decision I made for myself. I actually just bought the space I wanted to open my dispensary."

I gape at him. "What? Really? Kyrell, this is amazing news! Why didn't you tell me sooner?"

He laughs. "I didn't want to make a big deal."

"That's bullshit. You love a good party," I say. He lets out a bark of laughter. "But... wow, your very own dispensary, huh? That's amazing! You're doing what you said you would years ago!"

After Kyrell came back home from Louisiana State University he told me that his dream was to start his own dispensary. He can make some amazing edibles and of course loves marijuana.

He bows in his seat. "Thank you, thank you! I tried calling Hendrix to tell him, but he was too hung up on you posting a picture of some guy to even congratulate me."

I drop my sub sandwich back onto the paper I just unwrapped it from and lean back in my chair. "Hung up? No, he was on a mission! Do you know how many times he called me after I posted it? Twenty fucking times!"

Kyrell is smiling because he thinks it's hilarious when Hendrix gets his feathers ruffled. "You had to know that was going to happen, though."

I shrug and roll my eyes. "We aren't together anymore, Kyrell! He asked me to think about how it looks." I suck my teeth. "I don't give a fuck how it looks. It was an amazing picture. End of story."

He sighs, shaking his head. His shoulder-length locs fall into his eyes. "You know that you're going to have to be the one to cut things off, right? Because he never will. He truly believes that you two are meant to be together."

I take a bite out of my sandwich and chew on it. Am I ready to cut things off completely with Hendrix? Kyrell knows him just as well as I do, if not better. "It's complicated."

"I know. I'm not saying you have to cut him off right this second, but I am letting you know that in his head, you're his endgame."

"Yeah, I—" I lose my train of thought because Acyn is walking towards our table. "Speak of the devil."

"What?" Kyrell asks confused.

Acyn reaches our table. "Am I interrupting something?" he asks. I can tell he is trying to hide a smile.

I squint up at him and he moves to block the sunlight from my eyes. "Thank you and no, you're not. I'm just having lunch here with my friend Kyrell. Kyrell, this is Acyn, the guy from my Instagram."

Kyrell's face lights up. Oh shit, here we go. He stands to greet Acyn like he is the President of the United States. "Hey man, nice to meet you." Kyrell is shaking his hand vigorously and I already know he is going to do something to really piss Hendrix off. He lives for it. It's all in good fun, Hendrix knows it, but he still lets it get to him.

"I'm the guy from Instagram now?" he asks as he pulls up a chair to our table.

Yeah, sure join us for lunch. I take another bite of my sandwich as I stare at him.

"It's a long story," I say.

"Care to share?" Acyn asks.

"No, I don't. Kyrell and I already talked about it."

"I was checking out your page last night. I don't have any ink, but I'd love to get some. How can I get booked with you?" Kyrell asks and then gives me a wink. I stare back at him wondering if he is being serious.

"I can see if I have any availability. I'm booked solid a year in advance, but I do make special accommodations for people... especially if they're friends with Harlow."

I almost choke on my sandwich as he says this because I am not used to him being the slightest bit nice to me. He must have noticed because he chuckles.

"That would be great, man. I don't know if Harls told you, but I don't live here."

Acyn gives me a questioning look. "Harls?"

"It's a nickname I've had since I was a kid and it stuck." I shrug.

"And you talk about Ace." I can't help but laugh because I know Harls isn't the cutest nickname but it's what they call me.

"Feel free to come up with a better one." I shrug but when I start thinking about it, he will probably come up with something atrocious. "Never mind, don't."

He tosses his head back and laughs. "Thought about it, didn't you?"

"It probably isn't the best idea," I say and go back to eating my sandwich. I glance at the time on my phone and realize I only have ten minutes left of my break.

Acyn takes his card out of his wallet and hands it to Kyrell. "Call me when you're ready to get inked. I'll find a time. Send me what you're thinking of, and I'll see what I can come up with."

Kyrell looks at me. "C'mon Harls, what do you say? Should we get matching tats?" He wags his eyebrows at me.

"Ummm... as tempting as that sounds, I—"

"Do you have tattoos?" Acyn asks me.

I feel the heat creep up my neck because of my small butterfly tattoo on my hip. You wouldn't be able to see it unless I took off my panties. "I do." I nod and try to leave it at that. Of course, Kyrell can't leave it there.

"Bullshit! Where?" Kyrell asks. His eyes bright with excitement.

Both of them are now staring at me waiting for me to respond. This lunch just became so awkward. "It's a small butterfly but it's on my hip near my—" I point to my jeans and Kyrell's eyes widen with recognition.

Acyn's ember eyes are on me and glittering with curiosity. At least I think it's curiosity. I'm not sure with him.

"Really? When did you get that done?" Kyrell asks.

I smile. "While I was in Bali. Marisa, Quinn and I all got one."

"See, now you have to get one with me," Kyrell says matter-of-factly.

"I don't know about matching, but I'll go with you when you do get it done."

He claps his hands together. "Sweet!"

"Wait, that's if you have enough time for the both of us?" I ask Acyn.

"Yeah, let me know when and I'll make it happen." He smiles at me.

I start to clean up my wrappings from my sandwich when West walks out. "Acyn DeConto! How have you been?"

I look between West and Acyn because I had no idea that they knew each other. Acyn gets up and gives West a dap. How in the hell do they know each other?

"I'm good. Just enjoying some conversation with Harlow and her friend." Acyn gives me a pearly white smile when he sees the confusion on my face.

"Well, I may as well invite you guys to the dinner we're having tomorrow," West says to Kyrell and Acyn. My eyes flit to West and then back to Acyn who is now looking at me with a raised eyebrow and a grin.

"If there is food, I will be there," Kyrell says to West.

He laughs. "Alright, I'll count you in." He looks over at Acyn, "What about you? I have to ask because Ava likes to know how many people are there so she can do all her planning stuff."

Acyn is looking at me. "Yeah, I'll go." His annoying, lopsided grin is still on his face.

I can't help but sigh with exasperation because I know he is only agreeing because it annoys me. "You don't even like me," I say to him.

Acyn leans forward and rests his forearms on the table. "Who says I'm going for you?"

West and Kyrell are looking between Acyn and I. I feel the heat creep up my neck again. "Oh, okay," I say with a shrug, "I'll just see my way out of this little bromance conversation that is going on." They all start laughing and I roll my eyes as I get up to throw my trash away.

"Oh, c'mon, Harls, don't be like that," Kyrell says.

I wave them off. "I have to get back inside anyway. I'll see you tomorrow."

They go back to talking but I can't hear what they're saying as the door closes behind me. I forgot about the dinner West and Ava are having tomorrow. It's in honor of West opening up the newest coffee shop. They had a celebration on the first day it opened, but Ava wants to do something more intimate for him. I love how they celebrate each other and have built each other up in their relationship. I can only hope that one day I find a love like that. One where I can grow and don't feel like I am having to erase myself for their benefit.

11
ACYN

I arrive at the party fashionably late. Social events really aren't my thing, but I am trying to put myself out there more. Even if that means I'll have to be uncomfortable for a few hours. I may own tattoo shops, but you can honestly never have enough connections. In the short time I've known West, I've learned that he is very well-connected, which isn't surprising given the fact that he has three successful business. As men of color, owning our own successful and thriving businesses is a big fucking deal.

I make my way to their backyard, and everyone is gathered around listening to music, talking, and eating. The vibe is right. I always worry about events dragging and being boring, but I can already tell that this will be anything but that. There are servers walking around with drinks and appetizers. I see that West is at the grill chatting with guests while Ava walks around conversing. They are a power couple if I ever did see one.

There's a guest house further in the back of their yard. That must be where Harlow lives. As I'm looking at the house, she comes out the front door wearing a short red sundress that hits her mid-thigh. She is laughing, as always, and is pulling Kyrell along behind her, telling him something that he is laughing at. Her hair is different; it's in waist-length twists that are adorned in gold hair jewelry.

She and Kyrell make their way towards where I am standing. Her eyes are observing the crowd of people and then they meet mine. She weaves and dances her way through the crowd which causes me to smile. When she reaches me, I'm startled when she gives me a hug. I let my creep tendencies shine bright and smell her subtly sweet, spicy perfume. She smells good, so no regrets.

"You made it. I didn't think you'd come. This doesn't seem like your scene," she says as Kyrell gives me a dap.

"It typically isn't, but West is different. So I thought I would make an effort."

She smiles. "Yeah, he and Ava sure know how to throw a party."

Know how to throw a party is an understatement. Their backyard looks like something you would see on TV.

"Have you eaten?" she asks. "Kyrell and I were just going to get something to eat. I know you're not here for me." She smirks. "But do you care to join us?"

I chuckle. "Yeah, I'll join you guys."

We make our way through the crowd of people; Harlow is leading the way. She reaches West. "Look who came," she says as she points to me.

West and I exchange greetings. "Thanks for coming. I hope you're hungry. I just finished some burgers, ribs, and hot dogs. Let me know if there's anything else you would like," he says.

"Nah man, that is more than enough to satisfy my appetite," I say as I eye the table that is filled with food. I wasn't hungry when I arrived but looking at all this food, I am going to eat like a king tonight.

"Enjoy," West says with a smile. "I'll catch up with you later."

We all fill our plates with a variety of foods and then make our way to sit down on some chairs that are away from the crowd. I am about to take a bite of my ribs when I hear a moan that catches my attention in more ways than one. When I look up Harlow has her eyes shut and she is chewing her food... and *moaning*. I can't help but stare at her.

She opens her eyes and gives me a dazed look. "This is sooo good!" she exclaims.

I have never in my life heard someone moan like that while eating food. My mind wanders as I wonder how she would be on top of – I stop the thought before I can finish it. I am still watching her eat because she looks like she is experiencing ecstasy and it's hard to look away. Kyrell is busy eating and doesn't seem to notice it. He must be used to this. I'm sure as fuck not, and neither is my dick apparently.

Her eyes flutter open. "Have you tasted it yet?" she asks.

I snap out of it and look down at my ribs that are apparently just as good as sex. "Uhhh, no, I haven't." I take a bite and I almost want to moan too. I haven't had ribs like this that are so tender that they melt in your mouth. "Damn, these are good."

She licks her fingers as she looks at me. "I told you."

I have to tell my dick to calm the fuck down. I don't know what is going on right now but we're just eating food, and she has somehow turned it into a whole different experience.

Thankfully, we start talking about shows to watch and she stops moaning. Not that I would complain if she started up again, but it makes it hard for me to eat. When we've cleared our plates, Harlow takes them and tosses them in the trash. The she collapses onto the couch and with a satisfied look on her face. "West sure can cook."

The sound of her moaning is on repeat in my head. "He sure can." A thought occurs to me, and I have to ask, "You don't call him Uncle?"

She shakes her head, "No." She laughs. "He said he's too young to be an uncle, so I dropped it."

I laugh. "He does look young to be an uncle. That's why I asked."

She shrugs. "Black doesn't crack either. My dad is forty-three and looks like a more polished version of West."

Kyrell cuts in. "Does anyone care to smoke with me?" He holds the joint in front of Harlow and her eyes light up, which surprises me. I haven't spent a lot of time with her and when I do see her, she's at work. I'm enjoying seeing this carefree side of her.

She reaches for it. "The perks of living on the west coast. Care to join?" she asks. "I understand if you want to mingle or don't smoke."

"I'll join. I don't care for small talk or mingling."

"Let me grab some blankets from my place to sit on. I'll meet you guys under the willow trees."

When she's gone, I turn to Kyrell as we walk towards the trees. "How long have you known Harlow?"

"Harls and I have known each other since sixth grade. She's like a sister to me."

I wasn't looking for an answer on their relationship status, but I can't help the small bit of relief I feel when he says that.

"That's a long time."

"Yeah, she's amazing. Are you and her friends or...?"

"I would say we are acquaintances more than anything. This is the first time I've actually spent time with her outside of the coffee shop."

"Careful." He nudges my arm and smirks. "You'll want her around all the time. She has a magnetic personality and is one of the few genuine people that I know."

He says it jokingly, but I can tell that he is serious. Since I've met her, I have found myself stopping in the shop whenever she is working. She's different to me because she is the first woman I've built a friendship with. Well... we mainly pick at each other, but that's more than what I usually have with women.

She catches up with us with blankets draped over her shoulders. Once we're standing under the shade of the willow tree, she lays the blankets out on the ground. She sits down and lays her head on Kyrell's knee. Their relationship is different. I at first thought that maybe they were sleeping together, not that that's any of my business, but after talking to him it's clear that they don't see each other that way.

I lay down on the blanket and try to remember the last time I hung out with people that weren't family in this way. Most people I know want to party and are living a faster paced life than I care to. I've always been a bit of loner and I keep my circle of friends small. I try to hang out with my best friends when I can, but we all have a lot going on. That becomes even more difficult when we don't live in the same area.

Kyrell's phone chimes with a text. "Hey Harls, I gotta go. I'm going to meet up with a lady friend before I head back to LA."

She snorts with laughter. "Lady friend?!"

"Yeah, what else am I supposed to call her?"

"Gee, I don't know, her name maybe?" She giggles.

Kyrell stares up at the cherry blossoms. "If I could remember what the fuck it is, I would." This causes even me to laugh, and he looks at me and shrugs.

"I'm keeping your weed," she proclaims as she gives him a hug. "Text me when you get home, okay?"

"Sure, Mom." He winks at her, then turns his attention to me. "It was nice to get to know you. I'll text you some ideas for the tattoos for the next time I'm in town."

"Yeah, you too, man. That sounds good to me. See you around."

Harlow twirls back around after watching him go. "You're welcome to stay if you want. I don't know if you have plans with a lady friend, too."

I chuckle. "Nah, no lady friends for me."

She sits up on her elbows and gives me a curious look. "You have no lady friends at all?"

I lay back down next to her. "Nope. Why does that seem hard for you to believe? Am I that good-looking that it's unbelievable I am not interested in entertaining women?"

She bursts into a fit of laughter. Harlow's laugh is contagious. Once you hear it, you kind of want to make her laugh again and again just to get lost in the sound. It's melodic and genuine. Sometimes when people laugh, it's forced or out of nervousness, but with her, she finds the joy in whatever you're telling her.

Once she catches her breath, she focuses her brown eyes on me. "You're alright." She raises the joint to her lips with a smirk on her face and inhales. She exhales, passing the joint to me. "Had a bad experience?"

The willow branches sway with the warm breeze and I wonder if I should give her the watered-down reason or real reason. She doesn't seem to water herself down for me, so I decide to be honest. "I want more," I say plainly. Her head turns towards me, and her eyes give me a searching look.

"More?"

"Yeah, more... I want a real relationship. Not some shallow hook-up shit. But that seems to be all that's available, or they want hook ups and money. I need for there to be some depth and not have it all be superficial. I have money? Cool. I have nice cars and clothes? Cool. But at the end of the day, all that shit doesn't matter. I want someone I can vibe with on every level. So, until then... I'm fine being solo. I'll know when I know." I am surprised about how honest I'm being with her. Maybe it's the weed or maybe I just feel comfortable with her. I don't know.

She lets out a sigh. "I know what you mean. About wanting more and not settling for someone who you don't really vibe with just for the sake of not being alone. That's why I refused my ex's proposal." Her confession alarms me and I sit up to get a better look at her.

"You refused his proposal?"

"I did." She gives me a half-smile and then looks away from me. "We've known each other our whole lives... but I still felt like I couldn't be myself with him. I felt like our relationship was more of an expectation than anything. If I had said yes, I would have had to erase myself to be with him. Everything was about him and his career. Everything. And he expected me to follow along... so I said no. I guess we're somewhat friends now... I don't know." She shrugs.

I want to applaud her for saying no to the fuckboy, but I can also tell see the sadness in her eyes. "Do you think you two will get back together?"

"No," she says without hesitation. "I just want to focus on myself and what I want to do... and make some friends. Since I was so wrapped up in him for two years, I didn't really have a lot of friends. I still don't." She covers her face with her hand and laughs. "Annndd that makes me sound like a loser."

"It's okay. I already knew you were. Sevyn told me you have no friends," I say with a grin.

She bolts upright with her eyes wide. "She did?"

"Yeah, she said to be nice to you because you have no friends." Harlow starts cracking up. "I told her not to put your business out there like that, but you know Sevyn."

"I can't believe she told you that. I am going to tell her something when I see her next. Please don't be my friend out of pity."

"I don't do anything out of pity, and Sevyn means well... in her own way. I think I would consider you a friend now... I think."

She gives me an incredulous look and puts her hand across her chest. "Acyn DeConto, are you considering me a friend?"

I chuckle. "Yeah, why not?" I shrug. "It's not like you have anyone else anyway." She shoves my arm, catching me off guard, and it causes me to topple over. She snorts with laughter as she collapses on top of me.

She sits up and pulls me by my shirt to make me sit up. "C'mon, we have to take a picture to immortalize this moment. You're admitting to being my friend and now everyone must know. Plus, it's golden hour." I can't help but smile because she looks truly happy about this. "Here." She shoves her phone at me. "Your arms are longer than mine. So, you take it and don't fuck it up."

"No pressure," I say with a chuckle.

She gets as close as she possibly can without sitting on my lap. Her temple is pressed to my cheek and we both smile at the camera, but it doesn't seem right, so I tickle her, and she erupts with laughter. I snap as many pics as I can with my arm wrapped around her while I tickle her.

"You jerk!" She squeaks as she cracks up. I eventually stop and hand her back her phone. She glares at me and snatches it from my hand. I lay down with a satisfied smile on my face because between the alcohol and weed, the buzz is kicking in.

She flips through the pictures on her phone. "These are actually pretty good, Acyn."

"I know. There isn't anything I can't do," I say smugly.

She smacks my chest and then rests her head on me, flipping her twists into my face. I start cracking up.

"You just had to flip your hair in my face?"

She giggles. "Okay, which one? I think this one." Her finger is pointing to one where my arm is wrapped around her, she is leaning into me, her hand is gripping the collar of my shirt, while she laughs uncontrollably, and I am looking at the camera smiling.

"I like that one."

"Me, too." She busies herself with uploading it. It's nearly dusk but the party is still going on. I almost don't want to go home, and I am not sure I can move at this point. I don't know what the fuck kind of weed Kyrell brought but I feel like I can lay here with her for days. My phone vibrates in my pocket, and I pull it out to see a notification that Harlow has tagged me in a post. I click on it and see the picture she chose with the caption: *Immortalizing Memories.*

There are two things that I learned tonight. Harlow is comfortable enough with me to be herself which makes me feel good because I think she spends a lot of time second guessing herself. The second thing I learned is that Kyrell is 100-percent right. She is magnetic.

12

Harlow

A cyn and I rejoined the party after the sun had set. We have eaten, because munchies, lost count of our drinks, danced, and have had the most fun I've had in a while. I could easily say that the weed or alcohol made me more comfortable with him, but the truth is that I have never felt uncomfortable with Acyn. Sure, he can be a bit of an ass, but I have always felt like I can be myself with him.

We fall onto one of the couches underneath a canopy decorated in twinkle lights.

"I think I should go home now. What time is it?" he asks.

I reach for my phone, and it takes my eyes a moment to focus on the time. "I think it's... almost three a.m."

He starts laughing. "You think?"

I can't breathe because I am laughing so hard. I already laugh at everything, and he is no help.

"I am properly intoxicated. Don't judge me," I say.

He puts his hands up in defense. "Aye, you'll receive no judgement from me because I was right alongside you. But if it's almost three... I should really go." I watch him and already know he isn't going to make it. He stands up for about five seconds and then falls back down on top of me. Which causes me to laugh... *again.*

With all of his body weight on me — he isn't light, but he smells so good — I try to help him sit up right. My voice is muffled because his back is pressed against my mouth. "Um, as your new friend, I cannot allow you to drive home. You're welcome to stay at my place, or you can stay in one of the guest bedrooms in West and Ava's house."

He is still lying on top of me. "I think you're right. So far, you're a good friend."

"Okay, can you be a good friend and get off of me? It's getting hard to breathe."

"Oh shit, sorry. I was comfortable." I shove him off of me with as much force as I can muster. He finally moves.

"Okay, so where are you staying? With me or in a guest bedroom?"

"I'll stay with you," he says and for some reason it makes me smile. He also doesn't have a choice. I wouldn't let him leave even if he wanted to.

"Alright, up! We've got to make it to my place. I need some water and my bed." This time he makes it to his feet and holds his hand out to me. I grab it and feel the electricity I felt the first day I met him. He wraps his arm around my neck, and I wrap my arm around his waist as we head towards my place.

I head for the kitchen to get water because I feel like I just walked through the desert. I offer him a glass that he downs also. Once he's done, he looks around my place with interest. "This is very... you," he says as he looks back at me with a lopsided grin. "Do you like sunflowers or something?" I have sunflowers in vases on both my coffee and kitchen table.

"Yeah, they're my favorite flower."

"That fits you, too."

"Why do you say that?"

He puts his hand in his pocket as he looks at the pictures on my wall. "You light shit up."

"Wow... a compliment." I curtsy. "Thank you."

He grins. "Yeah, yeah, don't get used to it. I'll be back to insults tomorrow."

"Wouldn't expect anything less. Do you want the bed or the couch?"

He turns towards me with his brows furrowed. "What kind of man would I be if I let you sleep on the couch?"

I cross my arms. "Oh, now you're a gentleman?"

"Yes, but only on Saturdays at three a.m." He winks.

I chuckle. "I'm going to go change. I don't have any clothes for you... unless you want a t-shirt. I think I have one big enough for you."

"Oh, I'm good. I sleep in my boxers anyway," he says as he flips through my record collection. I gaze at him a moment and try to ignore the butterflies in my stomach about seeing him almost naked. Friends or not... he is GQ material.

I nod. "Of course you do." He laughs as I walk to my bedroom to change. I rummage through my drawers looking for a t-shirt to put on when I hear Bob Marley's *Red, Red Wine* start playing from my record player. I smile because I remember dancing to this song with my mom. I head back out to the living room to see that Acyn has made himself at home as he digs through my fridge.

"Where did you get your records from?" He stands upright and turns around with a container of leftover pasta. Unbelievable.

"They were my mom's." I sit down at the table and watch him move around my kitchen. Instead of asking me where things are at, he opens drawers and stops only when he finds a fork.

"Were? She didn't want them anymore? That's a nice collection of vinyl." He sits down at the kitchen table with me and digs into the pasta.

I watch him eat a few bites and hug my knees to my chest. "Yeah... she died."

He stops mid-bite with a mouth full of pasta. "Shit, I am so sorry. I didn't mean to be a downer. You don't have to talk about it. We can talk about something else." The look in his eyes isn't one of pity but one of care.

"It's okay," I shrug. "I can tell you or we can talk about something else."

"Yeah, you can tell me."

I grapple with my emotions. I could easily keep the bandage on the wound as I have done for the past eleven years, or I can bare it and see what happens.

"My mom..." A smile tugs at my lips as an image of her appears in my head. "My mom was vibrant and full of life. She was our sun. Everyone always says I'm her spitting image. If you put our photos next to one another at similar ages it's hard to tell us apart." Acyn gives me a warm smile.

"She died when I was twelve." My palms start to sweat. I barely know him. Why the hell am I sitting here on the verge of spilling my guts? He doesn't say a word. I squeeze my arms tighter around my legs as he waits for me to continue. He's not looking at me expectantly or sympathetically. He's simply sitting next to me in this moment. Holding the space for me to let it out.

"On Friday nights we would get a pizza and watch a movie together. I looked forward to Fridays. I'm sure I was one of the few kids who actually enjoyed spending time with their parents and admitted it." I smile and Acyn chuckles. "My dad would usually pick up the pizza on his way home from work, but that particular Friday he had off. My mom worked as a curator for a museum and had Fridays off. Since my dad was glued to some game on TV my mom said she would go pick up the pizza. She invited me to go along and of course I said yes because it sounded more fun than watching a game I knew nothing about."

"She..." Tears sting my eyes. My heart is thumping in my chest but again Acyn says nothing and simply holds the space for me to continue on. "She and I went to pick up the pizza. I remember my mom and I were talking about what movie we were going to watch when we got home. And then everything happened so fast..." A tear escapes and I wipe it away. "A car hit my mom's side. I saw it coming but there was nothing I could do but scream. I remember screaming for her and then everything went black."

"Hours later I woke up thrashing and screaming for her in the hospital. I had a concussion and a broken arm." I show him the scar near my elbow of where the bone pierced my skin when it cracked. "My dad grabbed me, and it took me a couple of seconds to realize it was him. When I calmed back down I noticed he was sobbing. I asked him why he was crying. He didn't immediately respond. I got an unsettling feeling that it had something to do with my mom. I asked him again and he... he told me that she didn't make it."

I let out a shaky breath, "I didn't believe him. I thought there was a mistake. I wanted to believe there was a mistake. It was just an accident. People walk away from accidents all the time. The longer my dad kept sobbing the realer it became that my mom was gone. We were struck by a drunk driver. My mom was killed instantly..." I let silence fall between us for a moment.

My eyes find his. "For a long time after she died I had wished it was my side that got hit." I wait for him to protest but he doesn't. "So many people told me that I should be grateful to be alive or that it's a miracle I was alive... at that time it didn't seem like that. It felt like a curse or some sick joke to be in the same car with my mother who was killed and walk away with minor injuries. For a long time after she died everything was a blur. I remember bits and pieces. Trying to desperately function with my mom gone... forever."

"My dad blamed himself for a long time because he wishes it were him who picked up the pizza that day. I was wishing it were my side of the car that got hit. It was a rough few years after she passed. It's still hard but..." I exhale. "After a while I realized my mom wouldn't want me to live in misery. So I try to honor her as much as I can in all that I do. I have way more good days then bad days now..." Tears are streaming down my face. I'm startled when Acyn's rough hands wipe them away. My eyes meet his and he pulls me into a hug, wrapping his brawny arms around me. I don't pull away. I allow myself to melt into him and cry. We stay like this for what feels like forever. I'm sure it's only a few minutes but it feels like longer.

My ear is pressed to his chest, and I feel the deep vibrations of his voice. "All I can say is that your mom would be proud of who you are now. I also feel like a jackass for trying to leave while under the influence."

"Two compliments in one day? I don't know what to do with myself, Acyn." I hug him back. "You didn't know. Don't feel bad. Thank you... for listening to me."

"I may be full of myself, but I am a good listener."

I chuckle. He scoops me up in his arms.

"Um, are you insane? What if we both fall?"

"Then I will use you as cushion," he says with a smile. "Where is your bed?"

I laugh and point to my bedroom. Once we're near my bed; he tosses me onto it, and I start cracking up. "What the fuck was that?"

"It makes up for the two compliments I gave you," he says with a smirk. And then he starts fucking stripping. He grabs the hem of his shirt and peels it up. I feel I should turn away, but I can't. My presumption of every inch of him being covered in tattoos is correct. His abs are embellished with tattoos that wind around to his back and disappear beneath the band of his boxers. I feel like I am in the desert again. Then as if that weren't enough, he slides his pants off, his V is on full display, and I watch him step out of them. Standing in front of me with just boxers and tattoos, he folds his clothes and sets them on the chair at my vanity. I quickly pretend to be more interested in crawling under the covers then ogling him but then he leaves the room. I lay back against my pillow with a sigh and wonder what the fuck is wrong with me.

Acyn reappears moments later with a blanket and stage dives onto the bed next to me. "What the hell is wrong with you?" I shout as he sprawls out and almost pushes me off the bed. "Clearly your gentlemanly gestures have a short lifespan."

"Your bed looks more comfortable than the couch. I think I made the right choice," he says with a smug smile.

I climb out of bed to turn off the light and my shirt rides up exposing my ass cheeks. I turn back around as I try to pull it down and catch Acyn quickly looking away and smiling at the ceiling. Once I turn off the light, I crawl back in bed and snuggle up with my pillow.

We both lie still in the dark. "Tonight was fun," Acyn says.

"Yeah, it was."

He chuckles, "Even without seeing your face, I can tell you're smiling."

"I am. I'm glad you came."

He grabs my hand and holds it while placing it on his chest interlaced with his. I don't know what to do or say, so I don't do or say anything because my hand in his feels... *nice*. He rubs my hand with his other. It calms me, and I start to feel drowsy.

"Night, Acyn," I say sleepily.

"Night, Harlow."

ACYN

I roll over and open an eye as I slowly start to remember where I am. I look over towards Harlow's side and she isn't there. The smell of bacon makes my mouth water. Of course she's a morning person. If I don't have any clients, I sleep in until my cat meows at me like he's dying because he needs food. Even then getting out of bed is trivial.

I climb out of her bed and follow the scent of bacon to the kitchen. When I round the corner, I see her lip syncing and dancing. She is giving it her fucking all as she winds her hips, flips her hair, and rubs her hand over her body. My eyes are fixed on her hand as she rubs it over her breasts, down her torso, past the hem of her shirt, and I follow it back up her thigh as it rubs over her ass. Do friends get morning wood? In my defense, I just wanted some bacon and ended up with a show.

I decide to stop being a creep and let her know I am here. "Morning, Sunshine."

She whips around with her hand over her heart. "How long have you been standing there?"

"Long enough to enjoy your flash dance," I say with a smirk. "Why lie?

Her eyes go wide and then she shifts her gaze downwards. "Oh... uh... I'm not used to people being here and I really can't not move when I love a song." She goes back to cooking the food.

"Hey, this is your place. I'm just a guest. Do what you want, and I'll enjoy the show."

"Shut up," she says while shaking her head with a grin.

"Please tell me your cooking is better than your coffee making."

She glares at me. "You know, I don't have to feed you. You can just watch me eat."

"What about southern hospitality?" I honestly wouldn't put it past her to have me watch her eat. She is a sweetheart, but I can tell that there is a side to her that you don't want to cross. Something about the quiet ones.

She snorts with laughter. "That doesn't apply to you. But you're lucky today because I've already made your food." Turning off the stove, she removes the pan and makes her way to the table that is set with two place settings. "I hope you like orange juice."

"Sounds good, Sunshine. Thank you." I am honestly shocked that she even cooked me breakfast. When I am in the company of women it is mostly for dick and then they, or I, dash. There was no dick involved last night. It wasn't even on my mind. Okay, I'm fuckin' lyin'. When her t-shirt rode up and exposed her ass last night, I thought about it. But it wasn't a motive. I really just want to be in her space. I also didn't want to leave her alone after she told me about her mom. So I opted for the bed. I have never built a *real* relationship with a woman. I have never cared to because I already knew what it was.

"What did you call me?" Her voice cuts through my thoughts. I glance at her and there is a hint of a smile on her lips.

"Sunshine. It suits you and, quite frankly, is better than Harls." I shrug unapologetically.

She starts cracking up. "I was expecting something much worse than Sunshine coming from you."

"Have some faith in me." I wink.

We are mid-conversation when there is a knock at her door. Her hand slaps over her mouth as she stares at me with wide eyes.

"What?" The look on her face has me worried.

"I forgot your sister was coming over today!" She looks panicked and I can't help but laugh because what a fucking sight this is. She jumps up and dashes to her room. "I've got to find pants and you need to get dressed." Hopping on one foot as she tries to pull her pants on, she says, "Hurry, Acyn she is going to think that you and I—"

"Slept together?" I look at her with amusement. I have no plans of putting clothes on. She tries shoving me out of my seat, but I sit as solid as a tree trunk with a smirk on my face. Eventually she gives up and starts whisper yelling at me.

"Yes! Put your fucking clothes on." My sister knocks again, and Harlow's phone starts ringing.

I go back to eating my food. "I'm comfortable."

"Acyn!" she scream-whispers and her eyes narrow. "You fucking twat! Oh my god!" She runs her hands over her face and looks between me, her ringing phone, and the door. I continue eating my omelet with a grin on my face. Harlow slowly walks towards the door and only opens it a sliver.

"Hey, Sevyn." Her tone is a little too high and enthusiastic.

"Were you slee —" I tried my best to stifle a laugh, but I start cracking up. "Wait a minute, I know that fucking laugh!" Sevyn pushes past Harlow and sees me laughing at the table. She then stands there gaping between Harlow and I. Harlow looks like she wants to die. Her head is tilted towards the ceiling and her hands are covering her face. I on the other hand am extremely amused.

"Are you two... sleeping together?" Sevyn asks, still looking between Harlow and I.

"Sevyn, I can explain-" Harlow begins but I don't let her finish.

"We did sleep together."

"Acyn! Why are you lying to her?" Harlow yells.

I shrug. "I'm not, Sunshine. Did we or did we not sleep together?" I drink my orange juice as I gaze at her, waiting for her to answer the question.

Her hands are on the side of her head, and she looks at war with herself because, technically, we did sleep together. "I mean, yes, we did, but—"

Sevyn gasps. "You guys did sleep together? How long has this been going on?"

Harlow puts her hands up in front of her in protest. "No, we didn't... we didn't actually sleep together. I mean we slept together but – I am making this worse! Acyn, tell her!"

I give her a clueless expression and shrug. She gives me a murderous look and it makes me chuckle. I could easily explain but I am enjoying watching Harlow struggle with getting the words out.

Then, Sevyn squeals and hugs Harlow. "Oh, my God! Why didn't you guys tell me? This makes me so happy because maybe you'll become my sister-in-law!" She looks like she is about to burst with happiness. "Can you imagine if we became—"

Harlow pulls away and her brows are pinched. "You're not mad?"

"Hell no! This benefits me, not just Acyn. Forget about Acyn. This is a dream come true for me."

Harlow grabs my sister's face and looks her in the eyes. "Sevyn, Acyn and I didn't sleep together as in have sex. We just shared my bed. We are not together. We're just friends. I couldn't let him drive home in his intoxicated state and he wanted to sleep in my bed. But nothing happened."

Sevyn looks as though someone just told her the most devastating news. "You both suck. I was so happy for you two for a moment."

Harlow looks at me with a puzzled expression. I shake my head and shrug. "Sevyn doesn't care. As you can see, she would be elated if you and I were to get together."

Harlow grabs her chest and looks completely relieved. "I cannot stand you, Acyn."

I chuckle as I clear our plates. "You love me, Sunshine. Even if you don't want to admit it."

She gives me the middle finger and a glare. "I am going to go get ready. Are we still going shopping today?"

"Yes, I'll need a pick-me-up since you two just crushed my dreams," Sevyn says.

Harlow doesn't give her a response as she heads towards the bathroom. Sevyn turns her attention to me. I pretend to not notice her staring at me because I already know what she is going to ask me. "Do you like her?"

I scrub my hand over my face. "Here you go on your bullshit."

She shrugs defensively. "It's just a simple question. Do you like her?"

"I enjoyed spending time with her. We're friends. Can that be enough? Or do I need to buy a ring right now?"

"Touchy, touchy." A grin is pulling at her lips.

"Neither of us are looking for a romantic relationship. Stop trying to play matchmaker."

"Alright, alright I'll leave it alone but if you two do end up –"

"Sevyn, drop it!" Her mouth snaps shut mid-sentence. I rarely get short with people, especially my sister, but she knows how to push my buttons. Why can't a man and a woman simply enjoy one another's company? I don't understand this automatic relationship thing because we spent one night together as friends. It is exhausting to me and probably the reason why the few friends I do have that are women are fellow tattoo artists. It's all strictly business.

"Sorry," she mumbles without looking at me.

"It's fine."

I head to the bedroom to get dressed. I grab my t-shirt and pull it over my head. When I look up again Harlow is standing in front of me wrapped up in a robe. I can find my friend attractive, right?

She grins. "Leaving so soon?"

I grab for my pants so that I can form a thought and give her a response. I clear my throat. "Yeah, I don't want to impose on your shopping trip with Sevyn."

She disappears into her closet and then tosses her robe she was just wearing onto her bed. My mind immediately starts thinking of her naked but then her voice cuts through my thoughts. "You don't want to come with us?"

I shake my head attempting to shake the thoughts I just had out of it. "Nah, I'm good, Sunshine."

Reappearing from the closet with a smirk. "Some friend you are," she teases.

"Sounds like you like having me around."

"Mm, you're alright." She looks at me in the mirror as she applies her face moisturizer. "I feel like if I give you a compliment it's going to go to your already big head."

I let out a bark of laughter. "That's how you feel?"

"Only speaking facts." She walks towards me and holds out her hand. "Let me see your phone so I can add my number to it so you can text me. Sometimes I turn off my IG notifications." I pull my phone from my pocket, unlock it, and place it in her palm. "Oh my God! How cute are we?" she asks referring to my phone's background picture. I had changed it from me and my cat to the one we took yesterday under the willow tree.

"Just add your number. You don't have to ooh and aww. It will be back to a picture of me and my cat soon enough."

"No, leave it. I won't say another word."

I side-eye her.

"Aweeee, but Acyn look at us," she says.

I snatch my phone back from her – letting out a falsely annoyed sigh. "Are you done?"

She starts cracking up. "Yes, text me so I have yours and don't think you're a creep. Wait... already too late for that."

"I am second guessing this friendship." I shoot her a text and also quickly change her name from Harls to Sunshine in my phone and then lock it. "Alright, I better get going."

"See you around." She wraps her arms around me, and I kiss the top of her head.

"Later, Sunshine."

13

Harlow

My life went from being pretty mundane to full on Technicolor in a short time. If someone would have told me six months ago that I would be *thriving* in Seattle – living on my own – I would have called their bluff. I haven't been here long, and it already feels like home to me. I worried that I wouldn't be able to get settled after feeling unsettled for so long.

It also helps that I have been fortunate enough to cultivate a family of friends. West and Ava are wonderful but I know firsthand how limiting it can be to keep your circle a little bit too close knit. I have had to really push myself, like my dad suggested, to make new friends. The most unlikely person has been my ace. No pun intended. Acyn and I have become really good friends since the night we spent together.

Harlow: Do you want to go camera shopping with me? Sevyn is busy.

Acyn: Sounds boring but count me in, Sunshine.

Harlow: I'll pick you up after I'm done.

I signed up for two six-week photography classes that will start soon. Acyn told me to stop being indecisive and pick some because I can always take more in the future if I want to but I need to start somewhere. He also added, since I am a hands-on learner, that I should look for working as a photography assistant. I hadn't considered that and mentioned it to Ava, who had a photographer friend willing to take me on a few shoots with her. I'm excited because that means I'll be able to get some hands-on experience while building my portfolio.

My schedule right now is pretty full between the yoga studio and coffee shop. I was hesitant to add on another commitment because

I already feel like I'm spreading myself thin. But, if I don't start now, then when will I start? I'm tired of waiting for things to happen when I can make things happen instead.

Later that evening, I'm sitting in Acyn's car, playing DJ while he gives me shit about my music selection. Harry Styles is serenading us while Acyn looks like it pains him to listen.

"Tell me he can't sing!" I am dancing in my seat while he tries to hold back a smile.

"I am actually surprised he can sing," he admits.

"Aha!" I point my finger at him. "See, you like his music."

"Whoa, whoa." He holds up his hand in protest. "I didn't say that. I said he can sing. That doesn't mean I want to listen to his album on repeat."

I snort with laughter. "Would it kill you to admit you like something I like?"

He looks at me from the corner of his eye with a smirk. "I don't want to find out."

I turn the music up a little louder and give him a grin as I do so. He shakes his head and pretends he doesn't notice. I jam the rest of the way to the store, even catching Acyn drumming his thumbs against the steering wheel a few times.

When we arrive, I am faced with a million choices. There are a lot of cameras on display with very little variances between them. We spend an hour looking due to my indecisiveness. Acyn patiently leans against a counter in the aisle, watching me re-read each info card over and over... and over again.

He bends down next to me, with his hands on his knees, while I read one of the info cards. "Which one is your least favorite?" I immediately point to the one I am in front of. "Okay," he says, nudging me. "Then there is no need to read the info card again. Which one do you like?" I walk a little further down the row of cameras and point to another one. "Alright." He grabs one of the scanner cards. "Now, which one do you love?" I move further down the row.

"This one." I chew my thumbnail while staring at it.

"Why are you wasting your time reading the other ones then if you know you love this one?"

"Because," I look up at him as he stands next to me. "It's out of my budget." Even though I am a single person and work two jobs, I still have bills. I pay rent to West & Ava, pay for my own food, gas, paid for classes – that weren't cheap – and everything else that I need in between. I have the money, but if I were to buy it, things would be tight for a little while. And I don't like that feeling.

Acyn cups his chin in his hand, with his other arm folding against his abdomen, as he stares at the camera I love. "You know I could hel – "

I place my fingers over his mouth. "No, Acyn. Thank you... really. But no. I can buy the one I like and save for the one I love." I smile at him. While I am grateful that he is willing to help me, there is no reason why I need the more expensive camera. The one I like will get me started and that's all I need – a start.

"Alright, just an offer, Sunshine." He holds the scanner card for my camera of choice up in front of my face. "Are you ready then?" he asks, grinning.

"Yes." I take the card from his hand.

He does a dramatic sigh and looks up at the ceiling. "Thank fuck for that!" I shove him playfully and laugh.

"You said you wanted to come with me."

"I did, and like I said, it was boring."

I ignore his remarks and head for the checkout. Once they hand me the camera, I turn to Acyn with the biggest grin on my face. "Look, I have a camera!" He gives me a smile that matches my own.

ACYN

She is always happy, but in this moment, she is *ecstatic*. It's hard not to feel as excited as she is because it is radiating off of her.

103

"Hold on, I'll take a picture." I hold up my phone and snap a picture of her beaming and hugging her camera. "Okay, can we get out of here now?"

She laughs and takes my phone I am holding out to her to look at the picture. "Yeah, you grouch."

"I'm not grouchy. I'm just hungry. Do you want to come and eat at my place?" I ask as I open my car door for her.

She slides in and gives me a look of surprise. "You're asking me to go hang out with you at your place?"

"Don't make me regret it, Sunshine. It isn't a big deal. You're just coming to my place for food and to meet my cat."

I can tell she is trying to contain a squeal. She closes her eyes and breathes to calm herself. Smiling all the while. "Yeah, sure." She shrugs. "Whatever. Sounds good." I let out a laugh because she is trying so hard to not make it a big deal, when for her, it is. I guess it is for me, too. I haven't had a woman, aside from my sister and mom, at my place in a long time.

"Calm down, Sunshine. It's just my place and dinner." I shut her door and get in my side.

"You know how to cook? Or am I going to get food poisoning after this meal?" She looks at me with a raised brow and a hint of a smile.

"How else would I eat while living alone, smartass?"

She chuckles. "I don't know, but I am about to find out."

"Regretting my invitation."

She covers her mouth as she laughs. "Alright, I'll stop."

I quickly connect my phone to the Bluetooth because I am not going to be forced to listen to Harry Styles for the thirty-minute drive to my place. The guy can sing but I'd rather listen to something a little more my tempo. When I glance over at her, she is texting someone that she seems annoyed with by how fast she is typing and rolling her eyes... *repeatedly*.

"Let me guess. The ex."

She sucks her teeth and does an imitation of what I am assuming is his voice. "'You two are sure spending a lot of time together.' And? So what?"

I really don't understand how this guy still has a hold on her when they aren't even together. I also have never been in a long-term relationship so I am definitely missing something. It's always obvious when she is talking to him because her usual bright and bubbly attitude disappears.

"I mean, I have no words of advice other than fuck him." Really though, fuck him. He seems like a needy asshole. Although I am sure he thinks I am an asshole for simply spending time with her.

She looks at me and sighs. "You're right. Fuck him." She tosses her phone in her bag and starts messing around with her camera that she just took out of the box. "It has a little bit of charge. I am going to charge this at your place so I can try and snap some pictures of you and your cat." Her smile is back. She looks out the window. "How far is your house?"

"About fifteen more minutes. I used to live in the city in a tiny ass apartment with insane rent. Then my sister convinced me to buy a house outside of it and honestly it's the best decision I've ever made."

"Wow, twenty-five and you have your own house and businesses? Acyn, how are you single?" she asks with a grin.

I can't help but laugh because I do have my shit together for my age. A lot of people assume I don't given my appearance, but I have been working for this life that I have now since before I moved out of my parent's house. I got my first job when I was sixteen – pushing carts – and I have been working consistently since then.

"Are you admitting that I'm a catch?" I give her a lopsided grin.

"Mmm..." She closes her eyes and lays her head back against the seat. "You are. You'll make some woman very happy one day. Not just because of what you can offer but because of who you are." When she opens her eyes, she looks at me with a smile on her face and then looks out the window. "You live in a nice neighborhood."

Her words make me feel off kilter. I let them wash over me like an unexpected wave. She's a lot like the ocean, you know. Unpredictable and beautiful.

I clear my throat. "Uh, thanks. I tried to think of the future when I bought this house and not just right now." I park in my garage and turn to her. "I hope you like steak."

Once inside, my cat is waiting for me, per usual, and meowing like I am cruel for leaving him home alone all day. His meows stop once he realizes I have someone new. "Harlow, meet my cat, Six-Two-Six."

Her eyes are glittering with excitement. "Did you really name your cat Six-Two-Six after Stitch from Lilo & Stitch?"

"Yeah... my niece and nephew were really into it at the time I got him and I thought it was cool so..."

She finally lets out the squeal she had been holding in since the store parking lot. "Eee that is the cutest thing ever! He is so soft. Oh my God, I am going to steal him." And like the traitor Six-Two-Six is, he rubs against her legs. He loves the attention. Apparently, me providing him with ridiculous amounts of food, love, and a place to live is now subpar. She picks him up and he snuggles into her neck. Yeah, eat it up buddy. "It is so cozy here... I was expecting..."

"A bachelor pad?" I ask her as he looks around.

"Yeah." She grins as she holds and pets Six-Two-Six who is now purring in her arms.

"Nah, I went through that phase before I bought this house." I chuckle. "C'mon you can sit with me in the kitchen or feel free to stream something in the living room."

"Oh no, I am going to watch you cook. I love cooking, too. Plus, I need to make sure you don't poison my food," she teases.

Six-Two-Six only jumps down from Harlow's arms when I put food in his bowl.

"Do you want to come take pictures at the studio next week?" I ask her as I wash my hands.

"Next week?" Her voice sounds higher than usual. "Don't you want me to practice?"

"I know you're capable, so what's the hesitation?"

She chews on her thumbnail which I have learned she does when she is nervous or unsure. "What if you hate them?"

"Then I'll tell you, but I doubt I will."

She doesn't say anything for a few breaths while she watches me prepare the steak. "Yeah, I can."

"See... was that so hard?" I grin as I put the pan on the stove.

"No," she chuckles. "Now feed me."

"Aye, aye captain."

While I prepare the food, Harlow snaps pictures with her new camera, until it dies, and then switches to her phone. I have never met someone who has such a well-documented life. The majority of the pictures she takes don't make it to her social media. They are hanging all over the walls at her place. I wonder if she's always been like this or if losing her mom had something to do with it. I haven't lost anyone close to me but I imagine it makes you hold onto every happy moment a little tighter.

After we've eaten, Harlow and I sit outside on my back porch listening to the rain fall. I have become comfortable living alone but it's nice having her here tonight. Even Six-Two-Six seems happy to have someone around other than me. She sits snuggled up in the crook of my arm, wrapped in a blanket, with her head resting on my shoulder.

"Thanks for dinner tonight. It was delicious."

She was distracting me with her moaning – yet again. I can't act like I didn't feel some satisfaction that my food got that reaction out of her. "Told you I can cook."

"Who taught you to cook?"

"My mom gave me the basic knowledge and love for it."

"Ah, my mom loved to cook too. Do your parents come over to your house or just Sevyn's?"

"They come to my house, too. Sevyn and I swap Sundays. Now that it's summer though, they'll be traveling a lot. Visiting my other siblings and doing whatever it is that retired people do." She chuckles. "How's your dad?" I ask.

"He's good but misses me. I may go home for my birthday. I haven't decided yet."

"When is your birthday?"

"September twenty-second. What about yours?"

"I just celebrated mine in February, on the twelfth."

"Awe, a little Valentine's baby. That's cute."

I laugh. "I guess." I check the time on my phone and it's almost eleven. "You can let me know when you want me to take you home." I am half hoping that she'll stay. I've gotten so used to having her around. I have spent a few more nights at her house but it wasn't intentional, we just fell asleep watching shows.

"Are you kicking me out?"

"No, you can stay if you want." I try to sound indifferent when I was just hoping she would stay.

"I'll stay... for Six-Two-Six."

I start cracking up. "Oh, just fuck me, huh? Stay for my cat?"

"I am also unbelievably comfortable and the thought of getting up to have you drive me home sounds unappealing," she says while yawning. She readjusts herself so now her head is resting on my lap.

Sitting here, listening to the rain, and having her body weight on me is relaxing. When I first met Harlow, I didn't expect her to become someone that I would grow attached to. I have my guy friends that I do things with but it's not like we're going to snuggle up on the couch together listening to the rain. She brings a different kind of energy to my life that I didn't know I needed.

"Do you want to go inside and watch something?" There's no response. I look down at her and see that she has fallen asleep. I gently slide her head off my lap and get up so that I can carry her inside. When I lift her, she doesn't even stir. Six-Two-Six is watching me with a puzzled expression, wondering where the hell I am taking his pillow. I could put her on the couch but it's not the most comfortable place to sleep. I've fallen asleep there enough to know that you will wake up with aches and pains. I pass the living room and head for my room instead. I lay her down gently on my bed and cover her with some blankets. She loves her fucking blankets. Even if it's warm, she wants to be wrapped in a blanket.

I lie there, listening to her soft snores and drifting off to sleep, when she turns over and her hand lands on my chest. I interlace my fingers with hers. She lets out a sigh and her breathing slows again, and I fall asleep wondering how I became so attached to her in such a short period of time.

14

Harlow

With the addition of the photography classes – to my already busy schedule – I am feeling it both physically and mentally. I overslept and woke up with a headache from the depths of hell. I am flitting from room to room looking for my clothes because I am supposed to work at the yoga studio for two hours, the coffee shop for four hours, and then zip over to my photography class for an hour and a half. The shifts aren't long, but they wear me out because I am on my feet, moving the whole entire time. Even in my photography class I am not just sitting down and taking notes. I am active – *all day long*.

West did offer to cut back my hours at the coffee shop. I told him not to worry about it because I don't mind working at the coffee shop.

Okay, if I'm being honest, I enjoy working at the coffee shop because Acyn works a few blocks away. I've been so busy these past couple of weeks that the shop is the only place we get to see each other. At the end of the day, I am utterly exhausted. We still see each other in the evenings sometimes but I am not really fun to be around when I am falling asleep as soon as I slow down.

He hasn't complained and assures me that it's fine but I still feel bad. Hendrix is still bothered by our relationship – of course. I keep telling him that Acyn and I are just friends. I didn't tell him that we sleep together frequently. There is no way he could wrap his mind around that without thinking that we are having sex. It's just Netflix and Chill... without the chill.

Nothing, aside from hand holding, has happened between Acyn and I. Friends hold hands, right? It's not like I'm secretly pining for him. Except for when he smiles a certain way, or says some smartass remark, or does something sweet for me – like making me dinner – a feeling blooms within me that is beyond friendship.

I hustle out my door to my car and I get a text from Acyn.

Acyn: Morning, Sunshine! Are we still on for pics tonight?

I smack my hand to my forehead because I forgot I agreed to take pictures today.

Harlow: Of course, what time should I be there?
Acyn: 5 should be good.
Harlow: K, see you then! Stop by for shitty coffee.
Acyn: I wouldn't miss it.

He still won't admit that my coffee is good. Ass.

By the end of my yoga class, I'm feeling feverish. I brush it off because I did just teach back-to-back classes in a 100-degree room. I down a bottle of water and take a cool shower. I hope that I'll start to feel better by the time I reach the coffee shop. Except I don't. Even West notices.

"You don't look so good, Kid." He calls me Kid now, because my dad calls me Kiddo, and they refer to me as "the kid" when they talk.

"I don't feel good... at all."

He looks at me with a furrowed brow. "You know, I can handle it today. You've been doing a lot. Maybe a day off will do you some good."

I don't want to agree but the look he is giving me lets me know that I have no say in the matter. "Yeah, you're probably right. Don't burn the place down without me," I say over my shoulder as I walk out the doors I just came through.

Once I'm home, I have to run into my bathroom because I feel like I need to throw up. As soon I see the toilet, I pull back the lid and puke.

Once I puke everything up that I ate for breakfast, I lean back against the tub. I feel so drained and like I can't get up. I'd rather be in my bed than lying on the bathroom floor even though the cold feels good on my hot skin. After a few moments of resting, I get up, and the nausea hits me again. I puke and sit back down on the floor.

When I feel like maybe I can get up, I try again. I make it to my feet; the nausea is there but I am able to steady myself with the help of the bathroom sink and I make my way to my bed. Thankfully, it isn't far. I flop onto it and let sleep win.

ACYN

I glance at the clock; it's five-fifteen and Harlow still isn't here. I sent her a text earlier to let her know a tattoo I was doing was taking a little longer than expected, so her shitty coffee would have to wait. There was no response from her but I didn't trip because I know people go ape shit over coffee around noon.

It isn't like her to not show up for something. Especially something that deals with photography. After I finish with my last client of the day, I walk over to the shop, and am confused when I don't see her there. I see West and make my way over to him.

"Hey, West. Have you seen Harlow?"

"Yeah, I sent her home because she looked terrible."

"Terrible, how?"

"I think she came down with something. I had Ava check on her because she didn't respond to my text and she said Harlow's knocked out."

"Oh okay. Thanks, man. I'll see you around."

He raises his hands up. "What, no coffee? Is mine not good enough for you?"

I chuckle. "Nah, it's been a long day. Next time." I'm not about to admit to him that he doesn't provide me with the same company as Harlow.

"Understood. See you around, man."

I give him a two-finger salute and head out the door.

Once in my car, I drum my fingers on the steering wheel, trying to decide if I should go home or go see Harlow. If she's sleeping, I don't want to startle her but... I also don't want her to be alone. Or maybe... I don't want to be alone. If we don't physically chill with each other in the evenings, we're Facetiming. It's become our routine and now I don't know what to do without it.

I think for a few more minutes about what to do. Starting my car, I decide that I'll go and see her. I make a quick stop by the store to grab the ingredients for my mom's chicken noodle soup. When I'm walking to the checkout, some sunflowers catch my eye, so I buy those too because I know she loves them.

All the lights are off at her place. I'm sure I look like a level ten stalker creeping into her place at night. Hopefully, she doesn't freak out. I put the ingredients and flowers down in the kitchen before I head towards her room to see if she's still sleeping. When I get to her room, she is sound asleep. I sit on the edge of her bed, pressing my palm to her forehead. West was right; she's burning up. She groans and her eyes slowly open.

"Acyn?" she asks groggily.

"Yeah, Sunshine. You're burning up."

"I feel like shit. You shouldn't be here. I've been puking and I don't want to get you sick."

"Eh, I'm strong as an ox. I'll be fine," I say as I stroke her hair.

She starts to laugh but abruptly stops as she scrambles off the bed, dashing into the bathroom. Seconds later, I hear retching followed by puking. I follow her into the bathroom and she tries to protest.

"No –" She retches and starts puking again.

I crouch down next to her, pulling her hair back. She tries to push me away but she just rests her hand on my chest after she realizes I am not moving and goes back to puking. She flushes the toilet and leans back against the tub, wiping her mouth.

"You don't have to help me," she says weakly.

"I know I don't have to, but what if I want to?"

Her eyes are watery from puking as she looks at me. I can tell she wants to make a smartass remark but doesn't have the energy to. She closes her eyes and smiles. "Fine, welcome to my puke show."

I chuckle and sit next to her. "Front row seats, how did I luck out?"

She rests her head on my shoulder. "You said you wanted to. Can't back out now."

"I'm not. I'll be here for whatever you need."

"Good." She snakes her fingers through mine. "My whole body hurts. I want to take a hot shower."

"Can you stand to take a shower?" I look at her as she rests on my shoulder. Her eyes are closed and she looks like she could fall asleep right here.

"Probably not."

"How about a bath?"

"I guess that works, too," she says.

"I got you."

She moves her head off my shoulder as I get up to turn the bathtub faucet on. I look around the tub and see that she has a collection of bath products. I choose one and squeeze it into the water. The scent of lavender quickly fills the bathroom. I sit back down next to her and she rests her head on my shoulder. I bring my hand up to her cheek and gently rub my thumb along her cheek bone. We sit like that while water and bubbles fill the tub.

I check over my shoulder to see that it's filled. "Sunshine, you can get in the bath now."

She slowly slides to an upright position. "Thank you."

"Uh... I'm not trying to be a creep, but can you get your clothes off?" I observe her as she sits there with her eyes closed. Her color is dull and not as luminous as it usually is.

"If you want to see me naked, you just have to ask," she says with a grin and starts to peel her shirt off over her head. I quickly turn my head and find interests in other things in the bathroom. "Don't look, creep." I chuckle and watch her clothes as she tosses them near my feet. T-shirt, socks, jeans, bra, and then her panties. I hear her step into the water and let out a sigh as she lowers herself into the tub. "Okay, I'm in."

I swallow and turn back around. She is covered in bubbles up to her neck and she looks comfortable. I still feel awkward looking at her. I rub the back of my neck while looking at the floor. "Uh... I can just wait out there now that you're safely in the bathtub. You won't fall asleep, will you?"

She shakes her head. "Okay, I'll leave the door open a bit. Just yell at me if you need me."

Stepping out of the bathroom, I head towards the kitchen to put the stuff I brought for chicken noodle soup away and to find a vase for the sunflowers. I run out to my car to grab my phone so that I can text Sevyn to stop by my place and feed Six-Two-Six.

Acyn: Hey, would you have time to feed 626?
Sev: Where are you?
Acyn: Helping a friend.
Sev: Would that friend happen to be a girl named Harlow?
Acyn: Can you feed him or not?
Sev: Sure, tell Harlow I said Hi.

I shake my head. I love and hate her at the same damn time. I am closer with her than my other two siblings. I'm the only boy in my family. I have two older sisters and then there is me. Sevyn is the youngest. For whatever reason, she latched on to me as a baby and we've been close ever since. I don't tell her anything about Harlow and I's relationship though and I can tell it annoys her. There really isn't anything to tell her anyway, plus I figured Harlow would tell her. She hasn't either though – Harlow is a lot like me in that she keeps certain things private.

I go into her room to strip her sheets and put new ones on because when I arrived, she was drenched in sweat. There's a picture of her and I on her nightstand that wasn't there the last time I was here. I smile and then my attention is drawn to her phone that is vibrating next to the picture. The name Hendrix appears across the screen with an eye roll emoji after it. It stops ringing and then starts up again. Goddamn, bruh, let her fucking breathe. I thought he was supposed to be a professional athlete, so I don't know where he finds the time to blow up her phone. He must sit on the bench a lot.

I turn my attention back to searching for sheets. I look through her drawers but find nothing but clothes and... two vibrators. I slam that drawer shut as soon as my brain registered what I was looking at. I also curse myself for my dick responding to seeing those. I was just watching her puke but when you can't remember the last time you've been with someone... it doesn't take much for your mind to take you there. I went from dipping my dick, as Sevyn says, into everything to *nothing*. I've become well acquainted with my hand since then.

I push those thoughts out of my mind and eventually find sheets stacked in the top of her closet. When I'm done making her bed, I look up and she is standing there in her robe watching me make her bed.

Her mouth is curved into a smile as she leans against the door frame. "You're so...domestic, Acyn." She looks a little brighter than she did before her bath.

"We've already established I am a catch," I say with a wink as I fluff up her pillows and pull back the blankets. "It's ready when you are. Do you want water or anything?"

She holds her hand up as she walks towards her dresser. I avert my eyes because I know what's in there now and I can't unsee it. "No, I just want to lay in bed."

I glance at her as she is pulling her panties up her legs and I turn back around. "Uh, maybe I should go. That way you can get some rest," I say, rubbing my neck.

"I like having you here. You're not a bother at all," she says as she crawls into bed and buries herself under the covers.

"Alright, I'll stay, but let me shower first and throw my clothes in the wash."

She covers her face. "Did I get puke on you?"

"It's not a big deal, Sunshine. You're sick."

"This is embarrassing." Her eyes are wide as she stares at me through the slits of her fingers. "I'm sorry you – "

"People get sick and they puke. It's life." I shrug. It really isn't that big of deal to me. She has no reason to be embarrassed. "I'll be back."

I quickly shower, throw my clothes in the washer along with hers, and return back to the room to find that she is already dozing off again. Well, I thought she was.

She raises a finger, pointing to her closet, "There's some of your stuff you've left here over the past few weeks. If I didn't know any better, I would think you're moving in."

After the first few times of unintentionally staying over, the staying over became intentional.

"Thanks." I disappear into her closet and am surprised to find that she has given me a designated section. I am not sure how I missed this when I was looking for sheets earlier. I put on a pair of boxers and a white t-shirt. Instead of doing my usual stage dive – that annoys the shit out of her – onto the bed I decide to slide in next to her instead. She hugs my arm and rests her cheek on my shoulder.

"Thank you for taking care of me. Only my mom, dad, or my best friend back home have cared for me like this. It means a lot to me that you stayed... even though I puked on you."

I laugh. "Let the puke go. I am not even thinking about it, so neither should you." I can't help but wonder how someone she was with for two years didn't take care of her if she wasn't feeling well. "Your... boyfriend didn't take care of you?"

"Hendrix? No..." she scoffs. "The few times I was sick he wouldn't come near me. He said he couldn't be sick because of training. Had to be in tip-top shape." She sighs and I already know it was followed by an eyeroll without having to see her face.

"You did a lot for him though... didn't you?"

"More than I care to admit. He was... is very self-absorbed. It's always been all about him and how his future will be. I had to fit in where I could with him."

I knit my eyebrows because I am struggling to understand how a dude like that had Harlow by his side... and he fucked it up. I decide to drop it because I really don't care to know anything about him. "You should get some rest, Sunshine."

"Yeah," she says with a yawn. "You're right."

It doesn't take her long to fall asleep.

15

Harlow

I try to open my eyes but they are still heavy with sleep. Once I open them and focus, I glance at my clock and see it's a little past one p.m. Instead of getting up and scrambling out of bed like I usually do, I lay here a little longer. I've been running for so long and I think it finally caught up with me yesterday. My nausea has subsided but my body still aches and my throat is killing me. No doubt from all the vomiting I did yesterday. My stomach rumbles but I'm scared to eat. When I look at my nightstand there is a glass of water there.

There's a note next to it.

Hey Sunshine,
I had to work.
Hopefully you're feeling better.
There's soup in the fridge.
Ace

I smile and put the note back on my nightstand. I must have been exhausted if I slept through him cooking. Taking a small sip of water, I wait to see how my stomach responds. It doesn't hurt or make me nauseous, so I gulp down the rest of it. My stomach protests again, reminding me that I need real food and not just water.

I enter the kitchen which looks as though it hasn't been touched. Except for the vase of sunflowers on the counter. There goes those blooming feelings again. I open the fridge to find the soup he made me and it's still somewhat warm. He must not have left that long ago.

I warm it up to piping hot and settle on my couch to eat it. When the first spoonful of soup hits my tongue, I close my eyes and moan. It soothes my throat and tastes delicious. I have never had soup this good before. I am going to have to steal his recipe.

I quickly finish the bowl and warm up my second. While I wait for it to heat up on the stove, I go to find my phone. Of course, I have my usual missed calls from Hendrix – no surprise there. I also missed a few calls from my dad. I call him back and he picks up in two rings.

"How are you feeling, Kiddo? West told me that you weren't feeling well. Sorry I'm not there to take care of you."

I remove my soup from the stove and pour it in my bowl, "I'm fine Dad. I feel a lot better today."

He hesitates for a few seconds and then sighs. "Harlow, I think maybe you're doing a little too much. You essentially have three jobs."

I knew this was coming. He isn't wrong, but I don't want to think about slowing down right now. "People get sick, Dad."

"They do, but you also know that you have a lot on your plate right now. There is nothing wrong with stepping back from something."

To appease him, I agree. "You're right, Dad. I'll think about it."

I hear the smile in his voice. "Good. I still worry about you even though I'm not physically there."

I chuckle and take a spoon of my soup. "I know, Dad. I wouldn't expect anything else from you. My friend was kind enough to come over and help me out. He made me the most delicious chicken soup."

"Is this that Acyn fellow?"

"Yeah, can you believe he can cook?" I ask him as I almost gulp down the rest of the soup.

"I'm glad you have someone there with you. He sounds like a good guy."

"He is," I say with a smile.

"I'm going to let you get some rest, Kiddo. I just wanted to check in on you. I have an appointment and a meeting to get to."

"An appointment? How are *you* feeling?"

He chuckles. "Just a checkup. I love you and I'll check in with you later today."

"Love you, Dad. Talk to you later."

I end the call and contemplate another bowl of soup. A yawn escapes me and my bed seems more appealing than another bowl of soup. I make my way back to my bed and bury myself beneath the covers, feeling satiated.

I clear Hendrix's texts and calls from my notifications. I text Acyn.

Harlow: Thank you for the soup. It made me feel better.

He texts me a few minutes later.

Acyn: You're awake. Good. I'll be done here in a couple of hours. I'll stop by after.
Harlow: Aww, you're sweet.
Acyn: Stop that shit. I'm doing what any decent person would do.

I laugh because I know that was a subtle shot at Hendrix. He rarely says anything about him, but if he does, he usually isn't impressed. I find myself often wondering what the hell I was so impressed by all those years. Even before we got together. I don't have an answer and I may never have one. I let the thought go instead.

Harlow: I'm gonna sleep. I'll see you when you get here.
Acyn: Rest up, Sunshine.

I slide my phone under my pillow and get comfortable. It doesn't take long for me to find sleep.

When I wake up again it's four p.m. I haven't slept like this since I was in high school. I clearly took naps for granted. Acyn still isn't home. I correct my thoughts. He isn't *back* yet. I have to correct myself a lot because I often tell him, "Let's go home."

He always replies, "Which one?" He messes it up just as much as I do. We've blurred a few lines but neither one of us could find a fuck to give.

Feeling feverish again, I take a shower and then settle in front of the TV. I feel better than yesterday but I am still not 100-percent. I hate to even think that I am now coming down with a cold. My dad was right, though, I have been stretching myself as far as I can go and then some. Ava and West haven't dared come in my place. I don't blame them. Since Ava is pregnant, neither of them need to get whatever cold from hell that I have.

I text Acyn and ask him to pick some medicine up on his way back over here. I check my e-mails and my photography instructor assured me that most of the stuff I can do at home. Which helped me relax a little bit more.

My head snaps to the door when it opens and Acyn walks through it carrying grocery bags, flowers, and a duffel bag. "Moving in?" I ask with a smile tugging at my lips.

"Just an extended sleepover," he says with a smile as he kicks the door shut behind him. "I was ahead of you and picked up some medicine when I stopped at the store. Eli and Emery have happily volunteered to care for Six-Two-Six. I may not have a cat after this. So, you owe me a new cat."

I erupt with laughter. "Six-Two-Six must not love you."

"His loyalty is very shaky, if you didn't notice." He sets all the stuff he was carrying down in the kitchen. "How are you feeling?" he asks as he sits next to me on the couch and snatches the remote out of my hand.

"Jerk. If I had my strength I would – "

"You would what, Sunshine? Puke on me?" A smirk is on his face that I would love to smack off of it, but I refrain.

I sit there with my mouth slightly open, glaring at him, while he grins back at me. "I'm sick and this is how you treat me?"

He tosses his head back against the couch and laughs. "I asked you how you are."

"I honestly think I'm now getting a cold. My body really isn't having it right now."

"It's telling you to slow the fuck down," he says as he looks at me. I ignore him and get up from the couch to go rummage through the bags he brought. He follows me. "I'm taking next week off of work."

I gape at him. "Not for me, I hope!"

"No, I had already planned to take a week off during this time months ago."

I am instantly relieved when he says that. As much as I enjoy his company, I don't want him jeopardizing his work for me.

"What do you have planned?"

"I'm going to the Oregon Coast for the week. I rent a house there and just chill. It's simple but the views are... I think you would like it."

I still as I pour some medicine into the measuring cup. "Me? What does this have to do with me?"

"I wanted to invite you to go with me. After seeing how sick you've gotten, I think that a little time away could be good for you."

"Acyn, I don't want to intrude on your solitude if you've already had this planned for months." I stare at the small cup of blue liquid and make a face. I hate the taste of cold medicine. I have to mentally hype myself up to down it.

"I wouldn't invite you if I felt you would be intruding."

I down the disgusting medicine, chasing it with a cup of water. "You really want me to go with you?" I wipe my mouth with the back of my hand.

"Yeah."

I nod. "I would have to talk to Celeste and see if she will be alright for a week. She already told me to take some time off. I don't think West would mind either. In fact, he and Ava would probably be happy to get my sickly ass out of here."

He laughs. "You're a walking germ."

"You were so sweet just a few hours ago... when you weren't here."

"I have to keep the balance, Sunshine," he says with a smile.

"Uh huh." I put the new bouquet of sunflowers he brought into a vase. "Thanks for the flowers, asshole."

He chuckles and I set them on my coffee table. I take a picture of them because they are too pretty to not take a picture of. I upload them with a caption that reads: *when he's an ass but brings your favorite flowers*, followed by the hashtag #acetheass. I hear his phone chime in the kitchen where he is busy cooking something again. He starts cracking up as soon as he sees it.

"I'm Ace the Ass now?"

"If the shoe fits." I lie down on the couch so that I can watch cooking shows. A little while later, Acyn appears in front of me, holding out a hot bowl of something. When I look in the bowl, I see it's teriyaki with white rice.

"If I had known getting sick would cause you to become my own personal chef, I would have gotten sick sooner."

He chuckles with his mouth full of food as he sits down next to me. "Eat," is all he says.

I don't say a word as I eat because it is that good. Food is definitely a love language.

After we devour our bowls of teriyaki – that taste better than the restaurants' – I lie with my head resting on Acyn's lap while we watch cold case shows. I had never really watched them until I let him pick something one night and now I'm hooked.

Even though the bottles of cold medicine say "non-drowsy" they always make me sleepy. The cold medicine mixed with a full stomach – I didn't stand a chance. My eyes grow heavy and become harder to keep open. I hear Acyn talk to me but he sounds far away.

I hear him say, "Sleep, Sunshine. I'll be here." And then I drift back off to sleep.

After a few days of consistent rest and Acyn's cooking, I am starting to feel like myself again. This past week would have been hell if he weren't around to keep me company and care of me. I didn't have to ask him for a thing. He just did it. It was nice to be taken care of. Today is the first day that I've felt up to do anything aside from laying down or sleeping. It's Friday morning and I still have to talk to Celeste about taking next week off to join Acyn on his trip.

I am nervous to ask Celeste for a week off. West agreed without hesitation but I feel like I am abandoning Celeste even though she has never made me feel that way. I call her, chewing on my thumbnail, and wait for her to pick up.

"Harlow, darling, how are you?"

"I'm feeling better, Celeste. Thank you."

"Good, good I was worried about you. Everything okay?" she asks.

"Um, I wanted to ask you something... I was wondering if I could take this week off? Everyone keeps telling me that maybe I need to slow down. I think I agree. Even if it is reluctantly..." I don't know why I am holding my breath. I guess I feel like I owe Celeste something because I wouldn't be in Seattle if it weren't for her.

"Of course, you can! We'll manage without you just fine," she reassures me and I let out the breath I was holding. "Anytime you need something Harlow – just ask. Your health, in every aspect, is more important than anything."

"Thank you. That means a lot to me."

"Where are you heading off to this week?"

"My friend is taking me to the Oregon Coast. I've never been."

"Oh, you will love it. It is beautiful. Well, I don't want to keep you for too long. Enjoy your time off. I'll talk to you when you get back."

"Thanks, Celeste. I'll see you soon."

I end the call and let out a few breaths. I haven't been working for Celeste long but she has been nothing but good to me. Now that everything is setup for me to go away, the excitement settles in.

I shoot Acyn a text.

Harlow: All set!
Acyn: I knew she wasn't going to say no. Pack your shit.
Harlow: I'll have my 3 bags ready for Monday morning.
Acyn: 3?! What could you possibly be taking?!

Harlow: Everything I could possibly need, duh.
Acyn: It's a week, not a month.

I snort with laughter when I see the eye roll emoji. I'm rubbing off on him. He rarely ever uses emojis but now, when he texts me, he'll throw them in here and there.

Harlow: I'll try and narrow down my outfit options.
Harlow: Are you stopping by tonight?

I've gotten used to him being around. I see him more than I see Sevyn. We still talk constantly, but I didn't think that Acyn and I would end up being closer then she and I are. She doesn't seem the least bit bothered by it, though.

My attention is drawn to the door because someone is knocking. I'm not expecting anyone. I glance through the window near the door and see someone holding a box filled with red roses.

I open the door. "Good afternoon, are you Harlow Shaw?"

"Uh...yes..." I am sure my face looks as confused as I sound.

"We have a flower delivery from Hendrix Moore." Oh, for fuck's sake. I cover my face with my hands. "If you could sign here, and I will go get the rest."

"The rest?"

He gives me an apologetic smile which has me worried. "Um, yes, there are twelve more boxes."

Handing me the first box of roses, I read the side of the box, which says Venus Et Fleur. I have seen these all over Instagram. While they are pretty, what the hell am I going to do with twelve boxes of them?

It goes without saying that Hendrix was really bothered by Acyn's bouquet of sunflowers. Apparently, he now feels the need to flex. The more I think about it, the angrier I become. The delivery guy finishes carrying all the boxes into my living room, which is now covered in roses.

"Thanks," I say as I slam the door behind him.

I find a note attached to one of the boxes. It reads, "I could give you everything and more, if you'd let me." I scoff and rip it in half. I chew on my thumbnail as I stare at all the boxes. Why the hell does he have to do shit like this? I receive a call that I can only assume is from Hendrix.

"Did you get my delivery?"

"Yeah." My tone is clipped.

"You don't sound as happy as I was hoping you would."

"What the hell am I going to do with twelve boxes filled with roses?" I am waving my hand around like he can see me.

"I just thought it was a nice gesture. Since you've been sick... and I miss you."

I let out a bitter laugh. "No, these roses are a pissing contest."

"Do you know how fucking hard it is to see some guy you've only known for a few months get to spend all this time with you?"

"Hendrix, c'mon. Acyn and I are just friends."

"It's funny because that's what you used to say about us."

The retort that was forming dies on my tongue, because he isn't wrong.

"But when I said it, I meant it right? This whole relationship, or whatever the hell it is between us, has become so damn exhausting!" I enunciate every word. "I can't do shit without you having some opinion that nobody fucking asked for, about what I am doing or who I'm with. For fuck's sake, even when I'm with Kyrell, you have a damn problem!"

"I just want to be with you, Harlow. Do the past two years mean absolutely nothing to you?"

"No, no you want me to follow you around. To be there for you but... you don't really want me. You just want what I can provide for you. Which is funny, because you should know how that feels better than anyone, yet you fail to see it."

"Harlow, I lo – "

I cut him off because I don't want to hear him say it. "I'm going away for a week. I think it's best you just take some time to figure out what the hell you're doing because this... isn't it."

He doesn't say anything for a couple of breaths. "Are you fucking him?" I can tell he is trying to keep his voice steady.

I squeeze my eyes shut, gritting my teeth, and ball my hand into a fist. "I am going away for a week. I think it's best you and I don't talk for a while. There is distance between us but not enough space. I can't keep doing this back and forth with you. I'm exhausted. This is exhausting."

"Harlow, I'm sorry, I – "

"Save it, Hendrix. We're past the point of apologies." The tears are threatening to fall. I feel stupid for crying but I am so angry.

His voice is low. "Is he going with you?" I can hear his anger threatening to boil over.

"Yes! Yes! Acyn is going to fucking be with me. There isn't anything you can do about it." I know I sound like a petulant child but I am over him. "And for the record... I like sunflowers, not roses." I hang up the phone.

He doesn't call me back like he normally does. I know he is fuming just as badly as I am right now. I look around at all the roses and then I lose it. I start tearing them apart. Box by box, petal by petal, I unleash all the anger and annoyance that has been steadily building within me.

Tears are streaming down my face, my chest is heaving, my hands are shaking as I stare at my living room floor that is now littered with petals and torn boxes. A fake gesture of *caring*. I wipe the tears from my face and sit on the couch until my breathing becomes steady again.

It's dark outside now but I trudge outside to the fire pit. I grab the lighter and some kindling. Once it's lit, I tromp back into my living room and grab all the remnants of my meltdown and drag it back to the fire pit. I toss it in and watch it burn.

Thank God West and Ava aren't home so that I can self-destruct in peace. I grab another handful of the destroyed roses and start stomping back outside when I run directly into someone. When I look up, I am looking into Acyn's eyes that match the flames in intensity.

His brows knit together. "Sunshine, what's wrong?"

"Nothing," I say as I push past him and make my way back towards the fire. I toss another armful in. Acyn is standing there looking at me. I feel bad for snapping at him but I am finding it hard to calm down. I make a few more trips into my living room and back to the fire. When I finally get all the *trash* off of my living room floor, I sit outside by the fire and stare at it.

Moments later, Acyn comes and sits down next to me. He doesn't say anything. We sit in silence and watch the fire.

Acyn pulls me towards him and I let him. He still doesn't say anything, but he holds me tight enough so that I know he's got me.

"He... He didn't propose out of love or because he envisioned a life with me. He was afraid of losing me. If I had said yes, then he knew he would have me by his side. A perfect example is a delivery guy showing up with thousands of dollars worth of roses. He told me it was a gesture of love and caring but... I know it's bullshit. He's doing it because he's threatened by you. You got me the sunflowers because... you know me. He got me all these unnecessary burning roses to make himself feel better. Like he wasn't losing me. So... I destroyed them. As I tore through them, I just got angrier and angrier. Because..." My voice trails off. "Sorry, I'm rambling." I sit up. "You don't want to hear this." I hug my knees to my chest.

"You got angrier because?" he coaxes me.

I rest my temple on my knee and look at him. "Because... I still care. I feel stupid for caring about someone who so blatantly doesn't really care about me."

Acyn pulls me back into his arms. "You realize you're human, right?" I smile. "We can't just switch off emotions. You two were together for a long time. Over time you'll care a little less, until you realize that you don't care about him anymore at all. To get there... that's going to take time. I think you're being too hard on yourself, Sunshine. That's my job."

I laugh and wrap my arms around him. "What would I do without you?"

"Starve and have no friends."

I burst into a fit of laughter. "I wish Sevyn never told you that. It's sadly true, though."

16

Harlow

Acyn and I settle on the beach. There's a light mist along with a subtle breeze, but it doesn't stop me from fully enjoying where we are. I stare around in awe at the breathtaking views of the Oregon Coast. The beaches and lush greenery is unlike anything that I've ever seen. It's colder than the beaches I'm used to, but it has been nice to slow down in such a beautiful place. I didn't realize how badly I needed a break until I noticed that I haven't felt anxious or stressed since we arrived here.

I take a sip of my hot chocolate, wrap my blanket around me a little tighter, and watch the waves. Acyn is busy lighting a joint he takes a hit and then passes it too me. I inhale and close my eyes, listening to the wind, the seagulls, and feel at peace as I open my eyes and exhale.

"Thank you for bringing me here."

"No need to thank me, Sunshine." He lays back on the blanket and stares at the darkening sky. "It's nice to have you here."

I chuckle. "Even though I've made you stop a million times to take pictures."

"I've accepted that you're annoying," he says as he side-eyes me. I smack his leg and he starts to laugh.

"I tried to stay home but someone insisted on me taking a break."

"For your own good," he says matter-of-factly. "Have you considered not taking on so much once we're back home?"

"I have, but I don't know where to start." On the way here, he and I talked about my busy schedule and the possibility of me cutting back.

"I'm not trying to press you into making a choice, but when something is affecting your overall health, it isn't worth it."

"I know, but you also know how I make choices." I grin. We stopped at some little gift shop and it took me almost twenty minutes to pick out a postcard to send to my dad. He insisted that I am the only person still sending postcards in 2021.

"Okay, so we'll play a game of hate, like, and love. What do you hate?"

I finish my cup of hot chocolate and lay down next to him so I can gaze at the stars appearing in the sky. "Honestly... I hate teaching."

"Really?" he asks as he props himself up on his elbow next to me. "I thought you loved teaching?"

I shrug. "I did... but I miss being a student. The private classes I don't mind, but teaching is exhausting. I can take classes whenever I want, but I really don't want to take one after a day in the studio... no matter how much I love yoga."

"That's understandable." He nods. "Now..." He takes another pull on the joint and exhales. "What do you like?"

"The coffee shop," I say without hesitation. "I didn't think I would like to work there but I look forward to my shifts. Yeah, people can be assholes about coffee—" He laughs. "—but I still enjoy the people and the place."

"So, you like assholes is what you're saying?"

I cackle. "If I am sitting here with you, then yes, I must like assholes."

He lays back down next to me, laughing. "Alright, so then what do you love, Sunshine?"

"Photography." I exhale after taking a hit. "I love photography. I would love to have my own photography business."

He smiles. "You have your answers, then."

I sigh and rub my hands over my face. "It isn't that easy, though. I can't just quit on Celeste. She's the reason I'm even here."

Acyn sits up and looks at me. "Stop acting like you owe everybody something. You don't owe anyone anything. The only person you owe something to is yourself. It's okay to walk away from something that isn't working for you."

I gaze up at the stars. He's right. I appreciate all Celeste has done for me, for believing in me, but I can't continue on simply because I feel bad. That's how I ended up dragging things on for so long with Hendrix.

"I want to be you when I grow up, Acyn."

He chuckles. "You're pretty badass. You just need to believe it."

There go those blooming feelings again. I smile. "Thank you. I'm starting to."

"Would you be down to meet my friends... tomorrow?"

I sit up to face him. "You want me to meet your friends?"

He quirks an eyebrow. "Yeah... why do you sound so surprised?"

"I... don't know." I shrug. "I didn't expect you to want me to meet your friends."

"Why wouldn't I? We spend a lot of time together. I can tolerate you. Why not?"

I start cracking up. "Tolerate me? Is it such a burden to be around me."

"Sometimes I do question –" I smack his arm and he laughs. "I'm just kidding. Honestly, life was pretty fucking boring until you came along. You've grown on me... like a fungus."

I suck my teeth and laugh. "You are the king of backhanded compliments. I'm afraid of what your friends will be like."

"I would say they're nicer than me, but they're my friends so that's probably a lie. Asher and Greyson are good people though. I would trust them with my life if it came down to it."

A grin spreads across my face. Acyn keeps to himself for the most part, so the fact he has friends he is that close with makes me happy. "I'd love to meet them. I'm surprised anyone would want to be your friend."

Before I can react, he grabs me and throws me over his shoulder. I shriek with laughter. "I am going to throw you in the ocean!"

"Acyn! I will murder you if you throw me into that frigid ass water!" I yell as I latch onto his torso because he's got me all the way fucked up. It's dark and who knows what the hell is lurking in the water.

"I'd love to see you try, Sunshine." He keeps walking towards the water.

"Acyn!" I yell as if that is going to do anything. He is holding my legs too tightly for me to get off of his shoulder. I decide to do what any person in danger would: I bite him.

He yells— it's really almost a growl— and we tumble to the ground. I can't breathe because I am laughing so hard. Acyn is looking at me with wild eyes and in total disbelief because I just bit the shit out of his side. "What the fuck are you? A piranha?" he asks.

I am laughing so hard I'm not actually making any noise. "I did what I had to do!" I shout once I catch my breath.

"Bet," he says and this fucker picks me up again. Except now, he is holding me in front of him with my arms secured tightly in his. I scream at the top of my fucking lungs as he plunges both of us into the icy-cold water of the Pacific Ocean.

As we crash into the freezing water, I gasp. It shocks my system and steals my breath. I resurface coughing, sputtering, and grabbing around for Acyn like a mad woman as waves continue to wash over me. I hear him laughing next to me and I lunge for him but I miss and dive straight back into the water. He is laughing even harder now. I want to ring his fucking neck but I am so numb that my ability to move isn't the same.

Instead, I make my way back to the dry sand and start stripping off my clothes with shaky hands. Once he realizes what I am doing his laughter stops and he just watches me. I don't think he can see much. Oh, well. If he can, I have a plan. I reach my panties, peel them off, and launch them directly at his face. They hit him with a wet smack. I grab my blankets and wrap them around me. His ember eyes are still fixed on me. The moonlight must be brighter than I thought. I start to walk towards the house.

"Good luck getting inside, fucker," I scream.

I run like hell because I can hear him struggling to get out of the water to catch up with me. I have too much of a lead and make it into the house before he does. I lock the door seconds before he reaches it. I give him the middle finger and head for a hot bath.

Serves his ass right.

ACYN

Harlow lets me back inside *after* she takes a shower and uses *all* the hot water. Thankfully, she loves blankets and always has them at the ready. I was able to grab some from the car and wait like a locked-out puppy until she let me in.

She has the most satisfied smirk on her face as she opens the door. When she started stripping on the beach, I felt like I had plunged into the icy water all over again. Every ounce of air I had left me. I held my breath the entire time I watched her peel off her clothes layer by layer.

I thought she would stop once she reached her bra and panties. She didn't. Everything about her is fucking perfect. Then she threw her panties in my face. I could have easily came from that alone but I snapped out of it as soon as I heard her shouting. She got me. I think it may have been worth it, though.

The image of her bathed in moonlight – *naked* – will forever be seared into my memory. My dick immediately reacts as soon as I start thinking about it. I know we're friends, but it still doesn't stop me from rubbing one... or two out in the shower. It's been a long fucking while since I've been with anyone and being around her is a constant reminder.

The next morning, she doesn't say anything as I walk into the kitchen. I can feel her eyes on the back of me. I am sure they would shoot laser beams if she were capable. I turn around to face her as I lean against the kitchen counter, then smile at her as I slowly slurp my coffee. She hates when I do that so I know I'm not helping my case, but I find some satisfaction in annoying her. She turns to leave, headed to the door.

I follow her outside to the porch and plop down next to her on the bench. She lets out an annoyed sigh as she turns her back to me.

"Sunshine, are you going to be mad at me all day?"

She shrugs in response. I've pissed her off plenty of times, but never to the point where she won't utter a single word to me. I'll take insults over silence.

"Do you still want to hang out with my friends and I today?" I hope I didn't ruin the possibility of her meeting Greyson and Asher, because I have been looking forward to it. I usually don't give a fuck whose feelings I hurt, but her not talking to me is making me feel some type of way.

She rises from her seat to head inside. Her hand is resting on the handle of the door as she turns back around to face me with a grin. "Had you worried, didn't I?" She starts laughing.

Usually, I am a good reader of bullshit, but in this moment, I realize I would do anything for her.

I shake my head, smiling, as I wipe my hand over my face. "You're a fucking headache."

"Shouldn't have thrown me in the Pacific and I wouldn't have to be." She shrugs with a smile on her face. "Now excuse me while I go get ready."

Once she's gone, I walk across the deck and rest my forearms on the railing as I look out at the coast with one question on my mind. Are we blurring the line between friendship and... *more*?

I watch Harlow as she laughs with Asher, Greyson, and his girlfriend, Selene. We spent the afternoon on a boat crabbing, and then we came back to the beach house to hang out. Night has already fallen and surprisingly, neither Grey nor Ash have managed to embarrass me. I think they are too shocked by the fact I introduced them to a woman. They're probably not wanting to do anything that would scare her off.

Any women they have met in the past were by accident Even then, I never bothered introducing them by name. Both of them already knew what the situation was. But this is different. I wasn't even sure about inviting Harlow in the first place. Not because I didn't want her here, but because I didn't think that she would come with me.

Harlow looks over at me and smiles as she talks with Selene about yoga. They've already made plans to meetup once we get back home. Greyson lives in Seattle but is a pilot, so he's gone a lot. And Ash lives in LA, working as an architect, so we all try to get together when we can. This is the first time in a while that we've all been able to do so.

"Do you want to go find something on Netflix?" Selene asks Harlow.

"Sure." Harlow shrugs. "It's about the time Acyn starts throwing people in the ocean anyway." She grins over her shoulder at me as she walks into the house with Selene.

"He did what?" Selene asks. Harlow doesn't hesitate to talk as much shit about me as she can.

I smile and shake my head as they walk away and into the house.

Greyson turns to look at me once they are in the house. "Man, I never thought I would see the day that you actually introduced us to someone. I like her."

"Yeah, when you said you weren't doing the whole hook up thing anymore, I thought you were full of shit," Asher adds.

I laugh. "When have I said something and not meant it?"

"That's true." Greyson nods. "You're one of the few whose word is bond."

"We're just friends anyway. We like spending time together," I say with a shrug.

Asher snorts. "You're not just a friend to her, bruh."

My brows knit together. "What do you mean?"

"She looks at you a certain way," Greyson says.

"Damn, I didn't realize you two were so observant," I say with a chuckle. "She may look at me with annoyance or anger... but I don't know what look you two are seeing?"

"Nah, she looks at you like you're... everything," Asher says. I look at Greyson, who is nodding as if he agrees.

"Why aren't you two together?" Greyson asks.

"Neither of us are looking for a relationship. We're just hanging out and keeping each other company. Plus, she just got out of a long-term relationship and has voiced that she isn't ready for another relationship yet. So, I'm respecting that," I say.

That is the main reason why I'm okay with being friends with Harlow. I know she needs the space to figure herself out. I can appreciate and respect that. Most people hop from person to person, hoping that they'll find what the previous was lacking in the next.

"That's honorable of you," Asher says with a smirk. "How's your dick hangin'?"

"It's hangin' just fine," I say as I punch his arm and laugh.

"You know, Selene and I were friends for a while before we ever knocked boots." He thinks for a moment. "Okay, Selene made us wait before anything happened."

Asher and I start laughing. "Pussy whooped" perfectly describes Greyson Lee.

"But—" He raises his hands up. "—Hear me out. There is something about the prolonged anticipation that makes the first fuck something out of this world."

"Yeah, it's called pent up frustration, Grey," Asher says and I crack up.

Greyson shrugs. "You may be right, but what I'm trying to fucking say is, smashing at first sight isn't all it's cracked up to be."

"Well shit, it looks like I'm the last man standing," Asher says with a grin. "More women for me. I was getting kind of tired of all of them seeing your tats and you getting all the play, Ace. I'll have to thank Harlow for taking you off the field. Does she have any friends, though?"

I laugh. "You're not tired of chasing women?"

"Not when they're chasing me, bruh." He grins.

The three of us continue to talk into the night. When we get into the house, both Selene and Harlow are knocked out. I carry Harlow to her room and tuck her into her bed. I get up to leave, but she grabs my hand.

"Stay," she says. So, I do.

17

Harlow

My stomach is in knots and my palms are sweaty.

I am waiting for Celeste to get done with her class so that I can give her my two weeks' notice. This isn't a decision I made lightly. It was on my mind all week while at the coast. Acyn's words stuck with me. Staying in a situation because I feel like I owe someone something isn't going to get me anywhere.

I can appreciate what someone has done for me, but that doesn't mean I owe them something in return. I'm learning to have the courage to change my mind, whether it be about proposals or jobs – if they aren't serving me – I can move on without permission.

"Harlow," Celeste says as she kisses my cheek. "So good to see you healthy and well. How was Oregon?"

"It was beautiful." I force a smile even though my heart is racing.

"Peaceful, isn't? A nice place to reset." She leads us to her office. "Water?"

I clear my throat. "I'm fine, thank you." My voice is almost a squeak. Get a grip, Harlow.

Celeste sits down in her chair and smiles at me. "What did you want to speak with me about?"

Straight to the point. I wring my hands together as I stare down at them. "Celeste... I love working here at the studio with you. I've learned so much in such a short time." I force myself to look at her. "But right now, there is just too much on my plate. I thought I would find joy in teaching because I love yoga, but... I've realized that isn't the case. I miss being a student and it being medicine for me instead of a job. I decided that it's best for myself to resign from my teaching position." I almost apologize, but I swallow it instead because I'm not sorry about doing what's best for me.

Celeste leans back in her chair with a smile. "I knew it was only a matter of time before you were off to bigger and better things."

I let out a puff of air. "You're not... upset?"

"No, why would I be upset when you're being honest and doing what you want?"

My shoulders fall with relief. I'm glad that she sees it that way instead of me abandoning her. "I am trying." I let out a chuckle. "I guess I just feel bad for leaving since this job is what brought me here."

"Maybe that's all that was meant to happen," she says with a shrug. "Just because the job brought you here doesn't mean that you are tied to it. Life unfolds in interesting ways. If you hadn't moved here, would you have discovered your passion for photography?"

I knit my brows, not having thought of it this way. Ava is the one who said that I should try photography. "Honestly, probably not."

"See, you didn't move here just for a job. You moved here for yourself." She smiles.

The knots in my stomach unravel as I smile at her. "Thank you, Celeste."

"Now, I wanted to ask you if you would be able to take photos for the studio's website and social media pages?"

"Of course I can," I say without hesitation. "I'd love to do that."

"Great!" she smiles. "I have some ideas of places where we can take the photos. Of course, I do want some here at the studio, but I also think some outdoors would be wonderful, too. What do you think?"

Over the next hour, we discuss what vision and vibe she has in mind for the photos. This meeting went better than I had anticipated. I didn't think that I would walk away with a new project. Life truly does unfold in interesting ways.

I sit in Acyn's shop, sipping on an iced latte, waiting for him to finish up with a client. I didn't tell him that I was going to talk to Celeste today because I wasn't sure whether I was going to follow through with it or not. Now that I have, I'm excited to tell him the news.

I'm watching him work on his client's tattoo. He's hunched over with his tattoo machine buzzing away; he is completely in his element. His client is talking up a storm and somehow Acyn is able to carry on a conversation without missing a beat. Tattooing is like breathing for him. He could do it in his sleep. I admire the love and passion he has for his work.

I grab my bag and pull out my camera to capture a few shots of him. "Would you mind if I take some pictures?" I ask his client.

"Not at all. But be sure to get my good side," he says, grinning.

"Of course," I say with a chuckle as I adjust my aperture and shutter speed on my camera.

Acyn doesn't even look up from what he's doing once I start taking pictures. He's so used to me doing this when he's with me that it doesn't even faze him.

I take plenty of shots from different angles as he works. Acyn looks pensive most of the time, but as I watch him through my lens, he looks relaxed and happy. I capture a few shots of him laughing with his client. It makes me smile just watching him.

Riding my wave of inspiration, I wander around the shop taking pictures of things. There is a wall that is covered in art from floor to ceiling. Different intricate, framed, tattoo drawings from Acyn and the other tattoo artist line the wall.

I head outside to take pictures of the shop's sign and the exterior. I am not sure what Acyn wants for pictures, but hopefully he likes what I'm taking. It wasn't my intention today, but the inspiration hit me. I am in the middle of a picture when the guy who was just sitting with Acyn steps outside. I snap some more pictures of him standing in front of the shop, showing off his tattoo before he leaves. It's hard to look at Acyn's work and not want a tattoo for yourself. I would already have another one if I hadn't promised Kyrell we could get one together.

He's already booked our appointment, but he won't be back in town until after my birthday. I find Acyn cleaning up when I go back inside to sit down and look at the pictures. I can't wait to get these on my computer to edit them; I'm super proud of how they came out.

"Did you get some good shots?"

"Yeah." I smile as I continue to flip through the pictures. "I think you'll like them." Acyn sits down next to me and puts his head next to mine as we scroll through the pictures.

"These are really good," he says as I turn my head to look at him, not realizing how close we are. If I just move a little closer, we would be kissing. He notices too because I watch his eyes flit to my lips and linger there for a moment, as if he is contemplating closing the distance.

I almost close my eyes when he pulls away, rubbing the back of his neck. He clears his throat while I try to ignore the butterflies that are fluttering in my stomach.

"Um, would you want to come to my house this Sunday?"

"For your family dinner?" I ask as the butterflies start to dance again.

"You make it sound so formal." He chuckles. "It really is just dinner with my parents plus Sevyn, Zane, and the twins."

Sevyn has invited me before to the ones at her house but I've always said no because I don't want to intrude. Now that Acyn is inviting me, I want to say yes because it's him. I love Sevyn, don't get me wrong, but Acyn and I have developed a close friendship since we've started hanging out regularly.

I nod and smile. "Yeah, I'll go."

"Good, you can help me cook."

I start cracking up. "Why do I feel like I got swindled?"

"Because you did," he says with a shrug and a grin. "You can choose what we eat if that makes you feel better."

"Wow, here I was thinking you invited me out of the goodness of your heart and you really just want cooking help."

He lets out a rumble of laughter. "C'mon," he says as he holds his hand to me. "Let's go catch a movie at the park or something. I don't want to be inside."

I have never been to a movie in the park before. Needless to say, I am excited that Acyn brought us here. People are scattered around, sitting on blankets and lawn chairs. He must have had this planned because he had a blanket and sweaters in his car. It's not cold here anymore but with the setting sun, there will soon be a chill in the air. We pick a spot underneath a tree and then order nachos, popcorn, and soda.

"Do you come here a lot?" I ask as we settle down on the blanket.

"Yeah, with Sevyn and the kids. It's better than the movie theater because they can run around."

I've noticed that Acyn really enjoys spending time with Sevyn and her family, even though he acts like she annoys him. He doesn't really mention his other siblings too much. From what he's told me, they're older and moved away to start their own lives before he could develop relationships with them. Since he and Sevyn are a little over a year apart, they have always been close. I also don't think Sevyn would ever allow them not to be. Family is everything to them.

"I talked to Celeste today." I had the intention of telling him earlier but got distracted by our "almost" kiss.

He raises his brows. "You did? How did that go? Did she tell you that you couldn't quit because you owe her your life?"

I snort with laughter as I playfully push him. "No, you jerk. She said she was proud of me for doing what's best for me. Plus, she asked if I could do some photography for her studios. You know she owns the one here and in LA."

"What? That's amazing news!" He grins. "See, now you have room to do stuff like that and not feel stressed about it."

"I know. I'm excited. Thanks for giving me the push."

"Nah, all I did was verbalize what you've been thinking. This is all you, Sunshine."

I beam at him. We quiet down as the movie starts. I look at him with surprise when "The Goonies" starts playing. He doesn't say a word, he just grins and goes back to watching the movie. It's one of my all-time favorite movies. I mentioned it to him once in passing when we were scrolling through Netflix one night. On the way to the beach house, he surprised me with a stop in Astoria and took me to the house where the movie was filmed.

My eyes are on the screen, but my mind is on him. I start thinking about all the time we've spent together and how comfortable I have become with him. Not the mundane kind of comfortable, where you fall into a routine and then shit goes stale. It is the kind of comfort where I can be myself but he gives me room to grow and evolve.

I rest my head on his shoulder and he puts his arm around me, pulling me closer to him, as we rest against the tree trunk.

18

Harlow

A cyn picks me up to go to the store to get the ingredients I need to make my mom's spaghetti. I've only had to cook a handful of times since Acyn and I have hung out, so I don't mind making the meal tonight. I just hope his parents like it. I start chewing my thumbnail as I think of everything that could go wrong. I should have met them months ago. What if Sevyn's told them about me and me not wanting to stay for family dinner? What if they don't like me?

"Are you nervous?" Acyn pulls me from my spiraling thoughts.

"No," I lie as if I weren't just thinking of everything that could go wrong.

"Then why are you chewing on your thumbnail?"

I immediately stop and shove my hand under my thigh. Which is no use because I start bouncing my knee. I don't know why I am so damn nervous to meet them. I was actually excited until my mind started wandering. "Because... because I'm nervous."

I can tell he is trying his best not to laugh. "Why?"

I know I'm being ridiculous but once I start thinking about something it's hard to stop. "I'm just nervous." I shrug. "We spend a lot of time together, so I care what your parents think. What if they hate my food? What if they hate me? What if –"

"Chill, Sunshine. It really isn't as serious as you're making it seem. My dad is a lot like me." He pauses considering what he just said and adds, "Okay, that was meant to bring you comfort but I can see how that could possibly cause more anxiety."

I erupt with laughter because that was a very bad comparison if he was hoping for me to find comfort in it. Our first encounter wasn't exactly friendly.

"What I am trying to say is, that you have nothing to worry about," he says.

After laughing, I feel better. I resolve that it isn't my job to make them like me. Either they will or they won't and there isn't anything I can do about it. Not just with them but with anyone. It becomes exhausting trying to appeal to people. When you start being yourself, you attract people who you naturally vibe with. I mean, look at Acyn and I.

I feed Acyn a forkful of spaghetti once it's done. His parents should be arriving any moment with Sevyn and her family. The expression on his face says it all as he savors the bite I just gave him. He closes his eyes as he chews it slowly. I lick my lips as I watch him and smile when he opens his eyes like I wasn't just thinking of other ways to see that expression.

"Why have you been hiding this recipe from me this whole time?"

"I haven't," I giggle. "I usually only save it for when I feel like going all out because it takes a while to cook."

"That is so good." He grabs the fork to take another bite and I snatch it out of his hand.

"No, I've seen the way you eat and this will be gone in minutes if I let you have another bite. So you'll just have to wait." I move the dish of spaghetti to the table, which is already set for everyone. I turn back around and narrow my eyes at him. "Touch it and die. I have to go change before they all get here." He raises his hands up in defense as I back out of the dining room pointing my finger at him.

I go to his room and change into a flirty, off the shoulder, powder blue romper I had brought with me a few weeks ago when I couldn't decide on an outfit. I put on some white platform espadrille sandals which accentuate my long legs. I quickly apply some mascara, gloss, and give myself one last glance in the mirror before heading back out to the dining room.

"Sevyn said…" He stops mid-sentence as I enter the room, which causes me to look up from trying to fasten my bracelet. His eyes are trailing up my legs, over my body, and then his gaze meets mine. The fire that I saw in them when we first met is there again. I've noticed it more lately, which causes me to feel tingly and like I have butterflies coursing through my veins.

He swallows. "Uh… fuck… I just lost my train of thought. Let me help you with that," he says, closing the distance between us. He brings his hands to my wrist. His touch is gentle as he fastens my bracelet. My skin feels electric as his fingertips brush against the skin of my wrist. He gently sweeps his thumb across my quickening pulse. I don't dare move because I am enjoying his close proximity. He only moves to get closer to me… and then, his doorbell rings.

I blink and look into his eyes. "That's them."

"Yeah… you look beautiful, Sunshine." His voice is deeper than usual and it resonates in places that haven't been spoken to in a while. "Better go let them in," he says as he reluctantly tears his eyes from mine to go get the door.

I place my hand on my stomach once he's out of sight, trying to steady myself after that exchange. Even the simplest of touches from him have my body at full attention. I start to feel tingly again when I imagine what it would be like to be fully consumed by the fire in his eyes.

That thought is doused out when Sevyn walks into the dining room. Her eyes give me the up and down. "Okay, but I need to know who gave you permission to look this fine?" she asks.

I grin. "Who says I need permission?" I twirl on the spot to give her a 360 view and then give her a hug as we laugh together.

"I'll never understand how Ace spends all his time with you without devouring you."

"Sev, that's none of your business what other grown people do," Zane says as he stands next to her.

I smile and give him a quick hug. "I don't know why you try. She is going to say whatever she wants to say."

Zane chuckles. It isn't long before the twins are running at me full speed.

I pick up Emery, who gives me a hug, as Eli latches onto my leg.

"I think they may have missed you," Sevyn says with a laugh.

"And I missed them. How did you two grow to be so big in such a short amount of time?" They both giggle while they try to convince me one is bigger than the other.

Acyn appears seconds later with his mom on his arm. His dad is on his other side with his arms draped over Acyn's shoulders. I can see now that he looks like his dad and Sevyn is a spitting image of their mom. They both got the dark red hair color from their dad.

Emery is now playing with all the necklaces layered on my neck. Eli went off to pester Six-Two-Six. I smile at Acyn as I watch him with his parents and then he makes his way over to me.

"Mami, this is my friend Harlow. Harlow, I would like you to meet my parents. Gloria and Rafael." Both of them beam at me. My anxiety instantly melts away.

I hold Emery in one arm and hold my hand out to his mom first. She bypasses my hand, pulling me into a hug. "A pleasure to meet you," she says with a hint of a Spanish accent. His dad pulls me into a hug next.

"Our kids have told us so much about you. It's a pleasure to finally meet you," he says.

"Thank you, nice to meet you, too." I smile and am filled with a warm, fuzzy feeling. I can see why Acyn and Sevyn are such good people. They have two amazing parents. I don't need to talk with them for hours to know that they love their children unconditionally. It's apparent in the way they look at them with such pride and joy.

"Let's eat," Acyn announces. He places his hand on the small of my back, as we walk to the dining room table, and whispers so only I can hear. "See, Sunshine, they adore you."

A smile tugs at my lips as he pulls the chair out for me. I try to sit Emery next to me but she refuses. Sevyn tries to get after her but I assure her she's fine and that my clothes are washable. Acyn sits next to me instead and Emery stays seated on my lap.

"She loves you." Sevyn says as she serves herself. "You would think you're her mother the way she stays attached to you when you're around."

I shake my head and laugh. "She knows who her mama is. Don't you Emery?" She points to Sevyn with a grin. "See, I'm just a stand in."

We all laugh. One day I hope to start a family. I'm not in any rush but whenever I'm around the twins it's hard to not think of my future kids.

Everyone has served themselves. I'm feeding myself and Emery. She has only managed to drop a few pieces of spaghetti on my thigh. Acyn has been all too willing to help me clean it up which makes me giggle.

"Acyn, this meal is so good. How come you've never made it before?" his mom asks.

He smiles at me. "It isn't mine. It's Harlow's recipe. She cooked everything today."

Sevyn chimes in. "Harlow, you realize you're spoiling my brother, right? He is taking full advantage of this friendship." I erupt with laughter and so does everyone else.

His mom points her fork at me. "You must come to our house and teach me how to make this, okay?"

I nod and smile. "My pleasure. Let me know when and I'll be there." I didn't think I would feel this welcomed into their family. I glance at Acyn as he talks with his dad and Zane. An overwhelming sense of belonging washes over me as I realize he feels like home to me.

Later on in the evening, we all sit on the back porch listening to music, chatting, and watching Eli and Emery chase Six-Two-Six. I listen to Acyn as he seamlessly switches from speaking in Spanish to English as he talks with his mom and dad. I try my best not to stare at him because he sounds so sexy to me. Goodness, I am losing it. I need to sort out these feelings before I end up really blurring the fine line of our friendship.

"Alright my loves, we must get going," Gloria says. "We have an early flight to Dominican Republic tomorrow and you know how hard it is to get your father out the door on time." She kisses Acyn goodbye and then comes to give me a hug. "You are a beautiful young woman and I am happy that my kids have you in their lives."

I hug her a little tighter for two reasons. The first being that I imagine this is what it would feel like to hug my mom if she were here. The second is, she has no idea how happy I am to have Sevyn and Acyn in my life. His dad gives me a hug as well. "I can see why Acyn enjoys spending all his free time with you." I glance over my shoulder at Acyn, who I am shocked to see he is looking anywhere but at me as he rubs his hand along the back of his neck. He smirks and shakes his head as his dad embraces him.

Since his parents and Sevyn's family all came in one car, everyone is gone at once. As soon as we wave them off and close the door, Acyn grabs me and twirls me around. I shriek with laughter. "Told you they would love you. Worried for no damn reason."

We settle on the couch after he sets me down. "I love your parents. Makes me miss my dad. I didn't know you sing my praises to them so much, though," I say with a cocky grin as I flip my hair over my shoulder. He tosses his head back and laughs.

"I was really hoping my dad wouldn't say some embarrassing shit. Of course he saves it for the last minute as they're walking out the door." He slides my shoes off my feet and drapes my legs over his.

"It's cute. I've never seen you embarrassed before. I am going to catalog this in my brain to bring up when I can't think of a comeback fast enough."

He lets out a rumble of laughter. "I knew this was coming," he says with a smirk. "Do you want me to take you home?"

Since we now work in such close proximity to one another, we've been riding with each other to and from work. It's becoming more difficult to know where one of us begins and the other ends. I haven't had a friendship this deep before. I am not sure if we are crossing the line into something more or if we are still in friend territory.

I pet Six-Two-Six as he makes himself comfortable in my lap. I question myself, wondering if I'm getting lost in Acyn like I once lost myself in Hendrix. I want a relationship where I can still be my own separate being with hopes, dreams, and desires. Since I've met Acyn, he's only ever pushed me to do things for the benefit of myself. He's let me know that I always have a choice and that I don't owe anyone anything, him included.

"I have to be at the shop to open tomorrow. I don't want you to have to wake up that early just to take me to work." I asked West for the opening shifts because I knew no one else really wanted them. Most of his employees are college kids who stay up late and hate the morning shifts. I don't mind because it means that I get off at two in the afternoon and have the rest of the day to myself.

"I don't know why you act like you're an inconvenience," Acyn says.

"It's not about inconvenience, it's about being courteous and knowing that you aren't a morning person."

"I'm not but... I don't mind. How about this, do you want to stay and watch a horror movie with me?" he asks with a piqued brow.

I snort with laughter. "Now you know if we watch a scary movie I am not going to want to be alone so I will just sit my ass right here."

He grins at me. "No hesitation for that choice."

"Yeah, well I don't wanna be murdered in my sleep now, do I? At the very least I can use you as a shield. So I'll stay here."

He starts cracking up. I usually stay up all night after watching a scary movie. Every noise is a possible murderer or spirit lurking in the shadows waiting to kill me. Okay, I may be a bit dramatic, but I really struggle with scary movies. Acyn loves them though so I try to watch as much as I can. That usually means holding onto him for dear life and staring through the slits of my fingers, though.

"I would never let anything happen to you anyway," he says as he looks at me. I don't doubt those words. He's never given me a reason to ever doubt anything he does or says. I've noticed that if Acyn DeConto says something that he fucking means it. I swallow because my body is starting to tingle again.

"Pick out a movie while I go steal your clothes." I didn't plan on changing but I will now because I don't want to take things further with him. I find it more difficult to stay on the friend side of things without dipping my toes into the possibility of more. Hendrix, even though we haven't talked for a few weeks now, is still on the back of my mind. I wish I could snuff out that flame but I also don't want to push anything with Acyn right now. I value our friendship...relationship too much. I wouldn't want to jeopardize it by acting on feelings of desire.

Desire... is it just desire? No, if we were playing a game of hate, like, and love, I would be teetering on the edge of like. Ready to free fall into love.

19

Harlow

I inhale fresh air as I resurface from beneath the water of the pool. The sun is glistening off my body as I climb onto the edge to sit. It feels so good to be back in the water. It's one of my favorite summer pastimes. I peek over my shoulder at Acyn who is trying to pretend he wasn't just staring at me. I've caught him staring more than once. I can't blame him. There isn't much to my bikini other than some fabric barely doing its job held together by some string.

I arrived back home yesterday after a few days in LA taking photos for Celeste's studio. When I first met her I got the notion that she could and would make a lot happen for me. She has made so much happen for me in a short amount of time, more than I could have ever expected. I've gotten new photography clients after she revamped her website and social media pages with my photos. I am slowly starting to build clientele. Of course, she assures me that I put in all the hard work to get my name out there, but I'm still grateful for her help along the way.

This is the first time I've been able to indulge in Ava and West's pool in a few weeks. I've been busy, a good busy, between working at Holy Shot and doing photoshoots. I purposely took a few days off to slow down because I would prefer to not have a repeat of wearing myself into the ground. It's hard to do that when you're doing something that you love. Acyn helps remind me that I can't do it all and I won't miss opportunities that are meant for me.

When he asked me what I wanted to do today all I could think about is hanging out by the pool and listening to music. He may be regretting agreeing to that now because I am one of the few people who loves being in the heat of the sun. I get up from the pool's ledge and saunter over to where he is sitting. He has shades on but I can tell he is looking at me.

I sit next to him as he gives me a grin. "You know, pictures last longer."

He lets out a rumble of laughter. "What are you? Fifteen?"

"You're looking at me like I owe you something. I thought I would give you an easy solution," I say sassily.

"I am staring because it's hotter than the devil's asshole, yet you don't seem the least bit fazed."

I erupt with laughter. "I'm from Texas. A little 90-degree heatwave isn't gonna stop me." I search around for my phone, eventually finding it tucked underneath my towel. "Let me take some pictures of us and then we can go inside, you crybaby." He chuckles. I lean against his chest, getting comfortable, while I open my camera. "Look sexy, I know that's hard for you."

He cracks up. That's when I start taking pictures. "Fuck you, Sunshine. I look sexy all the time."

I open my mouth to say a smartass comment but my phone starts ringing and my dad's picture appears on the screen. I smile and answer it. "Hey, Dad!" Acyn puts his arm around my shoulders and starts scrolling through his phone.

"Hey, Kiddo and Acyn," my dad says with a grin.

Acyn gives him a two-finger salute. "Mr. Shaw, always a pleasure."

My dad has become used to Acyn being with me when he calls. He and Acyn even talk about me as if I'm not in the room. I think if they ever met, they would get along well. "What are you kids up to?"

Acyn answers before I can. "Dying in the heat."

I snort with laughter. "You're such a baby. We're enjoying the sun and pool, Dad. How have you been?"

"Good, just wanted to call to check on my favorite daughter." He chuckles. This is a running joke between him and I.

I roll my eyes, trying to be annoyed, but it always makes me laugh. "I am your only child, Dad."

"I know and what a lucky man I am. I also wanted to ask— well, more like Charlotte has been hounding me — are you coming home for your birthday?"

My face falls because, if Charlotte is asking, that means she is planning on throwing a party for Hendrix and me together. "Um, I want to, but I don't know about the party, Dad." I really do want to see my dad, but he has no clue about how things are going between Hendrix and me. There is nothing going between us. He'll send me occasional texts to check in but I don't always respond. It's for the best, honestly. I feel freer than I've felt in a long time.

"It's up to you, Kiddo. I'll just be happy to have you home."

I don't want to spoil the party. Even though my dad says Charlotte has been hounding him, I know my dad looks forward to my yearly birthday party. It's a tradition that my mom started with Charlotte. "Yeah, Dad, I'll be there." I force a smile because I am not sure whether I am going home for myself, my dad, or in memory of my mom.

"Great." He smiles at me. "I'll tell Charlotte. I am so happy to see you in a few weeks. I'll let you get back to baking in the sun. Love you."

"Love you, Dad."

I toss my phone aside and let out a sigh.

"Why are you bullshitting?" Acyn asks.

I turn to look at him. "What do you mean?"

"Why are you agreeing to shit you clearly don't want to do?"

I don't really want to go home. It isn't home for me anymore, but I do want to see my dad. He looked so happy about the party and seeing me that it was hard to say no.

"It's... I don't know." I shrug. "It's something my mom and Hendrix's mom started when we were babies... it's tradition."

"I'm going to support your choice, but also know you can stop saying yes to shit you hate at any given time," Acyn says.

I know he's right. "Do you want to go with me?" I think my question catches him off guard because his phone slips from his hand a little. "You can meet my dad and my friends back home." I've told Marisa and Quinn all about Acyn and they are dying to meet him.

"I would have to check my schedule and see if I could even take time off then. It's September twenty-second, right?"

"Yeah, it's no big deal if you can't come. It's kind of short notice with it being a little less than a month away." I do want him to come, but I also don't want him rearranging things for work on my behalf. Even though I know he would if I asked him to. That's one thing I love about our friendship; we spend a lot of time together but we still are our own people.

"I'll see what I got going on," he says. "But for fuck's sake, can we go inside where we aren't burning in this fucking heat?"

I start cracking up. "Alright, alright. I've got my sun fix. Let's go inside... weakling."

He gathers all our stuff. "What do you want for your birthday?"

I shrug, "Nothing really." Acyn could get me a cotton ball and I would be excited. All that would matter is that it came from him.

ACYN

I lean against the front desk of my shop as I scroll through my phone. "Riley, can you tell me what my schedule is like around of the twenty-second of next month."

She gives me a confused look. "Are you going somewhere?"

"I want to, but I need to know how busy my schedule is." I want to tell her to clear my schedule but I haven't missed an appointment with a client since I opened Crown Ink six years ago. People book me months in advance for a reason.

"You have one client for a small tattoo the morning of the twenty-first, the twenty-second is for a back tattoo, and the twenty-third you have nothing because it's a Saturday."

"Damn." There is no way I could swing that. Even though I know Harlow won't be disappointed, I am.

"Where did you want to go?"

"It's my friend's birthday." I don't give Riley much information because she is a chatter box. While everyone in the shop knows Harlow, they also know that I like to keep my personal life private. That doesn't seem to ever stop Riley from trying to get more.

"A friend, huh?" she says with a grin. "What are you getting said friend?" Her eyes are glittering with excitement.

"Uh, nothing. My friend said they didn't want anything."

She scrunches her face up and chuckles. "You believe that? If this is the friend I think you're referring to than you better get her something."

I quirk an eyebrow. "She said she didn't want anything..."

"Yeah so...?" She says with a shrug. "She can say she doesn't want anything but what she really means is she's leaving it up to you to figure it out. She expects you to get her something."

I knit my eyebrows together. "That's not what she said, though."

"Jesus, Ace, are you truly this dense? She probably said that because you two are close but I bet you anything she will be disappointed if you don't get her something or do something for her."

I open my mouth to say something, but then close it. Fuck. She's right... especially now that I'm not going to be able to go to Texas with her. Harlow usually says what she means with me but... I think that Riley may be right about this one. If I don't get her anything, she might assume I don't care. The only women I've ever bought stuff for are my mom and sisters. They've never hesitated to tell me what they want.

"What the hell do I get her?" I am mostly talking to myself but Riley answers anyway.

"You don't necessarily have to get her something. You can do something with her." She gives me a wink.

I scrub my hands over my face. "Riley... that's not the type of relationship we have."

"Oh, I just thought since you two spend so much time together that..." She cringes and shuts her mouth. Even if our relationship were like that, I wouldn't tell her. It's none of her business. I also know she tends to gossip and I don't want her telling everyone we are sleeping together.

I give her a fake smile. "Thanks for the help."

I spend the rest of the day trying to figure out what the hell to get Harlow for her birthday. While driving home, I get an idea that makes me drum my hands on the steering wheel with excitement. Maybe Riley was onto something. Harlow may have said she didn't want anything, but that doesn't mean I can't do something with her.

I grab my computer as soon as I get home to see if the idea I have in my head can happen. I'm not sure if it's the right season for what I have in mind.

It says that it is. I pick up Six-Two-Six who has been meowing at my feet for food while I was googling. "I think your human pillow is going to love this," I say with a grin.

I decide not to tell her. I'll just make sure to ask her about her schedule for next week so I know what day to do it. I'm not sure who will be more excited, me or her.

It's the day of Harlow's birthday surprise. I told her that she and I have plans this afternoon and to wear something nice. Of course, she took offense to me telling her to wear something nice and accused me of politely calling her a bum. I would find her beautiful even if she were wearing a trash bag.

As soon as I step into her place, she is asking me twenty-one questions because my typical sneakers, jeans, and t-shirt are gone. I went for a dressier look and put a white button up shirt on with nice slacks and a pair of dress shoes.

"Acyn! You look... very dapper." She bites her bottom lip and gives me a hug. "I've never seen you dress up before." Her eyes roam over me as she pulls away.

"You look stunning, as always." I'm starting to like summer, since she's always either in bikinis that barely cover anything or sundresses that hug every single curve. She has legs for days that I would love – alright, maybe now isn't the time to think of that.

"Thank you." She curtsies which causes me to chuckle.

"There is one thing..." I say.

"What?" she asks with her eyebrows raised.

I pull a yellow, satin blindfold from my pocket. "I am going to need you to wear this."

Her left eyebrow raises as it always does when she is unsure of something. "A...blindfold? Am I going to end up on Cold Case?" she teases.

I laugh. I knew she was going to be skeptical when I pulled the blindfold out. "No, I just don't want you to see where we're going. Do you trust me?"

"With my life." She turns around, waiting for me to tie it on her.

"Can you see?" I ask her once it's tied.

"No."

"Good, because I was flipping you off."

She erupts with laughter. "Jerk."

"Alright, grab my arm so you don't bite the dust." She loops her arm through mine.

"Wait, wait take a picture." She pulls on my arm.

"Right, right. Pictures." I have learned the basics of taking pictures because somehow, I've become her personal photographer. "Are you going to pose or am I just going to take them?" She gives me a cheesy grin. I chuckle and take a few pictures so she can choose her favorite. "Alright, are you ready now?"

"Yes!"

Harlow hasn't stopped smiling since I picked her up. I haven't either if I'm being honest. I hope she is this excited when she sees where we are. I pull into the parking lot. "Alright, we're here." She lets out a squeal that I am sure she was holding in.

"Can I take off the blindfold yet?"

"No, not yet. Let's walk a little further and then you can."

I place her arm on my hand and lead the way.

20

Harlow

I grasp Acyn's arm as he leads me to wherever we're going. We're not in the city because it's quiet. I feel the crunch of gravel beneath my feet and then the softness of dirt. I don't think where he's taking me is going to be indoors. We walk for a few more minutes, then he stops.

"Ready, Sunshine?" he asks, standing behind me.

"Yes!" I clasp my hands together with excitement. I can honestly say that I have never been this excited for anything in my life.

"You already know that I'm not going to be there with you in Texas for your birthday. You also said that you didn't want me to get you anything. However, you didn't say that I couldn't do something with you." He unties the blindfold and says, "Happy birthday, Sunshine."

It takes my eyes a moment to adjust but when they do, I blink in disbelief. We are standing in the center of a sunflower field. The golden yellow leaves are illuminated with the warm glow of the afternoon sun. I look at Acyn and then back at the sunflowers because I feel like I'm in a dream. I get closer to one standing in front of me. It's much taller than I am. I reach up to touch it to be sure that I'm not dreaming; this is all so surreal.

"Do you like it?" he asks.

A lump is in my throat and tears prick my eyes. "I love it Acyn." I stand on my tip toes and give him a kiss on the cheek.

He wraps his arms around me. "I've had this planned for weeks. That's why I kept asking you about your schedule because I wanted to be sure that we got here before golden hour so you could take some good pictures."

I don't want to let him go. "This is the sweetest and most thoughtful thing anyone has ever done for me. Thank you." I give him one last squeeze and then reluctantly let him go.

"Never need to thank me, Sunshine. I brought some stuff for a picnic, too."

I notice that there is a picnic basket sitting next to his feet.

My God, and they say chivalry is dead. "Acyn... I am... I feel like I'm dreaming." I grin. "This is the best birthday present ever."

"Shall we?" he asks with a grin.

He thought of everything. There's champagne, fruits, and a charcuterie board filled with bread, meats, cheeses, and jams. Everything is perfect. Even him.

"This is a day I will never forget," I announce as I stuff my face with food and sip champagne.

He chuckles. "Good. I was worried that it was a stupid idea."

"What? Why?"

"I guess because it isn't a physical gift," he says, shrugging. "But I knew that I wanted to do something special for you. Especially since I'm not going to be there for your birthday."

He was more disappointed than I was when he told me he wouldn't be able to get the time off to fly home with me. I had already suspected that would be the case, but I can tell he still felt bad.

"Acyn, this—" I wave my hand around the sunflower field. "—Is so much better than you being at my party in Texas. Trust me, I already know I am going to get a bunch of meaningless bullshit gifts." I look down at the bubbles rising in my glass of champagne. "You know me so much better in the short time I've known you than people who have known me my whole life." I look into his ember eyes. "Stop feeling bad for not being able to be there. This is amazing."

He gazes at me as if searching for a lie on my face. When he doesn't see it, he nods. "Alright. I'll stop mentioning it... maybe."

I laugh. "It's almost golden hour. I want to get some pictures."

Acyn snaps pictures of me amongst the sunflowers. I must admit that he has become quite the photographer. It wasn't my intention, but I'm not surprised because I'm always asking him to take pictures of me doing something. As we walk through the field I spot some people and ask them if they can take a picture of us.

Before we leave, Acyn buys me a huge bouquet of sunflowers that has various other flowers mixed in with it. It's gorgeous. I can't wait to get it home and in a vase.

I rest my head against the window of his car as we drive back to my place. "What would I do without you, Acyn?"

"I ask myself the same question about you." He keeps his eyes on the road as he grabs my hand to hold it.

"So, are you two together yet?" Quinn asks during our weekly morning video chat over coffee.

I scramble to find my ear buds because Acyn is still sleeping and my volume is all the way up on my phone.

"Keep it down," I hiss.

"Oh my God!" Marisa exclaims. "Is he sleeping over again? How do you keep your hands to yourself?"

I rest my head in my hands. "Had I known this was going to be an interrogation, I wouldn't have answered the call." They both laugh at me.

"Marisa does have a point though," Quinn says with raised eyebrows.

"How?"

To be honest, I am questioning my own self-control at this point. Especially after my birthday surprise. I am seeing him in a whole new light. My fingertips are slipping off the ledge of *like*. One by one. "Because I don't want to ruin what we have now."

"Please don't tell me you're still hung up on Hendrix," Quinn says.

They know everything that has gone down between us. My contact with him has still been minimal. He lives his life and I live mine. I know that he still keeps tabs on me on social media because he is always the first to view my stories and like my photos. Even the ones with Acyn in them. I think by liking them he is trying to show some maturity.

"I don't think I feel the same way for him that I used to. I guess I'll know more when I see him next week. That's if, he's even there." I think Acyn was right. With time, you start realizing people who were once your world matter a little less to you each day.

Marisa cackles. "Like he would miss an opportunity to see you. I bet his bags are packed right now, waiting at the door."

I shake my head, laughing because she is probably right. "I cannot stand you two. Can we talk about something else?"

Acyn appears behind me in the camera, and it makes me jump. He, of course, thinks it's hilarious. I swat at him. "Ass."

Both Quinn and Marisa are begging to see him in my ear. I flip the camera around to face him. "Say hello to your little fan club."

"Hi," he says in his low, gravelly, sexy morning voice. Acyn doesn't seem to care that he is only wearing boxers and neither do we.

"Morning," Marisa and Quinn say dreamily.

I roll my eyes and turn my attention back to them while Acyn busies himself in the kitchen. "Alright, I've gotta go."

"That man is a God. I think I saw his morning salute," Quinn says.

The heat of embarrassment creeps up my neck. I cover my face with my hand, thankful I have ear buds in and he can't hear what my thirsty friends are saying.

"Yeah, yeah, yeah, I gotta go. I'll see you two soon." Rolling my eyes, I wave at them.

They both giggle. "Bye, babe! See ya!"

I wasn't thrilled initially to go back home but after talking to the girls, it's hard not to be excited to see them. I've contemplated asking Hendrix when he'll be arriving back in Galveston. It's going to be weird to be around him and not be friends or lovers anymore. I'm more worried about still feeling something for him. It's easy to ignore someone when they aren't physically in your space. I've wondered if maybe there is still a part of me that hopes he and I could work things out.

After we broke up, that was my hope. That we could somehow find our way back to each other. For the first few weeks in Seattle, he was my life jacket. Helping me feel secure in a new place by holding onto something familiar. But I found my footing, and then our relationship became exhausting because he was treating me as if we were still together. As if he had a say in what I did and didn't do. Slowly, the hope of working things out faded. I didn't want to put forth the effort for a friendship with him. Let alone a romantic relationship.

But then... Acyn happened.

21
Harlow

"Sunshine, you realize we have to be at the airport... now," Acyn calls from the other room as I scramble around my place, trying to gather the last of my things for my trip. I have accepted that I am perpetually late. Acyn has not. Bless him for trying his best to get my ass out the door on time for things.

"I know, I know. I'm coming, I am commiinnnggggg," I yell as I find the flats I tore my room apart for. I throw open my already stuffed suitcase and cram them in on the side.

"You know you're only going to be gone four days...," he says as he eyes my three bags.

"Yes, but... who knows what will happen. I had to have enough outfits to choose from. You know how I am." I sit on my suitcase as I zip it up.

"Wouldn't it be logical to take less instead, then? Take less and suddenly you don't have so many choices," he says with a smirk.

"Are you going to help me with my bags or are you just going to give me lessons on decision making? This is who I am as a person, babe. Take it or leave it." I go in my closet and take one last glance through my clothes to make sure I'm not forgetting anything. Acyn follows me, picks me up, and places me back in front of my bags. I don't even fight because I already know I'm being unreasonable.

He places his hands on my shoulders and brings his eyes down to mine. "Breathe." I narrow my eyes, ready to say something, but he raises an eyebrow, so I close them and breathe. "You cannot take your entire closet with you. You are going for four days. Put your shoes on or you will miss your flight."

I open my eyes and stare into his. He grins at me, giving me a wink. "Fine," I huff. "But if I am missing something –"

"You can tell me you told me so when you get back. It's not like you can't buy something while there."

I raise my hands. "Alright, alright. Let's go."

Acyn looks up at the ceiling and lets out an exasperated sigh as if he is thanking the heavens.

He loads all my bags into his G-Wagon and I hop into the front seat to scroll through IG. My heart rate picks up when Hendrix is first on my feed with a picture of him in his parent's backyard with the caption: *home to celebrate my twenty-fourth.*

I start chewing on my thumbnail because I don't know why I was hopeful that his baseball schedule wouldn't allow him to be there. Charlotte is throwing the party. Professional baseball player or not, she would expect him home regardless of what he has going on.

Acyn gets in and swats my thumb out of my mouth. I snort with laughter. "I can't stand you."

He grins as he starts his car. "You love me and my bullshit." I roll my eyes and laugh, but in my head, I know he isn't wrong.

I put my camera on him and record for my IG stories. "Acyn, are you going to miss me?"

He scrunches up his face and sucks his teeth. "Can one miss someone as annoying as you?"

I erupt with laughter. "Stunt for the gram. I feel you."

We pull to a stop at a light and he looks directly at me. "I'll always miss you when you're not with me." Butterflies are coursing through my veins now and I am grinning like an idiot. I am thankful when the light turns green so he has to focus on the road.

When we get to the airport I am cutting it close like Acyn said I would be. "I told you we should have left earlier," he says.

"Are your observations going to help me get there faster?" I ask as we practically run towards check in. I still have to make it through security.

He chuckles. "No, but it's fun to tell you I told you so." I ignore him and hand the agent all the stuff she asks for to check in. Once my bags are checked, Acyn walks with me to the security line.

I wrap my arms around him when we get to the point he can't go past. "Wish you could come with me, but I'll see you when I get back."

He hugs me back. "I'll be here. Enjoy time with your dad and friends. Call or text when you can."

Standing on my tippy toes I give him a kiss on the cheek. He grins and waves me off.

I feel like I can't breathe when I step off the plane. I forgot how thick the humidity is in Texas. My clothes cling to me as I wipe the sheen of sweat from my forehead. "Ah, the great state of Texas," I mutter to myself.

My excitement grows as I near baggage claim. I can't wait to see my dad. It's been months and I really miss his hugs. As I near, I see him waiting with a smile on his face. I grin and walk as fast as I can without running because my carry-on is pretty heavy. I can hear Acyn laughing at me in my head.

"Harlow," he says, giving me a bear hug. "It's so good to see you, Kiddo."

I cling to him. I missed his hugs, his voice... everything. This is the longest I have been away from him. "I've missed you, Dad."

"Missed you, too. I'm happy you finally came home to see your old man."

I laugh as I pull away from our hug. "You know you can come see me anytime you want, right?"

"I know, I just like to give you a hard time." He nudges my arm and we wait for my bags to appear. When we get my three bags of luggage my dad gives me a look of incredulity. "Three bags? Really?"

I put my hand up and start laughing. "Look, Acyn already laid into me about it. I know it's over the top, but I also like options." I grab two of the suitcases. "Are we going home or are you going to judge me, too?"

"Still dramatic, I see." He chuckles and leads the way to his car.

An hour later we are pulling up to the home that I was born and raised in. I am feeling nostalgic. Growing up, I didn't think I would ever move away. Especially after my mom passed, the thought of leaving terrified me. At that time I couldn't have imagined moving and leaving my dad alone. When you lose someone it makes you acutely aware of how fleeting time is. When we consider time, it is for appointments, birthdays, milestones, celebrations, et cetera. We don't consider time being a series of moments we will eventually miss.

"Nothing's changed," my dad says as he pulls into the driveway.

I've been away for half a year. Staring at the front door, it feels like an eternity. I think about how much I've changed since I walked out that door six months ago. I inhale the familiar scent of this house. It instantly makes me feel at ease.

"It's good to be home with you." I smile at my dad.

"It's so good to have you in the house again. I put fresh linens on your bed. If you want to crash, be my guest. I bet you're exhausted after the flight." He squeezes my shoulder then leaves me alone while he goes to get the rest of the bags.

I climb the stairs to my room. A smile tugs at the corners of my mouth because it is exactly how I left it, except the comforter and sheets are different. I exhale as I collapse onto my bed. The exhaustion of travel settles over me. My mind wanders to Acyn as my eyes grow heavy. I forgot to power on my phone when I got off the plane. The excitement to see my dad blocked out everything else.

Harlow: Made it.
Acyn: Good! Glad you didn't miss your flight.
Harlow: Why are you living in the past?
Acyn: LMAO enjoy your time with your dad!
Harlow: Wish you were here.
Acyn: Me too.
Harlow: I'll text you in a bit. I need some sleep.
Acyn: Pack your bags the night before and you wouldn't be.
Harlow: I like to live life on the edge.
Acyn: Get some rest, grandma.
Harlow: I am going to remember this for when I am back.

Acyn: Shakin' in my sneakers, Sunshine.
Harlow: LMAO. To think I thought I missed you.
Acyn: You do even if you don't admit it.

I send him the middle finger emoji and put my phone into do not disturb mode. I didn't think I was tired but now a nap seems appealing. My dad brings my bags in but I am half asleep and don't say anything. He kisses the top of my head before he leaves my room. It feels good to be home.

The next morning my dad and I walk along the beach.

"Have you spoken to Hendrix?"

I don't immediately respond even though I expected the question. I've tried not to think about seeing Hendrix again because it distracts me from enjoying the few days I have with my dad.

I let out a sigh. "No, we don't really talk like we used to. I think it's for the best." I may be filled with uncertainty but I can't deny that it has been good for Hendrix and me to take a break from talking all together. Trying to be in each other's lives post-breakup probably wasn't the best idea.

"He's asked about you every time I've seen him over the past few months. I am telling you this because I think he still has hope that somehow you two will still end up together."

Ever since I came home crying after our breakup, my dad and I talk about so much more than just surface things. I tell him practically everything now like I used to when I was younger.

"I know he does but... I don't believe he and I will ever be compatible. I want to be an individual and he wants me to follow him around," I say. "I didn't think it would be an issue for me to be back here seeing him again but it's a lot easier to think that when someone isn't in close proximity."

"If you don't want to go to the party tomorrow, we can do something else."

I smile at my dad because I know he just wants me to be happy. I squeeze his hand. "Thank you, Dad, but I'll be okay. I'm not the same girl I was when I left here six months ago."

That is what I'm telling myself, anyway. My fear is that I'll look at him and realize nothing has changed at all. I don't want to fall back into old ways because familiarity is so comforting.

"You're not, and I'm proud of you, Kiddo."

Later that afternoon I get a text from Kyrell asking if I want to get together for Hendrix's pre-birthday bash today. Since Hendrix and I are only twenty-four hours apart, our parents would alternate which day we would actually celebrate our birthdays. The years that our birthday bash doesn't fall on his birthday, he throws a pre-birthday bash. He started that when we were sixteen. It tends to be a wilder party then the birthday bash that our parents put together for us.

Harlow: Who all will be there?
Kyrell: Everyone.

I roll my eyes because everyone means all their high-school buddies they really don't give a shit about. But they all like to party, so I guess it works out. Marisa and Quinn are my only real friends that are attending the party tomorrow. Besides, Hendrix will be there. I don't know that I voluntarily want to hang out with him before I have too.

Harlow: I think I'll pass. That's not my scene.
Kyrell: Ah, c'mon, Harls.
Harlow: I'm good love, enjoy.

If this were before I had moved to Seattle; I would have said yes without hesitation. I am channeling Acyn at this moment because I am not going to say yes to shit I hate. I hate hanging out with people who don't give a damn about me and who I don't give a damn about. Why pretend?

Kyrell: LMAO fine, can I stop by after I am done?
Harlow: I don't care but don't bring anybody from high school. I don't
want them at my house.
Kyrell: You're so friendly.

I ignore his last text because he knows that I don't talk to those
people. Not that my high school experience was terrible, but they
weren't people I cared to carry on lasting friendships with. Hendrix
and Kyrell were really my only two friends. I didn't it mind it that way
because I liked to keep to myself. I was "friends" with everyone else
by association.

My phone rings and it's someone that I actually want to hear from.
I answer the video chat.

"Hey, Sunshine."

"Hi," I say with a grin. "Are you done with work already?"

"Yeah, today was a chill day." He sits down in the tattoo chair. "What
are you doing?"

I sigh and cradle my chin in my hand. "Kyrell wants to hang out later."

"That's right." He nods. "I forgot he's good friends with your ex."
Acyn never calls Hendrix by his name. He has dubbed him *the ex*.

"Yep." I smile. "But enough about me. What are you doing this..." I
look at the time because he is two hours behind me. "Afternoon?"

"I..." He gets distracted by another call. "Hey, let me hit you back. You
should go out and have fun while you're there though. Forget everyone
else." He gives me a lopsided grin.

"Alright." My mouth curves into a smile. "Talk to you later and I'll
consider." He chuckles, gives me a two-finger salute, and ends our call.

I tap my fingernails on the counter, trying to decide whether I want
to go to this party with everyone or not. It would be nice to get out
of the house and enjoy the beach, but I can't get past all the people I
know will be there. Then I will have to deal with them tomorrow too.

I text Marisa and Quinn to see if they want to go shopping for a
birthday outfit with me. They both immediately respond in the group
text that they will meet me at the mall in an hour. Apparently, Acyn was
right. I would end up buying stuff here instead. He knows me well.

I gaze at my birthday outfit for tomorrow as it hangs in my closet. It is a floor-length, sheer, tulle skirt paired with a bodysuit that is embellished with rhinestones. One can never go wrong with a little extra sparkle on their birthday. Excitement is buzzing through me. I've always loved celebrating my birthdays. I thought maybe the glamour of them would wear off as I got older, but it hasn't.

I didn't celebrate the first few years after my mom passed away. It was hard to do things without her. I also felt like I was betraying her by doing happy, exciting things. Sometimes I still do. Except now, I do things in honor of her and to celebrate her. My very existence is a celebration of my mother, even if she isn't physically here with me.

I hear our doorbell chime at the same time my phone does. I ignore my phone to go answer the door.

I see Kyrell through the glass. "Hey!" I say, grinning at him. "I didn't thi –" my words get lost in my throat. I see Hendrix stepping out of the car behind him. I narrow my eyes at Kyrell. "Are you trying to ambush me?"

He gives me a cringy smile. "I texted you."

"You sent the text after you rang the fucking doorbell!" I whisper-yell at him.

He mouths, "I'm sorry," as Hendrix gets closer to the door.

Hendrix looks so good, if not better, than the last time I saw him. His black curls are a little longer and he has more muscle on him. The corners of his mouth turn up as he approaches me. Yep, he still has a smile that takes your breath away a little.

"Hey, Harls. Hope you don't mind me being here with Kyrell."

Kyrell is now looking awkwardly between Hendrix and me. If I had telepathy, I am sure he would be apologizing for doing me like this.

"Hey Hendrix," I say clumsily. "You look good." Wait... what the fuck? My eyes go wide, and I just stare at him because I didn't mean to say that. Well... I did but I didn't mean to say it out loud for them to hear.

Kyrell is now looking at me with raised eyebrows, probably hopeful that I won't kill him later. I knit my eyebrows together as I give him a look of contempt. His eyes find the floor once he realizes that I am still not happy about this surprise tag-along visit from Hendrix.

"You look gorgeous," Hendrix says, bowing with a nod of his head. I can do nothing but watch him because what do you say to a person who you know is still in love with you?

"Um, thanks." I tuck a stray curl behind my ear. "Um... lemme go get my bag and we can go somewhere that isn't here." I start to close the door, so they know to stay on the porch and not come inside.

"I asked Kyrell to bring me with him," Hendrix spits out. "He had mentioned he was going to skip the get-together tonight and come hang out with you so – "

"You thought you would tag-along?" I ask with a quirked brow and hand on my hip.

"Yeah, so don't be mad at him."

Kyrell gives me a plea in the form of a grin. Instead of responding, I roll my eyes and shut the door in their faces. Maybe they'll think I'm not coming back and leave. I mean, I know I could just tell them to leave, but they already know that I'm not doing anything tonight. I sigh as I slowly climb the stairs to my room to get my bag and phone. I don't know why my brain didn't consider this scenario earlier when I gave Kyrell the greenlight to stop by. I expected him to stop by much later than this. The sun hasn't even set for the day yet. I wonder why Kyrell didn't want to go the get-together. He loves shit like that.

I alert my dad that I will be going out with Kyrell and Hendrix. He gives me a look of surprise. I wave him off with my hand. "I know, I know. He tagged along and well... we're here now. I'll be back in a few hours. Love you." I exit the room before he can ask me any questions. There is nothing to say anyway. I would have to see Hendrix eventually. Our birthday party is tomorrow. May as well rip it off like a band-aid.

We eventually find ourselves sitting in the backyard of Kyrell's parents' house. They're out of town, as usual. His parents weren't around a lot growing up and apparently they still aren't now. The third time we had gone over to his house in middle school I finally asked him where they were. He shrugged and said he didn't know. I remember thinking his life must be lonely in a house this big. When we were younger, most of his time was spent with Hendrix or me. They really only started hanging out here when they realized it was cool to throw parties in high school. What better house to throw a party than one where parents are rarely home.

I settle into the plush pillows of a hanging swing. Kyrell offers me a brownie bite. I gladly take it because hopefully it will take the edge off of my nerves. Or maybe I'll need some nerve. Too late, I think as I swallow the bite. Hendrix refuses because he could be fined for using marijuana.

"You're such a buzzkill, Hendrix," Kyrell says with a mouthful of brownie. I snort with laughter because it's kind of true. Wait, be nice Harlow.

Hendrix looks at me and smiles. I grin, shaking my head as I look away.

"How have you been, Harls?" Hendrix asks.

"Good." I nod. "Working at Holy Shot and taking on photography gigs wherever I can." I pick at the fray of my cut off jean shorts. I'd rather look anywhere but at him right now.

"How's the photography thing going?" he asks.

I stop picking at the frayed strings and look at him. I'm shocked that he is showing interest in something that I'm doing. "Great, actually." I smile. "I just had a shoot in LA."

He grins at me. "That's amazing! I'm happy for you."

All I can do is blink at him because I am not sure how to react to him genuinely being happy for me. I can tell by his tone that he's being sincere. Maybe he has changed with a little time and distance.

"You were in LA and didn't bother to text me? I'm hurt." Kyrell holds his hand over his heart as he fake cries.

"It wasn't for pleasure." I laugh. "Well, it was pleasurable for me but I was there for a job with not much downtime. Besides," I say, shrugging. "We are supposed to hang out in two weeks anyway for our tattoos."

Hendrix leans forward, resting his forearms on his knees. "You two are getting matching tattoos?" he asks with his brows furrowed.

"Yeah bruh, I told you about this. Her friend is doing them," Kyrell says matter-of-factly.

"Who?" Hendrix asks when I know he already knows the answer. I only have one friend with tattoos that I hang out with.

"Acyn..." I say.

"Oh, that's cool. Maybe when I have more downtime, instead of a day or two, I can hit him up for one."

I blink and then look at Kyrell, who is also looking at Hendrix like he's gone mad.

"Um... you," I say, pointing my finger at him, "want a tattoo from Acyn?"

Hendrix shrugs. "Yeah, you two are friends, right? Any friend of yours is a friend of mine."

Kyrell is now looking back and forth between us as if we are playing a game of tennis. I wasn't expecting this reaction from him. I also can't help but feel like he asked about us being friends for him to know whether Acyn and I have become more.

"I'm sure he would be down." I know that's a lie. From what I've gathered, Acyn doesn't care too much for Hendrix. He's never spoken poorly of him but will make remarks here and there.

"Will you take me to the sunflower fields next time I'm in town?" Kyrell asks with a grin on his face. I am not sure if he is trying to elicit a response from Hendrix or not. Knowing him, he probably is. I know Hendrix saw all of those pictures because he liked every single one.

"Uh yeah..." I side-eye Hendrix, who still seems unbothered. "Acyn would have to take us though because I was blindfolded the whole way there."

"Aw, fucking sweet," Kyrell says with a huge grin. I don't understand why he likes to bother Hendrix so much. They usually end up fighting at the end of it all.

"A field of sunflowers..." Hendrix nods. Almost as if he is contemplating whether he wants to comment or not. "He seems like a nice guy."

I am not sure how to take this side of Hendrix. I thought it was going to be difficult to be around him and that he was going to throw a fit if Acyn was brought up. Maybe he really does want to be in my life now.

I guess the problem is I don't know if I want him in mine. There is so much history there and I'll always wonder if he's being genuine or just hoping I'll let my guard down. Kind of like I am now.

"You guys cancelled your birthday party?" I ask, wanting to change the subject.

"No, we showed up for a little bit and then left." Hendrix shrugs. "It's not fun like it used to be. People and priorities change," he says as he looks into my eyes.

"They do." I nod and watch the fan whirling above my head. Kyrell and Hendrix start talking while I zone out. My body is physically here but my mind is on my birthday party and Acyn. I can hear the boys talking, but I am only half listening and responding when necessary. Hanging out with them hasn't been as bad as I was anticipating. I don't know what I expected from Hendrix, but it wasn't this... more mature version of him.

My phone rings, bringing me out of the trance the fan had me in. The edible must have kicked in. I steady myself as I stand; Hendrix reaches out his hand to help me and I grab it before I topple over. We hold hands for a few seconds longer than necessary before I remove mine from his. "Thanks." I smile and get my phone from my bag.

"Damnit," I mutter when I see I missed a call from Acyn. I hadn't heard from him all day and I kind of missed him.

"Everything okay?" Hendrix asks.

"Yeah." I chew my thumbnail as I look at my phone because his phone goes straight to voicemail. "Just missed a call."

He runs his hands through his curls, as he does when he's annoyed, and doesn't say anything in response. I am sure he knows who it is. I have posted pictures with my other friends in Seattle, but Acyn is the one person I am with consistently.

I look at the time and realize it's getting late. Deciding I don't want to look like a zombie tomorrow, I ask Kyrell to take me home. "Hey, Kyrell. Do you think you could run me home? I have a lot to do in the morning before the party tomorrow."

"Yeah, whatever you want, Harls. Lemme go find my keys." Kyrell leaves Hendrix and I alone for the first time all evening.

"It's been good to see you in person and not just in pictures," Hendrix says as he leans against the counter of the outdoor bar.

He is awfully close now. I can smell his cologne. "Yeah." My voice is a squeak and I quickly clear my throat. "This went better then I imagined it would."

"Why?" He chuckles and tucks a stray curl behind my ear. The action causes me to look him in the eyes. It reminds me of old times. For a second I get lost in his eyes like I used to. The familiarity of them, the warmth. His eyes travel down to my lips as he licks his own. I glance quickly at Kyrell who is walking towards us holding the keys in his hands. When I look back at Hendrix, his lips meet mine.

My eyes are wide open as I stare at his long, black lashes as his lips are pressed to mine. The way I was just looking in his eyes I thought this kiss would elicit more of a response from me but... it doesn't. I don't feel the same way I use to. I place my hand on Hendrix's chest and push him back. I initially look down at my feet unsure of what to say. I glance at Kyrell who is staring between the two of us.

"Hendrix..." I take a few steps away from him. "I don't feel the same way you do." An apology is on the tip of my tongue but again, I swallow it. I am not going to apologize for something I am not sorry for.

"Is it because of Acyn?" he asks bluntly.

"No," I lie. Acyn is the first and last person on my mind every single day. Even with Hendrix's lips on mine I was thinking of him. Wishing I was kissing him instead of Hendrix. I think... I'm in love with Acyn. Or maybe I've known this whole time and this kiss just confirmed it.

"Then what is it?"

"People change, Hendrix. Feelings change." I wrap my arms around myself. "We've changed. I am not the same person I was six months ago, and neither are you."

Kyrell is still staring at us as if he is watching a soap opera.

"But you're still the same girl I've been in love with." He grabs my hand, but I slide it out of his.

"I –" There is nothing more for me to say. No matter how I package the delivery of the words, he is still going to think that we will somehow mend things. Instead I turn to Kyrell. "Can you take me home now, please?"

"Uh... yeah, yeah, sure. C'mon."

I quickly walk away from Hendrix and past Kyrell making a beeline for the car.

I let out the breath that I was holding in during that whole exchange as I lean against the car door. Kyrell reappears moments later, unlocking the door for me to get in. I slide into the seat and shrink against it as I see Hendrix walking towards the car. Kyrell stops him and talks to him for a moment before he comes to the car. Hendrix stands there staring at him and I can tell that he is contemplating doing whatever it is that Kyrell just told him not to.

Kyrell gets back in the car. "He wants to know if you'll still be at the party tomorrow?"

I sigh. I kind of forgot about the party tomorrow. "Uh, yeah... I guess I have to go."

He gives Hendrix the thumbs up and he responds with a smile before he disappears back into the house. "Kyrell, what the fu-"

The engine revs to life as he turns the key and begins to back out. "Harls, listen, I had no idea that was his intention or I wouldn't have let him tag along with me."

I cross my arms and stare out the window. "What did you tell him in the driveway just now?"

"He wanted to come with to drop you off so he could talk to you. I told him I think you need some space."

I could have all the space in the universe from Hendrix and it still wouldn't be enough. I am now dreading the party tomorrow. I let out a groan. "Kyrell, why does he always do this? Why is his timing always fucked up?"

His eyes remain on the road and the music is the only sound between us. "Hendrix will go after whatever he wants because he's used to getting whatever he wants. He's having a hard time understanding that you don't want him like he wants you. He thinks that if he tries a little harder that maybe you will change your mind."

I bang my head against the headrest in exasperation. "If I were going to change my mind I would have done that months ago." I enunciate every word as if he is in the car with us.

"I know that." Kyrell taps his fingers on the steering wheel. "So you and Acyn, huh?"

A laugh escapes me. I cover my face with my hands. "Why are you bringing him into this?"

He shrugs and grins. "Thought I'd ask to see what kind of reaction I got from you." I don't say anything in response. "You know, I've watched you go from making everything about Hendrix to being your own person and creating your own life. I'm fucking happy for you."

I place my hand over my heart. "Aw, Kyrell," I say it jokingly, but I can feel tears forming in my eyes. "That's really nice of you to say."

"I have my moments." He grins and pulls into my driveway. "Don't worry about tomorrow. I think it will still be fucking amazing."

"I won't." I smile and give him a kiss on the cheek. "I'll see you tomorrow." I shut the door behind me and run up to my front door. Kyrell waits for me to unlock it before he starts pulling back out. I wave as he leaves.

Once inside, I rest my back against the door. Hendrix's actions tonight didn't shock me but I had hoped we would be able to be around one another without him feeling the need to profess his undying love. I really hope that he doesn't pull that shit tomorrow.

I pull my phone from my bag to see if Acyn texted or called me. He didn't. Knowing him, he's probably passed out on his uncomfortable couch with Six-Two-Six. Letting out a sigh, I climb the stairs, wishing I were home with him.

22
ACYN

*E**arlier that same day...***
Harlow hasn't been gone that long and I am already concerned because I miss her so much. I really need to get a fucking grip.

I just finished up with a client and decide I may as well call her to see how things are going in Texas. She picks up almost immediately and it is so good to see her face. You don't notice how much time you spend with someone until they aren't there with you. She seems happy, like a ray of fucking sunshine, to be home with her dad.

She is in the middle of talking about hanging out with Kyrell when I get a call from the client I am seeing tomorrow. He's been coming to see me since I first started when I was eighteen. I'm pretty sure he has more tattoos then I do. I end the call with Harlow and switch over to talk to him.

"Hey, Ace!"

"Hey, Elijah, what's up man? Everything good with you?" I hope he didn't interrupt my call with Harlow to shoot the shit with me. We'll have plenty of time to do that tomorrow.

"Yeah, I had a family emergency come up and I won't be able to make it tomorrow."

I pinch the bridge of my nose in annoyance. Why the fuck couldn't this family emergency of happened days ago so I could have been at Harlow's party. Oh shit, wait he's still on the line.

"Damn, is everything alright?" I try to sound concerned.

"Oh yeah, just some things I need to handle."

"I can have Riley call you and set up another time if you want." My annoyance is growing with each word that comes from his mouth.

"Yeah, sounds great. Sorry to cancel last minute."

"No worries. I'll see you another time." I end the call and squeeze my phone in my hand. Harlow and I are just friends. I shouldn't be annoyed that I am missing her birthday when – wait... unless.

I pull up flights from Seattle to Houston. Maybe I can still make it there in time for her party. "Yes!" I shout and Riley's head snaps up to look at me from behind the counter. There is a flight that leaves tomorrow morning at eight a.m. and arrives at two p.m. in Texas. I would need to get a hotel so I could shower and change. Excitement builds when I realize I can do this. But I have one fucking problem. I don't have her address. I think of asking her uncle, but they aren't in town either and I don't have his number.

I stare at my phone as if it is going to give me an answer. Then I remember that Harlow said she was going to hang out with Kyrell later. I bet he knows her address. Luckily, we have been texting back and forth about the tattoo he wants to get in a few weeks. I pull up his texts with a smile on my face.

Acyn: Hey. I need your help.
Kyrell: You name it and I got you.
Acyn: I need Harlow's address. So I can surprise her at her birthday party.
Kyrell: My man Acyn! Let me ask her because I only know how to get there I don't know the actual address. I'm with her right now.

While I wait for him to text me the address I purchase the ticket before the last few seats are taken. He texts me back a minute later with her address.

Kyrell: The party starts at 6. She is going to lose her shit!
Acyn: Thanks man! Are you going to be at the party?
Kyrell: Hell yeah! See you tomorrow.

I hop up from my seat and stop at Riley's desk before I dash out the door.

"I am going out of town tomorrow and I'll be back on Monday."

"Are you okay? You're smiling more than usual."

I haven't stopped smiling since I realized I can be in Texas with Harlow for her birthday.

"Yeah, I'm fucking great! I'll call Hunter and let him know that I'm going to be out of the shop and unavailable for a few days. He knows what to do."

"Okay," she says with a smile. "Where are you going?"

"I'll see you Monday." I give her a smirk and walk out the door. She may have helped me with Harlow's birthday present but that doesn't mean I'm ready to tell her anything that I don't have to.

Once in my car, I make a mental list of everything I have to do before I leave tomorrow. I call Harlow but she doesn't answer. Maybe it's best I don't talk to her until I see her because I'm sure I would let it slip that I am on my way to her. I don't know how the hell I am going to sleep tonight because adrenaline is already pumping through my veins. Once I'm home, I text Sevyn to let her know where I am going and to ask her if she can take care of Six-Two-Six. Of course she doesn't hesitate to say yes.

Harlow is more than just a friend to me. We started off there but it has developed into more. I think she knows it, too. Sometimes I can see it in her eyes when she looks at me. I am sure that she sees it in mine. There have been a few times over the past few weeks where I have wanted to kiss her but I haven't. When she talks about her ex, even though she tries to be indifferent, I can tell her feelings about him are mixed. I don't think she knows how to feel about him.

I find myself not wanting to wait anymore.

I step out of the shower at the hotel. I am not sure how people survive the humidity that is already sticking to my skin. I have about an hour before the party starts. She may be worried about me at this point because I haven't wished her a happy birthday or responded to the messages she's sent me. She'll understand once she sees me, though.

The GPS tells me in a quarter of a mile my destination will be on the right. I am fashionably late. It's not something I intentionally do, but I'd rather skip the awkward early party phase of sipping drinks and staring at one another. My heart rate picks up because parties aren't really my thing, but there isn't anything I wouldn't do for her. It's apparent which house is her dad's because it is generously decorated. I find a spot, park, and grab her present from the back.

I send Kyrell a text.

Acyn: I'm here. Should I just walk in?
Kyrell: I can meet you out front. I want to record her reaction.

I head towards the house and Kyrell comes out seconds later. He throws his hands up in the air to greet me. "Acyn! I never thought I'd see you in the great state of Texas!" He wraps his arm around my shoulders as we enter the house.

"Neither did I." I chuckle. I'm doing a lot of things I wouldn't typically do since I met Harlow.

"C'mon, everyone is out back. Do you want a drink or anything before we go back there?" he asks as he gestures towards the kitchen were passing.

My mind is on Harlow. Drinks can wait. "Nah, I'll worry about that later."

"Let's do this then," he says with a grin and pulls out his phone.

We enter the backyard that is packed with people, but my eyes find her instantly. She is stunning. Her hair is in a braid that wraps around her head. It gives the fitting illusion she is wearing a crown. Her skin is illuminated by the sun and she is fucking perfection. She is standing in the middle of a group of people. A guy is with her and from the pictures I can tell he is her ex. He has his arm around her shoulders as they laugh and talk to the people around them. To my surprise, she graciously moves out of his hold and stands between two girls instead. One whispers something in her ear and she starts laughing.

No one laughs as much as she does. She is genuinely that carefree and fucking happy. I've learned that laughter is her medicine. If it were bottled up and sold, I would buy a lifetime supply.

Her friends are talking to her but she scrolls through her phone and chews on her thumbnail. It makes me realize she must be wondering why she hasn't heard from me on her birthday of all days. The guy to the right of her is trying to get her attention but she doesn't listen to what he is saying.

"I can't wait until she realizes you're here. She is gonna flip," he says as he continues to record. We haven't been standing here longer than two minutes.

Then as if she senses someone is looking at her, she looks up and scans the crowd. At first, her eyes pass over me but then they snap back to me and she blinks a few times. She gawks at me as if she isn't sure whether I am there or not. I smile and wave at her.

She starts running towards me as fast as she can. Everyone around her looks at her like she is crazy. I toss the gift to Kyrell. I brace myself to catch her so we don't both fall on our asses. She crashes into me, I pick her up off her feet, and spin her around.

"Acyn!" she squeals with her arms wrapped tightly around my neck.

"Hey, Sunshine. I thought I would come say happy birthday instead."

"I told you today would still be fucking amazing," Kyrell says with a grin as he continues to record.

Harlow's feet touch the ground and she stares between us with a shocked expression. "You knew?" she asks Kyrell with her hand over her heart and a grin on her face.

"Yeah, I knew since yesterday." He stops recording. "But Acyn wanted it to be a surprise."

She hugs me again. "Wait, did you know you were coming?"

"No." I hold my hands up, "I didn't know until yesterday when my client for today cancelled. That's why you haven't heard from me. I had to get ready and then I was on the plane."

"I'm not sure what to do with all these surprises Acyn." She places her hands on her cheeks. "You're here!"

The two girls she was talking to before walk towards us. She smiles at them as she grabs my arm, pulling me towards them. From their weekly video chats and photos back at her place I know that they are Marisa and Quinn.

"Guys," she practically squeals, "this is Acyn! Acyn this is Ma – "

"Marisa and Quinn. I've heard so much about you two." I extend my hand out to both of them and neither of them look sure of what to say.

Quinn eventually finds her words. "You're clothed."

Marisa nudges her and Harlow slaps her hand over her mouth as she looks at me. The guy who I think is her ex has been glaring at me but is now standing within earshot. And he looks pissed.

Kyrell quirks an eyebrow. "You have an OnlyFans or something, bruh?"

I start to respond, but Harlow interrupts. "It's an inside joke, right you two?" she says.

"Yep, you definitely wouldn't understand," Marisa says. "It's nice to finally meet you in person. Harlow has told us everything about you." She shakes my hand. "You have such nice arms. I mean tattoos."

"Wow, so this is what it's like to have embarrassing friends," Harlow says laughing as she covers her face with one hand and holds onto my arm with the other. The ex is still lurking. I have never had someone stare at me this hard without wanting to fuck me.

"C'mon, you can meet my dad!" She starts to pull me along behind her.

"Harlow..." the ex says as he steps in front of her. He looks from her to me as if he is making a silent demand of her. I pull Harlow towards me and she settles against my chest. I wrap my arm around her neck as if it's second nature. She doesn't pull away from me like she did to him. Instead, she relaxes into me and places her hand on my forearm.

"Uh, Hendrix..." She looks back at me. "This is Acyn." She keeps her eyes on me. "Acyn, this is Hendrix." I don't make any movement to extend my hand. Neither does he...initially. Then he reaches out his hand and I glance at it for a few seconds before I shake it.

"Nice to finally meet you. I know you two spend a lot of time together." His tone is slightly accusatory.

"We do," is all I give him. What Harlow and I do or don't do is none of his business. Even though he so badly wishes she were still his business. I bend forward a little to her so my mouth is next to her ear. "Let's go find your dad, Sunshine."

"Yeah, he's going to love you." She grabs my hand and sidesteps the fuckboy. I grin as I walk past. The fake-ass smile he had on during the introduction is now a sneer.

We find her dad at the BBQ. I am a little nervous to meet her dad. I now know how she felt when meeting my parents. Harlow was right; he and West could be twins. Except Harlow's dad seems more traditional. She taps his back and he turn around to face us.

He gives me a genuine smile when he realizes who I am and shakes my hand. "Acyn. Nice to meet you in person."

"A pleasure to meet you, sir."

"You made it! Harlow had said you weren't going to be able to join us."

"A fortunate change of plans happened for me." I smile and my stomach growls because I haven't eaten anything since yesterday. I've been running on pure adrenaline.

"It's great to have you here. I'm sure Harlow will show you around, but enjoy your time. We can catch up later."

It went better than I expected meeting her dad. I didn't really know what to expect because I have never intentionally met someone's parents. In the past it was more of a "stay away from my daughter" type of thing. I wasn't a "bad" kid, I simply didn't care for rules. I like to push boundaries. Her dad's boundaries were ones I didn't want to test, though.

"Have you not eaten?" Harlow asks.

"Nah, I was just focused on getting here. I haven't bothered to eat," I admit and a smile tugs at the corner of her lips.

"I won't have you starving on my account. Let's get some food. You met all the important people... well three important people."

I erupt with laughter because I know she didn't intend on introducing me to her ex but he made it hard not to.

We sit underneath the gazebo to eat our plates of food with Marisa, Quinn, and Kyrell. I notice that there are a lot of people here but they seem to be here more so for her ex than her. She hasn't bothered to introduce me to anyone else, but now I see why she wasn't initially thrilled about the party.

Harlow nudges my arm as she sits next to me. "I'm glad you're here." She briefly rests her head on my shoulder before she looks at me and smiles.

"Me too, Sunshine."

"Aww," Quinn squeals. "He calls you, Sunshine?" If the heart eyes emoji were a person it would be the look on Quinn's face as she looks between us.

"He's always called me that. I don't know why you're squealing about it," Harlow says with a shy look as she glances at me.

"I know, but it's different hearing it in person."

I didn't realize her ex had joined the table.

"What's wrong with Harls?" he asks as he takes a seat. Everyone's eyes snap to his as if he in an intruder. It makes sense now; he must have given her that nickname.

"I don't like it," I say with a shrug. "I think Sunshine is more fitting for who she is as a person. Especially after the first night we spent together. It just... stuck. You know what I mean?" I ask him without breaking eye contact.

Everyone is looking between the ex and I who is now glowering at me. I guess he didn't know how much time we spend together. Whoops. Harlow is trying her best to hold back a laugh. He opens his mouth to say something but is interrupted by Quinn.

"Do you have any brothers by chance?" she asks hopefully.

I chuckle. "No, no brothers. I only have sisters."

"Damn," she mutters, crossing her arms. Marisa and Harlow start cracking up.

"How come I've never met your sisters, Ace?" Kyrell asks with a mouthful of food.

"Would you want me to introduce your sisters to a guy like you?" I ask plainly with a piqued brow. Everyone starts cracking up.

Kyrell shrugs. "Touché."

My sisters are too old for him and Sevyn is married. It doesn't matter though, because even if I did have sisters single and his age, I wouldn't introduce them. He isn't a bad guy but I can see myself in him. I wouldn't have wanted my sisters to meet a guy like me when I was going through the phase he's in now. He's looking for a good time and that's it.

We all continue to talk while her ex observes us all, not saying anything. Kyrell says something funny and Harlow buries her face in my chest as she cracks up. Her ex looks like he wants to try and break my neck in that moment. I get the sense he is used to Harlow doing what he wants because it made things easier for him and her. While I simply want to be in her company and will take her anyway I can get her.

"Are you two ready to open gifts now?" her dad asks.

"Yeah," she says and then looks at her ex. "Are you ready?"

He stands and holds out his hand to her. "Yeah, c'mon."

"Oh..." She glances at me and then back at him. "Um, I'm going to stick with Acyn since he doesn't know anybody."

I can see his jaw flex with annoyance. "Right." He gives me a curt smile. "Wouldn't want him to feel lonely."

"Don't mind him," Kyrell says. "He is just realizing his place."

"C'mon." Harlow pulls me by my hand towards the table that's covered with gifts. She stands next to her ex once we reach the table. He gets ready to place his arm around her, but she pulls me next to her and he stops. I smirk because she wants me around and I know that bothers him.

"Thank you all for coming for the twenty-fourth birthday of Harlow and Hendrix," a woman who looks like her ex announces. "We are so grateful to have both of you home and are proud of who both of you have become." She gives Harlow an appraising look as she says this as if she doesn't mean it for her, but has to say it because people are around. This has to be the ex's mother then. "Let's open gifts. Then we can drink and dance the night away."

Everyone applauds and they start passing gifts to them.

Harlow gets a lot of stuff that isn't really her. It's shit you would buy someone you don't know very well. I understand that she didn't have a big circle of friends but she grew up here. I would think that the people she grew up around would know her a little better or at least have an idea of what she would like.

"This is for you," her ex says as he holds a gift out for Harlow. She hesitates before she takes it from his hand.

"Thank you Hendrix." She smiles. "I didn't think we would be getting each other gifts this year..." Her words hang between them. "I feel bad now." She gives him a sympathetic smile.

"It's just something that reminded me of you, Harls," he says.

She starts to unwrap the box that is in her hands. Everyone's eyes are on her and its apparent she is uncomfortable, but she handles the situation with grace. Harlow opens the box and looks inside. She looks at me, then at the box, and then at her ex. Then she pulls out a baseball. "Oh...um..." She is damn near speechless and so am I.

When she starts turning it around in her hand I can see that he signed it. It takes everything in me to not fall out laughing.

"It's a baseball..." Harlow awkwardly holds it up for everyone to see and they act like it's the best gift in the world. "Thank you, Hendrix." She puts it back in the box and her ex gives her this awkward hug and tries to kiss her cheek but she pulls away.

"Is that all the gifts?" she asks.

"Oh shit," Kyrell yells from the back of the crowd. "No, hold on. There's one more I set down inside." He disappears inside the house and reappears with my gift. A grin pulls at my lips because the timing of this is just too perfect. "It's for Harlow from Ace."

Harlow turns around to face me with her eyes wide. "You got me something else?"

"Yeah, nothing major." I shrug. "Just something that reminded me of you." May have been petty to say that, but it's true.

She grins and takes the package from Kyrell.

"Sorry my wrapping skills are shit," I say, but she playfully swats my arm like she always does when she thinks I'm being ridiculous.

Her fingers tear at the wrapping paper and she instantly knows what it is when she sees the box. Her hands still for a moment as she glances at me and then continues unwrapping it. Once it is completely unwrapped, she places her hands over her mouth as she stares at it. "Acyn..." She is looking at the box like it is everything she ever wanted.

"What is it?" Kyrell asks.

"The camera that I love." She looks at me again and has tears in her eyes. Then she wraps her arms around me in a tight hug. "Thank you."

I hug her back. Everyone is staring at us but we don't fucking care.

Quinn breaks the ice. "So does this mean we're going to get professional photos before you leave? I mean, I wasn't gonna ask but since we're here..." People start laughing and Harlow gives Quinn of a look of appreciation for not making things awkward.

I can't help myself and I wipe a tear from her eye. The gesture garners a look of disdain from her ex, who now looks like I just stole his favorite toy from him.

"Uh yeah..." Harlow says. "I can take photos of you guys... and anyone else who would like a professional photo."

The woman who looks like the ex speaks, "Okay, gifts are done. Enjoy the rest of the evening, everyone. The servers will be around with cake if you would like some." She glances at me and I give her a look of annoyance that matches her own. I can tell she wasn't expecting that and clears her throat. "And make sure to talk to Harlow if you would like a picture."

As the crowd disperses, Harlow says thank you to those who gave her gifts.

Kyrell approaches her. "I didn't get you anything because I already paid Acyn for our tattoos."

She smiles and hugs Kyrell. "Guess I can't back out of this now, can I?"

"Fuck no. Sealed your fate months ago when you agreed to my wild idea." He laughs. "Happy birthday, Harlow. It's good to see you genuinely happy." He walks off without saying another word and the ex follows behind him. I can hear him asking questions about Harlow and me but Kyrell just shrugs him off by giving him bare minimum answers.

"And you." She turns to me, "Thank you for making this so much better than I thought it would be."

"What else are friends for?" I ask her as I lean against the table with a grin on my face.

She stands between my legs and grabs the collar of my shirt. My heart thumps in my chest at the simple gesture. "I think..." She raises the camera to her eye. "We may be..." She snaps a picture. "Past that."

"Past what?" I ask her. I think I know what she is going to say but I want to hear it from her lips.

"Past –" we're interrupted when Marisa and Quinn come up to us and wrap their arms around Harlow.

"We're ready for our closeup, babe," they announce. Harlow laughs as they strike exaggerated model poses.

"You know, you guys could have just asked me to take pictures whether Acyn gave me a camera or not."

"Yeah." Marisa shrugs. "But you're here for fun and we didn't want to ruin that."

"Are you kidding? I love taking pictures. It's gotten worse now. Ask Acyn."

I chuckle and look at her. She looks so fucking happy. "Uh, yes. She goes nowhere without a camera. Which makes me wonder. Why were you not taking pictures of your birthday party?"

"I didn't have a reason to. Now I do," she says as she grins at me.

23

ACYN

Harlow spends the rest of the evening snapping photos of everyone and anything she can. I take a few photos of her with her friends and her dad. I'm even nice enough to take a picture of her and Kyrell that her ex sneaks into. After a while, Kyrell appears with some edibles and joints once the older people have gone home.

Harlow eats half of a cookie and then feeds the other half to me.

"So, what do you two do back in Seattle when you hang out?" her ex asks.

Everyone is having a good time, but this dude looks salty as hell. She doesn't bat a lash as she shoves the other bite of cookie in my mouth and laughs when frosting gets on my lips. Using her finger, she wipes it off my lip, and then licks it off her fingertip.

"Umm... when we're home..." She looks at me and starts giggling. "I guess it would depend on which house we're at. We call each other's houses home." It's clear the edibles have hit her. She doesn't censor herself like she does when she isn't lifted. I am not gonna stop her from telling him what we do if he wants to know that damn bad. "We hang out a lot." She shrugs. "And do whatever we feel like really. It's always fun to get together with his family and –"

"You've met his family?" he asks as he tugs at his hair. It doesn't seem to take much to annoy him.

"Oh yeah," she says, nodding. "I'm really good friends with his sister too. That's how we met. Then he recently introduced me to his mom and dad, who I love, a month or so ago." Harlow doesn't seem to register that this is making him upset. Or maybe she does and just doesn't give a fuck. She turns towards me and asks, "Do you wanna dance?"

"Sure, Sunshine." I stand and reach my hand out to her. "Excuse us," I say with a smirk to her ex, who glares at me.

"Wait for me," Kyrell says as he pulls Quinn and Marisa towards him. "No offense, Hendrix, but you're a fucking buzzkill lately."

Kyrell is the only person who is honest with him. Maybe that's why she stayed with him for so long. He is used to getting his way and it seems like he makes things difficult when he doesn't. Harlow grabs a glass of champagne from a server as we head towards the dance floor. It's her birthday and she is finally acting like it.

Harlow's hand is linked with mine as she pulls me into the center of the dancing crowd. She downs the rest of her champagne and wipes her mouth with the back of her hand as a smirk pulls at her lips. "Can you even dance?"

I look her up and down. "Can you keep up is the real question?"

She tosses her head back, laughing, as she presses her body into mine. I place my hand onto the small of her back, pulling her as close as we can be, as she starts to move to the beat. I match her movements and she looks at me with surprise.

I chuckle. "I meant what I said."

The song switches and so does the rhythm to a quicker pace. She spins around pressing her back into me. Okay, wait, let me rephrase that. She grinds her ass on my dick. I respond by gripping her hips and moving with her. She lifts her arms up and her fingertips caress the side of my face, trailing down my neck, and then she runs them down her own body. Goddamn, she is killing me. My body is focused on hers but my mind is imagining her legs wrapped around me as she calls out my name.

I am so lost in the movement of her body and my own dirty thoughts that I don't notice the song ending. Until she releases the pressure she was just applying to my dick and turns around to face me. She rests her cheek on my chest as the tempo of the song slows. I start to wrap my arms around her when someone taps my shoulder. I turn to the left to see her dad next to me. Oh shit, great, he just saw me feeling up his daughter in every way possible.

"Can I cut in?" he asks with a grin.

Thank fuck because I really was about to tell him I had absolutely no regrets for feeling on his daughter if that's what this was about.

"Be my guest," I say as I lift her hand to his and bow out. Harlow smiles at me and begins dancing with her dad.

I make my way off the dance floor to find a drink. Kyrell and the ex are standing next to the table. This should be interesting. I would avoid the situation entirely but I need something other than alcohol and weed in my system. Kyrell greets me while the ex is looking sour. Shocking.

"Enjoying the party?" Kyrell asks.

"Yeah, it was worth the flight," I say as I down the bottle of water. "When are you heading back to LA?"

"I head back tomorrow. I hate this fucking place," he says bluntly.

I don't think I've ever heard something negative leave his mouth before. I side-eye him and he chuckles.

"A story for another time," he says.

I nod, deciding to leave it at that. If he wanted to tell me, he would. I turn my attention to Harlow and her dad as they dance and laugh.

"I'm going to go take some pictures of Harlow with her dad," I say. I can feel the ex's eyes on me and if Harlow isn't around I'm not going to watch what I say. Hell, even if she is around. But I'd rather not start a fight and ruin a party she is just starting to enjoy.

"Being a good boyfriend." Kyrell laughs. I don't try to correct him, but the ex does.

"They aren't even dating," he scoffs and sneers at me.

I pick up Harlow's camera from the table she left it on. I contemplate whether I should say something or just let him have his moment. "Yet..." I say as I turn on the camera. "We aren't dating yet." I grin at him and his face is now flushed as his jaw ticks.

"Excuse me while I go take pictures of my gorgeous ass friend for now." I don't even know how Harlow feels about me, honestly. Sometimes I can see it in her eyes but I haven't heard it from her so it makes it hard for me to believe. Her ex doesn't know that though.

I walk away and hear Kyrell telling the ex to chill. If he wants to throw it down here I will. I am sure he thinks because he is a professional athlete he has the upper hand. I don't go to the gym and run daily for nothing. Once I am closer to Harlow and her dad, I start taking pictures. I have no clue if they're good. I shoot and hope for the best. When the song is over I take some of them standing together. She thanks me and asks her dad to take her camera inside.

She wraps her arms around me as another slow song starts. It must be getting later. They aren't playing dance music anymore. I wrap her in my arms as she rests her cheek on my chest.

"You smell good," she says. "I mean you always smell good... or maybe I just missed you." Her arms wrap around me a little tighter.

I chuckle. "You could also be a little bit tipsy and on cloud nine right now too..."

She nods as she laughs. "That too. That too. But it was all worth it. I've had fun tonight. May feel differently depending on the severity of my hangover in the morning but tonight... I'm fucking happy."

I smile as we continue to sway to the song. "I'm happy for you, Sunshine."

Harlow and I dance for a few more songs. We aren't really talking, just holding onto each other and slowly swaying.

"Acyn..." she mumbles against my chest. I think she's falling asleep.

"Yeah?" I stop us from moving and look down at her.

"I'm tired," she says with a yawn. "And my feet hurt from dancing in these fucking heels."

I grin and kneel down to take them off of her feet. I am honestly surprised she's kept them on this long. She is either barefoot or in flats most of the time.

"Take me to bed, please?" she asks with her arms outstretched, waiting for me to carry her.

I start laughing but oblige. I pick her up in one fluid motion and she wraps her arms around me. She buries her face in my neck as I head for the house.

"Thank you for coming. You were the best surprise." Her lips brush against my neck. My body responds as it always does to her touch.

I stop when I come toe-to-toe with the ex, who is now looking outright murderous.

"Harls, are you okay? Do you want me to take you upstairs to your room?" he asks.

He's bold and has me fucked up if he thinks I'm going to pass her off like a fucking relay baton. I guess if she says yes to him I don't really have a choice, though.

She lifts her head and her eyes focus on him. "Acyn's got it, Hendrix. Thanks, though."

Then she buries her face back into the crook of my neck and wraps her arms a little tighter around me. I smirk at the ex who now visibly looks ready to lunge at me. His fists and jaw are clenched. I am sure the only thing stopping him is that I am holding Harlow in my arms.

It looks as though every hope and dream he had with Harlow is slowly being crushed by *me*. I'll continue to stomp on them, fucking dance on them, if I have too. His eyes bore into mine. I maintain my cocky grin I know he so badly wants to wipe off of my face.

"Are you sure about that, Harls?" he asks.

She groans, "Acyn and I sleep together all the time Hendrix. He's got it."

"Yeah man," I say with a smirk, "we sleep together all the time. I've got this." I throw him a wink.

I move past him and Harlow calls out, "Night, Hendrix. Good seeing you again."

I'm an asshole. I turn back around and address him by his name for the first and last time. "Night, Hendrix. Good meeting you."

All he can do is stand there gawking at us as I take the woman of his dreams inside with me.

"Where's your room?" I ask once we're through the door.

"Upstairs, second door on the right," she mumbles.

I make my way through her house and climb the stairs. Once I find her room, I enter and kick the door shut behind us. I gently lay her on the bed and toss her shoes next to her suitcases strewn all over the floor.

"Uh... are you wearing that to bed?" I ask as she tries to get comfortable to fall asleep but is wrapped up in her skirt.

She groans. "I was going to but this shit is itchy."

I start laughing as she sits up and strips it off of her. She now has on what looks like a bathing suit. She removes the straps from her shoulders with her eyes half closed and then peels the top down over her breasts. I wasn't ready.

"Fuck..." I mutter to myself.

"Get me a shirt from my drawer please," she says casually as if her breasts aren't out.

I open the drawer and of course it's her panty drawer. I slam it shut and, thankfully, the next drawer has shirts. I grab one and throw it at her face. She is dramatic and falls back against the bed when it hits her. She laughs. I fucking love that sound.

"You jerk." She giggles. "I am intoxicated. I could have suffocated!"

"Right, you really were in danger with a light cotton shirt hitting your face," I say as I start to take off my clothes.

It's fucking hot as hell still and it's three a.m. She takes off the thing that looks like a bathing suit and tosses it at my face and starts laughing again. When I remove it from my eyes, I'm met with a view of her ass cheeks as she crawls up her bed to her pillows. I am momentarily rendered speechless and unsure of what to do with myself. I don't think I can sleep in just boxers like I normally do because... well now my dick is at full attention.

She flops down onto her bed and pats the spot next to her. I stand there, contemplating my options. I can lie next to her or I can take a shower and rub one out. "Acyn, lay with me," she says. So I do.

I would rather be buried inside her but I also don't want to make a move on her when she's drunk and half asleep. I want her to be fully aware of everything I am doing to her body. Every single touch, stroke, suck, lick, and moan – *all of it*.

I try to think of anything other than the fact she is half naked next to me. Harlow cuddles up to me when I get comfortable. She doesn't say anything but places her hand on my chest for me to hold. I really hope she doesn't try to sling her leg over me because she is going to feel my dick that is still fully erect. Not sure when that will go away. Or if it will go away.

Harlow sits up. I hope she isn't going to puke on me. I can she is looking at me in the dark with her face silhouetted by the silver moonlight coming through the window. She doesn't puke. She straddles me and I'm not sure whether I should stop her or see what she does. Placing her hands on my chest, she slowly spreads her legs apart as she lowers herself onto me. A moan escapes her when her pussy presses against my dick. I can't help it when it twitches in response. She rakes her hands down my abs as she slowly rocks her hips. I inhale sharply and move my hands up her thighs until they are holding her hips. I should stop her. But I don't. I will follow her lead, though.

She suddenly stops and lays her head on my chest. "Just let me listen to your heartbeat. It reminds me of home," she mutters.

I hold her as she drifts off to sleep...wondering if she'll remember this when she's sober.

24

ACYN

We spent our last full day in Texas with her dad. That's all she wanted. Her dad is planning to come visit Seattle for the holidays and that made Harlow happy. I know she loves her dad, but I also know that she no longer considers Texas home. Since we bought our plane ticket at separate times, I change my ticket to match hers for our trip back home.

On the flight home, we talk about everything other than what happened on the night of her birthday. I don't want to press her into talking about it, but I also am not going to forget it. It isn't about just sex with her. It's about the fact that I can't see myself without her in my life now. I've never been in love before, but I imagine this is what it feels like.

"Home sweet home," Harlow says as we enter her place. "Ah, never thought I would have ever loved having my own place, but it turns out I do," she says as she sets her phone and bag on the kitchen counter. "Thank you for flying all the way to Texas for me."

"No need to thank me, Sunshine. It was pleasure to meet your dad." I set her unnecessary bags on the living room floor. Yeah, I still gave her shit because she filled half of my suitcase with stuff she bought while she was there.

"He loved you by the way," she says as she slips her sneaker off of her foot. "Everything will be Acyn this and Acyn that from now on." A smile tugs at her lips even though she pretends to be annoyed. "I'm gonna go shower now. Feel free to stay and make yourself at home like you always do."

I chuckle. "I'll wait until you're done. I may shower here. I've just barely stopped sweating from all the humidity we've been in the past few days."

She tosses her head back and laughs as she heads for the bathroom. I hear her call out, "Weakling," right before she shuts the door and locks it. Smart move on her part because I probably would have gone in there after her.

I flip on the TV and start rummaging through the fridge while some murder show plays in the background. Her phone starts ringing and I turn around to see who it is. Surprise, surprise it's the ex. I have to chuckle because she changed his name to "The Ex," and there is a zombie emoji next to it now. After it goes to voicemail I resume my mission for food when her phone starts ringing again.

"For fuck's sake," I mutter to myself as I watch it ring.

Why does he call her like that? When it goes to voicemail a text comes through seconds later and... I read it.

I know I shouldn't, but I can't help myself.

The Ex: I loved spending the night with you and kissing those lips again.

I knit my eyebrows together and read it again before her screen goes black. She... spent the night with him? When would this have – oh, when she hung out with Kyrell. I think she had said he would be there. But she tried calling me back when I tried calling her. When I texted Kyrell he said he was with her. She even sent me texts but... maybe she did hook back up with him.

At her party she didn't seem like she did. It looked like she couldn't be bothered to give him the time of day. Maybe that's because I was there. I don't know how their reunion went. I didn't even bother asking. I figured if there was anything of importance she would have told me.

I know I don't have a right to be annoyed or even angry... but I am. We aren't even together but I still can't help but to feel fucking disappointed. At the end of the day we're just friends. I don't know that she would tell me if she did sleep with him. Because again, it really isn't any of my business.

They have a lot of fucking history. Maybe I need to give her space to sort herself out. Fuck... I still want to be in her life. Even if that means I have to give her space to try and get my feelings in check. Fuck. Fuck. Fuck.

She comes out of the shower in just a towel. "Are you okay?" she asks.

I'm at war with myself. I want to rip her towel off of her and claim her in every way I can but I also can't stop repeating that text in my head.

"Yeah," I lie. "I'm just tired. I think I'm going to go home to shower, sleep, and check on Six-Two-Six."

She looks slightly disappointed and I hate to be the cause of that look.

"Alright." She smiles. "We did just travel and I'm sure Six-Two-Six misses you."

I can't help but chuckle in spite of feeling... disappointed, angry? For reasons that aren't even valid because she isn't mine. We're just fucking friends. "I'll text you." I know I said I want to give her space but all I can do is physical space right now.

"Okay." She approaches me and stands on her tip toes to give me a kiss on the cheek. "Tell Six-Two-Six his human pillow says hello."

I smile. "I will." I want to ask her what happened between her and the ex but I don't. I leave it there and head home.

Harlow

I grab my phone to text my dad but roll my eyes when I see a text from Hendrix on my screen. Delusional is the only word that comes to mind. I send him a text back.

Harlow: Hendrix, things are over between you and I. Don't make this any more difficult then what it has to be.
Hendrix: He isn't going to love you like I do Harls.

Harlow: That's the whole point. I don't want him to love me like you do. I want him to love me in only a way that he can.

Hendrix: He isn't right for you.

I don't have time for this. I try to be cordial but it's hard when he is being pushy.

Harlow: Neither were you but I'm still standing. I am none of your concern any longer. Let me go.

I block his messages and calls. I am not going there with him again. He needs to accept that I have moved on. I smile to myself. It feels good to finally be able to say that to myself.

It's been a few days since we've arrived home from Texas, and I can't help but to feel like Acyn is avoiding me for some reason. He stopped into Holy Shot the morning after we got back but I haven't seen or heard too much from him since. I'm trying not to be clingy but at the same time I want to know what's going on with him.

Harlow: Hey. Do you want to hang out after work today?

I've never been nervous to send him a text but I can feel that something is... off. I rack my brain as I wipe down tables, wondering what could have happened between Texas and home. Or even over the past few days. I thought everything was good. In fact, everything felt better than good because I knew there was nothing holding us back anymore.

Unless... maybe he – my phone chimes. I have to keep myself from running across the shop to get to it.

Acyn: I can't tonight.

My shoulders slump and I feel like an idiot for being so disappointed. I let the feeling settle in my stomach, twisting it into knots. No explanation. He has been saying that for the past four days. It's been almost a week. At first I thought that he was just tired and then busy with work. I can respect that and give him space to do whatever he needs to do. But now I feel like he's intentionally avoiding me.

I check the time to see that there are only five minutes left of my shift. I start making his favorite cup of coffee after deciding that I'll stop by his shop so he has to give me a real answer instead of these three-word texts.

I see him through the window of his shop and he isn't even busy. In fact, he is sitting in the chair scrolling through his phone. I enter the shop and Riley gives me a smile from behind the desk.

"Hey Harlow! How was your birthday?"

I force a smile because I really don't want to talk to her. "It was good. Thanks for asking." I look over at where Acyn is sitting and he is still on his phone. I see from here that he has earbuds in. I turn back to Riley, "Can I go in?"

She laughs. "Like you have to ask. Go ahead."

My heart starts to thump in my chest. I don't know why I am so damn nervous; I've been here a thousand times. But those thousand other times I knew that he wanted me here. Now I'm not so sure. I stand in front of him and hold out the cup of coffee. He looks up from his phone and into my eyes. I don't think he expected me to stop by because he looks slightly shocked that I am standing in front of him.

I offer him a smile. "Thought I would stop by and see you."

He removes his earbuds. "What are you doing here?"

I blink and my smile fades. I wasn't expecting that question from his lips. My confusion must show because he tries to correct himself. "I mean... I have a client in twenty minutes and–"

"I just wanted to stop by and bring you a cup of coffee since we haven't been able to hang out this week." He then looks at the cup of coffee in my hand and almost looks afraid to take it. "It isn't poisoned...," I joke, trying to lighten the mood.

A smile tugs at his lips as he takes it from my hand. It reminds me of the first time I gave him a cup of coffee. The electric feeling of his fingertips brushing against mine. His fingers linger a little longer this time before he takes it from my hand.

He clears his throat. "Thanks Sun – Harlow."

My brows knit together. He's never corrected himself when he calls me Sunshine.

"Do you maybe want to get together this weekend?" I shift uncomfortably to my other foot. "If you're not busy."

His eyes don't meet mine. "I can't, Harlow." I nod and swallow the lump that is forming in my throat. Why is he being like this?

"Oh, okay...um –" the door opens and a woman walks in with waist length jet black hair. That must be who he was waiting on. She stands at the desk with Riley for a few minutes and then makes her way over to us. Acyn smiles at her which makes me quirk an eyebrow. I try to keep my emotions in check because this is his client after all and jealousy has never been my thing. I sure feel like making it my thing now, though.

"Ace," she says as she walks towards us. She gives him a hug and a kiss on the cheek... like I do. "I'm so glad we got to catch up the other night."

His eyes flit to mine as she takes a seat, unaware of the fact that we are now in the middle of a stare-down. So this is why he hasn't been talking to me. He's been going out and meeting people. I nod my head slowly as tears prick my eyes.

She turns to me. "Are you his apprentice? You're learning from the best, you know."

Acyn looks like he doesn't know what to say. It's clear that he didn't mean for me to know about her.

I look at her. "I'm no one." I give her a weak smile and look back at Acyn who now looks at war with himself. "I'll see you around," I say.

I walk as fast as I can without running as I exit his shop. I can't help but to look at him through the windows. He's still staring at me and holding the cup of coffee, while the woman talks to him animatedly as if nothing is going on. He didn't have to say anything to me.

I force myself to look away from him. I can take a fucking hint.

I don't cry on the way home or when I finally climb into a hot bath. I don't even bother checking my phone. I turn it off instead. For the first time in a long time I simply want to be alone.

I toss and turn that night like I always do when something is heavy on my mind. Ripping the blankets off, I make myself some hot tea and sit on my couch in the stillness of the night. I can either take this time to focus on myself or do what I know how to do so well: focus on someone else. I am not trying to make my life about Acyn, but I do want him in my life. He doesn't have to tell me that he is seeing other people. We aren't together.

Maybe I've been reading our relationship all wrong this whole time. This really could just be a friendship. But I can't ignore the chemistry between us. Perhaps I took too long to sort out my feelings with Hendrix and he got tired of waiting. Or he could've never been waiting in the first place and the feelings I feel aren't mutual.

What the fuck do I even feel? Sadness, loneliness, hurt... *love?*

All of the above.

I don't understand why he wouldn't just talk to me. The funny thing is, everyone makes communication sound so easy when it clearly isn't. I rub my temple with my fingertips, letting out a long sigh. I think about turning on my phone but if I do that I for sure won't be able to sleep. I don't even bother with my tea. I pour it down the sink. The only thing I can do right now is focus on myself. I can't make someone want to be with me and I *won't.*

Sevyn stops by Holy Shot with Eli and Emery. I haven't told her anything about what's been going on and I doubt that Acyn has either. The twins wipe that thought from my mind as they climb up the barstools to hand me a piece of paper.

"What's this?" I ask them with a grin. I tear through the twenty stickers they used to close the paper.

"It's a surprise," Emery says.

"Yeah, a surprise. Open it! Open it!" Eli chants.

I open it and read the paper that I now see is an invitation to their third birthday party. I gasp. "You can't be turning three! You're too little," I tease them.

"We are turning three!" they say and then start giggling.

"Can I please have a hot chocolate and a muffin?" Emery asks. She is always straight to the point.

"Me, too," Eli adds.

"Can you come?" Sevyn asks me.

I think about Acyn. He wouldn't miss their party for anything in the world. "Um... yeah." I smile as I make the twins their hot chocolates.

She piques a perfectly shaped eyebrow. "What's up with you?"

"Nothing." I shrug but I don't meet her eyes.

She narrows her eyes at me. "I'll ask again. What's up with you?"

I laugh. "Why are you giving me the mom glare?" She continues to glare at me and it is very intimidating. Her eyes are the same color as Acyn's. "Fine," I let out a sigh. "Acyn and I aren't really on speaking terms."

She cradles her head in her hands. "Don't tell me he fucked this up."

I don't respond. I just shrug because I really don't know that anyone is to blame.

"I am going to kill him," she says.

I hand the twins their hot chocolates and muffins.

"No." I raise my hand. "Just leave it. It's fine. I'll still go to the party but I don't know that I'll stay for the entire thing."

Sevyn raises her hands up in exasperation. "I was rooting for you!"

I start laughing because it reminds me of the Top Model episode where Tyra Banks yelled that.

She lets out a sigh. "I won't say anything but I am for sure going to be a subtle bitch to him."

I snort with laughter. "Thanks Sev. I appreciate your loyalty," I joke even though I really do. "I couldn't miss Eli and Emery's party, could I?" I ask them.

"Are you bringing presents?" Emery asks.

"Of course I am," I reassure her. "What would you like?"

"Oh God, she wants the world. Don't ask them that. They really are happy with anything," Sevyn reassures me.

Eli and Emery are now busy telling me all that they want. I hear a unicorn and an alien which makes me laugh. I stop abruptly when Acyn walks through the door.

Sevyn turns around and then back to me. "Oh, yeah," she cringes, "I told him to meet me before I knew you two were at war."

His steps momentarily falter but he makes his way towards us.

"It's fine," I say as I slip my apron over my head. "I'm off anyway. I'll see you and the little ones this weekend." I smile at her and disappear in the back to grab my things.

When I reappear Acyn is looking at me but I don't keep my eyes on him. I wave to the twins and Sevyn. Walking past Acyn he touches my arm and I glare up at him. It must say enough because he releases me as though I've singed his fingertips.

As I am walking out the door I hear a loud *whack*.

"Argh!" Acyn yells. "What the fuck was that for?"

"Language!" Sevyn retorts. "And you know what it was for!"

I bite back a laugh as I head to my car.

Celeste put me in touch with one of her friends that lives in NYC who is looking for a photographer. When she first suggested me for the shoot I told her that there are tons of photographers in NYC, why would they reach out to me? She told me that while there may be a ton of photographers in NYC, that I am not there and that I need to start valuing my work.

"When will this be?" I ask her during our phone call.

"Wednesday through Friday of this week. All expenses paid and of course generous compensation. All you have to do is show up. I'll be there, too."

I look at the calendar and see that Kyrell and I are supposed to get our tattoos on Thursday. I contemplate whether or not to take it. I really don't want to say no to this opportunity but I also don't want to leave Kyrell hanging when we have had this planned for months.

"Uh... yeah, sure, I'll be there," I say in a rush before I change my mind and end up staying here just hoping to see Acyn.

"Perfect," Celeste replies. "I'll email you all the information."

I end the call and look around my place. I haven't picked up my camera since we got back from Texas, mainly because Acyn gave it to me and also because I haven't been in the mood for pictures. This will definitely be a good way to get back in the groove of things. NYC is one of my favorite cities although I doubt I'll be able to enjoy it because I'll be so busy.

With that in mind, I start packing and surprisingly don't pack much. I chuckle to myself because Acyn would probably be proud of me but at the same time, *fuck him*. I'll talk to West after he's home later tonight. He's never said no to me requesting time off because I am the only employee he has that is willing to work any shift.

My phone chimes with a text and then there is a knock at my door. I already know who it is.

"Kyrell," I say with a grin as he pulls me into a hug. "Why do you always text me before you knock?"

He shrugs. "In case you're running around naked or something."

I snort with laughter. "Only you would think of that."

He flops down on my couch as if he owns the place.

"You're here early," I say as I bring my suitcase out to the living room.

He piques an eyebrow. "Are we going somewhere?"

"No, I'm going to NYC," I say, avoiding his eyes. "I have a photoshoot."

"Are you breaking up with me?" he asks with smirk as he looks up at the ceiling.

A smile tugs at my lips. "I could never."

He sits up on the couch and pulls out a joint from behind his ear. "What are you running from, Harls?" He lights up the joint and takes a pull as he observes me.

I give him a blank expression and shrug. "I don't know what you mean."

He nods and scrubs his hand down his face then holds the joint out to me. "I've noticed, every time something happens that affects you in a major way... you do something drastic. So"— he leans forward — "I'll ask you again, what are you running from? I've known you since sixth grade. It isn't like you to dip on me. I expect that from everyone else, but not you."

His words sink into me. I peer at him and then look at the floor. It just occurred to me that Hendrix was never my best friend. It's always been Kyrell. I start to think back on our friendship. Kyrell spent more time with me than Hendrix did after my mom died. I remember Kyrell telling me that it made Hendrix "uncomfortable" to be around me when I was sad. Not Kyrell though, he'd sit with me for hours, not even talking, just to keep me company.

Then when Hendrix and I did get together, Hendrix always called him for advice. It's clear now that Hendrix had realized Kyrell knew me better than he did. Most of the gifts that he got me were because Kyrell had suggested them. Then, when I moved here to Seattle, he was with me a lot my first few weeks because he knew I needed the support.

The night we went out dancing I told him that I was considering going back home. He told me not to do that because I would eventually regret it. That I just needed to get used to being here and meet more people. Shortly after that, I met Acyn.

I sit next to him on the couch and take the joint from his hand.

I take a hit and hold it for as long as I can before I let out a steady exhale. "Acyn and I aren't talking," I admit.

"What happened?" he asks with genuine concern.

I don't look at him because I really don't want to cry over him. I've cried enough. I shrug. "I don't know... everything was fine when we came back from Texas and then it wasn't." He props his feet up on my coffee table and I lay my head on his lap.

"There has to be a reason," Kyrell says.

"Really?" I ask him. "Why does there have to be a reason? He could have just got tired of waiting for me."

"Nah, not with the way he looks at you and the lengths he goes to for you. There is a reason he is pushing you away. Not that a reason makes it acceptable, but there has to be one."

I don't say anything and he runs his fingers through my hair while he thinks. At this point, I don't know that I care to know his reasoning. He could have simply talked to me.

"What do you want me to do?" he asks after a few minutes. "Do you want me to punch him in the balls?" I erupt with laughter. "Cause I'll fucking do it." I am wheezing so it takes me a moment to respond.

"No, no don't do that," I say as I hold my stomach and laugh.

"So does this mean I can't get my tattoo? Are we just saying fuck him?" That's one thing about Kyrell. He won't allow you to stay down for long.

"Get your tattoo. I know you've been looking forward to it." My stomach and cheeks hurt from laughing so hard. "I'm sorry to leave you," I say softly after I calm down.

"I get it. Sometimes you just got to get the fuck away. Why do you think I moved out to California? We've gotta do what's best for us, Harls. No one else fucking will."

He's right. At the end of the day all we have are ourselves.

25

ACYN

The past two weeks have been fucking awful. Not having Harlow in my life has made shit almost unbearable. Yet, I still can't find the courage to talk to her. Especially not after the look on her face when Isabella mentioned that she and I caught up the other night. Harlow has never looked at me with such disappointment and contempt.

My intention was to give myself some space to reel my feelings in if she wanted to kick shit off with her ex again. I want every single piece of her, not just pieces of her. I've never shared well and I don't want to play ping pong with her ex. I've typed out thousands of texts since I last saw her and haven't sent a single one.

After I saw her at Holy Shot and she gave me a look of loathing I knew a text wasn't going to do it. I probably shouldn't have walked in there like I owned the place or tried to touch her after pushing her away, but I'm fucking drawn to her.

The only reason I'm going in today and not saying fuck it all to hell is because she and Kyrell are getting their tattoos today. Maybe I can grow a pair and actually talk to her. Even Six-Two-Six misses her. Since she hasn't been coming home with me lately he ignores me and goes back to laying on my bed. My entire life is a fucking mess. I'm pretty sure Sevyn knows, too, because she has been more passive aggressive than usual, at least since she dropped off the birthday invite to Harlow.

I scrub my hands over my face and get out of bed to start this shit show of a day. Maybe I should stop by Holy Shot and gauge how she is feeling so I know whether to hide sharp objects.

To my surprise, I don't see Harlow at the counter. It's West.

"Acyn, it's been awhile." Oh fuck, he knows. "Your usual?" I let out an exhale when I realize he doesn't know.

"Uh yeah... where is Harlow?" I ask as I peer around the coffee shop, waiting for her to come up behind me wielding a pot of hot coffee.

"She didn't tell you?" he asks as he hands me my cup of coffee. "Harlow is in New York for a few days for a photoshoot. I dropped her off at the airport yesterday. I think she said she'll be back tomorrow but she said she was thinking of staying for a while longer because she loves it there."

Regret washes over me. She was so excited to get that tattoo with Kyrell and I fucked that up for her, too. Apparently Ace the ass is a more fitting nickname than I thought. I nod as I pick my coffee up off the counter. "Thanks, man. I'll see you around." He waves me off as I head to my shop.

I'm proud of her for getting a shoot in NYC but I also know that she is there to avoid seeing me. Fuck.

I told myself I wasn't going to ask Kyrell about Harlow. That lasts for about five minutes.

"Have you talked to Harlow?" Fuck that shit. I want to know how she's been. He knows her better than anyone else. I try to sound casual but I know I don't.

"Yeah," he says, "she said she thought it best not to come today. But what I want to know is what happened after Texas? Because it seemed to me that you two would finally get off that friends bullshit, bang, and make it official. How did you possibly fuck that up?"

Typically, I can carry on a conversation while tattooing as if it's like breathing. I can't though when he asks me this question. I have to stop and look at him.

I really don't want to admit that I saw the text or that it is what started this hell on earth. But it is the honest truth and the only valid answer. Maybe he can tell me what happened that night if anything. I shake my head, trying to clear it, and let out a sigh. "When we got back"—this sounds ridiculous now that I am about to say it out loud— "I saw a text from her ex that said something along the lines that he had a good time with her the other night and enjoyed tasting her lips again. Or some bullshit like that..." I shrug. I resume working on his tattoo again, not only to give myself something to do but so I don't have to look at him.

Kyrell snorts, which startles me, and then falls out of the chair as he laughs. He inhales as soon as he sits back up in the chair but is still chuckling to himself. I really want to be let in on what he finds so funny, because I have no idea.

He opens his eyes and looks at me with a grin on his face. "Hendrix said that?" he asks and then starts cracking up again. "Man, you're a dumbass. You believed that funky ass text message?"

"That's what the text s—" I start to say.

He sucks his teeth. "Fuck that text. You realize you could have avoided this whole situation if you would have just texted me and asked me what happened?" A chuckle escapes him and now I feel really fucking stupid. "I was there the whole night with them. Matter of fact, it wasn't even the whole night. Harlow only stayed until midnight because she had all the shit to do for the party the next morning. Hendrix kissed her and when he did she pushed him off." He looks at me. "She said she didn't feel that way about him anymore. That's it. Case closed. She didn't fuck him. She didn't kiss him back."

I place my head in my hands as my heart starts to race. I fucked up big time. I really fucked up. How the hell am I going to fix this? Kyrell sees the distress written all over my face.

He rests his hand on my shoulder. "Look, you fucked up. It happened. One thing I know about Harlow is that she is forgiving to those she loves."

I pique an eyebrow, "Loves? Did she say that?"

"No," he sighs, exasperated. "I see the way she looks at you and the way you look at her. I'm an observer and I spent a lot of time with her and 'the ex,' as you call him. She never looked at him the way she looks at you. I knew she loved him"—he shrugs— "but not in the way she loves you. Don't fuck this up over some exaggerated texts from Hendrix fucking Moore."

I shake my head, annoyed with myself. "How the hell do I even fix this?"

"I don't know," he says sarcastically, "maybe you should try doing what you should have done in the first place and talk to her."

I chuckle in spite of my despair.

"If all else fails then... grovel," he says with a shrug.

I really should've just talked to her, but we're here now. I go back to his tattoo but my mind is fucking reeling. After a few minutes he starts laughing again.

"You feel like a dumbass, don't you?"

I start cracking up. "Yeah man, I do."

I shoot a text to Sevyn to have her come help me carry in the gifts for Eli and Emery. I got them the electric cars they've begged me for every time we've gone to Target.

Sev: I'll be out in a second let me change their outfits.

I toss my phone onto the seat and see Harlow for the first time in days walking across the lawn. My stomach feels like it's dropped down to my feet. I have to talk to her now or I may not get another chance. "Fuck," I mutter to myself.

I hop out of my car, opening the backdoor to try and make it look like I was busy and wasn't just staring at her. When I hear her approach, her steps stop for a few second, but she starts to walk past me.

"Sunshine..." I croak out. She keeps walking past me as if she didn't hear me and then she stops between our two cars. Scoffing, she looks up at the sky and then whips around to face me. Her eyes flash with anger.

"Oh, it's Sunshine now. Fuck you, Acyn."

Okay, at least she spoke to me. She turns around to open her car and I reach out to her. "Wait... can I talk to you?"

Her eyes meet mine. "What could we have to possibly talk about right now?"

"Everything." Even though she looks like she could set my soul on fire, I don't break our eye contact. She crosses her arms and leans against her car. I relax a little because at least she isn't trying to leave now.

"I'm sorry...." I start. She scoffs, but I continue, "I'm sorry for pushing you away."

"It doesn't matter." She shrugs as she looks anywhere but at me now.

"It doesn't matter?" I ask her.

"Yeah. It doesn't matter now. I don't want your apology. Is that what you wanted to talk about?"

"No," I run my hand down my face because this isn't going how I thought it would but at least she is talking to me. "I was distant because –"

"I really don't give a damn why you were distant, Acyn. That's your own personal business. Why the fuck would you want to share that with me now? Or did you forget I tried to talk to you multiple times?"

"I know." I guess the only way to get all this on the table is to blurt it out. "The day we came home from Texas I saw a text from your ex talking about spending the night together and that... he kissed you." Her brows knit together as she looks at me with confusion and then it must register what text I am referring to. "I know I don't have a right to –"

"Why does that matter to you?" She piques an eyebrow. "Tell me how it matters when you're spending the night catching up with people. You know if you wanted to see other people I would have been okay with it. I could have handled it. But you didn't give me a chance to handle it at all."

I regret, with every fiber of my being, asking Isabella to come to the shop that day.

"Because... you're mine," I say. My eyes lock onto hers.

She narrows her eyes at me. "I belong to –"

Before another word is out of her mouth, my lips are on hers. I pull away just enough to mutter, "Me," against her lips. I want to devour her. I grab the back of her neck, pulling her towards me greedily. Claiming her mouth again. Claiming all of her. She responds by wrapping her arms around my neck, pressing her body into mine. She moans into my mouth. I run my hands along every curve of her body, gripping her ass before grabbing her legs. I pick her up to wrap them around me, pressing her up against the car.

Her hands grip my shoulders as she grinds against me. I am completely lost in the taste and feel of her. She tastes sweet, like cake and mint. As intoxicating as I imagined her to be. I need to taste all of her. I release her legs from around me and trail kisses down her neck. I'm aware we're outside but I don't give a fuck at this point. I want a taste. I back her up so she is flush against me and the garage door. Hopefully, the only person coming right now is her. I kneel down, thankful she is wearing a dress, and rip her panties off. She gasps and looks at me with wide eyes. "Acyn there are people and –"

"Tell me you want me to stop, Sunshine, and I will." She bites her lip as she looks down at me. Fuck, she is beautiful. I hike her leg up over my shoulder, waiting for her to respond. It doesn't take her long to make up her mind and she shoves my head into her pussy. I run my tongue along her slickness, tasting every last drop. I flick at her clit. She grips my hair tighter as she moans. I suck, flick, and lick her slot until her legs start to shake. She is grinding against my face as I hold her up against the garage door.

"Acyn, Acyn..." It's a mix of a moan and cry. My name sounds so good spilling from her lips.

"Acyn I'm gonna cum..." she pants as she wraps her other leg around my shoulder and thrusts her pussy into my face. I don't let up. I quicken the pace of my tongue as she comes for me. A shiver runs through her, she stills for a moment, and then releases. Crying my name. I continue to suck on her as she relaxes against the garage door when another voice cuts through everything.

"What the fuck, Acyn?" Every word is enunciated. It's Sevyn's voice.

Harlow pushes me back hard enough that I stumble backwards from where I'm kneeling and smack my head against the bumper of my car.

"Acyn!" Harlow gasps. "Are you okay?" She kneels down next to me.

"Yeah, I'm great," I reply. Better then great, actually.

Harlow remembers Sevyn is standing there. "Sevyn, I can explain – we – I – " she holds up her hands and cringes, "I'm sorry."

"It's a good fucking thing I made the kids stay inside because they would have been traumatized forever. Harlow, put your fucking panties on." She points to the ripped material wrapped around her ankle.

Harlow looks completely satisfied and horrified all at the same time. She kicks them off into my direction, I gladly catch them, but she refuses to look Sevyn in the eye.

"You two better stay for the entire party now and help with clean up afterwards. You can fuck on your own time." She doesn't say another word as she carries one of the presents inside.

I start laughing as soon as she is gone. I forgot I had texted her to come help me before I saw Harlow heading towards me. It wouldn't have stopped me from eating her for lunch the way I just did but I got completely lost in the moment. Harlow looks at me with wide eyes.

"I can't go in there," she says, shaking her head.

I try to hold back a laugh. Her cheeks are flushed, not from embarrassment, but from the orgasm I just gave her. I can't wait to see this look on her more often. "I'm serious, Acyn, I can never see her again." She covers her face with her hands.

"Sunshine." I pull her hands away from her face. "Trust me. Sevyn doesn't give a flying fuck about what she just saw. I walked in on her and Zane one time at my house on my bed. We're even now." She stares at me with wide eyes and then erupts with laughter. "If you're wondering, I made them buy me a new bed. She will just have to live with a defiled garage door."

I pull her into a hug and she wraps her arms around me. "I'm sorry I pushed you away." I mutter into her hair.

"Apology accepted," she says. "On one condition..."

I look at her with a piqued brow. "What?" I ask.

"All future apologies need to go this way. Minus Sevyn interrupting." I start cracking up.

"Whatever you want, Sunshine."

26

Harlow

A cyn and I stay for the rest of the party out of fear that Sevyn will rain hell fire down upon us if we don't. I still can't believe we were caught but at the same time I don't regret it. When we got back into the house, Sevyn had already told everyone that we were together. Thankfully, she didn't tell them the dirty details.

His mom hugged me and told me she was so happy while his dad told Acyn it was about time. Apparently they all saw this coming before we did. We did, too, but I think we were too scared to face it. The past two weeks of stress are gone thanks to finally being with him and that expert tongue of his.

"I'm so happy for you two," Sevyn says as we clean up the mess in their kitchen and living room.

I grin. "Thank you. I'm happy too."

Eli and Emery run into the living room followed by Acyn chasing after them. The sight makes me laugh.

"I tried to stop them, but they are both so fast," he says, slightly out of breath.

"And you go to the gym for what?" I ask him with a smirk.

He gives me a lopsided grin as he approaches me. "I'll show you later."

I squeeze my thighs together with anticipation.

"Acyn, what is wrong with you? The kids!" Sevyn says.

"Sev... it's not like they know what I'm talking about. Do you?" he asks the twins while Sevyn glares at him.

"Harlowww. Can you read us a bedtime story?" Emery asks me as she motions for me to pick her up.

"Of course, I would love to read a bedtime story to you," I say as I scoop her up in my arms.

"Me too?" Eli asks as he grabs my hand.

"Two stories then." I glance over my shoulder at Acyn and he smiles. "I'll be up to get you in a minute. I guess I'll be nice and help Sev after we fucked up her garage door." Sevyn punches his arm and he cowers away laughing.

The twins and I cuddle up on Emery's bed and they are out before I even get to the third page. I'm not surprised considering how much they ran around at their party. They both fell asleep on me and I don't want to move out of fear of waking them. I close my eyes, too.

I wake to Acyn whispering my name. "Sunshine, c'mon."

"The kids," I whisper. I look for them but Acyn already moved them. He holds his hand out to me and I grab it. "Was I asleep long?" I ask rubbing my eyes.

"Nah, only like an hour. Let's go home." His fingers interlace with mine.

I don't even bother asking him which one because, wherever I go with him, I know that I'll always be home.

As soon as I step through the door, Six-Two-Six wraps himself around my legs and meows. "Aww, Six-Two-Six you missed me didn't you? Acyn is mean, isn't he?" I say with a grin as I side-eye him. He just shakes his head and laughs at me.

I follow him into the kitchen where he sets out more food for Six-Two-Six who is now purring in my arms, completely uninterested in what Acyn has to offer. "You've deprived us of cuddles for two weeks. He needs time to adjust."

"I'm trying to cuddle you right now," he says. "I never thought a cat could be a cock blocker." He leans against the counter.

I set Six-Two-Six down in front of his bowl. "There. I'm all yours," I say with a grin as I stand in front of him, placing my hands on his chest.

He piques an eyebrow and looks at me. "Are you?"

"What?" I ask knowing perfectly well what he is implying.

"Mine..." He slowly rubs his thumb along my bottom lip. "I want to hear you say it." His voice is hoarse and his eyes look like they are on fire. I become aware of the growing need between my thighs.

I hold his gaze. "I'm..." I grab his hand and place his thumb in my mouth, twirling my tongue around it. He inhales sharply. I slowly suck and then release. "...yours," I say as I look into his eyes.

I pull him towards me until his lips meet mine. The kiss starts off slow but quickly becomes fevered. He backs me up into the living room. I stumble over something but he doesn't let me fall. We keep kissing as we head toward his room. His lips never leave mine as his hands roam over my body. We bump into the wall in the hallway and he presses me against it. I grope at his shirt, wanting it off of him.

I take a moment to admire his abs as he pulls it over his head. I run my fingertips, like I've been craving to do, along his tattoos. Once his shirt is off his lips are back on mine. He hoists me up and I wrap my legs around him. I hear the ripping of fabric as he tears my dress off of me. I bite his lip as he mumbles, "I'll buy you a new one." I could give a damn about that dress. My panties already bit the dust hours ago.

In his room, he sets me on the bed and trails kisses down the length of my body before standing up to remove his jeans. I lick my lips in anticipation as he grabs the hem of his boxers, pulling them down. His dick springs free. All that I can think about is riding him into the sunset. He is all mine and I want to feel every inch of him.

"Spread your legs for me," he commands. I do as I'm told, opening my legs for him. I slide my fingers over my clit, rubbing slowly, as my moan fills the space between us.

"Fuck..." He mutters as he drinks me in, slowly stroking his dick from head to hilt. My pussy is dripping and all I want is for him to be buried in me. He kneels on the bed, trailing his hands up my legs.

"You couldn't be any more perfect," he whispers.

He sucks my nipple into his mouth, gently grazing it with his teeth, and I let out a moan. I surrender to him as he slowly kisses his way down to my center. My heart rate quickens with anticipation.

I cry out and tangle my fingers in his curls as he his warm tongue meets my pussy. He makes slow circles around my clit. Each swirl is bringing me closure to the edge of ecstasy. Moaning and moving my hips, I beg him not to stop. I need this release so badly. With one more swirl of his tongue, my toes curl, and I come undone. I buck off the bed but he holds me in place as he continues to suck every last possible drop from me.

He kisses his way back up my body. I bring his lips to mine, eager to taste me on him. I suck on his lip and murmur, "I want you inside me."

He responds with a growl and sits up to position himself at my entrance. My eyes lock onto his. He takes the tip of his dick and rubs it against my sensitive clit. I let out a moan as he dips the tip into my wet pussy. Then he takes it out again and rubs my clit. I am in between pleasure and torture. The pressure he applies on my clit with the tip of his dick and then entering me slowly brings me closer to the edge.

"Are you going to cum for me?" he asks. I nod as I pant, letting out a moan, and my breath hitches as he enters me and buries himself in me as far as he can go.

"Acyn..." I cry out. I see stars behind my eyes as I enter euphoria. He keeps the pressure on my clit with his thumb as my orgasm shivers through me. I open my legs wider so he can go deeper and then he starts to move. His strokes are slow and my God, they feel so fucking good. He is stretching me out. Giving me the perfect mix of pleasure and pain.

"You feel so good. Tell me you're mine," he commands through gritted teeth.

"I'm yours," I cry out as he picks up the pace of his thrusts. I wrap myself around him and my pussy clenches as another orgasm hits me like a wave. I call out his name, biting his shoulder and clawing at his back. He pulls me tighter against his body as he thrusts into me.

"Fuck, Harlow, I'm gonna cum..." His voice sounds strained.

"Cum inside me..." I moan into his ear. He thrusts into me one last time as he moans and spills into me.

He lays on top of me. Our bodies are sticky with sweat. I keep my legs and arms wrapped around him, rubbing my hands along his back as our hearts pound together.

After a few minutes, he lifts his head to kiss me. "You're all I've wanted," he says.

"And you're all I've needed," I reply.

I tangle my fingers in his curls and deepen the kiss as we warm up for round two.

I open my eyes as I feel Six-Two-Six's paws on my face and hear the clinking of glasses. The corners of my mouth turn up when the activities of last night start to replay in my head. Acyn and I stayed up exploring each other until the first light of morning filtered through the windows. I roll over in bed and wipe the sleep from eyes. When they refocus again, Acyn is coming back into the room with a tray of food.

I blink because it isn't like him to be up before me. Apparently sometimes he is a morning person. My stomach growls when the smell of pancakes fills the room.

"Morning, Sunshine!" he says and then stage dives next to me. Clearly much hasn't changed. I glare at him and he laughs.

"Breakfast in bed?" I ask as I sit up to get a good look at what he brought in. There's pancakes, bacon, fruit, orange juice, and a single sunflower in a vase. I grin and look at him. He's never made me breakfast in bed before.

"Yeah, you've been upgraded to the full boyfriend experience," he says with a lopsided grin. I snort with laughter and then I can't stop because he looks so fucking proud of himself.

"Where's my phone?" I ask with a giggle. "I have to get a picture of all of this." He hands me my phone.

I snap pictures of the breakfast, of him, of us. Of everything. These are moments I would never want to forget.

"Can we eat now?" he asks after I spend five minutes taking pictures.

"Yeah." I grin. "We can. I need my strength to keep up with you."

He winks. "I told you I would show you why I work out."

He showed me over and over... and *over* again last night. I check the time on my phone and realize it's one p.m.

"It's late. What time did you get up?"

"Only an hour or so ago. You didn't work today, did you?" he asks with a piqued brow.

"No," I shake my head. "I took the weekend off. And after last night"— I smirk at him — "there is no way I am going anywhere today." He chuckles as he downs the rest of his orange juice. I grab my phone to upload the pictures I took to Instagram.

"Making this internet official?" he asks.

I grin. "Yeah... wait, unless you don't want me to."

"You've been posting pictures of me since I first met you. Now that I have you naked in my bed, you think I give a shit?" he asks.

I start cracking up because he has a point. I've never asked before. I did my own thing and he went along with it. I busy myself with uploading the pictures.

The pancakes are heavenly. "I am enjoying the perks of the boyfriend experience," I say with my mouth full.

"Not much has changed, just get to be buried inside you now," he says with a wink.

I shake my head and laugh. Looking through my camera reel, I see a few he took of me snuggled up sleeping with Six-Two-Six. I scroll a little more and see one he took of our intertwined hands. I lean across the food and kiss him. This is where I was always meant to be. I choose to upload a mix of photos he took and some of mine.

I add the caption, "I've been upgraded to the boyfriend experience courtesy of Acyn DeConto." I tag him and then click the blue checkmark to upload the pictures. Within seconds people comment and like the photos.

Kyrell is one of the first to comment: "Finally y'all banged and made it official! #teamacyn." I snort with laughter and show Acyn the comment.

He scrubs his hand over his face as he laughs. My heart almost stops when Hendrix likes the photos. I... *forgot* about him. I had blocked his calls and texts but didn't think about Instagram because I haven't been using it over the past couple of weeks. I side-eye Acyn when I see that Hendrix has the gall to leave a comment. "Happy for you, Harls."

"Um, I can block him if that makes –"

"I'm good," he says as he types something out on his phone. "He can watch us be happy."

I look at my phone after he stops typing and am surprised to see he left a comment. He's only ever commented on the picture I took of him in the coffee shop.

I read, "All I've wanted." I climb on top of him as I pin the comment and reply, "All I've needed."

I toss my phone to the side because all that matters is underneath me.

He places his hands on my hips as I straddle him. I see his dick getting hard beneath his boxers and I decide to let it spring free. I leave a heated trail of kisses down his abs. He watches me hover my mouth over him. I slowly lick from the base of his dick to the tip as he lets out a moan. I wrap my lips around him, swirling my tongue as I do. He grips my hair with his hands as he slowly guides my mouth up and down him. I wrap my hand around him as I continue to suck, moving my hand and sucking harder as I pick up the pace.

He's matching my sucks now with the thrust of his hips. "Baby..." he chokes out, "I'm gonna cum..."

I suck a little harder as he looks at me. "Fuck, Harlow... you want me to cum in your mouth?"

I respond by not releasing him. He tosses his head back against the pillow, gripping a handful of hair, and lets out something between a growl and grunt as he comes. I pop my mouth off his dick as I swallow his release and straddle him again. He gives me a dazed look, his skin glistening with sweat, as his eyes focus on me.

His hand cups my face as he rubs his thumb along the side of my mouth, wiping away his cum. I lick it off of him and see the fire flash in his eyes. He flips both of us over in one fluid motion so that he is now on top of me.

"Welcome to the girlfriend experience," I say with a grin as he looks at me with wonder.

He rests his forehead against mine and lets out a rumble of laughter.

"Want to shower with me?" I ask him.

"Is that even a question?" he retorts.

27

Harlow

This man is fluent in my body language. He worships me. I have never experienced this level of pleasure in my life. It isn't only a physical pleasure, but an emotional pleasure as well. The pleasure of knowing someone wants to know every curve, thought, and detail of you so they can take you to a state of bliss only they can.

I've lost myself in him but in exchange have also found myself in him. We are sprawled out on his bed watching some show that I am half paying attention to. His finger is tracing a small circle on my thigh and all my attention is focused on that one spot. You would think that spending all day together would be enough but... it will never be enough with him. I'll always want to be wrapped up in him.

My phone rings, cutting through the bubble we've created for ourselves. I'd almost forgotten the outside world exists.

"Mmm... who is it?" I mumble lazily against his chest.

He reaches for it. "It's your dad."

I sit up because I forgot today is Sunday. This is our usual catch up day to make up for the short conversations we have throughout the week. "I need a shirt." I announce as I scramble off the bed and grab one of his.

Acyn is laughing at me because this is the most I've moved all day unless I've been on top of him. I swat at his chest, fix my hair, and smile as I answer.

"Hey, Dad." I'm sure I look a mess. Acyn pulls me against his chest and I relax, forgetting about my looks.

"Hey, Kiddo. Just calling to check in on you. I tried calling earlier."

My mind immediately starts replaying all the positions Acyn and I have been in since we got home last night.

I smile. "I was... busy." Acyn is trying to hold in a laugh and I elbow his side.

"Hi, Acyn. What are you two up to?"

"Oh nothing, Mr. Shaw. Just enjoying the company of my girlfriend." I look at Acyn with a grin and then back at my dad.

"That's gre—" my dad starts and then he raises his brows as Acyn's words register. "You two are finally together?" he asks as a smile tugs at the corners of his mouth.

"Why do you have to say 'finally' like that?" I chuckle.

"Because I thought you two were together already. I didn't want to ask because I try not to be a 'nosy dad' as you like to call me."

A laugh escapes me. I haven't called my dad nosy in a long time. "Dad, you can ask me anything you want."

"No, no. I try to let you be an adult. I know you're in good hands and it's clear that you're happy. That's all I need to know." He gives me a warm smile. A timer goes off in the background. "I've gotta get the food out of the oven, Kiddo. Game day. Love you," he says excitedly. My dad loves his sports.

I laugh and wave at him. "Enjoy. Love you."

I wish he lived closer. It would be fun to hang out with him and watch a game. Acyn isn't really into sports but it would be nice to spend evenings with him and my dad regularly. Usually, we get together with Acyn's family but since we got together yesterday we're staying home tonight.

"I'm hungry. We should order food so we can lay in bed," I say.

"You're really not going to leave this bed today are you?" he asks with a chuckle. My only response is wrapping myself up in a blanket and snuggling closer to him. "Alright, what are you in the mood for?"

I shrug. "I could eat anything right now. Surprise me."

An hour later some Thai food arrives. I keep true to my statement and don't leave the bed. I wrap the blanket around my shoulders and dig in. On the show we're watching a girl with waist-length jet-black hair appears on screen. She reminds me of the girl from his shop. The one he spent the night with. I stop mid-bite and stare at the woman on the screen.

"You don't like it?" he asks.

I put the bite of food into my mouth and chew it slowly as I continue to watch the TV. Then I turn my attention to him.

"Who was the girl at your shop?" My palms become sweaty and the food suddenly isn't so good anymore. I shouldn't have swallowed that bite because now I feel it sitting in my stomach as I await his answer. We weren't together then but... I still want to know if he was spending his time with someone else.

"Isabella?" he asks with a piqued brow and a grin.

I want to wipe that grin off of his face.

"Oh, she has a name?" I reply haughtily.

I set my food down and lean against the headboard. Funny how he already knew who I was talking about. "Did you"— I reposition myself to look at him and narrow my eyes. — "sleep with her?"

"Isabella? No. She isn't into me like that."

I knit my brows and give him a scrutinizing look. "How would you know she isn't into you like that? She sure seemed happy to see you."

He has the audacity to chuckle and smile at me. "Aww, Sunshine, are you jealous?" He tries to cup my face with his hand and I move away.

I am trying to keep my growing annoyance at bay. "No, I just want you to answer the damn question."

"She isn't into me like that –"

I raise my hands in exasperation because I simply want to know if he was fucking her or not. I know I'm being petty because he wasn't mine then. Well, he was but he just didn't know it yet. "Acyn, answer the question..."

"Isabella isn't into me because she's into girls," he admits. I repeat the words in my head and then my eyes go wide.

I put my hand over my mouth as I gawk at him. "She is?" Relief pours over me.

Acyn starts cracking up. "I was trying to tell you. Look, I know I'm good looking..." I erupt with laughter and he continues on with a grin. "But not everyone is into me. She also asked me about you after you stormed off."

I splay my hand across my chest. "Excuse me, stormed off? Can you blame me? You didn't volunteer any information and she is gorgeous."

"Well, she thinks the same about you."

I quirk an eyebrow. "Me? Well what did you tell her?" I resume eating my food now that I know he wasn't seeing anyone else.

He shrugs. "That you're my girlfriend."

I can't help but smile. "But I wasn't…"

"Yeah, but she didn't know that and what is that shit you always say? Speak it into existence or some bullshit like that?"

I snort with laughter. I've been teaching him about manifesting and law of attraction.

"I didn't think you believed in that stuff…" I say as a I nudge his arm, grinning. "To be honest…" I let out a sigh. "I thought you were tired of me."

His brows knit together. "Tired of you? No, I could never tire of you. If the past twelve hours haven't proved that already." A grin pulls at the corners of his mouth. "I find you annoying but –"

I shove him playfully and he grabs my wrist, pulling me towards him. "But," he continues on, "you are my annoyance." I start laughing. "It's just you, Sunshine."

I sit up and press my lips to his. My appetite suddenly isn't for food anymore.

28

Harlow

A cyn and I have been together for a couple of months now. I swear he and I must have known each other in a past life because we get each other in a way that only we can. I mean, yeah, he still gets on my nerves but that's what partners are for, right? They know every button to push but you wouldn't want anyone else pushing those buttons but them.

Kyrell texted me shortly after we got together. He asked if we could get our tattoos now that Acyn and I are "banging," as he called it. We have plans to get them today. I'm still working at Holy Shot. West is slowly starting to step away from the business as Ava nears her due date. I've taken on the role of temporary assistant manager while he finds someone he's comfortable with to fill the manager position once their daughter is here. He wanted me to continue working there but it isn't where I see myself a year from now.

My photography business, Vision & Vibe, is taking off. What started as a hobby is turning into a real business. Even though West would love to have me stay on at Holy Shot, he also knows that I'm pouring every ounce of creative energy I have into my photography.

Acyn has been helping me get the business side of things sorted out. At first I mentioned the idea of renting a space for a photography studio in passing. That weekend, he took me around Seattle to see different lofts. By the end of the day we were contacting an agent to rent one that surprisingly isn't too far from his tattoo shop.

That's one of the many things I love about Acyn. I'll say something in passing but he picks up on the sense of longing in my tone and will do everything he can to help make it happen. There is still a lot of work to be done but I look forward to putting in the work to see my dreams materialize.

Acyn is also becoming a silent partner for a tattoo shop that his friend is opening in LA. Hunter is Acyn's right hand man at Crown Ink and he has asked Acyn if he would be willing to invest in his shop. He wasn't going to refuse because he knows Hunter will be successful wherever he goes, even if it isn't in one of Acyn's shops. After agreeing to help him with the startup, he and Hunter started traveling back and forth to LA a lot. Sometimes I go with them but this time I stayed because of work. I'll see him this afternoon, with Kyrell, for the first time in a couple of days.

But first, I have a date with Sevyn.

I'm sitting solo in the cute café Sevyn told me to meet her at... twenty minutes ago. My phone chimes with a text.

Sevyn: I'm one light away. I'm perpetually late. But you know this.

She may be late to everything but she is reliable. We get together at least once a week for what we call "luxurious girl dates." Friends are soulmates too, after all. Last week we went to a spa for facials and today we'll catch up at a French café.

I hear the click of her heels before I see her. Sev is always dressed to the nines. She thinks she is a hot mess but she always looks like she just came from a photoshoot.

Sevyn sits down with a huff. "Emery bawled her little eyes out because she wanted to come on our date. Eli doesn't care where I go as long as he has his shows and fruit snacks."

"Aww, poor Emery. Maybe I can take her on a date."

She puts her hand over her heart. "She would faint with excitement if you took her out."

Our server comes and takes our order. We get chocolate croissants, bowls of fruit, and mimosas.

"How is Vision & Vibe going?" she asks as she shimmies her shoulders with excitement.

I almost choke on my mimosa laughing at her. "Good," I say, nodding. "I think I found a space for the studio but I won't know whether I got it or not until next week."

"You'll get it," she says without hesitation.

"Are you signing up for school?"

She shrugs. "I don't know if I can do it with the kids and Zane."

"Oh, that's cool. Use them as excuses," I say nonchalantly, taking a bite of my croissant.

"You bitch!" She tosses her head back with laughter.

"Look, those are valid reasons to be hesitant but if not now, when? Zane and the kids will always be there. One thing I've learned is that you have to do things for yourself, too. Like these luxurious girl dates. We do this for us."

Over the past few months, Sevyn has expressed a desire to go back to school for fashion design. I have never met someone as fashionable as she is. She lives for fashion. She started a YouTube channel and already has a decent following but wants to further her education so she can work in the industry.

"I know but... what if I can't do it?" she asks, her voice laced with uncertainty.

"Sev, I know change is scary, but I also know that this is what you're passionate about. You need to ask yourself what happens when this all works out. Shift your perspective, babe."

She gets up from her seat and hugs me. "Thanks for believing in me."

"You can and will do this. I've always got your back." I hug her a little tighter. We break the hug when our server arrives with another round of mimosas. "So, when are you signing up?"

"Tonight." She smiles. "I can sign up for spring quarter."

"Yes, you can!" I exclaim. "If you don't, I am stopping by your house and cutting all the straps of your designer bags."

She gasps. "The mere mention of that made me have chest pains. We would have to physically fight."

I snort with laughter. "Then chase that dream, babe."

After my date with Sev, I head to Acyn's shop for my appointment with Kyrell. We decided on getting a tattoo of a wave with a sun behind it to remind us of where we came from and to always look forward to the better days on the horizon.

I see Acyn through the window when I walk past and can't help but smile. He still makes me feel like butterflies are coursing through my veins. Riley doesn't even bother looking up from her computer. She just waves now. I head for Acyn and he grins when he sees me.

"Sunshine." He plants a kiss on my lips and pulls me into a hug. "Did you miss me?"

"A little." I grin. "How was your trip?"

I plop down into my usual chair in the window. He busies himself with setting up his station. I take a picture of him and post it to my stories on IG, tagging Kyrell with the text: "Kyrell is always late." He responds almost immediately and says he was busy with a *lady friend* and he'll be here in less than a minute.

"LA is too fucking hot," Acyn says. "I'm glad he'll be living there and not me. But the shop is going to be dope when the renovations are done. Makes me want to renovate my shops here. Are you ready to get tatted today?" He turns towards me with a smile on his face.

"Yes. I –" I stop mid-sentence because someone walks in that looks like Kyrell but... he doesn't have his locs. I stare at him as he walks toward me with a grin.

"You cut your hair?" I ask in disbelief. He's had his locs since I met him in middle school. This is a huge change for him.

He shrugs as if it's no big deal. "Figured it's time for fresh beginnings and all that. What do you think?"

"You look good." I give him a hug. "I just wasn't expecting this." I run my hand over his low-top, curly fade.

"Who's going first?" Acyn asks.

Kyrell looks at me and says, "ladies first," with a bow.

"Is this going to hurt?" I ask as I take my seat in the chair. I wasn't nervous until this very moment. I decided to get mine on my ribcage on the left side of my chest. I am second guessing the placement now.

"You'll be fine, Sunshine. Not like you can't handle a little bit of pain," Acyn says with a wink. My eyes go wide as I look at Kyrell.

"Oh, y'all are freaky, freaky?" he asks with raised eyebrows.

I cover my face with my hands. "Can we just start the tattoo, please?"

They are the worst together. I didn't expect Acyn and Kyrell to become friends. I thought that maybe it would be weird given the fact that he is so close with Hendrix. But I'm glad they have a friendship because Kyrell is someone who has been a constant in my life since I met him. He's been with me through a lot and I couldn't imagine him not in my life.

Acyn gets about halfway through my tattoo, which doesn't hurt as bad as I was anticipating.

"Did you see Hendrix has a girlfriend now?" Kyrell asks.

Hendrix doesn't take up space in my head anymore. I wasted too much time on him to continue to do so when I'm happy.

"Nope. Have you met her?"

Kyrell shakes his head. "He and I had a falling out."

I look at him because he and Hendrix were almost like brothers. For them to not talk anymore, that's crazy. "What happened?"

He sighs and scrubs his hands down his face. "Do you remember Aubrey? The girl I was spending a lot of time with over the summer."

I already don't like where this is going but wait for him to continue on.

"Well Hendrix came out to visit and met her. Long story short... that's his girlfriend now."

I gasp. "What the fuck?"

Acyn shakes his head and scoffs.

"Why didn't you say anything?" I ask.

He shrugs. "What is there to tell? Besides, you were going through your shit with Acyn at that time."

I glare at Acyn who pretends like he suddenly doesn't have any hearing.

"This was recently then?"

"Yeah, I found out they were hooking up a day or so before I saw you last. But I just saw today that they're actually together and not just fucking."

"That's really shitty and I'm sorry you felt like you couldn't talk to me but... fuck him. And fuck her too. Clearly she isn't someone you would want to be with if she switched up so easily," I say.

Acyn finishes up with my tattoo. "I would have broken his jaw," he interjects, "but that's just me. He definitely isn't a friend and both of you are better off without him."

I kiss him and get up to check out my tattoo in the mirror. I grin; it's beautiful with the waves and the sun behind them. The words "rise & fall" are written beneath in small lettering.

"I love it!" I exclaim when I turn back around to face Acyn.

"My tattoos look good on you, Sunshine," he says with a grin.

"Rise and fall... that's all we know how to do, huh, Harls?" Kyrell fist bumps me as he gets ready to sit in the chair next.

"That's just life though isn't?" I shrug. "The rise and fall, the ebb and flow... at least we have each other, right?"

"Damn right," he replies.

29

Harlow

"**H**arlow..."

He only uses my name when he's trying to be serious. I'm too busy kissing and sucking his neck to give a damn.

"I'm going to miss my flight..." he mumbles.

I start tugging at his belt. It's cute he thought he was going to get out the door unscathed looking as fine as he does. He has a black button up on with the top few buttons undone and black slacks with a black Louis belt. He smells delicious.

"Mmm..." I bite my lip, meeting his gaze. "We can be quick." I kiss his lips.

We won't be apart for long. He's going to LA for the grand opening of Hunter's tattoo shop. I arrive tomorrow. He has to leave today to help with the finishing touches. I'm staying behind because they start the renovations on my photography studio today.

"Harlow..." He inhales sharply.

"Yes?" My hand is in his pants now.

"Why are you like this?" he groans. His eyes close and his head rolls back as I stroke him.

"Because... I want you to fuck me," I mutter against his lips.

That's all it takes. He flips me around, smacking my ass as he does. I gladly assume the position with my ass in the air. He rubs his fingers along the slickness of my pussy and then licks them.

"Always so wet for me, Sunshine."

My breath hitches and my fingers fist the sheets as he thrusts into me. His hand palms my ass while the other one finds my clit.

"This is what you wanted?" he asks through clenched teeth as he pounds into me.

"Yes!" I cry out. His dick filling me up and the pressure on my clit has me teetering on the edge.

"Then cum for me..." he commands.

I feel the tingle start in my toes and travel up to my center. I see stars behind my eyes as I fall into ecstasy calling out his name. After he ensures that every last drop of my orgasm is all over his dick, his hands grip my hips as he thrusts into me.

I meet his fevered strokes, throwing it back for him as he grabs a handful of hair. "Fuck..." He stills momentarily and lets out a growl, finding his release.

I slowly turn around to face him with a satisfied grin.

"You're unbelievable." He chuckles as he zips up his pants and buckles his belt. I place my foot on his chest. He leaves a trail of kisses that start at my foot and end at my lips. "I'll see you soon."

I pull him back to me by his collar and kiss him again. "See you soon. Go before you're late. You're turning into me."

"It was worth it," he says with a wink.

I'm looking forward to meeting Acyn in LA in a few hours but first I have stuff to do at my soon-to-be office. Excitement settles in as I walk around the studio with Ava. When I told her that I was renting a space for my photography she didn't hesitate to offer up her services. There are perks to having a highly sought after interior designer for an aunt.

She assures me that the studio won't need much work. There's a lot of natural light with floor-to-ceiling windows and hardwood floors throughout. When we walked into this loft, I knew it was the one. Ava is working on getting my office space and waiting area presentable. The idea of my own photography studio seemed farfetched initially. I didn't think that I would need or want one. After a bit of research, I realized that it is more beneficial to have one than not. Now to see this farfetched idea actually happening makes me happy.

"Okay, I was thinking we could –" Ava stops abruptly and rubs the side of her belly. I glance up from the mood board she is showing me to see her wincing in pain.

"Ava, are you okay?" I rest my hand on her shoulder. She is close enough to her due date that she could be in labor. I've never been around someone in labor. That thought alone causes my heart to race. What am I supposed to do if she is?

Her eyes flutter open and she smiles. "I'm fine. Just Braxton Hicks contractions is all. As I was saying, we could—" her sentence is cut short again and this time she grips my hand. I wince in pain from her grip being so tight. Her breathing becomes labored and she starts taking deep inhales and exhales. "I think we need to call West."

"Um, shouldn't I just take you to the hospital? You could be in labor. I just would hate for you to have –"

She nods her head vigorously with her eyes closed as she inhales and exhales.

I don't have time for panic to settle in because my only focus is getting Ava into my car. I put her arm around my shoulder and head for the elevator. She has more contractions on the short walk from the office to the elevator. I think my hand may be shattered from her grip at this point.

I call West as soon as we're in the car and tell him what's going on. The panic is present in his voice as he tells me he will meet us at the hospital.

Ava looks at me with tears in her eyes. "I can't do this. I don't know what the hell I was thinking, wanting to be a mom."

"Ava, you're going to be the best mom. Stop talking like that. Besides, it's too late to return her now."

She starts laughing but another contraction takes her breath away.

"Hold on, we'll be there soon," I assure her, knowing that Ava and West will be amazing parents.

After arriving at the hospital, I dash inside to get a wheelchair and alert the doctors that Ava's in labor.

"I think she is coming soon," she says. Her breathing is labored. "West better get here," she says through gritted teeth.

"He'll be here. Don't worry." They wheel her inside and Ava has a death grip on my hand, pulling me alongside her. I guess I will see my cousin be born today.

Once in the delivery room, everyone moves like fluid motion around Ava. West arrives a few minutes later, eyes wild and hair a mess.

"Harlow," he says, hugging me. "Thank you."

He rushes to Ava's side. She looks happy to see him but also like she wants to kill him. Watching her go through contractions, I don't blame her at all.

I fade into the background as they get her ready for labor. About an hour later, she starts pushing. I go between wringing my hands and chewing my fingernails. I silently ask the universe for her to make it here safely. They have waited so long for her. After what feels like forever, the smallest cry fills the room and tears prick my eyes because it is the most beautiful sound. She is finally here.

West and Ava are crying. "Hi, Mercy," they whisper to her. Even though Ava had a hell of a time during labor I know that one day I want this moment for myself.

After they tend to Ava and Mercy is snuggly in a blanket, West hands her to me. I look at him with wide eyes because I have never held a human this small before.

"You won't break her, Harlow," he reassures me.

I cautiously take her into my arms. She is the cutest thing I have ever seen. I walk around the room in total awe of her. It makes me wonder if my mom were still here, if I would have had a sibling.

My phone starts vibrating in my back pocket. I slowly walk towards Ava, as if walking too fast will disturb Mercy, and place her in her arms. "I'll be back," I whisper.

I pull my phone out of my pocket once I'm out of the room expecting it to be Acyn. It's a number I don't recognize. I answer it anyway because it could be a potential client.

"Hello."

"Hi, is this Harlow Shaw?" a woman says on the other end of the line.

"This is she. May I ask who's calling?"

"I'm Sarah, from Galveston Hospital. I am calling about your dad..."

My heart rate picks up, my vision gets blurry, and I feel like I can't breathe. This feels like my mom all over again.

ACYN

I walk around Hunter's shop. The grand opening is later today. It will be a red carpet event that Harlow is ecstatic about. I glance at my phone, waiting for her message. I'm supposed to pick her up in an hour, but she hasn't texted or called me since this morning when she was on the way to her studio. I know she's busy with the renovations. Knowing her, she's probably frantically packing last minute.

"You ready man?" I ask Hunter.

"As I'll ever be." The corners of his mouth turn up. "Thank you for all the support. I couldn't have done it without you."

Hunter started off as my apprentice at eighteen and he is now twenty-two, opening up his own shop in a prime location in LA. I didn't hesitate to invest when he asked. His work ethic is like mine. I know he is going to make himself, and me, a lot of money. It isn't just about the money, though. It's about jumping into something that you love and giving it your all. If you have the passion and drive then nothing else matters.

"I always got you." I give him a hug. "Alright, I've gotta get to the airport to pick up Harlow. Traffic is a bitch right now. I'll see you in a bit."

I arrive at the airport right when she should be getting off the plane. I wait by the baggage claim designated for her flight. I wonder how many bags she packed this time. The plan is to attend the opening tonight and then go to Palm Springs for a few days tomorrow. I never really used to travel before I met her. She lives for travel and going to new places. It doesn't matter where it is.

People start appearing from her flight. I am looking for her smile... but I don't see it. I check the time and the flight number again. I have it right. I try calling her phone but it's off. I wait for a few more minutes because maybe she had to use the restroom or something. Time ticks by and still no Harlow.

I check my phone to see if maybe I missed a call from her. I didn't. I try her phone again and I get her voicemail. I tap my phone against my hand, trying to think of what to do. It isn't like her to not show up. I know she was supposed to be with Ava today. Maybe West knows where she is, or maybe she actually missed a flight taking forever to pack her sixty-seven bags.

West picks up. "Acyn –" I hear the cry of a baby in the background.

"The baby is here?" That would explain why she is late.

"Yeah, yeah. She's here." I can hear the smile in his voice. "But Harlow. Her dad. He had a heart attack..."

The smile fades from my face. "What?"

"Yeah, she got a call shortly after Mercy was born. I was supposed to call you. I'm sorry but I've been trying to figure out how to go see my brother and –"

"No apologies necessary. Is he okay? Is she okay?" I scrub my hand over my face, looking around the airport. I can't imagine what Harlow is going through right now. All I know is that I've got to get to her.

"They didn't tell Harlow much other than he arrived and she is his contact. She took the first flight she could find."

"Alright, uh..." My mind is racing, "Thanks, man. Sorry this is such a bittersweet day for you guys." I end the call. "Fuck..." I mutter to myself.

I make up my mind to try and buy a ticket now in hopes that I can at least be there shortly after she arrives. I really don't want her to be alone right now. Especially if West isn't able to make it because he just had his daughter. I head to the first counter I see someone at. I explain to her what is going on and that I need a ticket to Texas today with a rental car if possible. Harlow must be in the air right now because her phone is still off when I try her again.

"We have one that leaves in thirty minutes."

Man, I am grateful to be at an international airport.

"I'll take it." I don't hesitate. I don't give a damn about the price. I just hand over my card and my ID while she sorts the rest of it out.

A few minutes later, she hands me my stuff along with a ticket. "I hope he's okay."

"Yeah, me too."

I try Harlow's phone one more time before the plane takes off. It goes straight to voicemail. All I can hope is that her dad and her are okay. I shoot her a text in hopes that she'll see it when is able to turn on her phone.

30

Harlow

I haven't stopped crying since the phone call. I stare out the window as the pilot announces that we are finally landing in Houston. This has been the longest flight of my entire life. My mind is racing with possibilities. I debated catching a flight as soon as possible or waiting to see if there was more news. I knew once I was in the air I wouldn't know what was going on. It's been torture.

I only know that I want to be with my dad. Waiting for them to park the plane after it lands is excruciating. At this point I don't have much of a thumbnail left. Once we are told we can exit the plane, I push past everyone. The only thing on my mind is my dad.

I rent a car and speed all the way to the hospital. If they were to try and stop me right now they would have to engage in a high speed chase because I'm not stopping for shit. Thankfully, I don't get pulled over. I run inside the hospital and wait at the nurse's station for someone. It's later in the evening so no one is there. I pace back and forth finally seeing someone.

"Hi, I'm here to see my dad. Felix Shaw. Can you please tell me what room he is in? Is he okay?" I am wringing my hands together and I am sure I look an absolute mess.

"Shaw..." She checks her charts and pulls his. "He was awake a couple of hours ago, honey, and he was alert. You can go back and see him. Room two-twenty-eight."

My body relaxes for the first time in hours when I hear that he is awake. I give her a smile, trying not to run down the hallway to his room.

I reach his door and try to steady myself. I lean against the wall trying to breathe even though it's hard. I am hunched over, dry-heaving in the hallway, when the nurse who was at the desk places her hand on my back.

"Oh honey, this is a lot. Sit down. Inhale." I listen. "Okay, exhale." I listen. "Do that a few more times for me. Focus on your breath. Your dad will be okay and so will you." People underestimate the power of kindness. "Are you ready to stand now?" I nod my head as she reaches her hand out to me and helps me stand. I feel much more stable than I did when I first arrived at his door. "Will you be okay?"

"Yes." I nod. "I just – this is a lot for me, and I was expecting the worst and he's alive. Thank you." I turn and place my hand on the doorknob.

"Let me know if you need anything. My name is Evelyn. I'll be the nurse on tonight."

I still, and a chill runs through me. Evelyn, well "Evie" is what everyone called her, was my mom's name. I turn around to face her. "Thank you. I will."

My dad doesn't wake when I enter the room. He looks just how I remember him. I was preparing myself for him to be dead and he is still here with me. I quietly pull up a chair next to him and sit down in it, grabbing his hand. He stirs. I stare at him to see if he'll wake and his eyes flutter open.

"Harlow…"

"Dad, it's me." I stand giving him a kiss on the cheek. "Sorry it took me so long to make it."

"You didn't have to come for me, Kiddo." His eyes are already closing again.

"I'm already here, Dad. Sleep and we'll talk in the morning."

He's already asleep again before I finish my sentence. A few minutes later, Evelyn comes in and hands me a few blankets to wrap myself in. Hospitals are always so cold. I forgot my bag and phone in the car. I think of Acyn and wonder if he talked to West. I wonder how they are doing with the new baby. I told West I would call him as soon as I landed but seeing my dad was the only thing on my mind. I curl up in the chair and wrap the blankets tighter around me. It's late there too and I don't want to disturb them. I will call him when I wake up again. I already feel myself drifting off to sleep. My dad is okay. He's still here with me. That's all I could ask for right now.

I wake to a kiss being pressed to my forehead. Opening my eyes, Acyn comes into focus. I blink a few times, a little disoriented. The beeping of the machine monitoring my dad's heart rate reminds me of what happened. I wrap my arms around Acyn's neck.

"Hi, Sunshine," he whispers.

I look over at my dad, who is still asleep, and point to the hallway. Acyn waits for me to get up and follows me out. He wraps me tightly in a much needed hug. I melt into him, letting him hold me for a while without saying a word. Tears prick my eyes and I don't even know why. My dad is okay. It must be from all the stress I've experienced since the phone call. I feel safe in Acyn's arms. I'm sobbing now but I can't stop. He doesn't say a word. He just holds me and that's all I need.

After a few minutes of crying, he holds my face in his hands and wipes my tears. He gives me a kiss despite the fact my nose is now running. It makes me laugh.

"I'm so glad you're here." I wrap my arms around him again. "When did you get here? What time is it?"

"About forty-five minutes ago and it is"— he glances at his watch — "four-thirty a.m. How's your dad?"

"Good. Stubborn. Told me I didn't need to be here."

A laugh vibrates through his chest. "Sounds like a typical man."

"I can't just leave him here alone now... you know that, right?" I was thinking about it on the plane ride that I can't and won't leave my dad living here alone. If he would move to Seattle with us that would be great, but I don't know if he would be up for that. I don't even know if a long distance trip like that would be wise given his current health situation.

"I know, and I wouldn't expect you to. I am here for whatever you need, Sunshine. You name it."

I hug him tighter. "I know, and that's all I need."

My dad wakes a few hours later. He beams at me when he sees me and I am finally able to give him a real hug. "You look amazing for just having a heart attack dad," I tease him.

"I told you I'm fine. There was no reason for you to stop your life for me."

I knit my brows together and stare at him.

Acyn clears his throat. "Uh... I am going to go get breakfast. I'll be back." He plants a kiss on top of my head and exits the room.

I go back to looking at my dad. Searching his face for a reason as to why he is acting like this is no big deal.

"Dad... what is going on with you?"

He won't look at me and instead focuses his attention on the television screen. I reach across him for the remote and turn it off. I know my dad is my dad but this isn't something we will avoid talking about. His health is at risk. Perhaps my reasons are selfish because he is all I have left but that's all the reason I need. He lets out a sigh, looking defeated. I have only seen this look on my dad's face when my mother passed away.

"I've known since shortly after you moved that I have high cholesterol. I saw a doctor for the diagnosis but didn't follow the care regimen." My mouth falls open and he holds up his hand. "I know, I know. I kept telling myself that I would get to it when I get to it. I'm pretty active as you know and I didn't think this would ever be a problem for me. I've been stressed at work but haven't retired because..."

I look at him, expectantly waiting for him to finish his sentence, but he doesn't. I lean forward. "Because... what, dad?"

"Because..." He lets out a sigh. "I – things haven't been the same since you left. The house is empty. It's the house you were born in, raised in, the house we created memories in with your mother," he says, his voice cracking. "When you left, I didn't think it would be that bad... but then you were gone. I hate being home in an empty house with so many memories. So even though work is stressful..." He shrugs. "It was better than being at home alone."

"Dad..." My tears fall into my lap. I had no idea that he felt this way. Whenever I talked to him on the phone he was always happy. When I saw him a few months ago he seemed fine. I guess that's the problem: I *assumed*.

"Why didn't you talk to me? I would have –"

"What?" He looks at me with raised eyebrows. "Stopped living your life when you have turned into this amazing young woman? No, you are meant to have your own life. Not be worried about me."

"I still want you in my life, Dad. I constantly daydream what it would be like for you to live in Seattle. You would be near West and me. There is nothing for us here, Dad, but memories. And –"

A nurse comes in, announcing that she needs to check my dad's vitals. His cardiologist will be by shortly as well. I lean back against my chair as my mind reels with this information. I had no idea that my dad felt so... lonely. The thought didn't cross my mind that there was nothing left for my dad here, either.

The cardiologist tells my dad that while he is doing well, he still needs to take this event seriously. I almost want to applaud him but I keep my mouth shut and listen to what he has to say. His heart attack was mild and his heart didn't suffer any severe damage. The small amount of tissue that was damaged should be fully healed within eight weeks. In spite of all of that, he still wants to keep my dad for a few days of monitoring.

Silence falls between us after he leaves. After a few minutes, my dad speaks first. "I don't want you to feel like you have to take care of me, Harlow..."

"Then don't give me a reason to feel that way. I hate to pull the guilt trip card, Dad but...when you're not taking care of yourself –" Tears well up in my eyes. "You are all I have left." I squeeze his hand. "Please consider moving to Seattle. I would take care of everything. From listing the house to finding you a place to live. You won't have to worry about a single thing." He opens his mouth to speak, and I interrupt him. "Please, Dad, just consider it. I'm an adult now. I can handle things. Let me handle things."

He squeezes my hand as he smiles. "I am sure lucky to have you as a daughter. I'll consider it. I'm going to some rest, and you need to rest, too." He pulls me into a hug. "I'm grateful you're here."

I squeeze him back before I release him. "Do you want me to bring you some food when I come back?"

"That would be nice." He smiles with his eyes closed as he settles in for his nap.

I step out into the hallway and see Acyn walking towards me. "I need a bed..." He raises his eyebrows and gives me a smirk. I giggle and interlace my fingers with his. "I mean we can do that but I need clothes, a shower, sleep, food. Everything."

He wraps his arm around my shoulder. "I got you."

Steam rises around us as we sit in the bathtub filled to the brim with bubbles. Acyn massages my back as I sit between his legs. The water trickling off his fingers as he lifts them out of the tub is the only noise between us. I am hopeful that my dad will choose to move to Seattle after given some time to think about it. Moving there was simpler for me because West already had a fully decorated guest house. I let out an exasperated sigh as I think of all that I have to do if he does decide to move. I don't mind it; I just hope that I can make it all happen like I said I could.

Acyn kisses my back and rests his chin on my shoulder. "What's on your mind, Sunshine?"

I melt into his chest. "I told my dad he should move to Seattle to be close to me and West. Then I started thinking about all that has to be done if he agrees. The most important thing is him having a place to live. I doubt he would want to live with me. He already feels like he is intruding on my life even though I've assured him he isn't. So now... my mind is racing with ways to make this happen. Surprisingly, I'm not at all worried about selling the house if he does say yes."

He intertwines our fingers. "What if you moved in with me?"

I whip around to face him, sloshing water over the sides of the tub. He grins. "That way, your dad could move into the guest house, and we could live together... like we already do."

"You *want* me to live with you?" I quirk an eyebrow. I never considered us actually living together until now. Moving in together would seem like a major step for so many people. For Acyn and I it feels... right.

"Yes," he says without hesitation. "We're always either at your place or mine but we haven't spent the night apart in a while. If you moved in then at least that would free up the guest house. Even if he only wants to stay there temporarily."

"I would love to move in with you." I grin, wrapping my arms around his neck. "This could actually work. I will have to call West and –" My eyes go wide. "Shit, I forgot to call West!"

"I've talked to him. I told him that your dad is okay but you should still probably call him so he can hear it from you."

I hold his gaze in awe. I wasn't expecting him to take care of anything. It feels good to have someone to lean on that can support me when I feel like I can't support myself.

"Thank you, babe."

He kisses my forehead. "You never need to thank me. I got you... always."

This is what it feels like to fall in love... to *be* in love. He is all I've wanted. All I've needed.

31

Harlow

T he day before my dad left the hospital he decided that he would move back to Seattle with me. I tried my best not to bring it up after I initially did. I knew that he needed to come to the decision on his own. After talking to Acyn about moving in with him I started to set things in motion in case he said yes. I called West and told him about my dad moving into the guest house. He happily agreed. West wasn't able to physically be here but he has done as much as he can from afar.

Ava had people from her office move my things and redecorate the guest house so that it suits my father's style. It is perfect for him even if he does decide to only live there temporarily. I contacted a real estate agent who assured me that our house will sell quickly, given the neighborhood it's in. She wasn't wrong. Within the first week after my dad agreed, and the house was listed there were multiple offers.

It has been a bittersweet time for my dad and me. This is the house he bought with my mom; I was born here, raised here. These walls hold so many memories. Our hope is that the family who bought the house will be able to create their own treasure of memories. It is time for us to move on and plant roots elsewhere.

My dad is sitting with me in his office, sorting through papers while I pack boxes.

"Should we have a going away party?" he asks, peering at me over the top of his glasses. We leave next Monday for Seattle. I am a little surprised my dad actually wants to have a party. He's always acted like they were a nuisance before. This is the place we've called home for so long. It would be a nice farewell.

"If it is a party you want..." I do a pirouette. "A party you shall have."

He starts cracking up. "I'm grateful that we get to live near each other again."

"Me too." I beam. "You'll love Seattle. Mercy is a doll. Ava sends me pictures daily and she has already grown so much over the past six weeks. My heart couldn't be happier."

I wasn't sure how my dad would react to living in his brother's guest house, but he seems to be really excited about it. I know that he's always wished he and West had a closer relationship. Hopefully, this move helps that happen.

Later on that day my dad texts me the list of people he would like to have over for lunch on Friday. He didn't want to have a dinner because in his words, "He didn't want to have people over all night." I told him he was getting old.

I quickly glance over the list and see that Hendrix's parents are on it. I can only hope that he is busy with something. He has a girlfriend now so I doubt he will try to attend. The rest of the people on his list are colleagues and friends. This will be a retirement and going away party rolled into one.

Acyn will be back tomorrow evening. He has been racking up frequent flyer miles with how much he's flown here over the past six weeks. He's been understanding and supportive throughout this whole process. Even though I feel like I'm falling apart, he comes along behind me and helps me put all the pieces back into place. Digging through stuff in the house has brought up a lot of emotions. He has been my soft landing space to process it all.

"Do you want me to do it? I mean, I'm enjoying the view..." Acyn is referring to my tennis skirt that is now giving him the best views as it flies with the wind. "But I'd rather you not break your neck."

I'm standing on a step stool, stretched as far as I can go, trying to hang a banner up for the party happening later this afternoon. "I..." My fingertips finally loop the banner on to the hook. "Got it!" I face him and bow with a satisfied smirk. He holds his hand out for me as I step off the stool. "How does everything look?" I turn on the spot, admiring all the navy and gold decorations we just put up.

This time with my dad has felt like a whirlwind. He's at an appointment with his cardiologist this morning. I am trying my best to give him space and not be a helicopter. He had to gently remind me that I am his daughter and not his caretaker. At first I was hurt by his words but Acyn reminded me that I need to give my dad the space to heal. He needs to resume his regular activities and he can't do that if I'm doing everything for him. It has been a learning experience for us both.

"It looks great, Sunshine. I think your dad will love it." He drapes his arm over my shoulders and I snuggle into him.

"I do," my dad says from behind us as he joins us out on the patio. He wraps his arm around me, too. I feel like the luckiest girl in the world standing between the two most important men in my life.

"How was your appointment?" I ask.

"Great. I'm doing great. He even set up an appointment with a cardiologist in Seattle for once we get there. I'm ready, Kiddo." I give him a tight hug and he squeezes me back.

I step away, wiping tears from my eyes. "Acyn and I are going to pick up the cake and the party platters I ordered. We'll be back in about an hour. Make sure you're ready, Dad." I point an accusatory finger at him. "Don't plop down in front of the sport's channel."

"It's my party," he says. I quirk an eyebrow and place a hand on my hip. "You look like your mother with that glare." The corners of his mouth turn up. "Okay, I'll go get ready," he says with a smirk.

Acyn and I laugh as he walks inside.

The party is in full swing. My dad is enjoying himself. It's nice to watch him laugh and carry on with everyone. I invited Marisa and Quinn who seemed happier to see Acyn again than me. They were sad when they learned that my dad and I would be permanently moving out of Texas but also understood why. I have gone through a rollercoaster of emotions over the past month and a half. It's hard to leave behind all that you've known but the horizon of new beginnings has a gorgeous view, too.

All of us are in the middle of a conversation when Quinn's face falls. I stop mid-sentence and peer over my shoulder, searching for what caused her reaction. My eyes meet Hendrix's gaze; there's some girl on his arm. After Kyrell told me what happened I can only assume that this is the girl who switched up on him. I turn back around, giving the girls a look.

"Did you invite him?" Marisa whispers.

Acyn looks over his shoulder and waves at Hendrix. I jab him in the side and he laughs.

"What? I'm just being friendly." He smirks. I roll my eyes at him and turn my attention back to Marisa.

"My dad put their family on the list. He is best friends with his dad after all." I let out a sigh, regretting sending them an invite. It was naïve of me to think that Hendrix wouldn't show up if given the opportunity.

Quinn is talking out of the side of her mouth. "He is coming over here. He is coming over here."

"Shut up!" I hiss as Hendrix comes to stand in our circle as if he belongs.

"Hey man," Acyn says. "Good to see you again."

I narrow my eyes at him. Knowing he is full of shit.

"Yeah, you too. Happy to see you two... thriving," Hendrix says as he extends a hand towards Acyn, but his eyes are on me. Could this be any more awkward?

"Who's your little friend?" Quinn cuts through the awkwardness as she eyes the girl on his arm.

"Oh, this is Aubrey." The girl offers a friendly smile that I don't return. "Aubrey, this is Harlow... and her friends."

"Boyfriend." I splay my hand across Acyn's chest plastering a fake smile on my face. "This is Marisa and Quinn, my best friends. We're just missing Kyrell. You already know him though, don't you Aubrey?" I narrow my eyes in her direction. She shifts uncomfortably and looks to

Hendrix, who offers her no comfort. Acyn looks at me with a mixture of caution and admiration. He interlaces his fingers with mine as silence settles between us.

"And this..." My dad cuts through the silence as he brings a friend of his into our circle. "Is my beautiful daughter, Harlow"—I smile, extending a handout to his friend— "and her boyfriend Acyn." He extends his hand out with a grin on his face. "I wouldn't have been able to get through this without either of them."

Hendrix has a sour look on his face as he disappears into the crowd of people. The rest of us fall into conversation about what the future holds for all of us. It has been a pleasant afternoon filled with laughter, food, and amazing conversation. My dad looks satisfied and happy. I was a bit skeptical when he first suggested a party but now I see he just wanted one last get together with friends.

"I'm going to get some more platters for the food table." The party is dying down but I still want there to be food available for the last people who may trickle through.

"Do you need help?" Acyn asks.

"No." I kiss his lips. "I got it. It will only be one anyway. I'll be right back."

"We'll keep him company," Quinn says with a smirk. I shake my head and laugh as I head for the kitchen.

There isn't anything in the fridge other than food for the party, so it doesn't take me long to find it. As I turn around with the platter in my hands, I am met by Hendrix's face. I let out an exasperated sigh, looking behind him to see if his girlfriend is anywhere in sight.

"Where's Ariana?" I ask, knowing damn well that isn't her name.

"In the bathroom." He leans against the counter. "You and Acyn are pretty serious, huh?"

I tip my head to the ceiling, asking the universe why this is happening now. "For fuck's sake Hendrix, does it matter?"

"Everything matters with you." He takes a step closer to me.

I roll my eyes, exhausted by this back and forth with him. "What do you want, Hendrix?"

"You."

I scoff and a shrill, almost maniacal, laugh escapes me. "You have Audrey! Remember? Your girlfriend that you ruined your best friendship for. What is going on right now?"

"She doesn't matter, Harlow. All she does is satisfy a need."

I feel the sting of bile rising in my throat. To think I spent so much time with him makes me sick.

"Well..." I swallow the vomit threatening to come up. "Let her fulfill your other needs, too. I'm not the one for you." I make a move to step past him and he blocks my way.

"Do you really think he can love you like I can? Provide a life for you like I can?"

"Hendrix," I say sharply, "I am in love with Acyn. I love Acyn. You've gotta move on. Let me go..."

His honey brown eyes are locked onto mine. "I don't want to let you go. I love you, Harlow." He steps closer to me. I can already tell what his intentions are. I back into the fridge as he runs his fingers down my arm.

The puke I just swallowed is threatening to come back up. "Stop, Hendrix," I warn him. I am ready to hit him with the platter of food but he flies back. I blink with confusion as I see tattooed hands connecting with Hendrix's face.

ACYN

I am only half listening to what Marisa and Quinn are carrying on about. Harlow has been gone for a few minutes now. Maybe she needs help.

"Excuse me ladies, I'm going to see if Harlow needs help," I say, excusing myself from the table.

As I enter the kitchen, I hear Harlow's voice.

"Hendrix, I'm in love with Acyn. I love Acyn. You've gotta move on. Let me go..."

My steps falter. I know she didn't mean for me to hear this. I don't know if I should keep walking into the kitchen or if I should pretend

I never heard anything and wait for her. Movement from the hallway catches my eye and I see that the ex's girlfriend is listening in on the conversation, too. They must have been talking for a minute. The ex professes his love for her. Not fucking surprising. I'm on high alert when I hear Harlow tell him to stop. I round the corner to see her backed against the fridge as he runs his hand along her arm.

There he goes touching what's mine again. I snap.

I rip him away from her and my fists connect with his jaw. Multiple times. I have been wanting to do this for a while. My fist slams into his nose. I am satisfied when I hear a crack. He cries out in pain.

I cock my fist back ready to punch him again when I hear Harlow's voice. "Acyn, this isn't what it looks like, I was trying to –"

"Oh..." I stand up with my chest heaving. "I know, Sunshine, but he needed to learn to stop putting his hands on what isn't his." I give him one last swift kick to the ribs and then turn around to face her.

There is a wild appetency in her eyes when my gaze meets hers. She doesn't pay notice to the pile of shit writhing around, screaming expletives beneath my feet.

"Did you hurt your hand?" she asks as she pulls me towards the stairs.

"I don't think so." It doesn't really matter if I did or not because it was worth it.

We reach the bathroom and she pulls me in behind her, locking the door as she does. I lean against the counter, she stands between my legs, and her lips crash into mine. I am stunned for a second because this isn't the reaction I was expecting for beating the shit out of someone. I'll fucking take it, though. Her hands fist my shirt as she kisses me with a sense of urgency and desire. I pull her closer to me, feeling her heartbeat wildly in her chest.

She pulls away only to peel her jeans off of her. I grip her ass while kissing her neck and slide my hand between her legs to feel her panties are soaked. I stand up and flip her around so we are both facing the mirror. Her eyes lock onto mine as I bend her over and pull her panties to the side. All she wants is me and I am going to happily give myself to her.

I slowly push into her wetness as I watch her face in the mirror. She moans as she closes her eyes, biting her lip, as her pussy clenches around my dick. When she opens her eyes again I lean forward, kissing her shoulder and her neck as I savor the feeling of being inside her. I grip her hip as she hikes her leg up on the counter. I thrust into her as her own hand travels down to her clit. We are watching ourselves get lost in each other in the mirror. I wrap my hand around her throat, applying light pressure, as I thrust into her. I feel her pussy clenching around my dick. I know she is going to cum, she doesn't have to tell me.

She lets out a cry, saying my name with a look of complete ecstasy on her face. I don't slow down; I want her release all over me. Her eyes flutter open once she's ridden out her orgasm and the look of... *love* in them sends me over the edge right after her. Both of us are now sticky with sweat. She gives me a lazy smile as she brings her leg down from the counter. I reluctantly pull out of her. It is my favorite place to be. She turns around to face me and I bring my lips to hers. "Violence is not okay..." Her voice is hoarse from just screaming my name. "But... watching you beat the shit out of him did things to me and I needed you inside of me."

I erupt with laughter. She wraps her arms around me with a grin on her face. "How long were you standing there?" I know she's asking because she wants to know how much I heard. I'm going to let her tell me she loves me when she feels the time is right for her. I doubt that is the way she wanted me to hear it.

"I didn't hear much. Just him professing his love for you." She snorts with laughter and covers her face with her hand. "Maybe he'll think twice about assuming everything is his."

"Oh my God." Her eyes snap to mine. "Your hand; is it okay? It sounded like you broke something."

"I doubt I did. I'm sure he broke something running into my fist like that." I bring my hands up between us and my knuckles are raw.

"Can you move them?"

"Harlow... I just fucked you into oblivion. You tell me?"

She snorts with laughter. My hands are working just fine.

"Are you okay, though?" I ask, searching for any indication that she isn't because I'll beat his ass again.

"I'm good," she says with a grin. And I know she means it. "C'mon, we should rejoin the party."

Once we're back outside, Harlow's dad approaches us. "Would either of you happen to know why Hendrix had a broken nose and a possibly dislocated jaw?" Harlow's eyes go wide.

"He doesn't know how to keep his hands to himself," I say bluntly. I would do it over again and he is lucky that's all he got.

Her dad nods as he pats me on the shoulder. "Hopefully, he learned his lesson."

I chuckle and Harlow hugs her dad. He has welcomed me with open arms from the beginning. I am grateful that he trusts me to take care of his daughter when and if she needs it. I don't think she needed it today but it sure felt good anyway.

32

Harlow

Walking into Holy Shot, I'm met with a sight that makes my heart swell. Acyn is sitting with my dad, Ava, Mercy, and West. They're talking and laughing. I can't help but smile watching them all together. I'm elated that my dad decided to move to Seattle. He has only been here for three weeks but he is so happy here.

We are so happy here.

I feel myself relaxing as I approach them. I love photography but that doesn't mean my days aren't tiring. Vision & Vibe is flourishing. It is nice to have a studio and not have to run around the city meeting people for shoots. I still travel if asked but it isn't a necessity now.

After sitting down in Acyn's lap, he pulls me towards him and kisses my temple. "Hey, Sunshine." Those words will always give me butterflies and put a smile on my face.

West and my dad are laughing about something while Ava holds Mercy on her knee. This has become normal for both our families. Gathering at Holy Shot, talking, and laughing.

"Do you two want to come over for dinner tonight?" my dad asks.

I love hanging out with them but tonight I just want to be home snuggled with Acyn and Six-Two-Six.

I hesitate in responding. "We have plans but we'll be there this weekend," Acyn says which surprises me because I wasn't aware that we had plans. "Are we still on for hiking Saturday morning? Maybe West won't sprain his delicate ankle this time." We all erupt with laughter except for West, who is staring at Acyn with his mouth opened.

"He does have a good point," my dad says, chuckling.

Last weekend, West sprained his ankle getting out of the car before their hike and they tease him about it every chance they get. "It was a serious injury..." West defends himself.

"Let's go Sunshine," Acyn says in my ear as they continue to carry on. I say goodbye to them all and let out an exhale as soon as we're out of the shop.

"We have plans?" I ask with a quirked brow.

"Nope, you hesitated. I can see it on your face that you need a chill night at home."

I hug him as we walk to his car. "I love spending time with them," I admit, "but I also like being with just you."

He opens the door for me and I slide in. "What do you want to eat?" he asks as he pulls into traffic. "Or do you want me to make you something?"

"Surprise me," I say with a smirk.

"Bet. I'll drop you off at home so you can shower while I go get the food. Sound like a plan?" I grin at him because he knows me so well.

"It's a plan."

I slip into my silk robe after a relaxing bath and head for the kitchen. My steps slow when I hear slow music. I smile to myself as I walk into the living room and see Acyn has made a space for us to have dinner in front of the fireplace. He appears behind me with plates of food from our favorite Thai restaurant. We settle onto the plush fur rug and oversized pillows. "What did I do to deserve this?" I ask.

He shrugs. "You exist. That's all you need to do." His ember eyes meet mine as he grins at me.

"I love you..." I blurt out before I even think about it. The overwhelming feeling of the love I have for him can't be contained any longer. I've known since the sunflower fields that I love him. Maybe even before then, but that's when I knew without a doubt that I had fallen for him. He slowly chews his bite of food, eyes locked on me, as he sets his plate aside. His eyes don't leave mine as he grabs my plate from my hands setting it off to the side.

"I'm sorry, Sunshine... I don't think I heard you." I see a smirk threatening to appear on his lips. He is inches from me now. I glance at his lips briefly.

"I said that..." I look into his eyes again. "I love you." My heart is thumping.

His hand comes up, brushing against my cheek, tucking a loose curl behind my ear. The simple gesture makes me hyper aware of his close proximity. His lips meet mine. It's a soft kiss. One that leaves me hungry for more when he pulls away.

"I love you, too," he says as he looks into my eyes. I hold his gaze for a few brief seconds before crashing into him, pushing him back onto the pillows.

I straddle him and he pulls at the ties of my robe, causing it to slip off and pool around my hips. I tug at his sweats, pulling them down, and letting his dick spring free. Positioning myself over him, I slowly lower myself onto him. His head drops back against the pillows as he enters me inch by inch. I toss my head back, reveling in the feel of him.

While gripping my breasts as I ride him, he starts rubbing my clit. I spread my legs further, welcoming the pleasure he is giving me. Each tantalizing wind of my hips elicits moans from Acyn's lips. The sound brings me closer to the edge. My breath hitches as I feel the flood gates of my orgasm slowly opening. "Acyn..." is all I manage to get out before my pussy clenches around him as the tidal wave of my release spills onto him.

He sits up, pulling me flush against him and wrapping his arms around me as he matches the wind of my hips with his thrust. I can tell he is near his release as his thrusts become more fevered as he drives into me. He shudders and lets out a grunt as he climaxes. We remain intertwined, panting, coming down off the high of being lost in each other. "I love you," I whisper into his ear.

He pulls away from me to look into my eyes. "I love you, too."

33
ACYN

Harlow hasn't stopped asking me what I want for my birthday. I told her all I want is to do is spend a few days with her on the Oregon Coast. She growls in frustration every time I tell her this. I know she wants me to give her some generic, material answer but what I want for my birthday isn't material. I knew she was desperate when she enlisted the help of Eli and Emery to find out what I wanted for my birthday. I jokingly told them that I wanted a black 1966 Mustang GT.

When she pulled up in one in front of my shop I thought I was fucking dreaming. She stepped out looking like a goddess, flipping her waist-length twists over her shoulder. Her eyes meet mine through the window with a grin on her face.

"Is this mine?" I'm almost afraid to touch it.

She grins. "All yours."

"How?" I don't know whether to thank her or fuck her... or both.

She shrugs nonchalantly. "It helps when your dad and his friends have a love for old cars and can help you find them at reasonable prices. So yes, she's all yours. And I am too."

She leans against the hood, dressed in an all-black skintight jumpsuit with black heels that I'd love to see draped over my shoulders. The only thought on my mind is thanking her by fucking her on the hood of that car.

That's exactly what I do. I drive us to somewhere secluded, where she can scream as loud as she wants, and dick her down. It's a fine start to my birthday week. But the real present awaits us at the coast.

"I'm glad you brought us here. I forgot how gorgeous it is," Harlow exclaims with the night sky reflected in her eyes as she stares at all the stars. It's a perfect night; there isn't a cloud in sight. She is laying against my chest as we sit snuggled up next to the fire.

"I brought you here for a reason..."

"Not to throw us in the ocean again, I hope." She will never forget that. I can't blame her because I won't either.

"No." I chuckle. "But that was a good memory."

She sucks her teeth. "For who?"

"Me. It was the first time I saw you naked."

She tosses her head back against my shoulder as she erupts with laughter. "I thought you were going to say something sweet!"

I intertwine my fingers with her. "This is also where..." I plant a kiss on her hand as I bring it to my lips. "I realized that I was in love with you."

She turns around to face me. "Really?"

"Yeah, I thought you were mad at me the next morning, remember?"

"Yes," she says with a grin.

My heart rate picks up as I get closer to the reason. "I realized then that I would do anything to make you happy. I knew I was fucked..."—she laughs— "and completely in love with you."

Her eyes are glistening now. I fumble around in my pocket and bring out a small yellow ring box with shaky hands. Her eyes widen with recognition as she stares between me and the box. I open it to reveal a glittering, two carat, round cut diamond ring.

"Harlow Shaw..." I press a kiss to her lips. "You're all I've wanted and all I've needed. Will you marry me?"

"Yes! Yes!" She holds out her hand. "I love you so much, Acyn."

"And I love you."

I slip the ring on her finger. "You gave me the best birthday present and you didn't even know it." She looks from the ring, sparkling on her finger, to me in disbelief. I pull her towards me and kiss her slowly because I know I have a lifetime to savor her.

There was no one before her.

There will never be another after her.

There is only her. Only us.

All I've wanted. All I've needed.

Harlow

M y ring glitters as I tangle my fingers in Acyn's curls. I begin to smile staring at it, still in awe that this man is all mine.

A chuckle rumbles from his chest. "Staring at your ring again?"

"Yes." I grin. "How did you know?" Our bodies are intertwined after getting lost in each other... *repeatedly.*

"Because you stopped massaging my head."

"Look at it," I say as I hold up my hand in the moonlight. "It's hard not to stare at."

He looks up at my hand, interlaces his fingers through mine, and brings my hand to his lips. "It's perfect, but you know we have to be up in three hours?"

"Excuse me." I snort with laughter. "I'm not the one who has trouble keeping my hands to myself. I was perfectly fine going to bed."

He laughs. "Bullshit. You wear one of my t-shirts to bed every night and tonight you somehow end up in lacey lingerie. Not that I'm complaining, but it takes two to tango, Sunshine."

I can't stop the giggle that escapes me. "I wanted to see what it looked like on."

"And I wanted to see what it looked like off," he says as he kisses my neck.

We spent the past two weeks on the Oregon Coast celebrating his birthday and our engagement. We love our families and they are very involved with all that we do, but for this moment, he wanted it to be us two. We spent time relishing in our engagement and each other. I didn't think it was possible to continuously fall in love with someone. But I find myself falling deeper in love with him every day.

"It's going to suck going back to reality tomorrow." I sigh. "Sevyn and Ava are apparently already planning our engagement party."

"Sevyn is going to be a force to be reckoned with until we say 'I do,'" he says. "This is the moment she's been waiting for since we first met."

Grinning, I snuggle closer to him. "What do you think of my coffee now?"

He smiles. "It still tastes like shit."

I let out a cackle. "*Really?* Even now that we're engaged you won't admit that I know how to make coffee?"

He plants a kiss on my forehead. "Apparently I'm a sucker for shitty cups of coffee."

Life has become a blur with our work schedules, planning the engagement party, and our wedding. With the engagement party only a few weeks away, there's a lot that needs to happen. I've been missing the two weeks we had alone. It feels like a distant memory even though it was a month ago.

It's Friday, and all I can think about is spending the entire weekend wrapped up in my future husband. I inhale the scent of plastic gloves, ink, and green soap as I enter his shop. It's a mixture of smells I never thought I'd find comfort in. Acyn doesn't bother looking up as I enter and sit down on my usual bench in front of the window.

"Hey, Sunshine. I'm almost done."

"Is this your fiancée?" his client asks.

I grin at the sound of fiancée.

"Harlow, this is Elijah. Elijah, this is my future wife."

Butterflies course through my veins and I can't help the foolish grin on my face. "Hi. Nice to meet you."

"Do you remember when I almost missed your birthday?" Acyn asks. "He's the reason I almost missed it."

Elijah lets out a roar of laughter. "Throw me under the fucking bus, huh? It all worked out though, didn't it?"

"It did." I laugh. "Acyn just loves to give people shit."

Acyn has a grin on his face as he sits up straight. "You're done for today, Elijah. I'll see you again soon."

Elijah stands up and puts his shirt on. He turns to me and extends his hand. "Pleasure to meet the woman who can put this son of bitch in his place."

I snort with laughter. "Pleasure is all mine."

"Yeah, yeah. Get out of here, Elijah," Acyn says as he steers him to the front doors. Elijah's laughter echoes through the shop.

"I like him," I say with a grin.

"Elijah's been good to me. Even if he is an asshole."

"So, what does that make you?" I ask.

He tosses his head back and laughs. "Guess he was right."

I put my feet up on the bench and watch him clean up for a few minutes. I've had an idea bouncing around in my head since he proposed. "Acyn..."

"Yeah, Sunshine?"

"Can we get tattoos on our ring fingers?"

He gives me a lopsided grin that makes my heart stop. "Now?"

I shrug. "Why not? Or we can do it another day if you just want to go home."

"Home is where I am with you. Let's do it now. Do you know what you want?"

"Yeah," I say as I sit down in the chair. "I want the ace symbol."

He stills for a second as he studies me. "I thought you said you didn't like my nickname."

"Oh, yeah." I shrug with smirk. "I said that because you were being rude. I still prefer Acyn but... you're my ace."

He leans forward, sweeps my curls out of my face, and kisses me. "I love you," he says as he runs his thumb across my bottom lip. "But I still think your nickname is fucking horrible. Harls? What the fuck is that? Sounds like someone is hacking. I have to suppress the urge to correct anyone who calls you that."

I erupt with laughter. "Only you could make an insult sound sexy. Sorry we can't all have"—I make air quotes— "edgy and cool nicknames."

He starts cracking up. "Who said that?"

"*You*," I exclaim and do my best impersonation of him, making my voice deep and copying his mannerisms. "You can call me Ace," I say as I roll my eyes. "With your stupid lopsided grin."

He is wheezing with laughter. "I don't sound like that. Stop that shit."

"Yeah, you do. You know you do. That's why you're laughing!"

"Wow." He catches his breath. "I had no idea you had so much pent-up frustration about my edgy and cool nickname."

"I don't. I just thought you were ridiculous for telling me to call you Ace."

He grins. "Well now look, you're getting an ace tattooed on you."

"I happily am."

"If you get it where your ring sits, you won't be able to wear it until the tattoo heals. Do you want it below it or do you want to take your ring off?"

I clutch my left hand to my chest. "I am not taking off my ring."

"Below, got it." He laughs as he preps my skin for the tattoo.

I start to remind him to take pictures but he beats me to it and pulls out his phone to take a picture of me before he starts.

"You know me so well," I say with a grin.

"It's second nature now," he says as he hands me his phone to look at the pictures and starts my tattoo.

It doesn't take him long to finish. It's small, black, and sits just below my knuckle. I move my hand side to side to admire it and grin. "This is perfect."

"I don't think that there is anything about you that isn't perfect," he says.

I press a kiss to his lips. "What are you putting on yours?"

"I already know what I want." He says as he pulls out a small sketch that he won't let me see.

"You already have one drawn out?" I ask in amazement.

"Of course," he says nonchalantly. "It shouldn't take long."

I watch, mesmerized, as his tattoo gun meets his skin. Watching him work is one of my favorite things. He looks so serene. The stencil he applied moments ago is starting to come to life.

"What do you think Sunshine?" he asks once he's done and holds his hand out to me.

I take it and stare at the sunflower that looks like the sun. The only thought running through my mind is, *this is my husband. This is my husband. This is my husband.*

"It's beautiful," I say as I look up at the ceiling, telling myself not to be ridiculous as tears sting my eyes. But it doesn't matter; a tear escapes and falls down my cheek. Acyn kisses it away and pulls me into a hug.

"I love you," I whisper against his neck.

"I love you too, Sunshine."

We stay like that until he breaks the silence. "We should lock up and get home. It's getting late. We can chill by ourselves this weekend. Sevyn can live without two days of wedding plans."

I grin. "That's exactly what I need." Planning our wedding is exciting, fun, and exhausting. Even though Ava and Sevyn are handling all the details, it's our wedding and I want to make sure it's what we want. "Let me take a picture of us first so I can brag about how amazing my husband is to the internet."

Acyn lets out a laugh.

I set my phone up on a portable tripod and position it in front of us. "Ready?"

"Always."

"It's on a –"

"I know the drill Sunshine." He says as he holds his ring finger up to the camera and pulls me into a kiss. I follow his lead and hold my ring finger up to the camera too.

While he cleans up, I scroll through the pictures. I can't help the grin that's on my face. I choose to upload two. One where we're locked in a kiss holding our ring fingers up to the camera and the other where I'm looking into his eyes like he has all the answers to the universe in them. I type the caption: *the beginning of forever.*

"Ready, Sunshine?" he asks with his hand held out to me.

"Always," I say as I interlace my fingers with his.

We're all deserving of happiness and of a love that's so deep that you only discover the depths to which it goes with each passing day as your love grows.

I squeeze his hand a little tighter as we walk into the night because I know I'm holding onto my forever.

The Beginning of Forever

A.E. VALDEZ

I
Sunshine

"Another six months?" I feel the reality of the situation crushing me.

"Miss Shaw, we realize it's an inconvenience but—"

"Thank you. I'll be in touch." I rise from my seat as I feel the sting of tears in my eyes.

This is a total disaster. The day that is supposed to be a dream has turned into a nightmare. I hurry out of the office to my car. Getting in, I exhale, and let the tears fall. All the plans we had are now ruined. I slam my palm against the steering wheel.

None of this is what I wanted.

I would've married Acyn the day he proposed. Just us two, right there on the beach.

But we wanted our families to share these moments with us. Now I'm wondering if that was a good idea. All the plans have become overwhelming, and it's feeling like our wedding isn't really 'our' wedding anymore.

Instead of going back to my studio like I had planned, I head home. There was some work that I wanted to finish up, but I couldn't concentrate on it now even if I wanted to. I call my assistant to let her know I won't be back in today.

"How'd it go?" Priscilla answers.

"Every direction but right." I let out a sigh.

"Oh no, what happened?" she asks sympathetically.

"I'd rather not talk about it right now. I wanted to let you know I won't be back in the office today."

"Don't worry. I got you covered. I'll finish up what I can and leave the rest for you to go over tomorrow."

"Thank you, Priscilla. Enjoy the rest of your day."

"You try to do the same."

I end the call, breathing a little easier, knowing I have the rest of the day to myself. Vision & Vibe is thriving; I opened the studio almost a year ago. I had to hire an assistant a few months in because, after working with Celeste, my former boss, on her ad campaign, I was flooded with opportunities.

Shortly after that, Sevyn asked me to go with her to New York Fashion week. I couldn't say no to a trip to New York City and an opportunity to photograph the newest collections from elite designers. It turned into more than I could've imagined.

After fashion week, a designer saw a picture I posted on my Instagram of her work. She reached out to me and asked if I'd be willing to work on an upcoming photoshoot with her. I've learned to say yes when opportunities present themselves. It opened the gate for me to do freelance fashion photography. It gives me a needed change of pace from my day–to–day when I get to jet off to a fashion shoot.

I turn up the music, roll down the windows, and head home, hoping I can salvage the plans we had.

Ace

I'm surprised to see Harlow's car already parked in the garage when I arrive home. Usually, she'll text or stop by the shop if she wraps things up early at the studio. As I enter the house, I hear "Under Pressure" by Queen and David Bowie playing and follow the music to the backyard.

Harlow's lying on a blanket in the grass with Six-Two-Six, our cat named after Stitch from *Lilo & Stitch*, resting on her chest while smoking a joint. I stand near her head and look down at her, blocking the sunlight from her face. She squints as she looks up at me.

"You're home." She exhales the smoke she was holding in.

"I am." I sit down next to her, and she moves to rest her head in my lap. "What's up?" I ask as she holds the joint up to me.

"Nothing," she shrugs, "just tired."

I take a pull of the joint, hold it in, and exhale before saying, "You're a terrible liar. What's wrong, Sunshine?"

She doesn't say anything for a moment and then sits up to face me with tears in her eyes.

"Harlow, you're freaking me out. What's—"

Her eyes don't meet mine. "I don't want this, Acyn."

"Want... what?" I ask as my heart jackhammers in my chest.

She finally looks at me. "The wedding."

There isn't enough air in the world for me to catch my breath. My whole body becomes rigid as I break out in a cold sweat and my heart stutters in my chest.

"You don't want to—"

Her eyes widen as she covers her mouth. "That came out wrong." She scoots closer to me and grabs my face. "I don't want this big ass wedding we have planned. I want you. You're stuck with me forever." Her lips meet mine, but I don't fully register the kiss.

I finally exhale as I clutch my chest. "For a few seconds there, I thought you didn't want to marry me, and I panicked. Kidnapping crossed my mind."

She doubles over with laughter. "I'm sorry. I knew that came out wrong. I'm just... frustrated with it all. It's been six months since you proposed. I would've married you that day without a second thought to colors, menus, and cake options."

Harlow has been trying her best to keep up with all the wedding plans. It's overwhelming, even for me, and I'm on the sidelines of it all. Now we have a little over a hundred and fifty people on the guest list, and we only care about handful of them. I guess that's what happens when you're the only boy in a family of girls who's finally getting married.

"I also got a call from the venue today." She picks at the grass.

"Oh yeah, about what?"

"Well..." She takes another hit of the joint. "The director wanted to meet to tell me they double–booked our wedding with someone else's.

I guess they had gotten a new system and things got messed up. It came down to a matter of who called first, and it wasn't us."

"So, what does that mean?"

Her shoulders sag. "It means we have to wait another six months, and all the invitations we sent out a few months ago are bullshit."

"Six months?" I scoff. "For their fuck up?"

"I know. I got up and left. There was nothing more to be said. I'm exhausted, Acyn. Months of planning, and for what?"

My jaw tenses. "It took them months to figure out their fuck up, and now we're having to pay for it?" I shake my head. "I'm gonna stop by there tomorrow. That's bullshit."

Harlow's eyes are alight with excitement. "I should rage with you right now, but seeing you all riled up does something to me."

I let out a rumble of laughter. "Focus, Sunshine."

"I am. I'm focused on you." She straddles my lap, wrapping her arms around my neck. "You're in my corner. That's all that matters."

"Always." I kiss her neck. "But we need to decide what we're going to do. Do you want to wait that long?"

"No." She shakes her head. "I don't even want all the people we've invited to be at our wedding."

"Me neither. Fuck it. Let's elope."

"Acyn, your mom would kill me." She groans. "She's more invested in this wedding than we are."

I wrap my arms around her waist. "Exactly. That's the problem. It isn't her wedding. It's ours. What do you want, Sunshine?"

She bites her bottom lip and looks away from me as she thinks. "To marry you." Her eyes meet mine. "That's it."

"So what's stopping us?" I pull her closer to me.

I've been down for elopement since I slid that ring on her finger. Harlow tries to meet others' expectations while I have a hard time finding a fuck to give about other people's feelings.

I'm fiercely loyal to my family, but Harlow is everything to me. The wedding plans are stressing her out, and I know she isn't enjoying it. There hasn't been a decision she's made without my mom's direct involvement. I love that they get along, but I think the essence of who Harlow is has gotten lost in all the plans.

"Acyn..."

"Sunshine, all I want is you. That's it. Fuck a guest list and expectations. It's us."

"Us." She smiles. "I'm all in."

There are no words left to be said. I pull her towards me until our lips meet. My hands roam over the familiar curves of her body. She moans into my mouth as she grinds herself against me. I slip my hand under her shirt and cup her breast while the other unfastens her jeans.

"Acyn..." She pulls away, but I pull her back to me and trail kisses down her neck. "Acyn, the neighbors."

"What about them?" I ask as she lets me pull her shirt over her head, her bra soon following.

"They'll—" She sharply inhales as I swirl my tongue around her taut nipple.

"Sorry. I didn't hear that." I smirk. "What did you say?"

She pushes me back. "They'll see us."

"Harlow, the Murphys are on vacation and Mrs. Brown is as blind as a bat. She thought Six-Two-Six was a dog, for fuck's sake." She giggles. "Now, if you'll excuse me. I'd like a taste of you." She squeals as I flip her onto her back, and I kiss her before sitting up to pull off her pants. She lifts her hips as I slide them down as she spreads her legs for me. Harlow is a masterpiece. I rake my fingers up her legs and over her stomach, appreciating the work of art she is and my art adorning her rich golden brown skin. Since her first tattoo with me, she's gotten more that are mostly in inconspicuous places that only I'll have the pleasure of seeing.

"Thought you didn't want to be fucked outside, Sunshine." I grab her ankle and pull her towards me. My dick is begging to be inside her as it presses against my jeans.

She simpers. "Stop talking shit and make me cum."

"With pleasure." I say, sinking between her legs. I kiss and nip at her thighs before pulling her panties to the side and slowly gliding my tongue along her pussy.

She drapes her legs over my shoulders and pushes my head into her center as she tries her best to hold back moans. I lick and suck on her clit as she hums with pleasure. Her body trembles as I dip my tongue inside her. I've been addicted to her since the first taste, and it's been one of my personal goals to make her come as often as possible since then. I've yet to miss an opportunity, which is why she's letting me eat her for lunch in our backyard. She arches her back and grips my curls. I loop my arms underneath her legs and use my hands to spread her thighs further apart.

I know she's about to cum from the way she's breathing heavily and grinding against my face as she teeters on the edge of her climax. I move my tongue in circles around her clit before sucking on it, causing her to unravel. She comes hard for me. Her cries reverberate around us, and there's no denying that every person on our block heard it. She claps her hand over her mouth as she continues to moan and tremble.

I stop sucking when her moans turn to satiated whimpers. The way she looks after coming, with hazy eyes hungry for me, is one of my favorite views. She sits up to unbuckle my belt and dips her hand in my boxers. Wrapping her fingers around my thick length, she squeezes as she pulls it out and then pumps her hands a few times, causing me to groan.

She lies back, opening her legs for me, and I push into her warmth. I let out a shuddering breath before I move my hips. She puts one leg over my shoulder as I grip her other thigh that's wrapped around my waist. I slowly pump in and out of her, watching my shaft become wet with her arousal.

"Goddamn, you're gonna be the death of me…"

"At least you'll die happy inside of me," she quips as she matches my thrusts.

She isn't wrong. I wrap my hand around her throat and pound into her as I feel the release I've been chasing steadily building in my core. Harlow looks like a goddess bathed in sunlight with sweat glistening off her rich golden brown skin and her hair splayed across the blanket. Just when I think she can't look or feel any better, her pussy tightens around me. Whoever discovered Kegels, I want to thank them because the way I'm about to bust, I may very well die. I desperately thrust into her as she squeezes her eyes shut and calls out my name.

"Ahh, fuck, Harlow…" I let out a harsh, throaty moan as my body momentarily tenses.

My release spills into her as my climax shivers through me. Harlow keeps moving her hips, determined to get every drop from me. Taking a sharp inhale of breath, I moan, reveling in the feel of her. I'm already thinking of round two when our neighbor interrupts my thoughts.

"Is Harlow alright, dear?" Mrs. Brown asks from the other side of the fence.

I collapse on top of Harlow to cover her up as she clasps a hand over her mouth and laughs hysterically. I'm still balls deep inside of her and the only thing she has on is her panties.

"Uh yeah... she's fine, Mrs. Brown. Thank you for asking." Harlow is laughing so hard I can see the tears in her eyes. I grin back at her as I shake my head.

"Are you sure? It sounded like a scream and—"

"I was laying pipe, Mrs. Brown." I respond.

Mrs. Brown gasps. "Oh no, did a pipe burst?"

Harlow is now silently wheezing with laughter.

"It sure did, but Harlow helped me fix it."

"She's a good girl, that one. I'm happy you two are getting married."

"She's a very good girl." I look into Harlow's eyes. "And she's mine." I add for only Harlow to hear.

"Well, I won't keep you. Tell Harlow I said hello."

"I will." I respond and then wait for the sound of her backdoor sliding shut.

Harlow laughs, shaking her head. "You fucking exhibitionist."

"Call me what you will." I chuckle. "I wanted you. Surroundings be damned."

She grabs for her shirt and then slips it over her head. "You can have me anywhere you want." Her lips meet mine.

"Unless you want to give Mrs. Brown another show, I suggest we go inside first."

"I really hope she is as blind as a bat, like you said."

"If she isn't, she got a nice view of my ass."

"Acyn!" Harlow cackles.

2
Sunshine

All the lights are off with candles lit and music playing in the background. Rain is pouring outside while Acyn lies next to me. It's the perfect time to plan our elopement. We decided that the best place for us to get married is the Oregon Coast. It's where we fell in love and he proposed to me—it's perfect. I wanted a beach wedding in the beginning, but with so many people involved in the planning process, it didn't turn out that way. I was nervous about eloping, but as we sit here and make plans together, I know in my heart this is perfect for us.

"What about this coming weekend?" I ask, while staring at my computer screen. "I don't need to go into the studio on Friday."

Acyn grabs his phone off the nightstand and opens his schedule. "Umm... that could work. I don't have any clients on Friday, so we could leave Thursday after we're done with work and head for the Coast. What day do you want to get married?"

My heart rate quickens as the corners of my mouth turn up. "This is actually happening?"

He looks at me. "This is actually fucking happening."

I squeal and throw myself at him. "I can't wait to officially call you my husband. Not that we need a piece of paper to prove that, but—"

"But it's what we want." He wraps his arms around me. "In a matter of days, you'll be Mrs. DeConto and stuck with me for the rest of your days."

"Happily stuck with you." I press a kiss to his lips before sitting up and grabbing my laptop. He sits up with me and drapes his arms over my shoulders. "We need to get an officiant, and I need to call my friend to see if she can go with us to the coast to take pictures. Thankfully, we already put in our marriage license application. I just need a dress, but I think I have that covered. We need to get you a tux. Do you have any ideas about what you want?"

We decided that we weren't going to use anything from the big ceremony. It would make it obvious what we're doing, and we want this to be ours.

"Believe it or not, I have a Pinterest board Sevyn helped me make."

I gape at him. "Truly the man of my dreams."

He chuckles. "I speak all your languages, babe."

"Okay, now let's pick an officiant. Hopefully we can find someone amazing on such short notice."

"We will," he assures me.

For the next hour, we search for an officiant and read reviews. Fortunately, there are a few who do elopements and are familiar with last-minute requests. I reach out to them while Acyn figures out where he's getting his tux.

"Alright, that's all done. This is a breeze compared to the months of planning we've endured."

"The best part is that you're happy, and that makes me happy."

I smile at him as I snap my laptop closed and snuggle up next to him. "Do you think our families will suspect anything?"

"Nah. We take trips together often enough that it shouldn't raise any suspicion that we're going to Oregon for the weekend."

We travel together a lot. Especially since I've been traveling more for photoshoots. He'll come with me if he can and sometimes even work with clients, depending on where we go.

"What are we going to do about the other ceremony?" I ask. "I still want to do the bachelor and bachelorette party in Vegas, and a reception would be fun to celebrate with people."

He rubs his hand up and down my arm. "We should chop the guest list down. I haven't seen half the people on my mom's list since I was a child."

"She wants people to see that her only son is getting married."

"Our love isn't a spectacle, Sunshine. It should be people who've been there for us."

"I agree." I snuggle closer to him. "We can go over the guest list together. Does that mean you still want to have the parties and the reception?"

"Yeah, Kyrell has put a lot into that bachelor party."

"I'm sure he has." I mutter, and he chuckles.

"Plus, it will be with people we actually want to be with. But the reception, I'm down for that if we comb through the guest list."

"How are we going to tell your mom?" I ask.

"Don't worry about her. I'm her favorite child. She'll be fine."

I toss my head back and laugh. "That's all the more reason for me to be concerned."

"This is about us, Sunshine. My only concern right now is making you my wife."

His words cause my worry to fade away as he brings his lips to mine.

My dad lives in a townhouse that isn't too far from us. His retirement didn't last long before he began working as an adjunct professor at the University of Washington. He loves it and can create his own schedule depending on how much he wants to work. After his heart attack, he did his best to become active and found a love for hiking. Acyn, West, and I join him on most hikes. Neither of us has been back to Texas since the move. It's been the best thing for us.

I find him in the kitchen making fish and chips. He recently went to the UK and has been determined to re-create what he tasted there.

"Hi, Dad." I kiss his cheek. "Do you need some help?"

"No, kiddo. Have a seat. I'm almost done."

"What are you doing on your Spring Break?" I pull off my mini Louis Vuitton backpack and set it next to me as I take a seat at the table.

"Umm…" he says distractedly, as he plates the food. "I think West and I may go camping for a night or two. You and Acyn are welcome to join us."

My dad and West have become closer since moving out here and have the brotherly bond he'd always longed for. It's been beautiful to watch them become best friends.

"We're actually planning to go to the coast this weekend, and our schedules are packed until then. Maybe we can plan something with the whole family this summer?"

He chuckles. "I don't know if Ava will be up for camping again."

The last time we went, Ava, my aunt, came across some poison ivy. She thought it was pretty and used it to make a flower crown. Unfortunately, none of us noticed until after she had it on for a few hours. Her rash lasted nearly two weeks, and she swore off camping after that.

"Maybe we can rent a nice cabin?"

"She may go for that." He sets a plate of fish and chips in front of me before taking his seat. "If not, maybe we can plan a nice vacation somewhere poison ivy-free."

I waste no time digging into my food. "I'm glad you took that trip to the UK. This may be one of my favorite meals."

"Thanks kiddo. What are you two planning to do while visiting the coast?"

"Just to visit and get away." I try to sound nonchalant.

"Are the wedding plans getting to you again?"

My dad knows how stressful planning the wedding has been for me. The weight I felt when the venue told us it would be six months before we could marry is gone. It left as soon as Acyn and I decided to elope.

"I actually wanted to ask you something."

"Yes?" he sets his fork down and looks at me expectantly.

"Would you mind if I altered mom's wedding dress a little? Just enough for it to properly fit me?"

His eyes glisten as he looks at me, and tears pool in my own. My dad gave me my mom's wedding dress when I was thirteen. It was a year after she passed and the first time either of us could bear touching her things. My dad thought it would be best to pack her stuff and keep it in storage because it was a constant reminder that she was no longer with us. We kept some things to remember her. My dad hadn't slept in their bed since the night she had passed. Instead, he stayed in the guest bedroom and left their bedroom frozen in time.

"She would've loved that. I would love that." He wipes tears from his eyes. "But didn't you, Gloria, and the girls already pick out a dress?"

A few weeks after Acyn proposed, I went on a trip with Gloria, Ava, Sevyn, and Acyn's two older sisters, Annalise and Nora, to shop for a wedding dress. I had wanted to wear my mom's wedding dress, but Gloria had suggested we at least look at other gowns. I found one that I love, but it doesn't have any meaning.

"Yeah, I did, but I want to wear mom's for some photos with Acyn."

"I can't wait to see them." He smiles.

I feel a momentary twinge of sadness for lying to my dad, but it's quickly soothed by the fact I know Acyn and I are doing what's best for us. My dad has only ever wanted the best for me.

Later that evening, I'm ringing Sevyn's doorbell. She's helping with alterations. I would've gone to another seamstress, but I trust her to handle my mom's dress with care. She can also get things done faster with only three more days to go.

She opens the door with a glass of wine in her hand. "You know you don't have to knock, right?"

"I don't know what you and Zane have going on. I don't want to intrude."

"Please, as if the twins would ever let us. It'd be great to fuck anywhere but in secret places or while they're asleep."

I snort with laughter. "Where are they, anyway? It's quiet."

"Zane went to his parent's house. Eli and Emery would never miss a chance to be spoiled."

"Smart kids, if you ask me." I follow her to her sewing room.

Sevyn began classes at the Fashion Institute of Technology to get her degree in fashion design. It's a year-long program that she'll graduate from in a few months. I'm proud of her for doing something that she is passionate about for herself. Over the past year, her sewing skills have improved. She never took it seriously until she started school. Her designs are amazing. I can't wait to do a photoshoot for her when she's ready.

"Alright!" She claps her hands together after finishing her glass of wine. "Show me this dress."

I hang the garment bag up on a hook and unzip it. Sevyn stands behind me and gasps when I pull the dress out of the bag.

"Harls, my God, this is gorgeous. I love that it's vintage." Her eyes glitter as she reaches out to touch the dress. "And no offense, but this is prettier than the dress you picked out."

"None taken." I smile because I know she's right.

"You have to wear this dress for the wedding, not just for pictures. It's not too late to change your mind."

I'm supposed to pick up the other wedding dress a couple of weeks from now. All those plans are currently up in the air. My only focus is marrying Acyn this weekend.

"Do you think you can alter it?"

She sucks her teeth. "Can I alter it? Is the sky blue? Strip and put it on. I'm dying to see you in it."

I take the dress and disappear behind the room divider and do as I'm told. It's a soft, romantic cream color off the shoulder dress with lantern style sleeves. The back has a corset closure. After the alterations, it will fit me like a glove. My mom was more endowed than me in the chest area. It has a snug-fitting, heart-shaped bodice, but there's a gap when I put it on. The rest of the dress is flowy, gorgeous tulle. The sides need to be brought in just a stitch as well, and whatever else Sevyn thinks will make me look like a dream.

I step out from behind the divider, and she gasps while covering her mouth with her hands.

"Harlow... Acyn is going to drool over you."

I giggle. "That's the plan."

"Hot damn, alright! Let me work." She holds out her hand to help me up on the platform she uses for alterations, then grabs her pins. "We'll bring the top in just a cinch to give you some cleavage. The beadwork on the bodice is breathtaking. And then I'll also bring in the sides so it hugs your waist. Do you want me to make the bottom a little shorter, or do you want it to flow behind you?"

"Leave it."

"Good call. I think you'll lose the romantic feel of it, but wanted to ask anyway." She stands back, turning her head from side to side. "It honestly doesn't need much work. Do you want me to do it now?"

I blink, not realizing how minor the alterations were. "Yeah... if you have time. I don't want to rush you."

"No rush. Let me do it now while I'm free of the little tyrants."

"Alright." I chuckle before stepping down to put my clothes back on.

Sevyn takes the dress from me and begins working her magic. I send a text to Acyn to let him know I'm gonna be a bit longer.

Harlow: Sevyn is going to do the alterations now.
Acyn: Alright. I paid the officiant. We're officially getting married on Friday.

I let out a squeal, and Sevyn's eyes snap to mine. "What are you squealing about?"

"Nothing." I grin. "Just something Acyn said."

She shakes her head. "You two are nasty."

I toss my head back and laugh. "Who said it was sex related?"

"It may not be, but I'd rather not know." She mutters around the pins hanging out of her mouth.

"Oh please, what about all the S.O.S. texts you send me to watch Eli and Emery so you and Zane can fuck each other's brains out?"

Sevyn doesn't think I know that date nights are code for them to have an empty house to do whatever they want. Acyn and I don't mind, though.

She doubles over with laughter. "Just wait until you and Acyn have kids."

"I'm not worried." I shrug. "I'll just drop them off with you."

She smiles. "I'm happy you're gonna be my sister-in-law, Harlow."

Without Sevyn, I don't think Acyn and I would've met. We became friends when we met at a yoga class. At that time, I was working at the yoga studio and my Uncle West's coffee shop. She brought him to the shop with her and we went from friends to falling in love with each other.

"I'm happy too, babe."

"Okay." Sevyn sighs a few hours later. "This should fit you like a glove, babe." She hands the dress back to me. "Try it on."

I disappear behind the room divider for a second time. As I pull on the dress, I know she's right. It fits me perfectly. "Can you help me with the corset?"

"Of course." She says, cinching it snugly, giving my breasts a boost, before tying the bow at the bottom. "Oof, girl! You are perfection." She grabs my shoulders, turning me to face the mirror.

I'm stunned when I see myself. I look like I belong in a fairytale. The only thing I can do is stare at my reflection as Sevyn smiles beside me.

"Damn, I'm good." She flips her hair over her shoulder.

I chuckle, but I feel a tightness in my chest as I run my hands over the soft fabric of the dress. Tears prick my eyes. I try to blink them away, but that causes them to fall down my cheeks.

"Hey..." Sevyn says softly, wiping my tears away. "Are you okay?"

I nod, trying to control them, but they keep falling. "I just wish she were here, Sev. It isn't fair that she has to miss all of this."

She wraps me in a tight hug. "It isn't fair, and it fucking sucks."

I hug her tighter, grateful that she doesn't talk me out of the pain I'm feeling right now. Sometimes I just need to miss my mom while wrapped up in a hug from someone I love.

3
Ace

S ince Greyson and Asher are in town, I drag them along with me to get my tux. Greyson protested, but I reminded him how I endured ring shopping for hours so he could propose to his girlfriend, now fiancé, Selene. Asher enjoys spending money and wouldn't miss a chance to buy a new Armani suit, even though he doesn't need one.

I've never been one to follow tradition or rules. After asking Kyrell to be my best man, I asked Grey and Ash to be best men, too. Kyrell's only request was that he get to plan the bachelor party. I sent him a text Sunday night when Harlow and I were making plans to tell him I'd be tux shopping on Wednesday afternoon. He said he'd try to come. With a baby on the way and opening a second dispensary, he has a lot on his plate. This morning he sent me a text that he'd just touched down with Quinn and to send him the address of the tux shop.

Ash is already inside, getting tailored for a suit when I arrive. I chuckle and shake my head.

"Is this shopping trip for me or you?"

"We can have our cake and eat it too, Ace." He winks.

Grey is right behind me, followed by Kyrell. I give both of them a hug. We've created quite the "bromance" as Harlow calls it. She can call it what she will, but I know these three men will always have my back.

"Getting married, Ash?" Kyrell smirks.

"Fuck no," he replies. "I need to try all the flavors first."

"And you wonder why women never call you back," Grey says as he takes a seat.

"Who said I want them to?" Ash raises an eyebrow.

"You talk all that shit now until you go home to an empty house and a cold bed at night," I say as I look around.

Ash doesn't respond because he knows I'm right. All that partying shit is fun until it isn't.

"Whatever you want, I got it." Kyrell says. "Think of it as one of my gifts to you and Harlow."

"You don't have to–"

"I know," he interrupts, "but let me anyway."

"Alright." I smile and nod.

Kyrell is already paying for the bachelor party, including hotel rooms and flights. Harlow and I tried to talk him out of it, but there's no sense in arguing with him because he'll do it regardless of what we say.

"I would help, but this wedding Selene is planning is gonna run me a grip." Grey says, and he looks a little worried.

I feel for him because weddings aren't cheap. While both our families are covering the costs of the wedding, I still see all the receipts and am grateful they offered.

"You knew Selene was high maintenance before you asked her to marry you." Ash checks himself out in the mirror.

"Fuck off, Ash. You're the last person I'd ever take relationship advice from."

"A wedding is a whole different ballgame," I cut in. "Something you'll realize if you ever walk down the aisle, bruh." I clap Ash on the shoulder, and he rolls his eyes with a smirk.

"Mr. DeConto?" the tailor appears. "Right this way. My name is Mauricio, and I'll be helping you today."

He leads us back to a private fitting room and there's a bottle of bourbon with glasses sitting on the table waiting for us.

"Wow, Ace. This is fucking nice." Grey picks up the bottle of bourbon.

"You look like you could use a drink, Grey." Kyrell hands him a glass.

"Pour me one, too," Ash takes a seat, being cautious of his suit he's still wearing.

The tailor wheels in a wrack with the suits I wanted to try on. The one I was most intrigued by catches my eye immediately.

"Which would you like to try first?"

"This one." I point to the one with the floral jacket.

Mauricio smiles. "That's my favorite too. You have good taste."

Grey, Ash, and Kyrell enjoy the bourbon, engaged in conversation. Mauricio points me toward the dressing room. When I re-enter the fitting room, Kyrell whistles, and they all stop talking.

"For fuck's sake." I chuckle.

"That's a nice suit." Ash nods. "Never thought I'd dig floral, but here I am wishing I would've bought it first."

"Let me borrow that for my wedding after you're done with it." Grey jokes, but something tells me he's serious.

The blazer is slim-fitting with a silk lining. The exterior is black velvet with rich crimson and oxblood florals and deep forest green foliage. You can't really tell it's a floral pattern unless you're close to it. The colors are vibrant, yet moody and dark. The pants are a slim-fitting black that I'll pair with some loafers.

"That jacket is going to photograph well." Kyrell nods. "Harlow will be proud."

I'm sure Kyrell knows we're up to something, but he hasn't asked. If it were just for pictures, Harlow would be here to help me pick it out.

"A cream-colored button down would look nice underneath this." Mauricio suggests.

"I trust your judgment." I smooth my hand down the front.

He disappears for a few moments and returns with a cream-colored collarless dress shirt and black slacks. I try it on with the jacket and Mauricio was right. It pairs well. It's classy yet has the edge I want. I think it will match Harlow's dress nicely. I haven't seen it, but she told me it's vintage and romantic. A lot like her. It doesn't take Mauricio long to mark up where the adjustments need to be made. Once he's done, I change back into my clothes and hand him the jacket, shirt, and slacks.

"Just a few minor adjustments, Mr. DeConto. I'll have this ready no later than tomorrow morning."

"That's perfect." I shake his hand. "Thank you."

Ash heads back out to the dressing room to change out of his suit and purchase it. Grey gets a call from Selene and steps outside. Kyrell leans back against the armchair with a smile on his face.

"I know this is more than just a trip to the coast for pictures." He tips his glass back to finish the bourbon. "I've known Harlow too long. She's a terrible liar."

Kyrell has known Harlow longer than I have. They're best friends. I turn to him with a poker face and open my mouth to say something, but he holds up his hand as he sets his glass down on the table. He gets up and embraces me, and I hug him back.

"Her mom would've loved to see her this happy." He releases me without another word and exits the room.

I just finished up with my last client when Harlow comes walking through the door with two cups of coffee in her hands. I glance at the clock, not realizing how late it is. The last client's tattoo took longer than I had expected because they kept needing breaks.

"Thought I'd stop by to see if you could use some coffee." She hands it to me, then presses a kiss to my lips.

I wrap my arm around her waist, pulling her closer to me, and kiss her neck. "Thanks, Sunshine."

"How did tux shopping go?" She takes a seat on the bench near the window.

"Got a tux. I'll pick it up tomorrow morning."

"Were the guys any help?"

"I think Grey will start losing hair soon because of wedding plans."

She snorts with laughter. "Can you blame him?"

"No, I can't, actually. And Ash is Ash," I shrug. "I'm not sure if he fears commitment or truly is content with being a player for the rest of his life. Sometimes he just seems... lonely."

Ash gives all of us shit for being in committed relationships, but sometimes it seems like it bothers him.

"He probably is. His two best friends are getting married, and Kyrell is with Quinn and is gonna be a dad. If that were me, I'd feel as though I'm looking through a shop window. Everything is right there, but not really within reach."

"Damn Sunshine. You're getting deep."

She chuckles. "Are you worried about him?"

"No, but I don't want him to feel like he isn't a part of the group."

"Please," she sucks her teeth, rolling her eyes. "Ash probably thinks he is the group."

I let out a rumble of laughter. "He is a little egotistical."

"Little is putting it nicely, babe. I'm shocked Kyrell and Quinn made it on such short notice. Her showing up at the studio was a pleasant surprise." She smiles.

"I think Kyrell knows..."

"Knows what?"

"That we're eloping. He said you're a terrible liar. Which I already knew."

"Excuse me!" She laughs. "I am not!" I side eye her. "It's hard to lie to people I love, okay? Besides, my dad bought it."

"Really? That's your gauge? You could do no wrong in your dad's eyes."

"Aha!" She points her finger at me. "Sevyn believed me."

"True." I nod, shrugging. "I also think Kyrell knows you better than anyone aside from me."

"That he does. But did you tell him we were eloping?"

"No. He didn't give me a chance to say anything. Just said your mom would've loved to see you this happy."

She looks at me for a few breaths. "He said that?" Tears well in her eyes before she looks away again.

I sit next to her and pull her into my arms. The wedding amplified the reality that her mom isn't here to see us get married. Trying on her mother's wedding dress was the first time I realized how bittersweet this is for her.

"I'm sorry..." She sniffles.

"Never apologize for feeling the way you feel."

"I just really miss her. I mean… I miss her every day, but I've been missing her more than usual lately. She would've loved you."

"How could she not, Sunshine?"

"Really, Acyn?" She laughs hysterically.

"You said she would've loved me, and I really wanna know how she couldn't."

She shakes her head with a smile on her face and wipes the tears from her eyes. "The real question is, what would I do without you?"

I kiss her. "That's a question we'll never know the answer to because you'll never have to know."

The next morning, I pick up my tux on my way to work. I was half tempted to tell Harlow that we should skip work and head out to the coast instead, but I've never canceled on a client. I'm always consistent and honest. The luxury of owning my business is that I tailor my schedule to fit into my life. But there are days I want to say fuck it and do whatever the hell I want. Today is one of those days.

My phone buzzes with a text and the chime lets me know it's Harlow. She's had her own ringtone since the first night we "slept" together.

> **Sunshine:** We should've skipped work today.
> **Ace:** I had the same thought.
> **Sunshine:** WE'RE GETTING MARRIED IN 24 HOURS!
> **Ace:** Final-fucking-ly.
> **Sunshine:** Dying of anticipation!

I'm typing out a text when a video call comes in from my mom.

"Hi, Mom."

"Hello, my love. I was trying to call Harlow, but she didn't answer."

"Oh, so I'm a last resort?"

Her shoulders shake with laughter. "No, no. Well... yes."

"The truth revealed." I chuckle.

My mom and Harlow are close. That is something I'm grateful for. I know my mom will never fill the void Harlow's mom left, but I think she at least makes that void a little less lonely.

"I was talking to Harlow earlier this week, and she said something about you two going out of town this weekend."

"Yeah, we leave tonight." Now I realize why Harlow didn't answer her call. She'd probably get nervous and tell her we're eloping.

"Where are you going?"

"The coast."

"Oh, Annalise and Nora are going to be in town this weekend. Maybe we should all go together."

I rub my eyes. "Mom, we wanted to get away. Just us two. Not have a family vacation."

"It wouldn't hurt to spend some time with your sisters, Acyn."

"And I will, when I want to." I smile.

"Alright. What are you two going to do there, anyway?"

"Harlow said something about engagement pictures and whatever else she wants to do."

"Isn't it a little late for engagement photos? Was she not happy with the ones you guys took?"

"Mom... I don't know. Whatever Harlow wants to do, I do." I shrug.

"As you should. Okay, well, I love you both and I'll see you when you get back."

"Love you, too."

I hang up and send a text to Harlow.

Ace: Avoiding my mom's calls?
Sunshine: She asks too many questions. We know I'm a terrible liar.
Ace: The worst.
Sunshine: Shut up.

My last client of the day walks through the front doors. A wave of excitement washes over me and I can't help the smile on my face. I get to marry the woman of my dreams soon.

The sun is setting as I load our bags into the back of my G-Wagon. I thought about taking the 1966 Mustang GT Harlow got me for my birthday, but I try not to push her, and the weather can be sketchy on the coast. Besides, Harlow over packed, as always.

"Funny you think you'll need clothes this weekend."

She wraps her arms around me. "Funny you think what's in those bags can be classified as clothing." She winks before kissing me.

I gape at her. "Now I want to see."

"Patience." She chuckles. "First we get married, then we do the freaky things."

"Wait... so what have we been doing this whole time? I thought you doing that little bendy thing you do is—"

"Make a PSA, won't you?" She swats at my chest.

"Pretty sure the way you call out my name is more than enough PSA for our neighbors." I smack her ass. "Now get that pretty ass of yours in this car so we can go."

"Yes, Zaddy!" She gives me a two-finger salute.

I chuckle and shake my head. I fucking love this woman.

Once I'm in the car, Harlow is ready to take pictures. I turn towards the camera with a cheesy, exaggerated smile.

"Why are you like this?" she laughs, shaking her head.

I wrap my arm around her neck and kiss her cheek as she snaps photos. She puts her phone down, places her hand over my heart, and kisses me.

"I love you."

"I love you, too." I kiss her again. "Onward into forever, Sunshine."

4
Ace

The coast is our place, giving us time to pause and just be. It always feels like coming home as we pull up to our little beach cottage we purchased together shortly after we got engaged. It's the same house we stayed in when I brought her to the Oregon Coast for the first time. Since I'd stayed here frequently over the years, I got to know the owners, Georgia and Joseph, pretty well. When they decided to sell, they reached out to me to see if I'd have any interest in buying it. They wanted it to go to someone they knew would appreciate it. We've already made countless memories here. It's where I realized I'd fallen for Harlow and then, a short while later, I proposed to her on the beach.

When I told her they offered us the house, we couldn't say no. It's a quaint three- bedroom, two-bath house that has everything we need for when we want to get away. Harlow's favorite part is the trail in the backyard that leads to a small private beach where we'll be getting married tomorrow.

"Who knew we'd eventually end up getting married here?" she asks as I park the car.

"I knew it was over for me when we took that first trip here." I cut the engine and we both get out. She meets me around the back of the car and leans against it while I grab our bags.

"That was a fun trip." She smiles.

"Even our swim in the Pacific?" I smirk, remembering when I threw us into the ocean.

"I could've easily died of hypothermia." She grabs the keys dangling from my pocket and opens the door.

"Nah." I kick the door shut behind me. "We would've been body to body before that happened."

"Damn." She turns on the lights as we head into the living room. "I feel I missed an opportunity."

I set the bags down. "We'll have countless opportunities now." I pull her into my arms. "How are we spending our last night as boyfriend and girlfriend?"

"Mmm... let's have dinner by the fire so we can eat under the stars. Maybe enjoy a joint or two. Then we can Netflix and chill, but we'll skip straight to the chill like we always do."

"That sounds perfect to me." I smile at her.

After we've settled in, Harlow makes us some blackened salmon and a side of Rasta pasta with shrimp in it.

"Taste it." She shoves a piece of shrimp in my face.

I open my mouth, and she puts it on my tongue. When she tries to pull her hand away, I catch her wrist and lick her fingers.

She giggles. "It's good then?"

"If I'm willing to lick it off you, it's good."

"I think the real question is, what wouldn't you lick off me?"

"Touché, Sunshine."

"Alright, you grab the drinks, and I'll take the food." She grabs the tray of food and heads out the backdoor. "Oh, and don't forget blankets!"

"Never forget the blankets." I chuckle as I grab the wine and glasses off the counter. Grabbing the blankets off the couch in the living room, I toss them over my shoulder and follow her outside.

She sets the food down on the table next to the fire that I started while she cooked.

"It's perfect tonight." She takes a deep breath, looking out at the ocean.

I watch her. I do that a lot—watch her do mundane things in total awe, appreciating being in her space. Although nothing with her is mundane. She lights up everything.

After we bought the house, she got all this stuff to have picnics on the beach. It's one of her favorite things to do when we come here. I should say one of *our* favorite things because I look forward to it too.

We settle on the blankets and pillows surrounding the low, candle-lit table and dig into our food.

Harlow moans as she takes a bite, and I chuckle. I like to think after a little over a year together that I'm used to it, but I'm not. My dick still twitches in response each time. It doesn't help that we're always trying to one up each other in the kitchen. We love to cook together and for each other. Either way, we're both winning because we make some bomb ass meals together.

"Are you happy we're eloping?" I put the last bite of food in my mouth.

She takes a sip of her wine. "Oh my God!" She exhales, placing a hand over her chest. "I am so happy. I felt like everything kept piling up. The venue, the never-ending guest list, all the pre-planning…" She takes a deep breath. "It was too much for me. Are you happy?"

"Of course." I give her a lopsided grin. "I didn't push elopement because I thought you were planning the wedding you wanted."

"It's not just my wedding, though. It's ours."

"Now it is." I smile at her as she goes back to eating her food.

Harlow could've said that we're skydiving into our wedding and I would've agreed. But I know her well enough to know that she wasn't happy with the wedding plans, long before the venue fucked up. She likes to make people happy, even if that means agreeing to shit that isn't really her.

"Are you nervous?" She sets her empty plate aside.

"Nah, I've been ready. Why? Are you?"

"No." She smiles. "I'm excited and happy because this," she motions between us, "is all I've wanted."

I've never felt the connection we have with anyone else. Even when we were just friends, the bond we shared was deep. We're on our own wavelength. I didn't believe in soul mates until her soul whispered to mine.

"You'll always be all I ever need."

Instead of going back inside once we're done eating, we sit on the beach talking and finish the bottle of wine. Harlow sits between my legs, wrapped up in my arms.

"We should probably get to bed. I need my beauty rest to marry you tomorrow."

"The moon and all the stars in the sky could never rival your beauty, Sunshine."

She sits up to turn around to face me, resting her hands on my legs. "So, how do you feel about immediately having babies?"

I put my hand behind her neck and pull her towards me, pressing my lips to hers. "A little one of us running around? Sounds like a shit show I'd love to be a part of."

Surprisingly, I'm awake before Harlow. We found it hard to fall asleep last night because our wedding day started with the sunrise. It's still surreal to me we're getting married. I doubt it'll ever stop feeling like a dream. I press a kiss to her cheek, to her forehead, and then one to her lips. She opens her eyes slowly, then closes them again. I chuckle, giving her another kiss.

"Why are you awake?" Her eyes are still closed.

"Because it's our wedding day, Sunshine."

Her eyes snap open as she springs upright. "It's our wedding day! Oh my God, we're getting married!" She squeals, throwing her arms around my neck and rains kisses all over my face. "You're gonna be my husband!"

"Yes," I say between kisses, "I am. And," she kisses me again, "you're," kiss, kiss, "gonna be," kiss, "my wife."

She kisses my neck and continues trailing kisses over my chest and abs. Sitting up, she rubs her hand over my morning wood before pulling my boxers down. I keep my eyes trained on her. I inhale sharply as she firmly wraps one hand around me and rubs the precum around the tip with the other, making it glisten. Her eyes meet mine as she slowly licks it off and then spits on it before rubbing it down my entire shaft.

"Shit..." I grunt.

She licks me from root to tip before taking me in her mouth. Her sucks are slow and hard. I brush her curls out of her face before gripping them tightly in my hand. I guide her up and down my dick, watching her with hungry eyes.

"Fuck, you look so good sucking on me." I groan.

She removes her hand that's wrapped around me and takes me further into her mouth. I fist her curls a little tighter. She rests one hand on my thigh while the other massages my balls. My head tips back and my eyes drift shut as I bask in the sensations.

She grips my dick again and sucks on the tip while still massaging me. I look back down at her as she swirls her tongue around the head. My breaths are shallow and sweat breaks out across my skin as she picks up the pace. I'm close to toppling over the edge.

I thrust into her mouth to match her sucks. "Fuck, suck me harder," I order her through gritted teeth. She sucks so hard my breath gets caught in my throat.

"I'm gonna fucking cum..." I pull her hair tighter.

A few more sucks and my muscles contract before I spill into her mouth. My hips stutter to a halt, but she keeps sucking on me until she's had her fill. She sits up and licks her lips with a smile on her face.

"Good morning to you, too." I say hoarsely and let my head fall back against the pillow. "I'm just gonna lie here for a minute."

She presses her lips to mine. "Wore you out? Gather your strength, Husband."

I open one eye to look at her. "Are you taunting me?"

"Me?" She splays her hand across her chest. "I would never. If I wore you out I–"

I'm off the bed and flipping her over my shoulder before she can finish her sentence. I smack her ass, and she yelps.

"Ace!" She giggles.

"You know I'll gladly fuck you into oblivion. Let me give you a preview of what you have to look forward to for the rest of your life." I hold her waist as I carry her into the shower.

Harlow grabs my arm to slip off her boots after our hike. We didn't want to spend the day sitting around just waiting. So, we went crabbing, then took a hike that ended with me fucking her up against a tree.

"I think I have bark in my panties. Words I never thought I'd say."

"I told you to take them off."

"Yeah? And what? Have my ass out if other hikers were to come along?"

I double over with laughter. "I'm not sure how having your panties pulled to the side is any better than having them off. Your ass is still out either way."

She tosses her hair over her shoulder with a smirk on her lips. "Look, it was worth it. But the couple we passed looked at us funny."

"You're loud." I shrug, slipping off my boots and unlocking the door.

"I love how you blame me when you started this exhibitionist bullshit."

I grab her as she walks through the door, wrap my arms around her waist, and kiss her. "Last I checked, you are a very willing participant, Sunshine."

"Always." She stands on her tiptoes and presses her lips to mine again. "But now..." she boops my nose with her fingertip, "I have to get ready to marry you."

"Did you just... boop me?" I quirk an eyebrow.

"Yes." She smiles and does it again. "Yes, I did."

I catch her wrist and pull her towards me. She squeals as I kiss her neck.

"Ace! I have to get ready, dammit. You've fucked me enough!"

"Oh, now you suddenly don't have shit to say? Where was all that energy from this morning?" She's too busy laughing to say anything. I hold on to her to keep her from falling over onto the floor. I make my voice high pitched and mimic her. "Wore you out, huh? Gather your strength, Husband? You better gather your strength, Wife, because as soon as we say I do, that bed upstairs is our home until we leave."

"Ohhh," she moans, "I love it when you talk dirty to me." She kisses me.

"Yeah," I nod. "We definitely belong together."

She snorts with laughter. "Okay, I seriously have to get ready now."

"Alright." I let her go.

"Do not enter the room, got it?" She narrows her eyes while poking her finger into my chest.

"Got it." I raise my hands up.

"See you soon." She kisses me again before turning and heading up the stairs.

I watch her and let out an exhale when I hear the door close behind her. I wasn't nervous until she said she had to get ready. It's a mix of both excitement and nervousness. The moment that once seemed so distant is now only a few hours away.

An hour and a half later, I'm putting on my suit. The photographer, Raven, who is also Harlow's friend, arrived early to help her with her hair and to take pictures of us while we get ready. At first, I thought it was ridiculous Harlow didn't want us to get ready together, but I'm glad we didn't. I can't wait to see her.

Once Raven's satisfied with her pictures, she heads back to the guest bedroom to help Harlow with her dress.

"Tell Harlow I'm heading outside," I say before she leaves the room.

"I will." Raven smiles. "She's almost ready. Just a few more details with her dress, then she's all yours."

My heart pounds in my chest as she leaves me alone again. I look at myself one last time in the mirror before grabbing my phone and sending a text to Georgia. I asked her to help me with a surprise for Harlow that she'll take care of while we're getting married. Opening the door, I set my phone on the dresser and head down the stairs. The officiant pulls up as I step outside. She waves and smiles from her car before getting out and heading toward me. She isn't very tall with warm brown eyes and is about the same age as my mom with short, white hair that falls to her chin with deep brown skin.

"Hi, I'm Sylvia. You must be the groom, Acyn." She extends her hand toward me.

"That's me." I smile. "I can walk you down to the beach. I'm waiting for my bride. She's still getting ready."

"Oh, no, no. That's unnecessary. If you point me in the right direction, I can find my way. Don't want to leave the bride waiting." She winks.

"Alright." I chuckle and point to the gate in the backyard. "If you follow the path just beyond the gate, it'll take you right to the beach."

"Perfect. I'll see you down there. Nice tux, by the way." She pats my arm.

Harlow is great at reading people. When we found Sylvia's website online, she said that she was the one who was going to marry us because of her energy. Everything is about energy to Harlow. All I know is she's never been wrong.

I head to the back gate and wait for Harlow to come outside. Now that Sylvia's gone, my heart returns to pounding in my chest. I've never been this nervous in my life. I try to focus on something else, but the only thing on my mind is Harlow.

Then, as if she heard my thoughts, I hear the backdoor open and slowly turn to see her.

I couldn't tell you the last time I cried, but when I see Harlow coming down the steps, she steals my breath and I feel a lump in my throat. She is a vision. I'm choked up as I try to catch my breath watching her walk towards me. Her dress looks as though it's made for her the way it hugs her breasts and waist before cascading down the rest of her body. She has a crown of flowers sitting atop her light brown curls that are flowing down her back.

When she's near, I hold my hand out to her, and she places hers in mine. I bring it to my lips without taking my eyes off her. There are tears in her eyes. I gently wipe one away as I straighten up again.

"Sunshine, you look divine. You are breathtakingly gorgeous. I should know because I still can't fucking breathe." She laughs and smooths her hand down the lapel of my tux. I grab her hand, interlacing our fingers.

"Are you ready to become husband and wife?"

"I'm all yours." She smiles.

5
Sunshine

A cyn has always been strikingly handsome, but him in this tux ready to marry me has me speechless and overcome with emotion. I can't take my eyes off him. It's tailored to his muscular frame perfectly. A few buttons are undone, giving me a nice view of his tattooed chest. He leads us down the path to the officiant. The sun is barely setting as we near the beach. This day couldn't be any more perfect.

"Acyn..."

"Yeah, Sunshine?" He stops walking and looks at me.

"I love you, and I'm happy I get to walk into forever with you."

He brings his lips to mine. "I love you, too."

We continue to walk hand in hand down the path toward the officiant until she comes into view. There's no décor, only the breathtaking view of the Pacific Ocean behind us.

"And you must be Harlow." Sylvia extends her hand out to me. "You are stunning, my dear."

"Thank you." I smile.

"Shall we begin?"

We say, "Yes," in unison.

"Then let us begin."

Acyn and I face each other. His ember eyes meet mine and there's the fire in them that's always been alight for me. Sylvia begins the ceremony, but all I see is Acyn. Even though we were just friends at first, he's always loved me as I am and encourages me to never dim my light. I fall madly in love with him every day.

"Sunshine..." Acyn gently squeezes my hand.

"Yes?" I'm lost in his eyes.

"The vows."

"Oh!" I let go of one of his hands to pull the piece of paper that I wrote them on out of my cleavage. Acyn raises an eyebrow while trying to hold back a laugh. "What? My dress doesn't have pockets. May as well hold it close to my heart."

He turns his attention to Sylvia. "You see why I'm marrying this woman?"

"I can." Sylvia laughs.

"Okay." I unfold the paper with shaky hands. I have it memorized, but looking into his eyes, there's a high possibility I'll forget. I take a deep breath, and meet his gaze.

"Ace, I found a home in you. Wherever we are, as long as I'm with you, I will always be home. I promise you'll always know love because I've loved you across lifetimes and will fiercely love you in this one and beyond."

I refold the paper, and before I can tuck it back into my dress, he takes it from my hand and tucks it into his jacket pocket over his heart. He kisses my hand that's still in his and pulls out a piece of paper from his pocket. My heart rate quickens as I watch his hands unfold it. Our eyes meet again as his deep voice fills the space between us.

"Sunshine, there aren't enough words in any language to express how much I love you. It's indescribable, but I can make sure you feel it. With everything that I am, I promise to show you every day for the rest of my days how much I love you. You're the heartbeat in my chest and the blood in my veins."

His words settle deep in my heart, and I feel like I can't breathe. He refolds the paper, kisses it, and then slips it into the front of my dress over my heart. His touch causes me to shiver and have goose bumps. He winks at me before holding both of my hands, and then I'm lost in his eyes again. Sylvia resumes the ceremony. Acyn and I say "I do" to each other and Sylvia turns her attention to Acyn.

"Do you have the rings?"

He pulls them out of his pocket, handing me his while holding onto mine.

"Let these rings not only be a reminder of your promises to each other but also a symbol of your eternal love and devotion to one another. Acyn, take Harlow's ring, and repeat after me."

He holds my hand and repeats after her as he slides it on my finger.

"With this ring, I give you my heart, love, friendship, and devotion for the rest of my days. I am yours forever and always."

"Harlow, take Acyn's ring, and repeat after me."

I hold Acyn's hand as I repeat after her and slide his ring onto his finger.

"With this ring, I give you my heart, love, friendship, and devotion for the rest of my days. I am yours forever and always."

"Now, by the power vested in me, I now pronounce you husband and wife. Acyn, you may—"

Before the words are out of her mouth, Acyn pulls me towards him and his lips are on mine. I wrap my arms around his neck and get lost in the kiss with him.

"Finally," he mutters against my lips before kissing me again.

I feel like I'm high. Our love is the best drug.

He pulls away to thank Sylvia. She congratulates us before wrapping us in a hug, and then she leaves. Raven stays a little while longer to get more photos of us before she leaves. And then it's just us.

"C'mon, Sunshine." He grabs my hand, pulling me toward the house. "I intend to keep my promise of making that bed our home."

We're both laughing as we run up the steps. I reach out to rush through the door, but he sweeps me off my feet, causing me to squeal.

"Gotta carry my wife over the threshold." A smile lights up his face.

I wrap my arms around his neck and kiss him. He carries me inside the house and kicks the door shut behind us. I'm ready to get out of this dress and on top of him. He takes me straight to the bedroom, as promised, and sets me down gently on the bed.

He whispers against my lips, "Open your eyes, Sunshine."

I open my eyes and gasp. "This is—you did all of this?"

There are candles lit all over the room, casting a soft, warm glow. Sunflowers and red rose petals are scattered across the floor. A bucket with a bottle of champagne and two glasses are sitting atop the bedside table. Twinkle lights are wrapped around the bedposts and music is playing softly.

"Yes, well, no. It's my idea, but Georgia put it together while we were getting married."

"Acyn." My eyes meet his. "This is gorgeous! I–" Instead of telling him, I show him.

My lips crash into his, and I pull him on top of me.

"You don't wanna take pictures?"

"Not as badly as I want you inside me." I turn around and brush my curls to the side. "Unwrap me."

"My pleasure." He presses a kiss to my shoulder, then one to my neck, and another just behind my ear.

My body shivers with anticipation. I feel him slowly untie the bow at the bottom of the corset. He gently pulls at the ribbons, one by one, and my dress slips a little further down my breasts each time. With one last tug, my dress pools around my hips. He pulls me flush against him, my back to his chest, as he trails his hands up my body until he cups my breasts.

"You're the greatest gift." He massages my breasts and kisses my neck.

Sliding my dress the rest of the way off, he drapes it over the armchair after setting the paper with his vows on the nightstand.

"And absolute perfection." He wraps his arms around me.

I traded the traditional white lingerie for black lace crotchless panties with a matching garter belt that's cinched around my waist. It's clipped to garters wrapped around my thighs. I chose black, not only because it's sexier, but it's Acyn's favorite color, and I'll do anything to please him.

Running my hands over the intricate lace, I smile at him. "You like?"

He pulls me toward him, threading his fingers through my curls as he guides my mouth to his. Our tongues dance around each other as my heart beats wildly. I doubt this feeling of bliss will ever fade with him. We fall back onto the bed, and I moan into his mouth when I feel the stiffness in his pants pressing against me.

"Why are you still dressed?"

He chuckles as he kisses my neck. "I was too busy admiring you."

I help him push his jacket off his broad shoulders before my greedy hands pull at his shirt. A button snaps off.

"Fuck it," I mutter against his lips and rip it the rest of the way off.

The buttons scatter around the room. There are too many fucking layers between me and my husband. He's already unbuttoning his pants and pulls them down with his boxers. My eyes take in every inch of his perfectly sculpted tattooed body. He climbs on top of me, crashing his lips into mine. I wrap my arms around his neck as he flips us over. Straddling him, I sit up and run my hands along his chest and abs. He grips my hips and guides me to move up his body until I'm hovering over his face.

"You know what to do, Sunshine." He smacks my ass, and I moan. "Sit like a good girl."

I spread my thighs further apart and lower myself onto his waiting mouth. His warm tongue tastes my center. He wraps his arms around me and palms my ass. My hands grip the headboard as waves of pleasure pulse through my body with each swirl of his tongue. These crotchless panties were worth every goddamn dollar.

I can't seem to catch my breath with the way his tongue is making love to my clit. I spread my thighs as far as I can, sitting on his face like it's my throne. He squeezes and smacks my ass in response, and I let out a cry of pleasure. Reaching down, I grab a handful of his curls. His hands grip my hips as I ride his face. My moans grow louder as I feel my climax building. He keeps one hand on my hip while the other rubs my nipples. The pleasure he's giving me is pure ecstasy.

"Acyn..." I moan. "I'm gonna fucking–" my words get lost in my throat as I fall over the edge into oblivion.

A guttural cry spills from my lips, and I grip the headboard to keep from falling over. My body shakes and twitches as my orgasm takes over me. My cries turn to whimpers as he laps up my release.

I collapse next to him on the bed, attempting to catch my breath. Acyn kisses my neck as his hands roam over my body. His lips meet mine, and I lazily kiss him back, spent from my earth shattering orgasm.

"Oh, Sunshine..." he kisses my lips. "Don't tell me you're already tired." He runs his fingers over my sensitive clit, causing me to moan. "Because I'm nowhere near done with you."

A smile tugs at my lips. "If you felt the orgasm I just had..."

"I tasted it, and I want more." He kisses my neck. "Every single drop that sweet pussy of yours has to give me. I want it. You're officially my wife. Officially all mine, and I intend to show you how much I love you for the rest of my days." His fingers massage my clit in slow circles.

My body warms up for round two of what is going to be an endless night of lovemaking. Turning on my side, I press my ass against his erection. He takes a sharp inhale of breath as I reach around, grab his dick, and run the head along my slickness before guiding him inside me.

He slowly pushes into me, letting out a shuddering breath while gripping my hip. Slinging one leg over his, I open myself for him to go deeper, and our lips meet. I moan into his mouth as he thrusts into me from behind. He pulls nearly all the way out before thrusting back into me, causing me to lose my breath.

"Mmm... yes, I love when you give it to me like that."

Wrapping his hand around my throat, he applies just the right amount of pressure while hitting my g-spot with each thrust of his hips.

"You feel so fucking good," he breathes out before lightly grazing my ear with his teeth, causing me to shudder.

I feel myself teetering on the edge of another climax. He teases my clit with one hand while the other moves from my neck down to my breast. His lips kiss my neck as he rubs and rolls my nipples with his fingertips. The feel of him all over me and filling me up pushes me over the edge into another orgasm. I call out his name as he thrusts into me. I throw it back at him to match his thrusts.

"Yes, baby. Bounce on this fucking dick," he growls as he grips my curls.

A few thrusts later, he falls over the edge with me. His body momentarily tenses as he grunts and then moans, spilling into me. I roll my hips, sliding up and down his length as his climax shudders through him. Our bodies slow as we melt into each other and the euphoric high of our release. He tightly wraps his arms around me, and I trace my fingertips along his tattoos.

"Can we stay like this forever?" I whisper.

He kisses my shoulder. "Of course, we have forever now."

6
Sunshine

O ur wedding couldn't have been any more perfect. We spent the weekend totally and utterly lost in each other. I know we kept joking about elopement, but now that we have, I realize it's what we were going to do all along.

It's Sunday morning and the first time I've worn anything since I had my wedding dress on Friday evening.

"Damn, you really didn't bring any clothes, did you?" His eyes and hands appreciate my lacy bodysuit, thigh-high stockings, and sheer robe.

"I told you, nothing in my suitcases truly classifies as clothing other than what I had on for the drive here and when we went hiking. I bought everything else with filthy thoughts of you in mind."

"Can I just have you for breakfast instead?" He kisses my neck as I flip a piece of French toast.

I turn around in his arms wrapped around my waist and kiss him. "I–" my stomach rumbles.

"Maybe we should eat?" he smirks. "Death by sex in the first few days of marriage isn't ideal."

I snort with laughter. "No, not when I'm trying to spend a lifetime with you."

He presses a kiss to my lips before unwrapping his arms from around me. "Do you need help with anything?"

"Nope. I got it." I flip the last piece of French toast on to a plate. "It's all done. Besides, I don't think I could wait for anything else to cook. I'm starving."

"I told you that bed would be our home, Sunshine."

"No complaints here. I am thoroughly loved and fucked at the same damn time."

He lets out a rumble of laughter. "As you should be."

I hand him his plate of French toast, bacon, and eggs with a cup of orange juice before sitting down to eat my own. We weren't completely confined to the bed the past couple of days, but sex was the higher priority. Being newlyweds added to the urgency of needing our bodies to be intertwined as often as possible. And we took full advantage.

The realization that we'll be leaving in a few hours causes another thought to enter my head.

"Do you think your mom is going to be mad?" I take another bite, chewing slowly.

Taking a drink of his orange juice, he shrugs. "Does it really matter? Would we have done things differently?"

"No, this has been a dream." I smile, feeling on top of the world with him.

"We can't make everyone happy, Sunshine. We did what's best for us. Even if she gets upset, it isn't going to change the fact that you're now my wife." He takes my hand and kisses it.

"You're the best husband." I lean across the table and kiss him. Getting up from my chair, I let out a sigh. "Guess we should pack, and I should put on some real clothes."

He smirks. "I'm not opposed to what you're wearing."

"If it were up to you, you'd have me running around with my ass out all the time."

"I love that ass." He smacks it, and I let out a squeal of laughter.

I push his plate to the side and sit on the table in front of him. "Does breakfast come with dessert?" I open my legs.

"It does when you're the option." He pulls my panties to the side.

His warm tongue meets my center, and I let my head fall back as he shows me I've always been his only option.

cAce

We arrived home yesterday evening, and now I'm in a trance watching Harlow do her morning yoga routine. She widens her stance before bending forward, and my eyes focus on her ass as she rests her head on the mat. My eyes flit to hers when she giggles and shakes her head. My phone rings, interrupting my thoughts before I can say something dirty.

"Hey Sev. What's up?" I ask with my eyes still on Harlow, who has moved on to another pose.

"Eli and Emery want to know if they can go over to your house tonight?"

I tear my eyes away from Harlow. "Of course, my favorite niece and nephew can come over. Just them, or will you and Zane come too?"

"Don't let Annalise and Nora hear you say that."

We may be siblings, but that doesn't mean we're close. Annalise is eight years older than me, and Nora is eleven years older. Annalise and Nora are only three years apart, while me and Sevyn are one year apart. The age gap made it hard to relate when we were younger. Now that we're older, we spend more time together since they moved back to Washington State, but I'll never be as close to them as I am to Sevyn.

"Sev, I'm pretty sure they know your kids are my favorite. Do you guys want to stop by at 6ish? Because I know regardless of what time I tell you, you'll be late."

"You know me well." She chuckles. "Yeah, that sounds good. I'll bring drinks and dessert."

"Bet. See you later."

Sevyn, Zane, and the twins arrive fashionably late at 7:00. It worked out for Harlow and me because we were both running late with clients. Instead of cooking a meal, we picked up pizza on the way home.

Eli comes running through the door at full speed. "Uncle Ace, look!" He points at his arm.

I kneel in front of him and see there's a small spider tattoo on his forearm. And this is why her kids are my favorite.

I smile. "Sunshine, look at Eli's arm."

She gasps. "Oh my God! That's the coolest tattoo, Eli!"

He giggles and smiles at us both.

"Who gave you your first tattoo, little dude?"

He points at Sev. "Mommy gave it to me! But daddy said I can't get a real one like you until I'm older." He pouts and crosses his arms.

I chuckle and put my hand under his chin so his eyes meet mine. "Maybe Mommy and Daddy will let me use some ink pens and draw a full sleeve on you."

His eyes light up. "Yes!" He turns to face Sevyn and Zane. "Please, please, please," he begs.

They both laugh at his prayer hands, pouty lip, and puppy dog eyes. It's hard to say no to the kid.

Sevyn tilts her head to the side, studying Eli for a moment "I don't know, Zane. What do you think?"

Zane crosses his arms, scratching his chin. "We'll probably get a call from the school."

"Probably." Sev shrugs.

"But he'll be the most badass kid at preschool." Zane smiles. "I guess he can get one."

I laugh as Eli jumps in the air, clapping his hands with excitement before hugging me.

"I want one too!" Emery whines, not wanting to miss out on the action.

"Oh yeah, bug? What do you want?"

Her eyes tip up to the ceiling as she thinks. "Mmm... can I have a unicorn?"

"Whatever you want, I'll make it happen." I smile at her before rising to my feet and then look at Sev and Zane. "Yeah, you two will definitely get calls from the school after I'm done with them."

A little over an hour later, we've all eaten our fill of pizza, pasta, ice cream, and brownies. Harlow is running around outside with the twins while Zane watches a basketball game and Sevyn helps me clean up. She leans against the counter after taking out the trash, and I feel her eyes on me.

"You and Harlow seem... different."

I ignore her prying statement and continue to load the dishwasher.

"I didn't think it was possible, but you two seem... closer. More attached. What did you do to her while on that trip?"

"Do to her?" I chuckle as all the positions we were in flash through my mind.

"Yeah... there's something different, and I can't put my finger on it."

I close the dishwasher, start it, and turn to face her. "You're reaching, Sev. As always." I pat the top of her head.

She sucks her teeth, shoving my arm away. "I saw the way you looked at her the first time you two met. I knew then that there would be something more between you. And I have the same feeling that you two are hiding something. Is she knocked up?"

"With the way I nut inside her? Probably." I shrug and give her a lopsided grin. Sevyn gags, and I laugh. "Why does it matter to you what Harlow and I have going on, anyway?"

"Because..." she looks down at the ground before her eyes meet mine again. "You're my big brother, and I love to see you happy." She shrugs. "That's all."

Her words catch me off guard. I know Sevyn loves me, but we spend more time joking and talking shit than saying it.

I pull her into a hug. "Can you keep a fucking secret?"

"Oh my God!" She pulls away from the hug, covering her mouth with her hands. "Fuck, yes! Are you going to fucking tell me?"

I look her up and down before sucking my teeth. "Nah."

"You asshole!" She punches my arm.

I laugh as she chases me out into the backyard with Harlow and the twins.

"Babies, get Uncle Ace!" Sev yells.

And like two wild animals, they listen and attack me. Harlow falls over, laughing as one latches onto my leg and the other to my arm. It's all fun and games until Emery's razor–sharp baby teeth attempt to take a bite out of my thigh.

"She bit me!" I holler as I fall to the ground.

Eli pulls my hair, and Emery jumps on my back. Harlow and Sevyn are both on the ground in a fit of laughter. Zane comes out moments later as Eli gets ready to sink his teeth into my shoulder.

"Oh, no!" he yells, drawing their attention to him. "Uncle Ace is being attacked by baby zombies."

The twins immediately stick their tongues out and tilt their head to one side. I laugh hysterically at their expressions. Zane helps me up, and then we stand back-to-back while the twins make growling noises, ready to attack again.

"Do you think we'll make it out alive?" I ask Zane dramatically.

"I don't know, but we'll die trying."

"Get 'em!" Harlow yells to the twins, and they lunge at us.

The girls laugh while Zane and I pretend to fight for our life. It eventually ends with all of us laying on the grass, laughing, underneath the stars.

"I'm tired." Eli yawns.

"Me too. Being a zombie is hard." Emery adds.

We all laugh as Sevyn says, "That's our cue to go."

"Yeah, gotta get these kids to bed. Thanks for having us over," Zane says as he rises to his feet. "And helping me fight the baby zombie apocalypse."

I stand to give him a hug. "Anytime, man." I kneel to hug the twins. "Bye little zombies. See ya soon."

Then they hug Harlow before Zane scoops them up. Sevyn tries to give me a hug, but I put my arm out, so she runs into the heel of my hand with her forehead. Harlow snorts with laughter.

"You two are ridiculous." She shakes her head.

"Fuck you too then," Sevyn says to me before hugging Harlow and kissing her on the cheek. "Bye, babe. Call me when you're tired of this idiot."

"She won't." I wrap my arm around Harlow's neck, kissing her temple.

"I'll see you Thursday," Harlow says to Sevyn.

"Ha!" Sevyn says. "See, she's already planning to be tired of you." She flicks me off before following Zane into the house and out the front door.

Harlow smiles and sighs. "I love when they come over."

"Me too." I smile. "Sevyn knows something is up, though."

"Did you tell her?" Her eyes meet mine.

"Fuck no!" She tosses her head back with laughter. "To be honest, I like the fact only we know."

She stands on her tiptoes, her lips meeting mine. "Me too. And I'd like to keep it that way for as long as we can."

I wrap my arms around her waist, twirling her around as she laughs. It was on the tip of my tongue earlier when I talked to Sevyn, but there will come a time when we'll have to tell everyone else. It's not that I'm not excited to tell them. I would broadcast it publicly to the world if given the chance, but I want to soak it up with her first.

7
Sunshine

Acyn may call me Sunshine, but there are days I feel like a thunderstorm. Today is one of them. A photoshoot that was planned months ago was a disaster. Nothing went right. The clothing items needed for the shoot weren't delivered on time. When it finally arrived and the model dressed, she was being difficult and not listening to direction. Then before I could take more than a few pictures, she fainted because she hadn't eaten anything all day and had to be taken to the hospital. My client is expecting these photos tomorrow morning, and I am working with a handful of pictures when I had hoped to capture hundreds.

I know these were all things entirely out of my control, but I still feel responsible. I'm a recovering people pleaser and try to bend over backwards for people even if I know they will be understanding. Staring at my computer screen, I try my best to work with what little I have. I jump when a bag lands on my desk and I look up to see Acyn.

Pulling my earbuds out, I smile at him. "I didn't hear you come in."

"You didn't answer your phone. I figured you were in the zone and stopped to get some Chinese food. Thought I'd chill with you." He presses a kiss to my forehead.

I stretch in my seat. "I could use a break. Today was a day."

"What happened?"

"Where do I even begin?" I ask, shaking my head and reach for the bag of food.

"Do I need to punch someone?" He smirks.

I snort with laughter. "No, it's not that serious. It was one of those days where all the little things added up."

Acyn settles on the couch with his food. I pull the box containing sweet and sour chicken with white rice out of the bag. My stomach growls at the sight of it. I had to skip lunch which didn't help my annoyed mood when I'm hangry on top of it.

I take a bite and moan. "God, I fucking love you."

Acyn chuckles. "I'd hope so. Since we've been married for almost a month now."

"I know! Isn't it crazy how time flies?"

After we became friends, I told him he'd make some woman very happy one day. I didn't realize that woman would be me.

"So... another celebrity booked me." He grins.

I gasp. "What? Babe! That's amazing. Who is it?"

"Macklemore."

"Are you serious?" My food nearly slips from my hands. "He's Seattle royalty! This is major."

He smiles. "I know, so I was wondering if you'd be willing to take photos?"

"Seriously? You're asking me if I'd be willing to take photos of my husband tatting up a celebrity?"

"I know." He rubs the back of his neck like he always does when he's nervous. "But I still wanted to ask."

"I'm so fucking proud of you."

I've learned a lot from Acyn. Not just about love, but about running a successful business. He's the best at what he does, yet humble and always looking for ways to improve and keep moving forward.

"Thanks, Sunshine."

We eat, and I tell him about my stressful day. After getting some food in my stomach and Acyn's good news, my mood lightens considerably. I put the last bite into my mouth and glance back at my computer, dreading the work I have to finish. I'd rather be home snuggled up with him and Six-Two-Six.

"I think I'll take this home and finish it."

He throws the food boxes in the trash and sits on the couch again. "I don't mind waiting for you. We both know you're less likely to get work done at home."

I groan, knowing he's right. "It's not like I have a lot to finish up, anyway."

"Your call, Sunshine."

Either way, I have to finish editing these photos tonight to have them ready for my client tomorrow. I'm kicking myself for telling them I could do it despite the setback of the clothing not being on time.

"I'd rather be home." I've been at my studio since 6:00 a.m., and I'm over it.

"Alright, do you want me to grab anything?"

"Can you grab the bag over there?" I point to the table. "I'll get my laptop and then we can go."

He grabs the bag, cleaning up my organized chaos along the way. It's the little things he does that make me feel all warm and gushy. I love when he just stops by my studio to spend time with me. I hope that never changes as time goes by. We walk out to his car, hand in hand. Since we work within a few blocks of each other, we take one car unless our schedules don't sync up.

When we pull up to our house, I let out a sigh. A hot, relaxing bath is on my mind as we walk inside and Six-Two-Six meows at us for taking too long to get home.

"I'm taking a bath." I say, stripping off my clothes as I head for the bathroom.

"I'm going to feed Six-Two-Six before he calls animal protective services on us."

"It isn't even that late." I chuckle.

We're usually home by 6:00 most evenings, but we're an hour late. He's a spoiled cat who likes his routine. When I get into the bathroom, I decide to take a hot shower instead of a bath because the work I have waiting for me. Once the hot water hits my skin, I relax. Letting the steam swirl around me as I finally breathe after a long day.

After my shower, I put on one of Acyn's t-shirts and head out to the living room to join him and finish up work. I hear him speaking to someone as I draw closer. When I get to the living room, I see his mom sitting there.

"Hi Harlow," Gloria says.

I glance at Acyn, and the look on his face lets me know the bubble we've been in for the past month is about to pop.

"Hi..." I give her an awkward hug before sitting next to Acyn and covering my lap with a pillow. "I didn't know you were stopping by."

"Neither did I." She straightens in her seat. "But when I called the wedding venue today to schedule a final walk-through with Ava for decorations and seating... they informed me you canceled the venue weeks ago."

I shift in my seat because I suddenly feel like I'm in the principal's office. "Gloria, I can explain–"

"Mom..." Acyn says. "The venue canceled on us because they double booked our wedding. The next available date is six months away."

Gloria places her hand over her chest. "Oh, they didn't tell me that. Well, six months is workable. Gives me more time to plan the wedding."

"We're not waiting six months, Mom." Acyn says, holding my hand, and his eyes meet mine. "We didn't wait. We already got married."

"I'm sorry... what?" she asks, blinking rapidly.

"We already got married, Mom. Nearly a month ago... when we went to the Oregon coast."

A pregnant silence follows Acyn's admission as she stares between the two of us. He rubs his thumb along my hand in his to calm my nerves. I'm not sure how he's not freaking out right now. I chew on the thumbnail of my other hand while she stares at us in stunned silence.

"It's what we wanted," I say.

Ace

Harlow's palm is sweating in mine. My mom never drops by unannounced, and I knew when I saw her, she was here about the wedding. She's still staring at us as if we betrayed her. I'll never regret marrying Harlow or the way we did it. Not even my mom can make me feel bad about that. I'm not so sure about Harlow, though.

"I'm disappointed in you both," my mom says after an eternity of silence.

"Mom—"

"Excuse me?" Harlow asks in a dangerously low tone.

My eyes snap to hers because I've only heard her use that tone one other time, and it's when I fucked up before we got together. She rarely gets mad, but when she does, it's palatable, like a storm coming. Everything shifts.

"You two ran off without zero consideration of others."

"Zero consideration?" Harlow's eyes narrow as she lets go of my hand, clasping her hands together as she takes a deep breath.

I hold my breath as I wait for her to speak. Whatever she's about to say will be heard whether my mom likes it or not.

"Gloria," she holds her hands in a prayer position in front of her face, taking steadying breaths. "I've done nothing but consider others for our wedding. *Our own wedding.*" Her voice rises in volume. "It is our choice," she motions between me and her, "how we wanted this to go. I was exhausted from all the planning for a wedding that neither of us wanted. But we're the ones with zero consideration? Why? Because we don't want two hundred people at our wedding? Acyn and I don't even know two hundred people we'd want at the wedding. So yeah, Gloria, I'm tired of considering others because all I've wanted since your son proposed to me is to marry him. And we did just that. I refuse to allow you to make us feel bad about it."

"After all the time I spent planning." My mom shakes her head with tears in her eyes. "What am I going to tell everyone?"

I momentarily felt bad for my mom until I realized she listened to none of what Harlow said. She's somehow made our wedding about herself. This is the first time I've had to experience it firsthand. Harlow's been dealing with this for the past six months. Makes me wish I would've asked her more about the wedding plans. Maybe she wouldn't have felt so overwhelmed.

"Gloria..." Harlow takes a deep breath. "You keep saying *I*. It isn't your wedding. It's *ours*. Mine and Acyn's."

My mom ignores Harlow, turning her attention to me. "Acyn, is this how you feel?"

I grab Harlow's hand. "Yeah, Mom. I wanted to marry her the moment I proposed. But we wanted to share it with you guys... not everyone you could think of to invite."

"Clearly you didn't want to share it with us bad enough if you left everyone out."

She's hurt. I get that, but she's making this all about herself and it's working every one of my goddamn nerves.

Harlow rises from her seat. "This isn't about you, Gloria. I'm not sure what else I can say to make you understand that." She turns to me. "I have work to do. There's nothing more for me to say. I will not sit here to be reprimanded like a child for something I'll never regret."

She walks out of the living room, leaving me alone with my mom. Once I hear a door shut, I turn my attention back to her.

"Acyn, I've never seen this side of Harlow before. Are you sure this is what you want? With her?" she asks, pointing down the hallway.

I get up from my seat. "Don't do that."

"What?" She shrugs. "I think it's a valid question."

I rub my eyes with the heels of my hands. "I get that you're hurt and upset, but you're not going to ever disrespect my wife. She has shown you nothing but respect. If you're questioning what Harlow and I have... then maybe you don't need to be in our lives. Maybe you shouldn't have been helping her plan the wedding in the first place."

"Acyn–"

I hold up my hand. "I'm not Annalise, Nora, or Sevyn, Mom. The guilt trip may work with them, but it won't for me. And for you to question my love for Harlow because you're angry..." I shake my head. "I think you should go because there truly is nothing good for me to say right now."

She looks at me, waiting for me to change my mind. When I say nothing, she grabs her bag, rises from her seat, and walks toward the front door. I follow behind her. She turns to look at me, opening her mouth, but closes it again and leaves. I lock the door behind her and rest my head against it before going to talk to Harlow.

I slowly open the office door to find her wrapped in a blanket with her computer resting in her lap and tears falling down her face. She doesn't look at me as I walk in but stops what she's doing as I sit next to her. I take her laptop and set it on the coffee table. Then I pull her into my arms and bury my face in her curls.

"I'm sorry, Acyn... I just couldn't hold it in."

"Don't apologize, Sunshine." I wipe the tears from her cheeks. "It's pretty fucking hot when you get mad."

She cackles. "Stop it!"

"I'm serious! I didn't take you down on the couch for obvious reasons, but... I sure as hell wanted to."

She covers her face with her hands. "You're ridiculous."

I gently tug on her arm to pull her hand away from her face. "Are you okay, though?"

She lets out an exasperated sigh. "I hate disappointing people. Especially your mom, and I love her, but I'm glad we got married. I wouldn't have wanted it any other way."

I softly kiss her lips once, twice, and then I pull her flush against me, claiming her mouth. She straddles my lap, and my hands caress her thighs, hips, and to my delight she doesn't have any panties on.

"Goddamn, and you had no panties on this whole time?"

"I wasn't expecting company and was hoping for some stress release."

"Let me help you." I say, pressing my thumb against her clit.

She spreads her legs further apart as she pulls her t-shirt off. I take a moment to appreciate the beauty that is her before leaning forward and taking her nipple into my mouth. A soft moan spills from her lips. I place my hand at the back of her neck and pull her towards me as our lips meet again. She reaches down to undo my belt, pulling my pants and boxers down. Wrapping her hand around my length, she lines the head up with her entrance and sits on me. She takes a sharp inhale of breath as I thrust the rest of the way into her.

Leaning back, she places her hands on my knees as she slowly moves up and down my shaft. She watches me disappear inside her with each wind of her hips. Her breasts bounce in my face as she moans, picking up the tempo. I rake my hand up her thigh before rubbing my thumb against her clit.

Her hips buck, and she lets out a sensuous cry. Sweat breaks out across her skin as she rides me, keeping one hand on my knee and using the other to grasp the back of my neck. Her pussy tightens around my dick as she nears her climax.

"Ah, fuck yes. I needed you inside me," she moans.

I smack her ass before gripping it as she bounces on my dick, desperate for release. Her moans grow louder.

"Acyn!" She gasps as her orgasm shivers through her.

I grip her ass cheeks as she rides me into my release, toppling over the edge after her.

"Jesus fucking Christ," I rasp, holding onto her.

I rest my head on her chest and hear her heart beating wildly. We stay entwined, hugging each other for a while before she pulls away, kissing my forehead and then my lips. I look up at her, and she threads her fingers through my curls.

"Just so you know... I'd fight your mama over you."

We crack up, but we also know we'd go to war for each other. And that's love.

8
Ace

Neither of us have heard from my mom since she left our house a few nights ago. I thought maybe she would have told my sisters, but I've talked to and seen Sevyn since then, and she didn't say anything. Even when she hung out with Harlow, she didn't say anything to her either. I worried that my mom trying to guilt trip us would have an effect on Harlow, but she just walked into my shop with a smile on her face and two shitty cups of coffee in hand.

She kisses me as she hands me a cup. "Hey. Do you have time to talk for a minute?"

"I always have time for you and shitty coffee."

"Fuck you." She laughs.

"What did you wanna talk about, Sunshine?" I ask, sitting next to her on the bench in front of the window.

"I want to tell my dad we eloped."

"Okay, do you want to stop by his place after work?"

"Yes." She smiles. "And I hope it's a better reaction than your mom."

I shake my head. "I'm still not sure what to say about that. But I bet your dad will be happy."

Her watch chimes, and she glances at it. "I've gotta get back to the studio to set up for my next client."

"Alright." I stand and hold my hand out to her.

She takes it and looks up at me as she stands. "You're okay... right? After everything?"

I wrap my arms around her and press a kiss to her forehead. "I'm good, Sunshine. It's me and you. That's all that matters."

"You'd tell me if you weren't, right?"

"Sunshine..." I grab her face. "I'd tell you if I felt any other way, but I'm happy." I kiss her. "And I mean that. My mom will have to come to terms with the fact that we're married in her own time."

She smiles after a moment of searching my eyes. "I just wanted to check in and make sure you're good."

"It helps that my wife is fine as fuck." I grab a handful of her ass.

She tosses her head back and laughs. "Alright, husband. I better go before we give everyone a morning peep show."

I chuckle and kiss her neck. "I'll see you later."

My phone rings while I'm in the middle of a tattoo. After going to voicemail, it vibrates with a text. I check my phone when I'm done with my client.

Dad: Do you have time to meet up today?

I scratch my jaw, letting out a sigh. My dad and I have always been close. But I'm not sure I want a lecture from him.

Dad: Just to talk.

I look at the time and decide I could go for lunch right now.

Acyn: Sure, do you want to meet at Pike's Place?
Dad: My treat. See you there.

I chuckle, shaking my head as I grab my keys and head out to my car.

When I arrive, I see my dad waiting outside of Pike Place Chowder for me. He has on some khaki chino pants, a white button down, and some boat shoes. He has rich copper brown skin like me with graying curly hair, the same ember brown eyes as mine, but he wears glasses. My dad looks nowhere near his age. Even with his salt and pepper curls, we're often mistaken for brothers.

"How are you?" he asks with a smile before giving me a hug.

"Good. Hungry as hell."

He chuckles. "Let's eat."

I follow him inside. I order a bread bowl of smoked salmon chowder and my dad orders the New England chowder.

When we sit at the table, I ask, "How's your week been?" before digging into my bowl.

"Good." He shrugs. "I'm having mixed feelings about retiring early. Not sure what I'll do with myself once I do."

My dad has his own accounting firm. He's the reason I've done so well with my business, aside from having the discipline and drive. Everything I know, I've learned from him.

"What do you want to do?"

"I don't know." He shrugs. "That's the problem. I retire, then what?"

"You rest, Dad. Do whatever you want to do."

"The downtime will be nice. That's what makes it so appealing."

He put everything he had into his company, and it paid off in the long run. As any business owner knows, the first few years can be tough. When he opened his accounting firm, I was old enough to remember how stressed and exhausted he was. Regardless, he stuck with it and saw it through. Now, a little over twenty-five years later, he's built one of the top accounting firms in the state of Washington.

"How's Harlow?" he asks after a few beats of silence.

"She's doing good..." I take a sip of soda. "Mom told you what happened, didn't she?"

He nods, "She did."

"I don't need you being the peacekeeper, Dad. We—"

"I support you both. You and Harlow."

I lean forward, resting my forearms on the table. "Oh... I wasn't—well, I don't know what I was expecting, but it wasn't that."

He chuckles. "Acyn, all that matters is the love you two have for each other. I'm no love expert, but I've been married to your mom for thirty-two years. One thing I know for sure is that other people's opinions of what you and Harlow do or don't do–don't matter. If you worry about that, it will inevitably create problems in your relationship. What matters is that you confide in one another because, at the end of the day, it's about you two creating a life together. Remember, you're committed to each other–not everyone else."

I take a deep breath, considering his words. "Mom made it seem like we betrayed the whole family by getting married."

"Your mom lost sight of what mattered. I don't know if you knew this, but we eloped too. We didn't have the money for a wedding. Even a small one."

"No, I didn't. Wait," I narrow my eyes, "then why does she expect us to have this extravagant wedding? She should understand."

"She should, but you'll always want better for your children. Even if what you consider best doesn't align with what they want."

"We tried to explain to her... but all she kept talking about was the plans she made and what she would tell people. Even asked if I was sure about Harlow." My jaw ticks as I remember.

"She was out of line for that and knows that you two belong together. Your mom handled most of the planning for your sister's weddings too, and I think she was expecting the same thing with yours. But... you and Harlow are entirely different from them. I don't say that in a bad way." He smiles. "I mean that you two care about what matters and not so much for the glitz and glamour of a situation. I'm like that too, and your mom and I have butted heads in the past about it. Still do."

"She's not talking to you, is she?" I smirk.

"Nope. Absolutely not." He chuckles. "But this is something I will stand my ground on. I'm happy for you, Ace, and proud of the man you've become. I love you and Harlow so much.

I rub my eyes, trying not to cry. "Uh..." I clear my throat. "Thank you, Dad. I really needed to hear that."

"She'll come around," he says, finishing his bowl of chowder.

"I know." I let out a sigh. "Thanks for meeting up to talk with me and for lunch."

"Of course. Maybe we can do this more often now that I'll have time."

"Yeah, I'd love that."

Harlow stares out the car window, nervously chewing on her thumbnail as we drive to her dad's place. I knock it out of her mouth, and she snorts with laughter.

"What? I'm nervous. I can't help it. What if he's pissed or hurt? Maybe–"

"Can we see what happens when we get there?"

I have a hard time imagining Felix ever being upset or disappointed in Harlow. He's always been understanding and supportive of us. I could be wrong, though. Harlow is his only child, and I hope he doesn't see me running off with her to get married as disrespectful.

"I guess." She rests her head against the window, letting out a sigh.

I chuckle, taking her hand in mine. "It'll be fine, Sunshine."

We pull up to her dad's place twenty minutes later. As I park the car, she's taking deep breaths while motioning her hands up and down. I shake my head, cutting the engine, and let her do her thing.

"Are you ready... or do you want to meditate for a bit too?"

She smiles, rolling her eyes. "Yes..." She breathes deeply again, shaking out her arms. "I'm ready. I'm ready. I am ready!" She claps her hands together.

"Sunshine, we're telling your dad we got married. Not going into a heavyweight fight."

"Acyn!" She grips my arm. "What if he's mad?"

I shrug. "Then he's mad, but honestly, we'll never know if you keep amping yourself up like you're going into battle."

"Alright, alright." She unbuckles her seatbelt and gets out of the car.

"Thank fuck," I mutter under my breath.

I follow her into her dad's house. He gave both of us a key after he moved in so we could stop by whenever we wanted and care for it when he's traveling. He's sitting in his chair, watching a movie.

"Oh, you two are here already!" He glances at the clock. "I sat down to watch a bit of John Wick, and here I am on chapter two already."

"It's fine, Dad." Harlow kisses his cheek. "We can just order out. Make it easy."

He rises from his chair, giving us both a hug. "How have you been, Acyn?"

"Good. Are we still on for our rafting trip next weekend?"

"Wouldn't miss it." He pats me on the shoulder with a smile. "I think West is coming, too. Did you want to invite Rafael?"

"Yeah, I'll see what my dad says."

It will give him a chance to see that there's a lot to do instead of just sitting at home after he retires. Harlow's palm is sweating in mine. I nudge her shoulder, giving her a reassuring smile.

"Do you want me to tell him?" I ask once he's out of earshot.

"No." She shakes her head. "I can do it."

"Rip that shit off like a band-aid, Sunshine." I wink at her.

She takes a deep breath as she heads to the kitchen to talk to her dad. He's leaning against the counter, going through a stack of paper restaurant menus.

"What do you kids want? I could always cook something too."

"Dad..."

"Yeah, Kiddo." He asks, distractedly. "Maybe Pho?"

"I–" she glances at me "–well, we have to tell you something."

He looks up from the menus and glances between the two of us. "Okay... what is it?"

"Acyn and I got married... about a month ago," she says all in one breath.

I glance between them both. Her dad takes off his glasses and rubs his eyes.

"Really?" he asks.

"Yeah..." she says. "We just—we wanted to get married and the wedding... it was becoming more than what either of us wanted, so... we eloped." She smiles, but it's a mix of a cringe and smile as she waits for his reply.

He sets his glasses and the menus on the counter and walks towards us. I hold my breath, not sure what he's going to do, but he wraps both of us in a hug.

"I am—" his voice cracks "—I am happy for you two. I just—God, Harlow. Your mom would have—she would have been just as happy and proud of you as I am." He holds onto us for a minute longer before letting go. "So, tell me all about it. How did it go? Did you wear your mother's dress?"

Harlow blinks. "You're not mad?"

He wipes his eyes with a paper towel he grabbed off the counter. "What? No. Why would I be?"

"It's just that..." her voice trails off.

I didn't expect her to be speechless. "My mom wasn't too happy about us eloping," I say.

Felix's face falls. "Oh, I'm sorry to hear that. What about Rafael?"

"I met up with my dad today. He's happy for us." I smile.

"You did?" Harlow asks.

"Yeah, you were too riddled with anxiety for me to bring it up on our drive over here."

She lets out a sigh, visibly relaxing. "This went so much better than all the scenarios I had imagined in my head."

I chuckle, pressing a kiss to her temple. "I tried to tell you."

"This is cause for a celebration." Felix smiles. "Why don't we go out to eat instead? Then you two can tell me all about it. I'd imagine you have an abundance of pictures."

"Oh!" She claps her hands together, looking at me. "Babe, can you run out and get the package on the backseat?"

"Yeah," I say.

She and her dad continue talking while I head outside. I hadn't even noticed she put a package on the backseat earlier. When I grab it, I realize it's a picture frame wrapped in navy blue paper with a gold ribbon around it.

"Here." I hand it to her.

She hands it to her dad. "This is for you. I'm sorry you weren't there, but—"

"Harlow, you don't have to apologize. Acyn asked me for your hand in marriage a couple of months before he proposed. I didn't have to be there to know that you're with who you were always meant to be with."

"Months?" she asks, looking at me.

"He didn't tell you?"

"No, I never knew." She looks at me expectantly.

"I asked him shortly after he moved here. My intentions have always been to marry you, Sunshine. It just took me awhile to find a ring, and once I found it, it was near my birthday... and I wanted you for my birthday so—"

She kisses me, wrapping her arms around my neck, and slipping her tongue into my mouth. The urge to fuck her on this counter is strong, but I remember this is her dad's house. I reluctantly pull away, clearing my throat and glancing at her dad. But he's not there anymore.

"Uh... your dad."

"Right. Sorry."

"No, I mean he's not here."

"Oh..." she turns around and then heads out to the living room to find him.

I follow behind her, and he's sitting on the couch, staring at the picture as he cries. When I get closer, I see it's of us at our wedding. Harlow looks stunning. Her dress is flowing behind her in the wind. My arms are wrapped tightly around her waist as I hold her up, and we're both laughing with her hands resting on my shoulders. That day was perfect.

"Harlow, you look like your mother... and you're wearing her dress. This is beautiful."

She sits next to her dad, hugging him. "Thank you, Dad."

Felix looks at me. "Get over here, Acyn. You're a part of the family, too."

We all laugh as I sit with them on the couch, and he wraps his arm around me and squeezes my shoulders. He looks at the photo for a minute longer before letting out a sigh.

"Alright, enough crying. Are you two ready to eat? I want to hear about this wedding." He rises to his feet, placing the picture on the mantle above his fireplace.

A few hours later, we've eaten our fill of food, and Harlow's face is alight with happiness as she tells her dad every detail about our wedding. I needed this as much as she did because I wish my mom could've been happy for us.

9
Sunshine

Before heading home, I stop by Ava and West's house to pick up Mercy, their daughter. They have an event tonight, and I volunteered to watch her. Pulling up to their house makes me feel nostalgic. It was the first place I called home when I moved to Seattle, and it will always be special to me. Mercy's little face is peering through the window as I park, and she bounces with excitement when she sees me. I laugh and get out of the car. Ava opens the door as I walk up the steps with a smile on her face, holding Mercy in her arms.

"Harlow!" Mercy shouts. She has trouble pronouncing my name. It sounds more like Harls-Low, but she tries her best.

"My Mercy girl! How are you, sweet thing?" I ask as she launches herself into my arms.

"She's been waiting by the window since I told her you were coming to get her." Ava smiles, shutting the door behind me.

"Play, play, play." Mercy repeats as I follow Ava to the living room.

"Yes, we'll play. We've got to get your things first." I smile at her.

Ava grabs Mercy's diaper bag. "I think I have everything in here." She looks around the living room, seeing if she missed anything.

"Ava, we've got her. If she needs something, we'll get it, but she'll be fine. Don't stress."

"She's almost two, and I still feel like I don't know where my head is half the time."

I chuckle. "If it's any consolation, you're doing amazing."

She lets out a sigh, and her shoulders relax. "Thank you."

"Hey Harlow." West greets me, walking into the living room. "Thank you for watching Mercy." He kisses Mercy's cheek, and she giggles. "Cousin Harlow is here and nothing else matters, huh, babygirl?"

"Ready for the event tonight?" I ask him. West has been nominated for one of Seattle's prestigious business awards. Tonight, they find out if he won. Even if he doesn't, it's great exposure for his businesses, but awards are always nice.

"Born ready." He smiles. "Ava, you look stunning. Are you ready?"

"Thank you." She kisses West. "Almost. Just need to finish up my hair and a few details with my makeup. C'mon Harlow, we can catch up while I get ready."

I follow her to their room with Mercy in my arms. She won't let me put her down, and I'm okay with that. Ava and West's home makes you feel like you're stepping into a magazine. It's perfectly designed by Ava, but it has all the cozy vibes one would hope to have in a house.

She sits at her vanity, removing pins from her hair as she looks in the mirror. "So, tell me, how have you been?"

I sit on the chaise, and Mercy only gets down from my lap to play in Ava's makeup. "Um... good. I have something to tell you."

She whips around to face me. "Are you pregnant?"

"No." I laugh, shaking my head. "But Acyn and I eloped in Oregon a few weeks ago."

She gasps, covering her mouth with her hands. "Are you serious? Aw, that sounds so romantic! Was it romantic? The Oregon coast is so dreamy."

"Yes, to all your questions." I smile.

Ava gets up and wraps me in a hug. "I'm so happy for you." Her voice is shaky, and I can tell she has tears in her eyes. "You've grown into this amazing woman since you first moved here. I'm just so proud of you."

"Thanks Ava..." I blink back tears. "For all you and West have done for me."

"Of course." She pulls away, looking into my eyes. "We're always here, if you need anything at all." She touches my cheek, smiling at me warmly, before she sits back down at her vanity. "Who else knows? I'm assuming Felix."

I tuck my curls behind my ears. "Um... no one knew until after, but yes, my dad knows, and he's elated."

"Of course." She smiles, applying some blush to her cheeks.

"And..." I let out an exasperated sigh. "Gloria knows... she wasn't happy about the elopement. She's currently not talking to either Acyn or me."

She scoffs, rolling her eyes. "That's bullshit." Her eyes widen as she looks down at Mercy. I chuckle, but Mercy is too interested in her makeup box to care about what Ava is saying. "She should be happy for you both. This isn't a time for selfishness. What made you decide to elope?"

I tell Ava about the venue messing up the booking. "Acyn and I didn't want to wait. The wedding was becoming something bigger than what we wanted. You were there for the planning. It was a lot, right? Or am I wrong?"

"From what you wanted in the beginning and what it was turning into, yes, it was a lot. The venue refunded the money, right? If not, I can go down there and talk to them."

"Acyn went down the following day and got the money back."

"I love that man for you." She smiles at me in the mirror.

"Ava... what if I put a wedge in the relationship he has with his mom? Or the one she has... had... with me?"

"Uh uh, Harlow." She turns around, pointing her makeup brush at me. "You didn't. If anyone is putting a wedge in the relationship, it's her. Don't let how she feels overshadow this moment. Soak it up. Be happy. What you and Acyn do is you guy's business. You need permission from no one."

I take in her words, knowing she's right. "Thank you. I really needed to hear that."

She smiles, resuming touching up her makeup. "Be 100% honest with me. Was that venue what you truly wanted? Or were you going with it because Gloria raved about it?"

"Honestly, because Gloria raved about it." I shrug, looking down at my hands. "I'm a recovering people pleaser."

"I know, and that's okay. But when you feel you're doing something for the good of someone else, be sure to ask yourself if it's for the good of you, too."

Ava is the closest thing I have to a mother figure. I know I can talk to her about anything, and she'll be there for me without judgement. "I'll remember that."

"You are happy with the reception venue, right? If not, have no fear. I can work my magic, and we can find somewhere else."

"I love where we're having the reception. Sodo Park is gorgeous. We're lucky to even be having it there, thanks to you."

Sodo Park in downtown Seattle was at the top of my list for places to hold the reception. They offer everything for the event, from catering to décor if you need it. Since Ava is a well-known interior designer and event planner in Seattle, she secured the venue for us. I would be insane to change that. It's the one thing about the wedding I am excited about.

"Good." She messes with her hair a little more before sighing and saying, "I'm ready."

"You look gorgeous, Ava."

"Thank you." She smiles. "Alright Mercy, girl. Time to go."

Mercy looks at her makeup bag, at me, and then at Ava. I chuckle. "You can bring your makeup. We can give Acyn a makeover." She clutches her makeup bag to her chest and walks over to me. I pick her up. "Ready?" She gives me a toothy smile and nods her head. I turn to Ava. "Thank you for letting me vent and the reassurance."

"Always here." She slips on her heel before giving me a hug. "We'll meet up for brunch this week and go over the reception details. How does that sound?"

"Sounds perfect. Wave bye to mommy, Mercy." She waves. "We'll see you guys later tonight."

I'm breathing easier after talking to Ava. We don't need permission from anyone for what we do. It's unfortunate Gloria isn't as happy as we are, but I won't let that damper my happiness. I'm finally married to the man of my dreams. Nobody can tell me nothin'.

Our original wedding was supposed to be two months from today. We're sitting on our porch, listening to music while sharing a joint, as we comb over the guest list to trim it down. Even though we won't have the wedding, we still want to have a reception. It's been a little over a week since the fallout with his mom. After talking to his dad, mine, and Ava we've both been in better spirits. Her reaction didn't change our minds, but that doesn't mean it didn't hurt.

"From two hundred people to seventy-five. This is doable. There was no way in hell I was going to deal with two hundred people. In fact–" he grabs the list "–I think we can cut it down a little more."

"No, Ace!" I laugh, snatching it back from his hand. "If I leave it up to you, no one will be there but us."

"What's wrong with that?"

"Because..." I say, looking down at the guest list. "I still want to celebrate us with people we care about, you grump."

"I'll always be the cloud to your sunshine." He kisses my temple.

"I'm not sure why that sounds comforting and ominous at the same time."

He chuckles. "Comforting for you. Ominous for anyone who fucks with you. What are you gonna do this weekend while I'm gone?"

He's going on a whitewater rafting trip with both of our dads, Zane, and West.

"Oh, ya know, probably hire some male strippers, invite Sevyn over, and have a wild weekend. Since I'll be so fucking lonely." I smirk.

"Really?" He quirks an eyebrow.

"Uh huh, big, burly, oily, male strippers... all for me."

He gets up, rolling his shoulders before stretching his arms. "You want a show, Sunshine?"

"Oh my God, Acyn! No!" I look around because some of our neighbors are outside.

He changes the song on the speaker to Ginuwine's "Pony", turning it up causing some of our neighbors to look at our house. I'm laughing hysterically while also being mortified.

"Nah, you're gonna get a show."

"Acyn!" I whisper yell. "Stop! They're staring at us."

"Shit, they'll get a show, too."

I try to get up, but he straddles my lap, keeping me in place. I glance to the side to see Mrs. Murphy staring at us with her mouth open. I wave awkwardly as Acyn does a body roll. He thrusts his hips forward and the bulge in his gray sweatpants brushes against the side of my face. My eyes focus on his abs and dick that are now in front of me as my neighbors watch my husband give me a lap dance.

"Are you sure you weren't a stripper before this?" I ask through laughter.

"You said you wanted a stripper, so you're gonna get a fucking stripper."

He grabs the waist of his sweats to pull them off, and I grab his hands.

"Acyn, don't you fucking dare!"

He winks at me with his stupid, lopsided grin. Of course, he ignores me and pulls his damn sweats off. Mr. Murphy has now joined Mrs. Murphy on their lawn.

"Take it off, Acyn!" Mr. Murphy shouts, and then whistles.

Acyn gives him a nod and two-finger salute before he resumes his dancing.

"For fuck's sake!" I giggle, trying to sink down into my chair, but I can't because Acyn's straddling me again.

He's giving it his all with his body rolls and his hips that I know he can move so fucking well. Mrs. Brown steps out on her porch, wondering what all the commotion is. It's at this moment that I realize she isn't as blind as a bat as she stares at Acyn. This would be worse if he couldn't dance, but the man can fucking move. I'd stare too. I smack his ass as he turns around. If I had cash on me, I'd put it in his boxers.

"Alright, okay!" I cackle. "No male strippers! Just you!"

"That's what I fucking thought." He says cockily before flipping me over his shoulder in one fluid motion. "Thank you! I'll be performing same time next week." He shouts to our neighbors.

I can barely breathe from laughing so hard as he carries me inside.

I'm sitting cross-legged on Acyn's back as he does push-ups, scrolling through my phone. He leaves in a few hours for his weekend trip. We're sending out new invites today for the reception. Since it's so last minute, I think our guest list will be smaller than we expect. I know our closest friends will be there, but I'm not sure about extended family. His mom still hasn't talked to us.

"Babe..."

"Hm?" He grunts, pushing me up into the air.

"We have to tell Sevyn before we send out the new invites."

He does a few more push-ups before he lowers himself to the floor. I slide off his back, sitting next to him, and he rolls over to look at me.

"Yeah, you're right. I have to leave in a few hours. If you invite her over now, she should be here when I'm getting ready to walk out the door."

I snort with laughter. "You're not wrong. I'll text her now."

"Alright." He kisses my cheek. "I'm gonna take a shower and pack my shit."

A few hours later, Acyn is finishing up packing his things. In true Sevyn fashion, she shows up as Acyn is getting ready to load his bags in the car.

"Nice of you to show up." He smirks. "We have something we want to tell you."

She tosses her purse on the couch. "I knew it! What is it? Spill it!"

"If you'd stop talking, I would."

"Acyn..." I nudge his side. "Just tell her."

"Harlow and I got married when we went to the Oregon coast."

She gasps, covering her mouth. "I knew you two were up to something! That dress was too gorgeous just for engagement photos. Damn bro, you really said fuck everyone else. Does mom know?"

"She hasn't told you?" he asks.

"No. Why? What happened?"

"I've gotta go, but Harlow can fill you in."

I follow him outside and wait for him to put his bags in the car.

He turns to face me. "I'll see you when I get back. Don't party too hard with Sevyn."

I wrap my arms around him, hugging his middle. "Oh yeah, a real wild night of facemasks, food, and Netflix."

He grabs my chin, tipping my face towards his, and kisses me. "Love you, Sunshine. I'll call when I can. You know reception is shitty."

"Love you too." I kiss him again. "See you when you get back."

I head into the house once he's pulled out of the driveway. Sevyn has already poured us glasses of wine and has popcorn waiting in a bowl.

"Wasted no time." I laugh, plopping down next to her on the couch.

"Nope. Tell me what happened with mom. I need to know."

Letting out an exasperated sigh, I tell her everything. I decide to leave out Acyn talking to their dad because I felt that was personal for him.

"You know, when I got pregnant... she didn't talk to me for months." Sevyn admits.

"Months?" I ask incredulously.

She nods her head yes as she takes a sip of her wine. "She was upset because Zane and I hadn't been dating for long and we were young. Then we found out we were having twins. She thought my life was over. It was hard at first, but then I decided it didn't matter what she thought. I knew Zane loved me, and I wasn't going to allow her to steal our excitement. Nearly five years later and we have a beautiful life."

I hope it doesn't take Gloria months to come around. I'd like her to still be a part of things, just not managing them.

"It'll be alright, Harlow." She reassures me. "Give her time. She's gotten better now. It just takes her time to process things."

"Mmm... I guess I can understand that." I can't ignore the uneasy feeling I have in my stomach, despite her reassurance.

"Now, tell me every single detail about the wedding. Even the sex!"

"Sevyn!" I cackle. "I'm not telling you about our sex life. That's your brother!"

"I know all you two did was fuck after you said I do."

"Oh my God." I cover my face with my hands. "Why are you like this? You're Acyn in female form."

"That's why you love me so much." She smiles and scoots closer to me. "Now spill it!"

I tell Sevyn all the details of the wedding, minus the sexy ones, to her dismay. How she doesn't find that weird, I'll never know. But she helps me get the new invites ready and drop them off at the post office, so they hopefully reach people with enough time. After that, our night is as eventful as we hoped. Facemasks, drinks, food, laughter, and Netflix. The twins stayed with Zane's parents for the weekend so Sevyn could have some time to herself. Sevyn is like the sister I never had but hoped for. I always thank the universe that she walked into the yoga studio when she did, because that moment changed my life.

I slowly open my eyes to the morning's light and feel like I'm being assaulted. My whole body feels the two bottles of wine we drank last night. Sevyn has her leg draped over my body with her foot in my face. I don't even remember falling asleep on the couch last night. Glancing at the television, Netflix is asking if I'm still watching Queer Eye. I grab Sevyn's foot and move it off my chest to get up. Groggily stumbling into the kitchen, I grab a bottle of water from the fridge and lean against the counter as I gulp it down.

I hear my phone ringing somewhere in the house but don't remember where I had it last and follow the sound of it to the coffee table in the living room.

"Hello," I answer hoarsely.

"Damn, aren't you a sight to behold first thing in the morning?" Acyn asks as he appears on the screen.

I snort with laughter, rubbing my eyes. "I know I look like hell because I feel like it." Getting up from the couch, I head to the bathroom to find a Tylenol and make myself presentable even if I have no plans today. "How was your first night?"

"Good. West almost started a forest fire. Got a little too carried away with the lighter fluid."

I shake my head, laughing. "Leave it to West to do that."

Uncle West isn't necessarily clumsy, he's just overzealous. It makes for a fun time at his expense, though. I prop my phone up on the bathroom counter and continue talking to Acyn as I brush my teeth, wash my face, and pull my curls into a messy bun on the top of my head.

"What are you and Sevyn doing today?"

"I would like to say nothing, but we'll probably end up getting our nails done or something like that." When I return to the living room, she's still sleeping on the couch. "If she ever wakes up." I jump when I hear a knock on the door. It's too early for packages or visitors.

"Is that the male stripper?" Acyn asks as I head down the hallway to the front door.

"No, thanks to you. Our neighbors now whistle at me each time I go outside."

As I get closer to the door, I see an outline of someone in the glass and hope it isn't a Jehovah's witness.

He grins. "It was all worth it."

I peer through the glass and see Gloria. "Um... your mom's here. Can I call you back? Or wait, just call me when you're back from rafting if you have service."

"Are you sure you wanna answer that?"

"She knows I'm home, Acyn. Both mine and Sevyn's cars are parked in the driveway, and your dad's with you."

He lets out a sigh. "Alright, just–"

"I'll be fine." I smile at him. "Love you. Enjoy the trip. You'll know if we get into a knock down drag out fight."

He lets out a rumble of laughter. "You're all sunny and cute until you get pissed off. I'm not worried about you. I'm worried about her."

I roll my eyes with a smile tugging at my lips. "I've gotta answer the damn door. Bye. Love you."

"Love you too, Sunshine."

I hang up the phone, take a deep breath, and open the door.

"Gloria." I smile, despite my nervousness.

"Good morning, I hope I didn't wake you, but I was hoping we could talk."

"Of course." I step aside to let her in and close the door behind her. When we get to the living room, Sevyn is barely waking up.

She looks between me and Gloria. "Um... morning. I will... go get coffee or something to let you guys talk."

"Looks like you two had a fun night." Gloria says, surveying the bottles of wine and snack wrappers littering the coffee table.

"You know me, Mom." She kisses Gloria on the cheek. "I love a good time. I'll go get breakfast for us. Be back in a bit." Sevyn squeezes my hand as she walks past and gives me an encouraging smile.

"Do you want to sit outside?" I point to the backyard.

Acyn and I turned the deck into a small oasis. There is an abundance of plants, a couple of fountains, and plush seating.

"That sounds great."

We settle on the chairs outside. I shift in my seat, waiting for her to speak. A silence settles between us as she looks down at her hands before her eyes meet mine.

She takes a deep breath. "I want to apologize for the way things went the last time I was here. Even though it's tough for me to admit, I lost sight of what is truly important. That's the love you have for each other. I know you love my son just as much as I do... and so much more."

"We didn't—we didn't intend to cut anyone out, but the wedding... it just wasn't what we had envisioned for us."

"I know that now. Acyn has always been different, not just because he's the only boy, but because he's never cared for... the extra stuff. He likes the meat of things, not the garnish."

"Yeah." I nod my head with a smile. "That sums him up perfectly."

"The only time I've ever seen him care about the extra stuff is with his art and... you."

Tears sting my eyes. "Thank you, Gloria. That means a lot."

"I hope you can forgive me. I love you both so much."

I get up from my seat and hug her. "Of course."

I tried to not let her not talking to us get to me, but it did. Gloria is a mother figure to me and until we told her about the elopement, she had always been loving and inviting. Her reaction was a slap in the face. It stung, but I can also understand where she's coming from. I sit back down in my seat and smile at her.

"What do you two want to do?" she asks, wiping tears from her cheeks.

"We're still planning for the reception, but we cut the guest list down. Did you want to look at it?"

"No, no." She holds her hands up. "I'm simply here to support what you two want."

"Okay." I nod. "Would you like to see the photos from the wedding?" I ask.

"I'd love to." She smiles.

I disappear into the house and grab an album I made for her and Rafael.

"Here." I hand it to her as I sit down. "This is for you to keep."

She places her hand over her heart, looking down at the photo on the cover. It's the same one I gave to my dad.

"You can tell me what photos you'd like framed, and I'll do it for you."

"All of them." She replies.

I toss my head back with laughter. "I can do that too."

She grabs my hand and squeezes it. "I couldn't have asked for a better daughter-in-law."

IO

Ace

I was relieved to hear that my mom apologized to Harlow. She invited us over for a family dinner tonight. I just got back from the whitewater rafting trip. I'm exhausted, but I'm looking forward to getting together with everyone. My mom also invited Felix, West, and Ava.

"Sunshine, are you almost ready?" I ask as I watch her apply lipstick in the mirror. "You talk about Sevyn, but..."

"First of all, we could be late, and we'll still arrive before them." She puts the cap back on her lipstick. "Serious question..." she says distractedly, as she looks at herself in the mirror.

"Yeah?"

"Do my titties look bigger?" She turns to face me and makes them bounce.

She's wearing a top that hugs them perfectly. It's hard to tell if it's the top, her making them bounce, if they really are bigger, or all of the above.

"I–this is a serious question? I mean, you're making them bounce in my face. How am I supposed to take this seriously?"

"Acyn, look at them," she says, squeezing them together with her hands.

"Oh, I am. And if you keep doing that, we'll never leave."

"Do they look bigger?" she says, making them bounce again.

I raise an eyebrow. "Do you want me to fuck you?"

She cracks up. "That's always a yes, but I really want to know if they look bigger, dammit. Turn your dick off your two seconds and focus."

"Turn my dick off? With you?" She gives me a look, and I clear my throat. "They look exactly like the titties I know and love."

"Huh..." she says while looking down at them. "I don't know. Maybe it's the top or this bra. Who knows, but I feel like they're bigger."

"If you want to take your top off so I could get a better look, I'd be happy to–"

"Nice try!" She laughs. "Let's go."

"Late for lipstick, but not for sex. Bullshit," I mutter as I follow her.

Harlow's sitting on the ground with Mercy in her lap. Emery is doing her hair, and Eli is telling her about his superhero action figures. Harlow isn't a fan of superheroes, but she's acting like they are the best thing in the world for Eli. The kids are always calm with her, but with me they act like I'm a human jungle gym. I have to admit, it's fun to toss them around and be a big kid.

Since Harlow's preoccupied and everyone else is in conversation, I step outside to watch the rainfall. It's nice to be hanging out with my family again. I complain about it, but it's something I enjoy. I hear the sliding glass door and turn to see my mom.

She loops her arm through mine. "You've always loved the rain. Even when you were a baby."

I smile at her. "It's calming."

"Acyn... I'm sorry for the things I said to you. And that I couldn't be happy for you in the moment."

I watch the rain, letting silence fall between us before I respond. "I've always been able to talk to you and dad about anything. For me to tell you about one of the most important moments of my life and then you question the love I have for the only woman I'll ever love... it didn't sit well with me. It still doesn't. Do you honestly question what we have?"

"You're my only son and–"

"That's no excuse, Mom. Whether I'm your only or fifth son, what you said... hurt. I never brought any women around you guys before Harlow because they didn't matter. But she... she's my heart. I know I may sound harsh right now, but I want you to know I won't tolerate you, or anyone else, ever questioning what we have."

She pats my arm and takes a few breaths before speaking. "I'm sorry I hurt you. I loved Harlow from the moment you brought her to that first dinner we had. She loves you as fiercely as you love her. I support you both, and I promise I won't plan anything else... unless asked."

I chuckle, feeling the tension I didn't know I had leave my body. "I love you, Mom."

"Love you, too." She says, resting her head against my arm as we watch the rain.

It's the day before we leave for our bachelor and bachelorette parties. Initially, we were going to have separate trips. But since Harlow's best friends, Quinn and Marisa, are planning the bachelorette party, Quinn suggested a joint trip to Las Vegas. We'll do some things together, but still have our separate parties and itineraries. I've been looking forward to this since Kyrell first told me he was going to throw it. Not because I want to get into fuckery, but because he knows how to have a good time. My phone chimes with a text, and Harlow tosses it in my direction from where she's sitting amongst our bags as she packs.

Kyrell: Are you ready to fucking party?

I laugh at his text, and Harlow narrows her eyes in my direction. She still isn't sure about the bachelor party, even though we'll be doing some stuff together. We're only going to be there for the weekend. We arrive early Friday afternoon. Saturday night is when we'll have our separate parties. Sunday is to recover from whatever happens Saturday, and then Monday morning we head back home.

Acyn: Hell yeah.

"You're cute when you're jealous, you know that?" I ask her.

"I'm not jealous. Why would I be jealous of a stripper who's paid to dance on you?"

"And the claws are out." I laugh. "Aren't you going to a strip show, anyway?"

"I am." She smiles smugly.

"Why are you jealous, then?"

"For the second time, I'm not jealous. I know you value your life too much to ever play with me. I also know you wouldn't do anything like that."

I sit down next to her on the floor and pull her into my arms. "Exactly, I never would." I kiss her. "But I'm gonna enjoy this fucking party."

"And I'll enjoy mine." She simpers.

"That sounds like a threat."

"It isn't." She shrugs. "I'm just looking forward to letting loose with the girls. It also means we're closer to getting to spend two entire weeks together on our honeymoon." She kisses me before sitting up again to finish packing her things.

We planned the honeymoon before we even thought about planning the wedding. Having time alone together after all the craziness was important for us. Since we both run our own businesses, we have to take into consideration the fact that we can't simply request time off. While we have people in place to manage things while we're gone, we still want to make sure everything is running smoothly so we can truly enjoy our time away together.

"We're almost there, Sunshine." I smile at her.

Our reception is next weekend, then we leave for our honeymoon. We'll be spending two weeks on an island called Seychelles that's off the east coast of Africa in the Indian ocean. I had never heard of it until she showed me pictures and I couldn't believe it existed. I don't give a damn where we go as long as I spend most of the honeymoon buried inside her.

Sunshine

Being met by neon "Welcome to Las Vegas" lights as we step off the plane amps up my excitement for the weekend with my favorite people. We all tried to get flights as close to each other's arrival times as possible. Ace and I flew in with Sevyn and Zane. Kyrell and Quinn's flight should arrive in fifteen minutes. Marisa, Greyson, and Asher will meet us at the hotel in an hour.

Sevyn throws her arms over my shoulders and squeals. "Girl, this is gonna be a fun weekend."

I grin at her. "I know."

To be honest, I thought a Vegas bachelorette was cliché initially, but now that we're here, I know we won't run out of things to do. Acyn and Zane grab our luggage. I anxiously scan the crowd of people, trying to catch a glimpse of my two best friends.

"What time are they supposed to get here?" Acyn asks.

"Any–oh, there they are!" I hold on to his arm as I bounce up and down while waving at them. "Oh my God! Look at Quinn's baby bump."

I throw myself at Kyrell when they get closer, wrapping him in a hug. He picks me up off the ground, twirling me around.

"Missed you too, Harls," he says.

Once he sets me down, I squeeze Quinn in a tight hug. "You look fucking amazing, babe! You're glowing!"

"Thank you." She smiles. "I'm just happy to not be sick anymore."

Acyn gives Kyrell a hug. "Thanks again for setting this up for everyone."

"Don't mention it. Anything for you and Harls." Kyrell smiles at him before turning his attention to Zane. "Why weren't you at the tux fitting, bro?"

Zane hugs Kyrell. "Not all of us are billionaire playboys." He jokes. "I'm a mere mortal who has to work."

"Nah, but you could be. Are you still down for a meeting with Titan Tech? They could really use someone with your brilliance."

Titan Tech was Kyrell's dad's company. He inherited it, and billions of dollars, after his dad passed away. Elias, his dad, gave him the option to keep the company or sell it. He chose to sell it because he didn't want to try and fill his dad's shoes and he wants to create his own legacy. Even though Kyrell isn't directly involved with Titan Tech, he still has the connections. Zane is a software developer and Kyrell has been encouraging him to consider working for Titan Tech.

"Hell yeah, I am," Zane says. "We'll talk more about it later, though. I'm here to let loose."

"And this is why I married you." Sevyn kisses his cheek.

Acyn chuckles. "Shall we head to the hotel?"

"Yeah, let's do this shit." Kyrell smiles.

The guys carry our luggage out to the car while Sevyn, Quinn, and I walk arm in arm behind them.

"I'm so excited! Once Marisa's here, we'll kick this weekend off with a lingerie party." Quinn smiles.

"A lingerie party?" I whip my head to look at her. "What is that?" In my head, I'm thinking of us running around in lingerie.

"We all got something to make your honeymoon a little spicier." Quinn winks at me.

"Why do I feel like your horny ass is behind this, Sevyn?" I laugh.

"Pinterest in the middle of a sleepless night always provides one with great ideas." Sevyn flips her hair over her shoulder.

"Greyson's fiancé didn't want to come?" Quinn asks once we reach the suburban awaiting us.

"Selene wanted to come, but she couldn't get the time off work."

"Oh, that sucks. She's really nice. I'll send her all the swag," Quinn says.

"She'd love that," I say.

The driver smiles as he opens the Suburban door for us. Me and the girls pile into the back row of seats and continue our conversation about our plans. Acyn, Zane, and Kyrell are talking about hitting up the casinos tonight.

I'm only half listening as I try to take in all the glitz and glamour of the Vegas strip. It's unlike anything else, and I can't wait to see all the neon signs glow at night. There's something to do every place my eyes look. And from what Quinn told me about the hotel we're staying in, there are an abundance of things to do there as well. One thing is for sure—Vegas is for fun.

"I thought we could go for drinks first," Quinn says.

I tear my gaze from the window, glancing at her belly, and snort with laughter. "Quinn, we can skip drinks, since it won't be enjoyable for you."

"No." She holds up her hand. "I'm not killing the vibe with my pregnant ass. I'll just get something virgin and an appetizer. No big deal."

"I'll have some virgin drinks with you." I smile at her.

I'm not really a drinker, anyway. I don't mind a good wine or mixed drink, but it's not what makes or breaks an experience for me. I'd rather have a joint or an edible. At least they don't make me feel like shit afterward.

"I support both of your decisions, but I am going to be drinking like a fish." Sevyn chimes in.

I toss my head back with laughter. "And we support that decision!"

"Don't worry, Zane will take care of me, if anything. Won't you babe?" She pats him on the shoulder.

"I love you, Sev." He turns to face her. "But it's every person for themselves this weekend." We all burst out laughing while Sevyn stares at Zane with her mouth open.

"You're so loud when you're drunk. It's not like he'll be able to ignore you even if he wanted to." Acyn smirks.

"Haha... ha." Sevyn narrows her eyes at them. "Fuck you both. I'm not loud am I, Harlow?"

"Huh?" I ask, pretending not to hear her.

Her mouth hangs open. "You're agreeing with them?"

"I–oh, look!" I point at the hotel. "We're here!"

The hotel is sleek and modern. As we get out of the car, my phone vibrates with a text.

Marisa: I'm here. Getting my bags.

Harlow: We just arrived at the hotel. Can't wait to see you!

I turn to Quinn as we walk into the lobby. "Marisa is grabbing her bags, and she'll be on her way."

"Perfect." She smiles.

The hotel lobby is all black, with immense columns that have LED screens that are playing clips of abstract art on a loop. I reach in my bag for my camera as I look around in awe.

"That didn't take long." Acyn chuckles beside me.

"I know, I was trying to not take a billion pictures... but I have to."

He wraps his arm around my neck and kisses my temple. "Take a billion pictures, Sunshine."

Acyn gets it. Photography is second nature to me. People ask how I enjoy the moment if I'm always busy taking pictures. Truth is, I am enjoying the moment–savoring it–with each photo my camera captures. I look for the little things that no one else notices but will want to remember. Through my lens, I see Quinn smiling at Kyrell as he palms her belly and talks to their baby. Zane stands behind Sevyn with his arms wrapped around her shoulders and a look of contentedness on their faces. And when I focus my lens on Acyn, all I see is the love and admiration he has for me. These are the moments I capture. I get to remember them forever.

Kyrell finishes up at the reception desk and turns to us, handing me a key. "I got you and Acyn a suite so you two can bang at your leisure." He smirks.

"You're so annoying, but thank you." I laugh.

Chuckling, Acyn shrugs. "At least you know what it is."

"The rest of us will stay in two separate suites." Kyrell says. "One for the ladies and one for the gents, but we're all on the same floor to make it easier to link up."

"We're doing our own thing tonight, right?" I ask.

"Harls, you know I never have a plan. I just go with what feels right." Kyrell winks.

"Yes, we're doing our own thing." Quinn chimes in. The calm to Kyrell's chaos. "We'll meet up for breakfast and some shows, but the night is our own. I figured we could get ready, have the lingerie party, and then go get drinks."

"Lingerie party?" all three men ask in unison.

We stare back at them. "You wouldn't get it." I smile at Acyn and continue talking to the girls. "Okay, I guess we'll all get situated. What time should we plan to meet up?"

Quinn glances at her watch. "Meet us in our suite in an hour for the party, and then we can go for drinks from there."

"Perfect."

"They already took your bags up to the room. I guess we'll meet in an hour, too," Kyrell says to Acyn.

We all pile into the elevator, and I send Marisa a text with the room number.

Marisa: Okay, Grey and Ash are with me too.
Harlow: See you in a bit!

We go our separate ways once we get to our floor. Acyn and I enter our suite, which is more like an apartment. Light is spilling into the room from the floor to ceiling windows. The walls are decorated with vibrant art. It's spacious, with a living and dining room that has a wet bar. It's nearly as big as the guest house I stayed in when I first moved to Seattle. I open one of the sliding doors that leads out to the wrap around terrace. The view is gorgeous.

"This place is unbelievable." Acyn wraps his arms around my waist. "I can't wait to see all the lights at night from up here."

"Are you happy we chose Vegas now?"

"Yes!" I turn around and kiss him. "Very happy."

My phone vibrates in my back pocket. I pull it out and look at the two texts.

Marisa: Hurry up and get ready!
Quinn: Don't forget we're meeting in an hour.

They know me too well. "The girls will have my head if I'm not knocking on their door in approximately one hour." I kiss him again. "I have to get ready."

"You know…" he kisses my neck. "We are in the desert. May as well conserve water and shower together."

"The exhibitionist turned environmentalist. I gladly support both of your causes."

He picks me up, causing me to shriek with laughter as I wrap my legs around his middle.

"I could fuck you on the balcony too, but I take it you want to be on time?" He carries me into the bathroom.

"I feel you're the higher priority right now." I pull my shirt overhead, tossing it on the bathroom floor.

He unsnaps my bra and trails kisses across my breasts before setting me down so I can take off my jeans. My lips meet his as he steps out of his own. He picks me up again before stepping into the shower and turning on the water without his lips leaving mine. Once steam billows around us, he presses me up against the glass shower door. I reach down between us, grabbing his length, and guide him inside me. My breath hitches as he buries himself. He presses one hand against the shower door and his other hand grips my ass as I keep my legs and arms tightly wrapped around him. A moan spills from my lips as he sucks on one nipple before taking the other into his mouth as he thrusts into me.

He trails kisses up my neck before meeting my lips again. "Turn around for me," he mumbles against my lips.

I untangle myself from him, turning around, and press my palms against the shower wall. Slightly bending forward, he grips my hip and pushes into my wetness. As he thrusts into me, I let out a moan that reverberates off the shower walls. He grips my hair, pulling me back flush against his chest, and his other hand plays with my clit. I spread my legs further apart and feel my climax building. The tingle starts in my toes as my body grows hot as he thrusts into me. He kisses my neck before gently grazing my skin with his teeth.

My body never knows what to do when Acyn touches me. I go into overdrive and short circuit at the same time. It's pleasure overload as he massages my center, grips my hair, kisses my neck, and fucks me at the same damn time. I quickly dissolve into pleasure as my orgasm shudders through me. I moan loudly while calling out his name. Acyn pounds into me as he chases his release.

He finds it moments later as his body tenses and quakes as he spills into me. I rest my head against the shower wall, trying to catch my breath. Acyn slowly pulls out of me and turns me around to face him. He kisses me softly.

"I'm addicted to the feel of you."

"What gave it away?" I wrap my arms around his neck. "The fact we're married or that we can't keep our hands off of each other?"

"Both." He chuckles, giving me another kiss before stepping underneath the rain shower faucet above our heads.

I watch the water soak his curls, making them longer, so they hang a little past his brows. My eyes follow the water as it flows over his closed eyes, soft lips, abs, and—

"Sunshine, if you don't get ready, you're gonna be late." His eyes are on me again with a smirk on his lips.

"Why did you interrupt my ogling?" I continue lathering my body with soap.

"Ogle away, but I know your friends and they'll kidnap you if they have to."

A little while later, I'm putting on my earrings as I look at myself in the mirror. I love the way my gold sequined mini skirt catches the light whenever I move. It makes my deep golden brown skin glow. I paired it with a white blouse that plunges low and loosely criss crosses in the front. Placing my hand on the wall, I steady myself as I slide on my ankle strap Christian Louboutin heels. I straighten up, fixing my curls as I turn side to side in the mirror.

"Sunshine, have you seen–" He stops in his tracks, and his eyes rake over my body. "You look incredible."

"Thank you." I smile. "You do too."

Acyn is wearing a black satin button up that has a muted shine with the top buttons undone, and it's tucked into his slim fitting black pants. It's clear he rarely misses a morning run or the gym. He's paired it with a black Fendi belt and loafers that have gold accents.

"Did you need something?"

"Oh." He tears his eyes away from my legs. "Did you pack my jewelry?"

"Yep, it's in my suitcase." His eyes are already back on my legs again. I bend forward, pretending to fix the strap around my ankle, and then slowly trail my hand up my leg.

"Those legs of yours. I look forward to them being draped over my shoulders with those heels by my ears later."

"That was a detailed description." I smirk. "I'll be sure to leave them on for you. For now, I have to meet the girls before they come for me."

He chuckles. "Alright."

"Love you. I'll see you when I see you because only heaven knows what you guys will get into with Kyrell. Enjoy your night."

"Have fun with the girls. Love you too, Sunshine." He kisses me again before I walk out the door.

II
Sunshine

Marisa wraps me in a neck breaking hug as soon as I step into their suite. I wrap my arms around her as I try to laugh.

"You're crushing my windpipe," I choke out.

"Sorry, sorry!" She loosens her arms from around my neck but doesn't let go. "I just missed you."

"Missed you too, babe."

"Is she trying to murder you, too?" Quinn asks as she enters the room.

"Yes." I snort with laughter. "Tell Acyn I love him."

Marisa finally releases me. "You two are so fucking dramatic." She rolls her eyes.

I rub my neck. "I feel our reaction is warranted."

Marisa looks different. Her curly black hair, that was once down to her waist, is now shoulder length.

"Your hair looks amazing! When did you cut it? I only saw you a week ago and you now look like a brand new woman."

We religiously video chat every weekend. With us all living in different places, it's the only way we can keep up with each other.

"I said the same thing." Quinn laughs.

Marisa fluffs up her curls. "Do you really think it looks good?"

She's had waist length hair since we met three years ago. Marisa is gorgeous with her deep brown skin, large hazel eyes, full lips, and toned curvy body from all the yoga she does. She could have the worst haircut and would still be beautiful.

"Yes! Do you not like it?"

"It's just taking some getting used to. It was a rash decision." Her eyes meet the floor.

"Did something happen?" I gently touch her arm.

Sevyn enters the room with a mixed drink in hand. She runs her fingers through Marisa's hair. "You're crazy to think it doesn't look good."

Quinn echoes my question. "Did something happen?"

Marisa smiles. "I'll tell you guys another time." She waves her hand. "We're here to celebrate and have fun. What are we doing first?"

I study her for a moment, wondering what happened that she's not telling us. She keeps smiling at me, and I decide to let it go. She'll talk about it when and if she wants to.

"The lingerie party!" Quinn says, clapping her hands together with a smile.

I look around their suite for the first time to realize it's decorated. There's a wall for taking pictures covered in lush greenery and sunflowers with gold letters hanging that say, "Miss to Mrs". It's surrounded by gold and white balloons. As I slowly turn around the room, I realize there are actually balloons and streamers everywhere I look. There's a table covered in beautifully wrapped presents and a table with various drinks, a charcuterie board, and a small gold platter with edibles.

"This is amazing, you guys. I love it." I beam at them.

"To be fair, Quinn did all the planning." Marisa says. "And all the decorating. We just gave a little input here and there."

"Oh, please!" Quinn waves her hand. "It was a group effort."

"Thank you." I smile at Quinn. She's the planner out of the four of us and clearly has an eye for design.

"Are we going to get this party started or what?" Sevyn asks. "I'm trying to get as many drinks into my system as possible."

"That's the spirit!" Marisa gives her a high-five.

"And this is why I'm not drinking. I can't leave Quinn to take care of all of us." I say.

"You're not drinking at your own bachelorette party?" Marisa gives me an incredulous look.

"Do y'all not remember the engagement party? The bad karaoke and then slipping off the stage. Acyn literally had to carry me out to the car, and I puked all over the seats—" They all laugh hysterically at the memory. "–And him. It was a fucking mess." I laugh. "Drinking is fun until you're puking everywhere. I'm fine with a couple of cute mixed drinks and an edible."

"Oh my God!" Sevyn wheezes. "I'm surprised you even remember that."

"I didn't. Kyrell showed me the video. I was so fucking embarrassed. Never again." I cover my face.

"It was your engagement party! You had every right to have a good time!" Marisa says through laughter.

"I'd rather not talk about this. Can we start the party?" I ask, desperate to change the subject.

"Okay, first up! We have something specially made for us by Sevyn." Quinn says, handing me a bag.

It's yellow with gold tissue paper sticking out of the top. Pulling out the paper, I reach into the bag and pull out a soft, white satin robe. When I unfold it, I read 'Mrs. DeConto' embroidered in black cursive on the back.

"Oh my God!" I squeal. "Sev, this is amazing." I get up and hug her. "Thank you."

"You're welcome." She hugs me back. "I wanted to do something different, so I thought why not Mrs. DeConto instead of the basic ass 'bride' on the back?"

"I love it so much!" I exclaim, hugging it to my body.

"She made some for us too, with our names on the back." Marisa grabs a bag off the table and pulls hers out.

"Babes... you know this means we have to take a picture, right?"

They laugh, already knowing what it is, as they pull out their robes and slip them on. We take countless pictures of us in front of the photo backdrop. Once I'm satisfied with the pictures, I take an edible, and they pass me the gifts on the table.

"There are some from everyone, including Gloria and Ava." Quinn says.

My eyes widen. "What? You told them to get me lingerie?"

Sevyn cackles. "You act like they haven't had sex before, Harlow."

"I know... but it's awkward."

Marisa sucks her teeth. "Girl, please! Free shit? Open it."

She has a point. Lingerie isn't cheap. For the next thirty minutes, I tear through gift after gift filled with the most beautifully designed, intricate lingerie I've ever seen in my life. Gloria gave me a gorgeous red silk slip dress with scalloped lace and foiled embroidery. Ava gave me a violet silk teddy that has ruffles around the thighs. I also received gifts from my assistant, Priscilla, and my former boss, Celeste. Aside from lingerie, each of the girls gave me a toy as well. Sevyn got me a vibrator, Marisa some divine smelling massage oils and black leather cuffs with a buckle closure, and Quinn gave me THC and CBD infused lube with a pretty rose quartz dildo. I'm looking forward to wearing and using all of this with Acyn.

"I'm low-key jealous Acyn gets to see you in all of this and not us," Marisa says.

"I know!" Sevyn whines. "I was trying to get her to tell me the dirty details of the post-wedding sex, but she was being a prude."

I cackle. "Sevyn! He's your brother, for fuck's sake!"

"It's not a secret, though. From the way you've stayed glowing since getting with him, we know the dick is sending you to other dimensions." Quinn side eyes me with a smirk.

I look at her belly. "You're one to talk."

"The dick was so good Quinn got knocked up." Sevyn cackles. "Been there. Done that. Have the kids to fucking prove it!"

"I'm going to tell our kid a beautiful love story that is worthy of being a book, okay?" Quinn says. "Not that Daddy was putting it down and Mommy couldn't get enough." We fall into a fit of laughter.

"Okay, okay!" Marisa says once she catches her breath. She grabs the bottle of tequila off the table and three shot glasses. "Do at least one shot with us."

"Yeah, you know your limits after the engagement party. A few couldn't hurt." Sevyn encourages me.

"Harls, this is your bachelorette party. Enjoy yourself." Quinn nudges my arm.

"I never said no to drinks. I said no to getting blitzed." I hold my hand out for a shot glass.

"I'd like to make a toast to Harlow choosing the same dick for the rest of her life." Marisa raises her glass into the air.

I snort with laughter. "I will gladly get on all fours, face down, ass up, for the rest of my life for Acyn!"

Quinn has her phone out recording and laughing while the three of us throw the shots back.

"One more," I say, and Marisa gladly pours us another round. I toss that one back too. "Okay, third times a charm, right?" I wipe my mouth with the back of my hand.

"Aye, that a girl!" Sevyn says, pouring herself a fourth shot.

"I need food in my system before these drinks and edible go straight to my head."

Quinn glances down at her watch. "Let's go get some food. The other two can get drinks and we can eat."

"I need food too. And more drinks." Sevyn smiles.

We stumble out into the hallway, talking and laughing. I met Quinn and Marisa when I didn't know who I was and met Sevyn when I was trying to find myself. Since it was only my dad and me, female support was something I was lacking and didn't really know. But now I have a group of amazing and endlessly supportive women in my life. I'd be lost without them.

The next morning, Acyn and I are the last to join everyone for breakfast. It's apparent it was our first night in Vegas because everyone but Quinn looks severely hungover. Kyrell is a seasoned partier and is guzzling water with a bottle of Tylenol next to him. Zane has his arm wrapped around Sevyn, who is resting her head on his shoulder with her eyes closed, as he drinks his coffee. Marisa has shades on with an oversized sunhat. She looks regal for being hungover. Asher is having a mixed drink with his breakfast and Greyson looks like he's still half asleep.

We take our seats next to Quinn and Kyrell. I lean against Acyn and let out a yawn, pulling my sunglasses down over my eyes.

"You good, Sunshine?" he asks, smirking at me.

"It'd be great if we'd stop moving."

He chuckles. "What happened to no drinks?"

"I wish I knew," I groan.

Last night I lost track of my drinks. We had an amazing time, eating, walking the strip, going into Casinos, and we ended the night dancing. Quinn texted Kyrell to let him know where we were, and the guys met up with us. When I looked at my camera reel, I had to laugh because the pictures progressively got blurrier. I wasn't engagement party shitfaced, but I was definitely flirting with that line again.

"Here. Eat something." He holds a strawberry up to my face from one of the many breakfast platters on the table. I open my mouth for him to feed me.

Food has no appeal right now, but I know I need it because it'll help me feel better.

"God, I love the way he cares for you," Marisa says with her chin resting in her hand as she looks at us.

I kiss Acyn. "You take the best care of me."

"Of course, I do. Cause I love you." He feeds me another bite of food.

"You're still single Marisa?" Asher asks from the other end of the table.

"Don't remind me." She sighs, leaning back into her seat.

"Being single isn't that bad," he says, taking a bite of pancake.

"Eh... it is when all your friends are in relationships. I'm in no rush, but I also want a man to dote on me."

"Preach, babygirl! Preach!" Sevyn says, waving her napkin in the air.

"If you're down, I'm down Marisa. The last two standing. May as well give it a shot." He leans forward, resting his forearms on the table.

"Thanks, Ash." She flips her hair over her shoulder. "But I don't need nor want a pity fuck."

We all laugh, even Asher. I think he may actually like her for real, though. They always pair up whenever we get together, but nothing has happened between them other than banter and flirting.

"You know where to find me if you ever change your mind." He winks.

Marisa stares at him a moment, considering his words, before turning her attention back to me.

"Ready for round two?" she asks.

I raise up my hands. "Hell no. Fuck that. You and Sevyn can keep it. I'll be joining Quinn on the sidelines."

"Had enough fun already, Harls?" Quinn asks, chuckling beside me.

"No, not enough fun. Enough drinking." I adjust my sunglasses, resting my head against Acyn's shoulder again. He hands me a glass of water that I drink in a few gulps. I'm slowly feeling better. "What's on the agenda for today?"

"Zip lining," Kyrell says.

"Are you serious?" I sit up and look at him with a smile on my face.

"Yep. We're supposed to be there at 1:00 this afternoon if everyone can get their asses in gear."

"I'm considering sitting this one out," Greyson says. "I'd be doing a public service because I'll probably puke on someone's head."

"I feel your pain, Grey," Zane says with a nod.

"Oh, please!" Sevyn says, sucking her teeth. "Men are so whiney. It's a hangover. Take some Tylenol, eat some food, and keep the party moving."

"Tell 'em, sis!" Marisa claps her hands while laughing.

"I didn't complain. I'm zip lining," Asher says. "Puke or not. It's their fault for walking underneath me."

"Your level of arrogance is–" Marisa starts.

"Sexy?" Asher flashes her a smile.

She narrows her eyes. "Unbelievable was the word on the tip of my tongue before you so arrogantly interrupted me. I have yet to see sexy coming from you."

I really need them to figure out what it is they have going on. They fight like this every time we're together. It has to be sexual tension because they both seem to enjoy it a little too much.

I grab Acyn's wrist to check the time. "Oh good, I can take a nap."

"You'll definitely need your rest." Sevyn wags her eyebrows. "We've got a Thunder from Down Under show tonight. Don't want you to miss all those oily, ripped bodies."

Acyn coughs as he takes a sip of orange juice.

"Are you okay?" I side eye him with a smirk.

"Yeah, I just–what time is this at?"

"Plot twist. I'm not the jealous one." I laugh. "No one has anything on your stripper moves, babe."

"Stripper moves?" Kyrell asks with a raised eyebrow.

"He stripped for me in front of our neighbors." Acyn tosses his head back with laughter.

"Dance stripped or took off his clothes stripped?" Marisa asks.

"Both!" I snort with laughter.

"She said she wanted a stripper." Acyn shrugs. "So I gave her a stripper."

"Was he any good?" Quinn tries to bite back a smile.

"Yeah, was he?" Marisa asks fanning herself with a napkin.

"Shit, I'm curious too," Kyrell adds and laughter ripples around the table.

"If I had cash on me, it would've been raining!" I swipe my hand across the other as if I'm throwing money.

"Ace, maybe you have a career in the performing arts." Zane says.

"I'm a man of many talents." Acyn grins.

We recap our night, laughing at each other for the dumb shit we did. Thankfully, none of us did anything too wild, but tonight is when our actual parties will be. After zip lining, I'm going to hang out with the girls for the rest of the day so they can help me get ready. It's been fun to spend time with the guys, but still do our own thing.

"Alright, I have to go prepare myself for a day of fuckery." Asher finishes his drink and slides his chair back as he stands.

"I should probably get ready too." Marisa takes her last bite of food and waves before heading back inside.

"Let's all meet in the lobby at 12:30. Sound good?" Quinn asks.

We all nod or say yes. Acyn and I sit at the table chatting with Greyson, Quinn, Kyrell, Sevyn, and Zane a little longer. By the end of breakfast, I feel much better.

"Are you ready to go, Sunshine?" Acyn asks, stretching in his seat and yawning.

"Yeah. We'll see you guys soon." I say to everyone still at the table.

As we head up to our room, I hop on Acyn's back. He grabs my thighs; I wrap my arms around his shoulders and kiss his neck. Once we're in the elevator, he sets me down and presses me against the wall before his lips meet mine. There's something about elevators. He wraps his arm around my waist, pulling me flush against him. His other hand roams over my body while my hands slip under his shirt to feel on his abs. I let out a moan when he dips his hand into the front of my sweats and applies pressure to my clit. He rubs in slow circles, and I let my head fall back as the pleasure washes over me. I have to admit, there's something thrilling about the possibility of getting caught. But in the heat of the moment, it's the furthest thing from my mind. I don't feel the elevator slow or hear the ding of the doors, but I hear the gasps.

I pull away from Acyn to see a group of women staring at us with their mouths open. Acyn's hand is still down my pants, and I'm not sure what to do. They already know what we're doing. We were so caught up in the moment that we didn't pull away. But now I'm trying to push Acyn off me, slightly mortified, but he refuses to move.

"Uh..." the woman says, blinking rapidly. "We can catch the next one and let you two... uh... finish." She smiles as she backs up.

"You do that," Acyn says, tapping the button for the doors to close, and his lips are on mine before I can utter a word.

I push against his chest, and he reluctantly pulls away from me. "Something wrong, Sunshine?" he asks, resting his forehead against mine.

"You're really going to pretend a group of women didn't just see you with your hand down my pants?" I ask, biting back a laugh.

It quickly turns into a whimper as he massages my clit again. "I know, but don't give a fuck. Now, we have about a minute before we reach our floor with the possibility of more stops. Let me make you cum." He dips his finger inside me before rubbing it over my clit again.

I can't give a verbal response as my body hums with pleasure. Instead, I lift my leg up to give him easier access and he grips my thigh as he rubs my clit while kissing my neck and makes me cum in the elevator.

12
Bachelorette Party

Zip lining was a blast, even though Quinn couldn't go with us because of her baby bump. She was on the verge of tears when she realized she couldn't join. Kyrell promised her another trip to Vegas once the baby's here. I couldn't blame her because it was a fun experience, but I also told her she wouldn't have to babysit tonight because I'd be sober. That seemed to lift her spirits a little.

After we're done zip lining, we go our separate ways.

"Don't run away with some Aussie, alright?" Acyn kisses my neck.

I snort with laughter. "Damn, that's been my plan this whole time."

He gives me a kiss that Sevyn interrupts.

"Alright, yeah! You've had enough of her. Save some for the rest of us." She pulls me away from him. "I'll make sure she only gets a lap dance, bro," she says over her shoulder as she escorts me to the car.

I toss my head back with laughter. "You're so comforting."

"You're telling me you don't wanna be tossed around like a rag doll by some ripped guy?"

"Uh... well, your brother already does that daily."

Sevyn gasps. "I fucking knew it!"

"Knew what?" Quinn and Marisa ask when we slide into our seats.

"That Acyn tosses her around during sex," Sevyn says loudly, and the driver tries to keep his eyes on the road but is now looking at Sev in the rearview mirror.

They both laugh. "How are you just now finding out Harlow is a freak?" Quinn asks.

"She won't tell me anything because he's my brother!"

"It doesn't bother you?" Marisa asks.

"I literally saw him eating her out against my garage door—" Quinn and Marisa gasp "—it doesn't bother me."

"Wait, what?" Quinn sits up a little straighter and leans forward to look at me.

"Yeah, when the fuck did this happen?" Marisa tilts her head to the side.

"Sevyn!" I groan. "You weren't supposed to say anything about that."

"I feel betrayed right now," Quinn says dramatically. "Keeping dirty little secrets from us."

"It's not even like that. I just..." My voice trails off.

"Then what was it like?" Marisa raises a brow.

Sevyn is sitting with her arms folded and a smug smile on her lips, waiting for me to tell them.

I let out an exasperated sigh. "It was when we got together. We hadn't been talking for two weeks and then he kissed me..."

"Okay, but how did his lips end up between your legs against Sevyn's garage door?" Quinn asks.

"Heat of the moment..." I shrug. "He got on his knees in front of me and—"

"Wait, he got on his knees in front of you?" Marisa's mouth hangs open. "That is the sexiest shit I've ever heard in my fucking life."

"Exactly! How was I supposed to tell him to stop? So, he just... ripped my panties off and ate me for lunch. Then Sevyn caught us."

"Ripped your panties off?" Quinn fans herself.

"Oh my God! You guys act like you don't have amazing sex." Heat creeps up my neck.

"Always the quiet ones, I tell you." Sevyn points at me.

I swat at her, laughing. "Shut up!"

"I'm definitely not having sex like that," Marisa scoffs. "I mean, it gets the job done, but they aren't worshipping me. This is when I hate being single."

"I'm sure Asher would love to change that for you." I smirk and look out the window. "We're not going back to the hotel?"

Quinn shakes her head. "Nope. We're going to the spa first, then we'll head back to get ready. I thought some pampering couldn't hurt."

The driver pulls up in front of an extravagant building and opens the car door for us. Walking into the spa makes me feel like I'm in Morocco, with the intricate design and décor. The aromatic scent of Palo Santo wafts around us. We have a reservation, but choose two services each so that we're all done around the same time. I choose a HydraFacial and a full body hot stone massage. Once we've chosen what we want, we're escorted to a dressing room where we change into plush white robes. I ask one of the spa staff to take a picture of us doing our best model poses. They take a few before inviting us back to begin our massages.

I slip out of my robe and lie face down on the massage table. When I was teaching yoga I would get regular massages, but then I focused more on my photography career and can't remember the last time I got one. As soon as the massage therapist's hands touch my back, I melt into the table. I can't help the moan that comes out of my mouth.

"Whatever massage you're having, I want it," Sevyn says.

"Shut up, Sevyn." I chuckle. "Quinn, I can tell you this is by far better than zip lining."

"I'm in heaven," Quinn mumbles.

"We're right there with you, babe," Marisa adds.

Talking subsides as we enjoy our massages. After a long night of drinking and dancing, this is exactly what I need. Sooner than I'd like, we're heading for our facials. To my surprise, the facial is just as relaxing as the massage. I've never had one before, but as I look at my dewy, supple skin in the mirror, I'll make it a regular thing. It's amazing how I'm glowing. Now that we're polished and radiant, we're ready to have fun with the men at the strip show.

Marisa applies lashes after doing my eyeshadow and eyeliner. I've never worn false lashes before and am anxious to see what they look like.

"I'm almost done," she mumbles distractedly. Moments later, she holds a mirror up to my face.

I gasp. "That's me?"

"Yes. Do you like them? I tried to keep them minimal, but just enough to make your lashes look fuller."

"I fucking love them!" I look at myself from every angle. "Can you come do my lashes for me all the time?"

"I wish I lived a little closer, then I totally would."

She lives a few hours away in Portland. She's close, but not close enough.

"I think a red lip would look fire on you with your leather and lace get up. Fuck around and really go home with an Aussie."

"Accents are nice," I smirk.

"A true weakness of mine." She gently grabs my face to apply the lipstick.

Since we're alone in the room, I decide to ask her about the haircut. "What happened with the hair?"

Her hand freezes. "It's a long story... and I don't want to dampen the mood."

"Where are we hiding the body?"

She laughs as she sits next to me on the bed. "Remember the guy I was telling you guys about that I met a few months ago at the bar?"

I nod my head. "You guys hit it off, right?"

"He was perfect. Handsome, charming... an actual dream, you know?"

I think of Acyn. Although I wouldn't have initially said he was charming. "What happened?"

"He was married... with kids. This whole fucking life."

"Did you know this or?" I search her face.

"No, I didn't know. I didn't have a fucking clue. Harls, he had an apartment and everything. I thought he was who he told me he was the first night we met." Her eyes well with tears, and I place my hand on her back.

"H-How did you find out?"

She hesitates, and we sit in silence for a moment. "His wife... I found out from his wife."

"Wait..." I sit up a little straighter. "What? How?"

"God, it was a fucking mess." She sighs and looks down at her hands. "She signed up for private lessons at my studio. She came in twice a week, and we hit it off. Even went to coffee and brunch together a few times. She told me all about her family and her husband. Then, after a couple of months of this, she invited me over to her house... *their* house for a dinner party."

I don't like where this is going, but I keep my mouth shut because I want to hear the full story. She continues. "I get to the dinner party and there are quite a few people there. And not just random people, but people who are prominent in Portland. People who can help you make a name for yourself. I was honored to be in such a space." She smiles briefly, and it fades.

"But then... he walked in. He didn't see me at first, but I saw him walk toward the woman I considered a friend and kiss her on the lips. And I felt... gutted. Everything I thought I knew was a fucking lie. The man who I let into my life, my heart, my bed... I let him into everything and there he was with his wife. It felt like a double-edged sword because I actually considered her a friend, too."

I hold her hand because I don't know what else to do as I listen to her tell me about this lying piece of shit. She inhales deeply. "She brought him over to me, and he knew he was fucked when his eyes landed on mine. All I could do was stand there frozen, staring at him, wondering what the fuck I'd done. As if things couldn't get worse, his wife made a toast introducing me as his 'whore mistress'."

I gasp, covering my mouth. "That bitch did not! What about her cheating, lying ass husband who can't keep his dick in his pants?"

"My thoughts exactly." She laughs. "After she did that, I sort of snapped out of it and told her maybe if she was more of a whore like me, he wouldn't be in my bed at night. Needless to say, I got a glass of wine thrown in my face, but it was fucking worth it."

I fall back onto the bed with laughter. "Marisa! You did not!"

"I sure as hell did. Fuck that bitch and her man, too." She laughs. "But..." she sighs, falling back onto the bed next to me. "I fucking loved him, Harls. I still do. And I hate that about myself. I feel ridiculous for falling for a man who only saw me as a novelty. It fucking hurts and I'm lonely. So... as any woman does who wants to change her life and the world after heartbreak, she cuts her hair."

I give her a small smile. "I'm sorry that happened to you. Marisa, you're gorgeous inside and out. None of this is your fault. There is no way you could've known that he was lying sack of shit. Fuck him and his wife, just like you said."

"I love you, Harlow." She hugs me, kissing my cheek.

"I love you too, babe."

Quinn peeks her head into the room before stepping inside. "Oh." She puts her hands on her hips. "You two thought you could have a romance without me?"

"I'm always down for a ménage à trois," Marisa says, holding her arm out.

"What are we talking about?" Quinn wedges herself between us. "Are you okay?" she asks Marisa.

"I am now, but I'll tell you another time." Marisa smiles at her. "I've gotta finish getting our Queen ready."

Marisa finishes my hair and makeup; now it's time for the outfit. I put on a black lace bustier top that gives the illusion my breasts are a split second away from spilling out. Then I pull on my black leather miniskirt that has a high slit on the front of the left thigh. I slide a glittery gold thigh chain on for a little extra detail.

"Can you guys see my ass cheeks if I bend over?" I bend forward slightly.

"Yes, but the skirt is cute. Wear it. It's Vegas, baby! Be a showgirl!" Sevyn shouts.

"That thigh chain in sexy as hell," Quinn says.

"Ow, ow, ow! Legs for fucking days!" Marisa whistles. "Put the heels on. I'm trying to get the full Harlow experience right now."

I giggle as they hype me up and put on my heels. They have a gold ankle strap with a gold heel, and black soles. I stand in front of the mirror, feeling like a total bombshell.

"Ugh, I'm feelin' myself y'all!" I run my hands over my body.

"That leather and lace is working for you, babe!" Marisa says. "You're gonna break necks."

"We all are." I turn around to look at them. "We came to slay, not to play tonight."

Marisa is wearing a high waisted mini skirt with a belt cinched at her waist, and a sheer body suit with embroidery detail that covers her nipples. She paired it with some strappy black heels. Quinn adjusts her baby pink slip dress with a scoop neckline and two high slits on the side that she paired with thigh high heels. Whenever I get pregnant, I hope to be as fashionable as she is. Sevyn is wearing red leather pants with a white bodysuit that has a plunging neckline, almost to her navel, and no back with black sky high heels. We are all definitely going to get some attention tonight, and I love that for us.

After a round of pictures, I immediately upload them to Instagram, and then we head out for our show. There's nothing like a little glam and your besties hyping you up for a boost of confidence. We're talking and laughing as we spill into the lobby from the elevator. I reach into my clutch for my phone when I bump into a hard chest.

"Oh, excuse me. I—"

"Look fucking incredible. God fucking damn," a deep voice that calls to my soul says.

I look into Acyn's eyes, and they're ablaze for me. "Thank you." I simper.

"No. Thank you for being my wife."

"Forever a pleasure." I smile at him before glancing at his entourage and realize we stopped them in their tracks. Mission accomplished.

Acyn turns to Kyrell, who's currently feeling up Quinn. "Do we really have to go out tonight?" His heated gaze is on me again.

"I was wondering the same shit, bro." He kisses Quinn's neck as she giggles.

"Well, this makes me feel like a lonely fucker without Selene here." Greyson says, looking at all of us. Acyn's about to respond when Sevyn raises her voice.

"Back up!" Sevyn smooshes Zane's face with her hand. "I have no time for this. We have a date with some male strippers. You can have your way with me after."

Marisa cackles. "He just wants to appreciate you looking like his last meal."

"Yeah, Sevyn. Let me show you my appreciation." Zane continues to feel her up.

"That's too damn bad! I've been looking forward to this all day. I am going to see sweaty, ripped men, and then I will come back and fuck my husband." Sevyn grabs my hand, trying to pull me in the opposite direction.

"Marisa, I can show you some appreciation right now," Asher cuts in.

"What is with you horn dogs?" Sevyn asks, exasperated.

"You're really one to talk, Sev," I snort with laughter.

Marisa gives Asher an appraising look. "We'll see if I go home with a dancer or not. I'll let you know." She smirks.

Acyn grips my ass and smacks it before kissing me. "I can't wait to taste you and hear you scream my name later," he whispers in my ear.

"You should probably know I don't have any panties on," I whisper back before Sevyn, Marisa, and Quinn pull me in the opposite direction.

I peek over my shoulder at him before we walk out the door, and I feel the pulse between my thighs at the look of desire in his eyes.

We arrive a little early for the show and they give us a round of jello shots. Despite saying I wouldn't drink tonight, the girls encourage me to take a shot.

"I refuse to rain on anyone's parade," says Quinn with a smile as I grab a shot.

I squeeze my eyes shut as it slides down my throat. "I won't get sauced. I promise."

I'm excited, but I had to take an edible to calm my nerves because I don't know what to expect at this show. I've never been to a strip club before, and I want to enjoy myself. Marisa and Sevyn down the rest of the shots. When they're done with them, they pop open a bottle of champagne.

"We're gonna have to carry them back, aren't we?" I ask Quinn as we watch them down glasses of champagne.

"It's only a matter of time before they pass out."

I giggle as the lights dim. A mixture of excitement and nervousness come over me. I could barely handle Acyn dancing on me, let alone watching professional dancers.

"Yes! Show us the dick!" Marisa shouts.

I slap my hand over my mouth, laughing hysterically. "Are we going to actually see dick?"

"I've heard these shows can get pretty wild." Quinn shrugs with a mischievous glint in her eye. "I guess we'll have to see."

The dancers come out on stage and the crowd goes wild. It's hard to tell what they look like because it's dark and their heads are down. I can tell they all spend hours in the gym, though. Music cuts through the cheering. When the beat drops, they look up in unison and begin their performance. Despite their size, they move around the stage effortlessly in sync. Marisa nearly drops her glass of champagne when they rip off their shirts. Quinn tosses her head back with laughter, and I can't help but giggle, too. I settle into my seat as the performance continues, realizing this isn't anything like I was expecting. They turn their backs to the crowd as the music stops and rip off their pants to reveal bright blue briefs. We gasp. I feel I should look away, but I can't, and the row of men flash their asses at the audience. The screams and cheers go up a notch. They pull their briefs up before facing the front of the stage again and thrust their hips so their packages bounce around.

I spoke too soon. *This* is what I expected. I've never been around this many dicks at one time in my life. Maybe another shot earlier wouldn't have hurt. I'm by no means a prude, but I truly don't know what to do with this many nearly naked oiled men dancing in front of me. Apparently, neither does Quinn as she stares at them with her mouth open. Marisa is definitely in her element, and Sevyn is downing another glass of champagne as she looks at them over the rim. Before I can take it all in, the men jump off the stage and come into the crowd. I feel the heat creep up my neck, and my face grows hot as one of them beelines for where we're sitting. All I can hope is he doesn't come for me.

But he does. Marisa, Quinn, and Sevyn cheer him on as he takes my hand and places it on his chest. My heart stutters in my own.

He leans down and asks, "Wanna come up on stage?"

I glance at the girls, realizing this is all a fucking setup. They think I won't go up there as they laugh at me. Well, the jokes on them. It's my bachelorette party, after all.

I turn my attention back to the man in front of me and say, "Yes."

He gives me a megawatt smile and holds out his hand.

"Atta girl!" Quinn yells.

I'm not sure what I'm getting into, but I soon find out as he flips me over his shoulder and carries me to the stage. For the first time in my life, I regret not wearing panties. I hold on to my skirt in hopes it's dark enough that no one gets a free show from me. My hand slips on his oiled back as I try to hold myself up, so I don't face plant into his ass.

He sits me on a chair that's center stage, and my heart races. I try to situate myself after being flipped around like a rag doll, and when I focus on his face, he still has a smile.

"Relax and enjoy yourself." He winks.

The crowd is cheering wildly, and the lights are brighter here on stage. But I forget about that once he grinds his ass in my lap. I clamp my knees together, and I don't know what the fuck to do with my sweaty hands other than keep them glued to the sides of the chair. When I steal a glance around his gyrating hips, I see the other dancers entertaining the crowd. I'm grateful all the attention isn't entirely on me, but I'm still torn between embarrassment and being impressed by how agile he is. I can appreciate his art... right?

He does a handstand in front of me, spreading his legs nearly into a full split, and slowly drops his ass back into my lap. I hear the girls over the crowd whistling and calling my name. I cover my face with my hands and can't help the laugh that escapes me. He continues to dance on my lap and around me, perfectly in sync with the rhythm of the music. Just when I think I can't take much more, the music fades into a new song. He picks me up as though I weigh nothing, carries me back to my seat, and sits me gently in it. Before he turns to leave, he kisses the top of my hand like a gentleman, as if he wasn't just humping in my face and grinding in my lap.

"You lucky bitch!" Marisa shouts over the music. "I didn't think you'd do it and lost $100 because of you!"

"You had bets?" I toss my head back with laughter.

"Of course! I was the only one who said you'd do it because you'd want to prove a point." Quinn laughs as she collects her $200 winnings from them.

"I thought you'd say no, and I would've gladly offered myself up." Marisa pours herself another glass of champagne.

"What did he feel like?" Sevyn asks. "The way he was grinding on you like he wanted to fuck you, I know you felt something."

"He's a stripper, Sev." I cackle. "He's supposed to grind on me. And to be honest... I was more worried about flashing my goodies to the audience in this short ass skirt. Warn a girl next time!"

"You look drop dead gorgeous," Quinn says. "A little peek of the kitty is a small price to pay. Now, don't play with us. What did he feel like?"

"He felt... rock hard. In more ways than one."

They gasp before we fall into a fit of laughter. You'd think none of us have been around men before the way we're acting.

"I want in on some of this action." Marisa downs her glass of champagne and adjusts her breasts. She stands and gets the attention of the dancer closest to us.

"Make us fucking proud!" Sevyn shouts, two sheets to the wind.

Marisa gladly gets picked up by him, and he carries her on stage. It's safe to say she's the wild card of our group. We're all free spirited in our own right, but she truly is on another level. Marisa is the woman they want on stage. I looked like a deer in headlights. She is eating it up and more than willing as the dancer practically fucks her on stage. I'm glad my dancer was somewhat of a gentleman. This guy clearly loves Marisa's energy. We cheer her on as she has her moment on stage.

"She's in her element!" I say to them, my voice hoarse from yelling.

"She read the assignment, that's for—" Quinn begins but stops abruptly.

"Oh, honey, no!" Sevyn shouts.

When I look back at the stage, Marisa is sliding her thong off her legs. I watch in shock as the dancer takes them from her hand and puts them in his mouth.

"C-Can he do that?" Quinn asks.

"I'm guessing this is the wild part..." I watch Marisa shove her head in the dancer's crotch.

"Um... this escalated quickly," Sevyn says with wide eyes.

I'm speechless as I watch her bow with the dancer before he brings her back to our table. Marisa is laughing hysterically, but stops when she sees the look of shock on our faces.

"What? I just wanted to have some fun." She shrugs, pouring herself another glass of champagne.

"W-We didn't say anything." Quinn stutters.

"No, but you're all looking at me like you don't know me."

"He put your panties... in his mouth." Sevyn enunciates each word. "You're a true legend."

There's a moment of silence before we all laugh hysterically. The shock of the moment dissolves.

"What happens in Vegas stays in Vegas, right?" I ask them as we enjoy the rest of our night.

13
Bachelor Party

E*arlier that same day...*
      After saying bye to Harlow and the girls, we await our ride to begin the bachelor party. It pulls up less than a minute later.

"Where to next?" I ask Kyrell as I get into the SUV.

"I can't tell you that." He smirks. "It's a surprise."

"Get off your fucking phone, asshole." Asher kicks Greyson's foot.

"It's Selene," Grey whispers.

"I know," Asher whispers back. "Tell her you forgot to pack your balls."

"Oh, he has some?" Zane scrunches up his face.

I try to hold in a laugh, but Kyrell cracks up, and I let it out. Greyson punches Asher's arm as he lies to Selene and says we're pulling up to our next stop.

"You're whipped, bro. They aren't even that bad." Asher points at Kyrell, Zane, and me. "And they worship the ground those women walk on."

"Yeah, and you're the lonely fucker hunting for pussy every night," Grey quips.

"That's part of the thrill." Asher winks.

"When was the last time you had a girlfriend, Ash?" I ask him, trying to recall if that's ever happened.

"A girlfriend?" he asks incredulously. "Damn, I don't even remember."

"And I thought I had commitment issues." Kyrell chuckles.

"I think Ash has us beat in a lot of things," I reply. Greyson's phone rings again and he stares at it, then back at us. "Man, I respect the love you two have for each other, but she fucking bothers."

"I told you," Ash says in a singsong tone, looking out the window.

"She just misses me." Grey shrugs.

"Mmm... that's not missing," Zane says.

"Yeah, there's a fine line between missing and suffocation," Kyrell adds. "You're a pilot. She should be used to you being gone."

"That's for work. It's different."

"Right... so you're saying she doesn't trust you?" Kyrell asks.

"What? Why would you say that?" Grey looks at him and his ringing phone again.

"You're in Vegas for a bachelor party, and it's known for getting wild. So, I'll repeat myself—there's a fine line between missing and suffocation." Kyrell sighs before looking out the window with a bored expression.

I chuckle, shaking my head because the confused look on Greyson's face lets me know he doesn't get it. "She thinks you're out here to do fuck shit, Grey. That's why she's blowing up your phone. While she may miss you, jealousy is what's really going on here."

Grey looks at his phone thoughtfully for a moment before turning it off and sliding it into his pocket. We weren't saying ignore her, but he'll figure that out in his own time. We can't spell everything out for him. Grey's a good guy. He's the nice one compared to the rest of us, but he's also a pushover and Selene takes advantage of that. Harlow knows she could ask me for the heart in my chest and I'd gladly give it to her, but I know she would willingly give me her own. Grey has been with Selene for three years, and I have yet to see that same energy from her with him.

About twenty minutes later, we pull up to what looks like a racing track.

"Are we watching a race?" I ask with a quirked brow.

"Fuck no. We're racing." Kyrell grins.

"What? For real?" I ask, looking around. I have a love of cars, both old and new.

"Ah, like a kid in a candy store." Zane smiles at me.

"Thank fuck it isn't a strip club." I let out a sigh.

Kyrell pulls his shades down. "Nah, that fuckery is for later—" I let out a rumble of laughter "—but for now you can choose between driving a Ferrari, McLaren, Lamborghini, or whatever else they have here."

Excitement courses through me as we walk into the building for registration. I wasn't expecting this. While Vegas is fun for gambling and partying, I'm happy that we're stepping outside of that box. Kyrell checks us in at registration and then asks for our driver's licenses. The hostess goes over what our driving experience will be like and then we get to choose our cars. I take nearly ten minutes to decide on what to drive because I want to try them all. I finally decide to drive the Lamborghini Huracan Performante.

"Good choice." The hostess smiles.

"Took you long enough." Zane nudges my shoulder.

He chose a Lamborghini, too. Kyrell chose a Ferrari, Asher went with the McLaren, and Greyson decided on a Porsche. Once we're all checked in, we're taken to a classroom to begin our training session with an instructor. They go over the mechanics, how to handle the car on the track, and safety procedures. It's mostly basic, common sense stuff, but it's easy to forget common sense when you're behind the wheel of a dream car.

After the training session, we're taken to a simulator room where we take virtual laps. We won't be driving alone. We're each paired with an instructor who helps us learn the controls of the car and the layout of the track.

"Do you feel comfortable?" the instructor asks me.

"Yes," I reply, eager to get behind the wheel.

"Alright, man. Let's get you suited up," he says.

I thought he was joking when he said we'd get suited up. It's a full racing gear outfit with the jumpsuit and helmet.

"We've got to take a picture," I say to Kyrell once we're in our gear.

"You really are Harlow's other half."

"Oh no, this is for me."

He tosses his head back with laughter. "Bet."

My instructor takes photos of us looking like wannabe bad asses by our chosen cars and as a group. After that's out of the way, it's time to play. I feel like a little kid with how excited I am to get behind the wheel of this Lamborghini. Opening the door, I slide into the seat and buckle up before making the engine rev to life.

My instructor, Lucas, asks, "Are you ready?" His voice resounds through my helmet.

"Hell yeah!"

"Alright," he chuckles. "Slowly pull out onto the track."

I listen to his instructions. There are already others on the track which makes me kind of nervous because I don't want to run into anyone or vice versa.

"Keep on creepin' out..." Lucas says. "You're clear to go."

With those words, adrenaline pumps through my veins. The only other time I've driven a Lamborghini was at Kyrell's place and it was on a residential road. But here on the track I have freedom.

"Up shift here," Lucas says. "Up again. There you go, and up again."

As we come up on the first curve of the track, Lucas guides me around it. "Break real firm... one down shift. Ease off the brakes as you turn. Light throttle for balance around the curves."

Once I get around the first curve of the track, I speed up as I get comfortable and reach speeds up to one hundred and sixty miles per hour on the straighaway. It's an exhilarating experience to have the freedom to drive at speeds you'd get a ticket for. With each lap, I go faster, getting more comfortable with the layout of the track and driving the car with more ease. We're doing ten laps, which sounds like a lot initially, until you're nearly going two hundred miles per hour. I even pass Zane and Asher without killing any of us.

Before I know it, Lucas says, "We'll stay wide and exit at the top."

"Exit?" I ask him, surprised it's already over. I could easily keep going.

He chuckles. "Yeah, those ten laps go by pretty quick."

I pull off the track and park the car, realizing now I want a Lamborghini. We'll see if Harlow will go for that later. I reluctantly get out, thank Lucas, and wait for everyone else to finish their laps. Kyrell is first, Zane second, Asher third, and Greyson last.

"How was that, man?" Kyrell grins, wrapping his arm around my shoulders.

"Shit, I'm wondering if Harlow would be down for me to get a Lambo."

He pats my shoulder. "When you're ready, I know a guy."

"Yeah," Zane says, "you're gonna have to set that meeting up with Titan Tech immediately. I need to drive fast cars regularly."

"This experience really just made me wanna buy shit." Asher agrees.

"When do you not wanna buy shit, Ash?" Greyson asks him.

We all laugh as we head into the building to the lounge. Kyrell gets me a copy of the video footage of me driving and all of us t-shirts. While I love to party as much as the next person, this has been my favorite part of this trip so far. Our driver pulls up in front of the building, and we all pile back into the SUV.

"Alright, let's get some food in our systems before the real fuckery begins." Kyrell rubs his hands together.

I already know this is going to be an interesting fucking night.

Back at the hotel, I head to my room to get ready before we eat. After a shower, I put on distressed dark wash jeans, with a V-neck army green t-shirt, and black Nike Air Max sneakers. For jewelry, I put on a layered gold necklace that Harlow bought me a few months ago and black obsidian crystal bracelets. She says that obsidian protects me from negativity. I'm not sure if that's true, but I rock with it because she's never been wrong about energy, and they look nice. Before I walk out the door, I spray myself with the cologne Harlow got me called Spicebomb.

I head to the guy's room and knock. Greyson opens it seconds later, unsurprisingly on the phone with Selene, who sounds like she's yelling. Poor guy. Asher's pouring himself a drink.

"Do you want one?" he asks, holding up a bottle of whiskey.

"Yeah." I shrug.

"Pour me one too." Zane enters the living room, smoothing his hair out of his face.

"So... how long has Greyson been getting yelled at?" I take a drink of whiskey.

Zane chuckles. "She's still going?"

"God bless the bastard." Asher raises his glass into the air before tipping it back.

I down the rest of mine. "Where's Kyrell?"

"Aw, you missed me?" He appears seconds later. "Looking like this is an art, y'all." He smooths his hands down his shirt.

"Shut the fuck up." I shake my head, laughing.

Asher offers Kyrell a glass of whiskey. He takes it and tosses it back and opens the fridge, pulling out a bag of edibles.

"Where's Greyson?" He hands an edible to each of us.

"Getting bitched at," Zane says, putting the edible in his mouth.

I head back to where the rooms are to find him still arguing with Selene. "Bruh, let's go."

"Selene, look, I love you, but I gotta go. I'll talk to you later tonight," he says, hanging up the phone.

"You good?"

"She's gonna drive me fucking nuts," Greyson growls.

I chuckle. "I think that's how it's supposed to be. Let's go eat and get into whatever Kyrell has planned. Maybe once you're both cooled down, you can talk."

"Yeah." He sighs, following behind me.

"Finally!" Kyrell says when he sees me with Greyson. "Let's roll out."

We decide to go to a restaurant within the hotel since there are countless options to choose from. After we clear enough plates of food for a football team and a few rounds of sake later, we head out to the lobby to start our night. I see her before she sees me, stopping dead in my tracks at the sight of her. Kyrell runs into the back of me.

"What the fu—" he begins before stepping aside and stopping in his tracks too.

All of us stop, staring at Harlow and the girls as they get ready to go off to some male strip show looking like a group of super models. She runs right into me as she digs through her purse. I grab her and pull her flush against my body as she apologizes for running into me.

"Excuse me. I—"

"Look fucking incredible." I finish her sentence for her. "God fucking damn."

She looks up at me with a smile on her face and a million filthy thoughts run through my head.

"Thank you." She simpers.

She's thanking me when I'm the lucky bastard who gets to be with her for the rest of my life. The urge to throw her over my shoulder and carry her up to our suite is strong. I turn to Kyrell to ask him if going out is necessary and see he's feeling up Quinn.

"Do we really have to go out tonight?" I ask him.

"I was wondering the same shit, bruh." Apparently, he has the same thoughts as me as he kisses on Quinn.

I turn my attention back to Harlow as Greyson declares he misses Selene. We may give him shit, but I'd honestly miss Harlow too if she weren't here with me. Sevyn's loud voice interrupts my thoughts of Harlow as she talks to Zane.

"Back up!" Sevyn says to Zane with her hand in his face. "I have no time for this. We have a date with some male strippers. You can have your way with me after."

Marisa cackles. "He just wants to appreciate you lookin' like his last meal."

"Yeah, Sevyn. Let me show you my appreciation." Zane continues to feel her up.

"That's too damn bad! I've been looking forward to this all day. I am going to see sweaty, ripped men, and then I will come back and fuck my husband." Sevyn grabs Harlow's hand, attempting to pull her in the opposite direction, but I keep my arm around her.

Sevyn is always cock blocking someone. I'm sure that's why she's the youngest child. She probably cock blocked our parents from ever having another opportunity. While Asher tries to get with Marisa for the millionth time, I focus my attention on Harlow. My mouth is watering to taste her.

"I can't wait to taste you and hear you scream my name later," I whisper in her ear.

"You should probably know I don't have any panties on," she whispers back.

Her admission causes my arm around her waist to slip, letting them pull her out of my hold and in the opposite direction. She looks at me before they walk out the door, and my dick twitches at the look in her eyes. All I want is to feel her on me.

"So... now that we officially have blue balls aside from Greyson," Kyrell says. "Shall we go to a club?"

"Yeah, fuck it," I say. Not sure that anything will get my mind off of wanting to be balls deep in Harlow right now, but I'll join in.

As we walk outside to wait for our car service, Asher stands next to me.

"Hey, man..."

"Hey..." I side eye him.

"Do you think..." he hesitates, rubbing the back of his neck. "Nah, never mind."

"Do I think what?"

He lets out a sigh, seemingly frustrated with himself. "Marisa man..."

I try to bite back a smile. "Yeah... what about her?"

"She just... I mean, I usually don't have to do much, right? C'mon look at me." He points at his chest and I chuckle. "But she... she..."

Asher and I have been friends since we were thirteen and I've never seen him like this before. It's kind of funny.

"Do you like her, or do you just wanna fuck her?"

"I don't fucking know." He shrugs and falls silent as the SUV pulls up.

"Wow Ash, I think you may actually like someone." I pat his arm and climb into the car.

I can't remember the last time I came to a strip club. When I was young and dumb, I would blow cash at them like I had something to prove. Asher and Greyson were alongside me, doing the same dumb shit. Then we started making real money in our careers and realized there were better things to blow it on.

"Here." Kyrell tries to hand me a stack of cash.

"Nope." I shove my hands into my pockets. "I'm not taking your money."

"Why not? They did." He points to the guys behind him who have cash in their hands.

"I'm not taking your money." I back away from him. Kyrell may have more money than he'll ever know what to do with in his lifetime, but I never want him to feel taken advantage of.

"Will you fucking take the goddamn money?" He waves it in my face. "Look, I enjoy doing shit for people I care about, and I care about you... a lot. You're like a brother to me. Do you think I'd do this shit for any random motherfucker?"

I'm momentarily at a loss for words as I stare at him from behind the cash he's holding in my face. "Uh... no, I don't."

"Then take the fucking money." He shoves it at my chest, and I take it.

"Thanks, Kyrell... I feel the same way about you."

He holds up his hand. "Don't make this fucking weird."

"Alright." I shrug. "I won't... but I love you too," I add and wait for his reaction as I try to keep from laughing.

"Goddammit, Ace!" He gives me a hug, and I toss my head back with laughter.

"Are you two done with your little bromance? I'm trying to see some ass and titties." Asher smirks.

"Don't be jealous," Kyrell says smugly, wrapping his arm around my shoulders as we head inside.

Upon entering the club, a scantily clad woman escorts us to a VIP table. The crowd is going wild for a girl who is dropping it on the pole. Asher still loves this environment and throws some money on the stage as we walk past. When we get to the VIP section, there's a hookah on the table with two buckets of beer and a bottle of Grey Goose.

I sit on one of the chairs and grab a beer. The woman who seated us takes it from my hand.

"Here. Allow me." She smiles, opening it.

"Thanks." I nod as she hands it back to me.

"Anything else I can assist you with?" she asks.

"No, I'm good. They may need help, though." I point to the other guys.

"Let me know if you need anything else." She runs her hand along my shoulder as she walks toward Asher.

Asher is the only one of us who's single and in situations like these, he thoroughly enjoys himself. Sure enough, once she opens his beer, she sits on his lap and is giggling at his terrible jokes. While Asher enjoys the attention, Kyrell, Zane, Greyson, and I smoke some hookah. It's not really my thing, but it gives us something to do other than sitting around and drinking beers.

"So... if I get a lap dance–"

"Sevyn will fucking kill you, Zane." I take a swig of my beer.

Both Kyrell and Greyson crack up.

"Remember when you complimented that girl?" I ask and Zane nods. "Right. Now, take that up ten notches and imagine your funeral."

"Wait, wait, wait. What happened?" Kyrell asks through laughter.

"We went to an event once and for whatever reason, Zane complimented another woman on her dress in front of Sevyn. She had just had the twins and was already feeling some type of way. Then this dumb ass says something like 'oh, that color is nice on you' to the woman. Anyway, I had to hold Sevyn back from tearing him apart. She kicked him out of the house for a week, and he had to stay with me."

"Damn, that big brain of yours only speaks in computer code or what?" Greyson smirks.

"It was a terrible lapse of judgement that she still brings up to this day." Zane hangs his head.

"And you know damn well she'll find out." I point my finger at him. "She's better than the CIA at digging up shit on people. You're better off enjoying a few beers, some hookah, and watching them swing around the pole."

"Would Harlow care?" asks Greyson.

"She doesn't have to care because this doesn't interest me." I shrug. "And..." I take a deep breath. "She would wipe me from the face of this earth."

Kyrell cracks up. "I was about to say."

Some dancers enter our section and Zane immediately tenses. I can tell he's already mentally apologizing to Sevyn from the look on his face. One of them gets close to talk to him and he drops his beer at her feet. Kyrell and I laugh hysterically as he profusely apologizes and tries to clean it up.

"My name's Sasha. Would you like a dance?" an overly sweet voice asks.

I turn to see a dancer standing in front of me. I hadn't noticed her because I was too busy laughing at Zane's conundrum.

"Oh, nah. I'm—"

Before I can finish my sentence, she whips her glitter covered hair in my face. Hitting my eye and giving me a mouthful. I gag and am momentarily blinded. Her head connects with the glass beer bottle in my hand, causing it to clatter to the ground.

"Fucking shit!" I grab my eye while pulling strands of hair out of my mouth.

I can hear Kyrell's laughter over the blaring music. The dancer pops her head back up, and from what I can see with my good eye, she looks mortified.

"Oh my God!" she gasps. "I am so sorry about that. I didn't mean—I'm so sorry. It's my first night. I just—are you okay?"

She reaches out to touch me, and I move away from her, nearly tipping over the chair. "I'm fine," I say, still holding my stinging eye. She's just trying to do her job, albeit she's terrible at it, but I still have the urge to tell her to get the fuck away from me.

"I—I can get you guys another bucket of beer, or maybe you'd want to go to a private room?"

"No, no, no!" I hold my hands up. "No private room. It's fine. I'm good. We're good."

She stands there, staring at me, and tears well in her eyes. I glance at Kyrell, who can barely breathe from laughing so hard, and he shrugs.

"Uh... it's okay. It was an accident..."

"I don't want to get fired. I need this job." She sobs.

I stare at her in disbelief, wondering how this escalated so quickly. Zane is looking at me, wondering what I'll do next. While Greyson is rolling on the couch laughing. I let out an exasperated sigh. "Look, I'm sure worse shit happens here. It was an accident. No harm done." I shrug with my vision still blurry in my right eye.

I dig in my pocket for some bills and hand it to her. "Shit happens."

"Are you serious?" she looks down at the cash in her hand.

"Yes." I am so fucking serious. Even if she could dance, I don't want her near me. She takes a step toward me, and I put my hands out in hopes she won't come any closer.

She stops in her tracks. "Thank you," she whispers before turning around and practically running out of our section.

I shake my head, rubbing my eye, and turn my attention back to Kyrell. "I appreciate the effort, but this definitely isn't my scene anymore."

"To be honest, mine either, but that shit was hilarious!" He's still laughing with Greyson and Zane.

Sucking my teeth, I glare at him. "Then what the fuck are we here for?"

"It's Vegas and a bachelor party." He shrugs. "It seemed fitting."

I can't help but laugh. "If I have any damage to my eye, you're footing the bill."

"Bruh, she nearly knocked herself out on that bottle!" Kyrell exclaims. "I kind of felt bad for laughing, but fuck. And it's her first night too! She's got a long road ahead of her."

"Yeah, she'll feel that tomorrow," I say as my vision clears.

"Wanna go back to the hotel and hit up the casino? The night is young, and I refuse for it to end at," he glances at his watch, "midnight."

We've only been here for an hour, but the smoke, flashing lights, and blaring music are getting to me. "Yeah, that's more my tempo."

I glance at Asher, who is in the corner with two women dancing on his lap.

"Aye," I say to Asher. "Are you staying?"

"You're done already?" he asks with his eyes trained on the dancer's ass.

"This doesn't do it for me anymore. You know that."

"It's your party. I'll follow whatever you wanna do. I can find a girl to dance on my belt anywhere." He smirks. "Ladies, ladies, I've thoroughly enjoyed all you've given me tonight." He stands up and slides more cash into their bras and panties.

"Such a gentleman." I smirk.

"Damn, partying isn't as fun when you're the only one enjoying all the play."

"Nah, partying loses its appeal when your priorities change," Kyrell says, taking a final drag on the hookah.

"I enjoy my freedom," Asher says.

"Is it really freedom if you're fucking lonely, though?" Kyrell asks him.

For whatever reason, Kyrell gets away with saying the rawest shit to people. If Greyson or I had said that to Asher, I think he would want to fight. Kyrell is nonchalant in the way he says things and truly means no harm. He's like Yoda. Asher stares at him for a moment. Probably deciding whether or not he wants to argue. He must decide against it because he scrolls through his phone in silence. We head outside to wait for our car service, and I open up Instagram to stalk Harlow. She posted a story two minutes ago, and it's of a very drunk Sevyn and Marisa singing at the top of her lungs. When the camera flips to her, she's laughing at them with Quinn.

"Sevyn is gone with the fucking wind," I say to Zane, showing him the video.

"Yep... that's my wife." He grins.

We pile into the SUV and head back to the hotel to blow some cash before we call it a night.

14
Ace

After winning a jackpot on a slot machine, I head up to the suite to find Harlow. Today was an unforgettable experience in many ways. Winning some money is the perfect way to end the night. Well... I can actually think of a better way.

I see her silhouette on the balcony illuminated by the Vegas lights. While I enjoyed today, the only person I want to spend time with is right in front of me.

"Sunshine..." I place my hands on her hips and kiss her neck.

She leans into me and smiles. "I felt you before I saw you."

I wrap my arms around her shoulders, resting my chin on top of her head, and watch the fountain dance below us as the lights change colors. "Did you have a good night?"

She places her hands on my forearms. "It was fun. Marisa took off her panties, and the dancer put them in his mouth. She nearly went home with him at the end of the show. Quinn and I had to talk her out of it while Sevyn cheered her on."

I laugh. "That sounds like something Sevyn would do."

"Yeah, they're in the room now... hopefully sleeping. Poor Quinn had to help me get them both back to the room."

"You could've called us. Zane would've picked up Sevyn's drunk ass."

"No." she turns around to face me. "We got them up here..." Her voice trails off as her brow furrows. "Why is there glitter in your beard? And your right eye looks... red."

"Oh... uh. A stripper—" her eyes narrow "—wait, let me finish. A stripper whipped her hair in my face, nearly blinding me. She almost knocked herself out too when she hit the side of her head on the beer bottle I was holding with her aggressive ass hair flip. Then she started crying, telling me it was her first night dancing." I let out a sigh. "Your husband isn't about that life no more."

She glares at me before she tosses her head back with laughter. "Please tell me you tipped her!"

"I did out of fear she'd come near me again." Harlow laughs harder. "Yeah, yeah. Hilarious." I smirk. "What else did you get into?"

"Me?" she asks, swallowing. "Oh ya know, just a show with the girls... got carried up on stage by a stripper, possibly flashed hundreds of people my vagina, and then I got a lap dance from him in a tiny blue speedo before I nearly died of embarrassment. Your wife isn't about that life either and apparently never was."

"You got a lap dance." I raise my brow, "And I got blinded? Something isn't right."

She buries her face in my chest, laughing, and wraps her arms around my middle. "I'll give you a lap dance," she purrs, looking up at me.

"Mmm... I've only had one thought all night." I turn her around, grabbing her hips, and pulling her flush against me. I wrap my hand around her neck and kiss it while my other hand squeezes her breast. A moan spills from her lips that makes my dick twitch.

"Being inside you has been my only thought all night," I whisper in her ear before grazing my teeth along her neck.

Rucking up her skirt, I shove my hand between her legs, rubbing my fingers along her wetness. She grips the balcony railing, spreading her legs apart for me as she rests her head against my chest, melting into my touch. Her wetness drips down my fingers when I dip them inside of her warmth. Pulling them out, I rub her clit in slow circles, coaxing her to unravel for me as I unbutton my pants with my free hand. Once they're undone, I caress her curves that I've committed to memory. Her skin feels like velvet beneath my fingertips. Brushing her hair aside, I trail kisses along her shoulder and across her back and see goose bumps break out on her skin as she shivers.

"Acyn..." she whimpers as her knees buckle and she grips the railing a little tighter. I wrap my arm around her waist to keep her steady. Her soft moans become louder, and she makes a strangled noise.

"Don't hold back, Sunshine. I want to hear you call out my name."

She cums, calling out my name. I keep one hand on her clit while gripping the back of her neck and bending her forward with my other hand. As she's cumming, I bury myself in her wetness. Her breath hitches, and I groan at the feel of her tight pussy around my dick. She hikes her skirt further up her hips, giving me a perfect view of her ass cheeks bouncing on my dick as I pound into her. I move my hand from between her legs to her hip and grab a fistful of her hair with my other.

"Harder, Acyn!" she pants, throwing it back for me.

I grab both of her hips and thrust into her, giving her what she wants and I need.

"Take all this dick, baby," I growl.

Her pussy puts my dick in a vise as she cums for me again. The tension that has been building all day finally snaps. I topple over the edge, holding onto her, seeing stars in my eyes as my climax shivers through me, and my cum spills into her. My thrusts slow as I ride out my orgasm. I bury myself deep inside her before leaning forward and kissing her back.

"I never thought I'd be cumming while enjoying this view," she says hoarsely, leaning forward and resting her head on the balcony railing.

"I'm all about adding to the experience," I say, pulling out of her and smacking her ass before covering it with her skirt.

She straightens up and turns around to face me, wrapping her arms around my neck. "Wanna stay up the rest of the night drinking champagne and watch the sunrise?"

"I've got the goods." I pull a container with a pre-rolled joint out of my pocket that Kyrell gave me earlier.

"You're speaking to my heart." She smiles, and I kiss her lips.

We spend the last couple of hours of the night stretched out on a lounge chair, talking, sharing a joint, and finishing off a bottle of champagne until the sun rises.

Sunshine

Shortly after sunrise, I fell asleep laying on Acyn's chest that's now covered in my drool. Sitting up, I wipe the side of my mouth, and Acyn stirs. He throws his arm over his eyes and pulls me back on top of him.

"What time is it?" he asks in a raspy, deep tone.

"Uh..." I fumble around in his back pockets to pull out his phone. "It's just past noon."

"I'm fucking starving," he mumbles with his eyes still closed.

"Me too. Should we order room service and then we can get our shit together to see what everyone else is doing?"

"I'd be surprised if anyone is even coherent right now."

"Actually, I know for sure Quinn is." She's the only one who couldn't get drunk.

"Hit her up. If Kyrell's awake, then we can get some food with them. Unless you wanted to have breakfast in bed?"

"We can see who else is up because I'm sure we're not the only ones starving."

I climb off Acyn to find my phone sitting on the table next to my clutch. Grabbing it, I head to the bathroom and call Quinn as I turn on the shower. She picks up on the second ring.

"You're alive," she says happily.

"Barely," I say groggily. "Have you eaten?"

"I had a smoothie, but Kyrell just woke up and said he needs food."

"Is anyone else up?"

"Nope. Just Ky and I."

"Do you wanna go get food together?"

"Of course. I'll tell Kyrell. Want to meet in the lobby?"

"Yeah, give us twenty minutes to shower and get our shit together.

"Sounds good. See ya soon."

I hang up the phone, strip out of my clothes, and step into the shower. Acyn comes in after me, pressing me up against the shower wall.

"I told them…" he kisses me, "twenty…" he kisses me again, "minutes."

"Then we better be quick, Sunshine."

We head back up to the suites after lunch. Quinn and I decide to wake up the girls. Sevyn is in the shower, but Marisa is nowhere to be found. Her bag and phone are where we left them last night on the counter.

"Have you seen Marisa?" I ask Sevyn as she comes out of the shower, drying her hair.

"No, to be honest, I don't remember much after we got food last night."

Quinn laughs. "I bet you don't. We had to carry you back up here."

"I'm sorry." She cringes. "She's not in her room?"

"No. Her bag and phone are still here, too."

"Maybe she went out to grab some coffee or something." Sevyn sits at the table to apply her makeup.

"Mmm… I don't know. I think she would've said something." Quinn says.

"What if something happened to her?" I look around the room.

Sevyn sucks her teeth. "Please, I know she was just as drunk as I was. If she went anywhere, she didn't go far."

"She has a point, Harls. Let's ask the guys if they saw her."

We head across the hall to the guys' suite. Kyrell and Acyn are watching something on TV when we enter the room.

"Have either of you seen Marisa?" Standing in front of them, I block their view.

"No. Is she not in her room?" Kyrell asks.

"She isn't," Quinn says, looking around the suite.

"Oh my God. What if something happened to her? We shouldn't have left her alone." I pace the room. "Where could she have even gone? She was shitfaced."

"Chill, Sunshine. This isn't an unsolved mysteries episode."

"No," I point my finger at him. "But they always start like this."

"Normally I'd think Harls was being dramatic," Quinn says. "But she left her phone in the room."

Marisa rarely goes anywhere without her phone. I left it on the counter last night because she has a history of sending drunk calls and texts. But even then, she would've grabbed her phone.

"Did you see her after we carried her to the room?"

"No, I spent the night here with Kyrell. I'm actually impressed she could get up after we got her in bed."

"Marisa can hold her alcohol." I sit on the armrest next to Acyn on the couch. "It's not like her to not say anything, though."

"Let's ask the other guys." Acyn says.

Zane enters the living room. "What'd I miss?"

"Did you see Marisa last night or this morning?" Acyn asks.

"No... I probably wouldn't remember, anyway. I was high and drunk by the time we got back to the room. Went straight to bed." He shrugs, leaning against the counter as he twists the cap off a bottle of water.

"You sound exactly like Sevyn." Quinn smirks.

"We're married for a reason." He smiles before downing the bottle of water. "Maybe Grey saw her? Ash was talking to some girls at the casino the last time I saw him. I don't even know if he came back last night."

"I can—" Kyrell starts but is interrupted by the door opening.

Greyson comes into the suite, dripping sweat. He stops in his tracks, slowly removing his earbuds as we look at him. "Um... am I gonna need a lawyer?" he asks.

"Nah, we're just trying to find Marisa," Kyrell says. "Although we're not sure she's lost. And why the fuck are you working out on vacation?"

"For real, bruh, why?" Zane asks.

"Selene," Grey grumbles.

"Did you happen to see Marisa while you were out?" Acyn asks Greyson.

"Marisa? No. The last time I saw her was with you two last night," Greyson says, pointing at Quinn and me.

The door of the suite opens again. I hold my breath, hoping it's Marisa. "Oh, it's just you," I say as Sevyn appears.

"Damn, what a warm welcome." She laughs and heads for Zane, giving him a kiss. "Still haven't found our girl, yet? I'm sure she's fine."

"No, we—"

"For the love of god, can you guys keep it down? Some of us have hangovers," Asher says as comes out of his room, pulling a shirt over his head.

"Have you seen Marisa?" Acyn asks. "None of us have seen her."

"Have I seen Marisa?" He smirks. "Have I seen—Risa, love!" he hollers from where he's standing. My eyes widen as I look at him and then at Quinn, who looks just as shocked as I do. "Come out here so they can see you're alive and well!"

It's silent as we all look at each other in disbelief that this is actually happening.

"Risa?" Sevyn asks. "Is Risa Maris—"

"I'm gonna fucking kill you, Ash!" Marisa screams and seconds later she comes out wielding her stiletto from last night dressed in Asher's sweats and t-shirt.

Asher jumps over the back of the couch, trying to get away from her as he laughs.

"They... slept together?" Quinn gasps as we watch Marisa attempt to wipe Asher off the face of the earth.

"I'm better off missing than admitting to ever having fucked you!" She lunges at him and smacks him with her shoe. Asher's faster and runs aways from her to hide behind Kyrell and Acyn who are laughing hysterically. They move to the side.

"You did this to yourself, man." Acyn laughs.

"Oh, c'mon baby," Asher says as he stands behind a chair, holding his hand out in front of him. "You know you needed the release as much as I did."

Marisa grabs the TV remote off the couch and hurls it at him. He isn't fast enough for her anger, and it hits him square in the forehead.

"Fuck!" he shouts, falling to his knees. "You know I like it rough." He groans, rolling around on the floor, holding his forehead.

Zane and Sevyn are laughing so hard they're wheezing. Greyson comes out of the bathroom with his toothbrush hanging out of his mouth, eyes wide, wondering what the hell he missed. Acyn and Kyrell haven't stopped laughing since Marisa hit Asher with her stiletto. And I'm in shock, along with Quinn, that Marisa actually slept with him after all the shit she talked.

"I can't fucking stand you!" Marisa screams. "I told you not to say shit! Do you wanna tell them how you lasted less than a minute the first round?"

"Wait... you fucked him more than once?" I ask, biting back a smile.

"I had to," she says defensively, "so I could get off properly."

"Don't lie on my dick, Risa!" Asher yells, getting up off the floor. He seems more pissed off about her saying he lasted only a minute than the fact she just hit him with the remote. "I had you saying my name like I'm your God." He ducks behind the couch as she hurls her shoe at him. She misses this time. "Just admit you enjoyed yourself!"

Quinn turns to me. "He has a nickname for her?"

"I've had better!" Marisa screams before I can answer.

Quinn, Sevyn, and I exchange a look, knowing damn well that's a lie.

"Really?" Asher smirks. "I couldn't tell from the way I just made you cum for me less than twenty minutes ago."

"Um..." I say, unsure of what to do. Quinn looks at me, cringing, and shrugs.

"This is better than reality TV," Zane says.

"Hell yeah, it is." Kyrell laughs.

"Keep your fucking trap shut!" Marisa screams at him, and I step in front of her before she can lunge at him again. Her chest is heaving, and I imagine this is what murder looks like in someone's eyes.

"Marisa..." I grab the sides of her face. "Look at me. You've gotta calm down. It already happened. Let's go back to our room, yeah? We can talk shit about Asher."

"Hey!" Asher says from behind me.

"Say another fucking word, Asher, and I swear to the Devil and all things unholy, I will shove that stiletto up your ass," I say to him without taking my eyes off her. "Marisa, let's go."

"I—" Asher begins.

"Leave it, Ash." Acyn warns him. "You've said enough."

"You're a real dick, Asher. You know that?" Quinn says, wrapping her arm around Marisa and following us out the door.

"It was just for—"

"Some shit isn't just for fun, Asher." I scoff, rolling my eyes. "Not everyone pretends to be devoid of emotion and disconnected like you."

I guide Marisa out the door with Quinn on her other side and Sevyn right behind us. It was funny at first until Asher kept going and putting intimate details out there for all of us to hear. When we're out in the hallway, Marisa turns around and hugs me. She lets out a sigh and pulls Quinn into the hug.

"Get in here, bitch." Marisa says to Sevyn. She laughs and wraps her arms around us all. "Fucking Vegas. Thanks for getting me out of there, but can I tell you guys a secret?"

"I–I'm not sure what other secrets you're withholding that Asher didn't just put on the table..." I say, pulling away from her and opening the door to their suite.

"Yeah... what more are you not saying?" Quinn asks.

"I hate to admit it..." Marisa lets out an exasperated sigh, "but Asher has a big dick, and he knows how to use it."

We fall into a fit of laughter as I kick the door shut behind us.

15
Sunshine

That afternoon, I learn more about Asher than I ever cared to. It's one of those things you don't want to know, but you're curious about how it happened.

"Wait... so it's clear the dick was phenomenal, but how did you end up in his bed in the first place?" I ask as we sit huddled on the couch after ordering some snacks and room service.

"I woke up dying of thirst, and there was no ice. When I went out to the ice machine, Asher was coming down the hallway. Our casual conversation turned into him taking me to his bed." She shrugs, putting a piece of chicken into her mouth.

"I feel this has been building for a while," Quinn says.

"Yeah... that back and forth between you guys was bound to explode," Sevyn adds.

"He's arrogant, but... he's also so goddamn sexy. With those full, soft lips, honey brown eyes, smooth brown skin, and his muscles... the muscles!" She clutches her chest. "His abs are just," she does a chef's kiss motion with her hand, "and then his face. Why are all the gorgeous men assholes?"

"You're gonna fuck him again, aren't you?" I snort with laughter. Sevyn and Quinn laugh hysterically.

"Look, I'm not gonna make a liar out of myself by saying yes or no. It's on a case-by-case basis at this point," she says, not looking any of us in the face.

"If you wanna fuck him, fuck him! We support you!" Quinn says. "Kyrell and I started out in a friend's with benefits situation. And now..." she puts her hands on her belly.

Marisa looks at her with wide eyes. "I need to buy Plan B now that you mention it."

I fall back onto the bed, cracking up. "For fuck's sake, Marisa!"

"Aye, at least get him to pay for it," Sevyn says with laughter.

"Good idea, Sev." Marisa points at her. "Where's my phone?"

I sit on Acyn's lap, looking at all the pictures we took as we wait to board our flight. For our last night in Vegas, we went to dinner and a Cirque du Soleil show. It was the perfect way to end our weekend. If we hadn't eloped, I'm not sure we would've been able to enjoy this trip as much as we did. It was a relief to enjoy the time with our friends and not have the wedding looming in the back of my mind. Even Acyn's grumpy ass is looking forward to the reception.

Greyson was able to get us some deeply discounted tickets since he's a pilot, which means we're flying first class. They call for us to board and Acyn grabs our things. Quinn and Kyrell are coming back to Seattle with us so Quinn can help me with reception stuff. Marisa wanted to come too but has a yoga training that she's teaching the first half of the week. She'll be there a few days before the reception. Asher had to get back to L.A. for business meetings but will arrive the same day as Marisa. It'll be interesting to see what happens with those two. If anything more even happens at all.

We settle into our seats, and I rest my head on Acyn's shoulder. Vacations are always exhausting even if they are relaxed. This was our first time in Vegas, and I know it won't be our last. There's too much to do here to fit it all into a weekend. Acyn holds a piece of paper out to me as the plane takes off. I grab it from his hand and realize it's a check. My eyes meet his and he has his signature lopsided grin on his face. I look at the check in my hand and read the number.

"Are you–" I slide my sunglasses up to the top of my head. "Is this... legal?"

"Yes, I don't know who does illegal business with checks."

"You have a point. But... ten grand is a lot. Did you win this at your bachelor party?"

"Yeah, after the strip club incident, we hit up the casino. I placed a $4 bet on a slot machine. Mind you, I had lost nearly a grand before that."

I snort with laughter. "Does the grand matter when you won ten?"

"No, but it sucks losing money. You know how I am."

Acyn is excellent with money management. He's not filthy rich, but money isn't something he has to worry about. He calls it comfortable. I call it well off.

"What are you gonna do with it?" I ask.

"We, Sunshine. Always we." He interlaces his fingers with mine and kisses the back of my hand.

I smile as butterflies ignite in my stomach. "What are we doing with it?"

"We talked about building a house and—"

I gasp, covering my mouth. "We're gonna do it? Now? Like as in soon?"

"Yeah, well, if you still want to."

"I love our house, but I would love for us to build one together."

"Let's do it then, Sunshine."

I squeal, wrapping my arms around his neck. After watching some home improvement shows after we first got engaged, I told him it would be fun to build our own house someday. Acyn bought the home we live in before we met with the idea he'd get married and have a family in the future. Now we're married, and I could see us raising a family there, but building a house from the ground up together would be a beautiful legacy. Acyn suggested we open a savings account specifically for this house we'd "someday" build. Over the past year, we've been putting money into it and now someday is here.

"You make all my dreams come true." I kiss him.

"Make sure you build a room for me." Kyrell smirks.

Quinn laughs. "Let them have their moment."

"Where's my house, Zane?" Sevyn asks.

"We have one that you—" Zane sighs, resting his head against the seat. "Thanks for setting such a high bar for the rest of us, Ace. I always appreciate it." He smirks.

After a hectic morning at work, I finally take a moment to sit down at my desk and breathe. My phone rings. I let out a sigh, wishing for a moment of calm. Glancing at the screen, I see that it's Gloria.

"Hi, Gloria."

"Good morning, love. How was your trip?"

"Good." I ease back in my chair. "Acyn and I had an amazing time with our friends."

"I'm happy to hear that," she says warmly. "Are you guys ready for the reception?"

"Yeah." I let out a yawn. "We just need to go over who RSVP'd. I'm going to do that later today when I get a moment."

She hesitates. "If you want—well, never mind. I only wanted to call to check in on you."

Despite going with a small, intimate party, there's still a lot to do. Looking at my desk, I can already tell it's going to be a later night then usual as I prepare to be gone for two weeks.

"Gloria... if you're not busy, I'd love to have some help this week with preparations. Quinn—"

"Done!" she says, and I chuckle. "Whatever you need, consider it done."

Things may have been rocky with the original wedding plans, but I want her to be involved. With her, Quinn, Sevyn, and Ava—I know I won't have to worry about a thing.

"Thank you so much, Gloria. There's more to do than I expected before we leave for our honeymoon."

"You two are leaving right after the reception?"

"Yes, we'll catch our flight about three hours after it ends. So straight to the airport after." I make a mental note to begin packing our things tonight.

"No pressure, but I'm hoping for more grand babies soon."

I chuckle, biting my lip. "I'll be sure to tell Acyn."

"Alright, darling. I'll keep you updated. Love you."

"Love you too."

Hanging up the phone, I toss it on the desk. I got my IUD removed shortly after our engagement party. Not because we wanted to have a baby, initially, but because it was time to get it replaced. When I told Acyn about it, we talked about kids and when we wanted to have them. We realized there's nothing holding us back. Instead of getting a new IUD put in, I decided to stop birth control. The doctor told me it could take a few months for me to get pregnant. We decided if it happens, it happens. But it's been more than a few months and in the back of my mind, I can't help but wonder if we'll ever have kids. I think I'd be more worried if I were tracking my fertility and we were actively trying to get pregnant. But it's not something I think about until someone mentions us having kids. Then I quietly obsess about it for a while before it falls into the back of my mind again.

Like right now, as Acyn strides into my studio with Kyrell at his side. A smile pulls at my lips. "To what do I owe this pleasure?"

"Mom said you sounded stressed and scolded me for not helping."

"Don't you have work to do?" Getting up from my seat, I give him a kiss.

"Do you think she gives a damn about that?" He imitates her voice. "You can't just sit back and let her do the work, Acyn."

I snort with laughter as I give Kyrell a hug. Gloria knows Acyn spoils me, but she never misses a chance to tell him if she thinks he's falling short.

"And I brought food." Kyrell places a bag on my desk.

I grab the bag and the smell of tacos wafts out of it. "You brought me tacos? I love you forever."

"I know." Kyrell grins, taking a seat and propping his feet up on the desk.

"He didn't even get those." Acyn side eyes Kyrell.

"Can't let me have anything, can you Ace?" He shakes his head. "You've already married her. Let me have glory for the tacos."

"Not sure you've noticed, but Acyn has a bit of a sharing problem."

"Well shit, so do I. What's up?" Kyrell throws his hands up in the air. "If we want to get technical, I was here first."

I roll my eyes, taking a seat on the couch. "You two are a mess."

Acyn knocks Kyrell's feet off the desk before he joins me on the couch. They fight like brothers and, to be honest, it's cute and makes my heart skip a beat.

He wraps his arm around my shoulder as I take a bite of taco. "Since my mom told me I'm a mediocre husband, do you need help with anything?"

I chuckle. "No, it's decorations and last-minute things for the reception. I don't think either of you wants to help with that."

"I feel I should tell you I'll help you with anything here, but you also know me well enough to know decorating isn't my forte."

"Yeah, it's a hard pass for me, too," Kyrell says, fiddling with things on my desk.

"Wow, you guys are so helpful," I tease.

"Does support count?" Acyn grins.

"It does. And that's all I need. I'm not worried about it. There's just a lot to do here before we leave."

"Do you need me to be your assistant for the day?" Kyrell flashes me a smile. "Models love me."

"Not sure how Quinn got past your arrogance, but God bless her," I say, and Acyn lets out a rumble of laughter.

"She knows all my toxic traits and loves me, anyway." He shrugs.

"Actually… if you want to assist me today, that would be great. I have a shoot with some babies. It could be good practice."

"Whatever you need, Harls."

"I really wish I could stay to see this, but I've gotta run back to my shop. Elijah is stopping by."

"Aw, Elijah!" I smile. "Tell him I said hi and he better be coming to the reception."

Elijah has been getting tatted up by Acyn since he was an apprentice. He is also the reason he nearly missed my twenty-fourth birthday, and Acyn makes sure to never let him forget that.

"I think he's afraid of you and wouldn't dare miss it." He kisses me and turns to Kyrell. "Don't make the babies cry, alright?"

"Fuck you. Children love me." Kyrell tries to punch Acyn's arm, but he dodges it.

"Later, Sunshine." He gives me a two-finger salute before leaving.

I finish eating my tacos. As I'm chewing, a thought occurs to me, "Kyrell, have you ever been around babies?"

He's been around Sevyn's kids, but they're older and do a lot for themselves. Kids under the age of one are entirely different. They're into everything. Basically a drunk, tiny, carefree human.

"Nah." He shrugs. "But how hard can it be?"

I toss my head back with laughter. "This is going to be interesting."

After a few hours of giggling, crying, and sometimes screaming babies, Kyrell beelines for the bathroom. I follow close behind him.

"Is that all they do?" Kyrell asks me as he vigorously scrubs his Gucci shirt with a wet cloth. "Shit, puke, laugh, and repeat?"

I laugh hysterically as he makes the shit stain on his shirt worse the more he rubs. One baby had a blowout in the middle of the shoot, and Kyrell was holding him.

He throws the towel into the sink. "Fuck. This is ruined. You knew this was going to happen, didn't you?" He smiles as he slips his shirt over his head.

Holding my stomach, I take in a deep breath and try to control my laughter. "How would I know a baby was going to poop on you?"

"I don't know. You seemed a little too eager to see me struggle with those babies."

"I thought your confidence would carry you through like it always does."

"Damn." He scratches his jaw, letting out a sigh. "I'm fucked, aren't I?"

"No! You're gonna be a great dad. Your kid is lucky as hell."

His carefree demeanor falters as his brow furrows. "Harls... I'm gonna be fucked up for the rest of my life."

"Is that how you see yourself? Fucked up?"

He crosses his arms, shrugging his shoulders. "Yeah... it is. Some days are alright and some days I miss my dad so much that getting out of bed is the last thing I wanna do."

After losing his dad only months ago, Kyrell has been struggling to keep his head above water. He's doing better than he was, but that doesn't mean it's easier. We unfortunately have losing our parents in common. I understand what he's going through on a soul level.

"Kyrell, you need to allow yourself some grace. You can have good days and shit days. And fuck anyone who says otherwise. You got people around you who can ease the load when it feels like it's too much. But I can guarantee you, no one sees you as fucked up." I lean against the counter next to him. "That's just a lie you told yourself."

"I have a tendency to do that." He chuckles.

"You know what?" I nudge his arm.

"What?"

"Your baby will love you as you are. Just like Quinn does. Like we all do."

He takes a deep breath. "Thanks, Harls." His eyes meet mine. "I'd hate to know where I'd be without you."

"We'd both be lost at sea. I'm always here for you, and I love you." I hug him and pull away, covering my nose. "You smell like baby puke and poop."

"I can't fucking help it." He laughs.

"C'mon, you're in need of a shower. Thanks for helping me today. It was fun to hang out with you."

"Anything you need, Harls." He wraps his arm around my neck as we head out to my car.

16
Sunshine

After the craziness of the week, I'm happy to be sprawled out on my dad's couch as he cooks lunch for us. I scheduled a half day because I thought I'd be running around taking care of last-minute wedding preparations. True to her word, Gloria handled everything with the help of Quinn, Sevyn, Marisa, and Ava. Since we'll be gone for two weeks, I worked late every night and am happy to have the rest of the day to breathe. Well... almost the rest of the day. One would think Vegas would've been enough partying, but our friends planned a get together tonight before our reception tomorrow.

I hear the front door open and Acyn appears a few seconds later with a small black bag in his hand. He presses a kiss to my forehead.

"Ooo, what did you get me?" I reach for the bag.

He moves it behind his back. "Not shit."

I cackle. "Damn! Why are you so aggressive?"

"I'm not." He grins as he sits on the couch. "It's something your dad asked me to pick up."

"From where?" I sit up, reaching for it again.

He presses the palm of his hand to my forehead. "Nowhere, nosy!"

I laugh, falling back against the couch. "You two are keeping secrets, and I intend to find out what they are."

"Good luck with that, Sunshine." He pulls my legs onto his lap. "Where's Felix?"

"Cooking. You know him, always making us some new recipe he found online." I smile.

He nods his head. "Are you ready for tonight?"

"I wanna know whose idea it was to throw a party the night before the reception."

"Take a wild guess."

"I know it wasn't Kyrell, so it had to be Asher."

"Bingo." He chuckles. "He'll use any occasion to be in the center of a party."

I groan. "Is this happening at our place?"

"I could tell him to have it at Greyson's, so we don't have to deal with the cleanup. That's where everyone's at right now, anyway."

"I love the way your mind works."

He pulls his phone out of his pocket and types out a text and his phone chimes a second later with a response. "Grey says he knows what we're doing, but he supports it."

I snort with laughter. "He's the real MVP."

My dad appears in the living room. "Ah, Ace, you're here." He smiles as Acyn gets up to give him a hug. "Did they have it?" my dad asks in a hushed tone.

"Yeah." He hands him the bag.

He glances at it before patting Acyn on the shoulder and giving him another hug. "Thank you."

"Just pretend I'm not here." I sit up on the couch.

They turn toward me, and Acyn has a glimmer in his eye. He's enjoying this way too much.

"Let's eat first, then we'll get to what's in the bag." My dad smiles warmly.

I roll my eyes at Acyn, who chuckles and interlaces his fingers with mine as we walk into the kitchen. My annoyance with them is quickly forgotten when the smells of what my dad has been cooking hits my nose and makes my mouth water.

"Whatever you made smells delicious."

"Philly cheesesteaks. You'll have to let me know how it tastes," he says as we sit down at the table. "Are you two ready for tomorrow?"

"Yes," we answer in unison and laugh.

"Good." My dad chuckles. "I'm looking forward to it."

I grab my sandwich from the plate. "What will you be up to while we're gone?"

"I'm back to teaching. I'll be busier than I probably care to be, but I enjoy it."

"It makes me happy that you found something you enjoy doing." I smile at him.

"Me too, kiddo," he says before taking a bite of his sandwich.

I take a bite of my own, and it tastes better than it smells. "Mmmm..." I close my eyes. "This is perfection. We're gonna have to steal this recipe." I say to Acyn.

"Be my guest. Are you guys all packed for your trip?" my dad asks.

"Surprisingly, Harlow finished packing a few days ago." Acyn smirks.

"What?" my dad asks, shocked. "She did?"

"I'm not that bad, you guys." I roll my eyes. "We're going across the world. I had to be sure we're prepared."

Again, clothes aren't really on the agenda for the honeymoon, but I won't write off the possibility of sightseeing while we're there. We have access to a private beach and the bungalow has a butler and everything we'll need while we're there. It'll be two weeks of sun and healthy doses of my husband. Absolute bliss.

We clear our plates, and I insist on my dad letting Acyn and me clean up while he heads to the living room to relax. It doesn't take us long before we join him. He's watching *Lord of the Rings* kicked back in his recliner. It's the same one my mom got him the Christmas before she passed. He's kept it in wonderful condition over the years.

"I wanted to give you something." He sits up and grabs the little black bag Acyn wouldn't let me near, holding it out to me.

I take it from him and sit down on the couch. Acyn makes himself comfortable beside me. "Thank you, Dad." I smile.

The bag is tied at the top with a black velvet ribbon. I recognize the name 'Asterin' scrawled across the bag in gold. It's the jewelry shop where Acyn got my wedding ring custom designed. I pull a small box out and open it.

"Y-You..." My voice trails off as I glance at him, then back at the box. My vision blurs as tears pool in my eyes. I'm hesitant to touch the glinting contents. "I thought... it was still with her."

"When you and mom got in that accident..." He takes a steadying breath. I focus on him, wiping the tears from my cheeks. "They took off all her jewelry and gave it to me after... after she passed. I remember while I waited for you to wake up, all I could do was stare at this bag of her of her blood stained jewelry... remembering where each piece came from." He wipes away his tears. "I realized in that moment all you'd have are memories of her... pieces of her. Her necklaces I gave to you because—"

"I asked for them." When I was thirteen, I asked my dad if I could have her necklaces. I rarely take them off. There are four. All gold and varying lengths, with different gems and chains. The pieces are timeless, like my mom.

"Yes," he smiles. "But her wedding ring... I wasn't sure whether or not to bury her with it. In the end, I kept it because I felt she would've wanted you to have it for when you got married someday. Just like her wedding dress. Acyn helped with your ring size and got it resized for me. I know how you feel about your wedding ring—" I sniffle and laugh because I protect it with my life "—so I had it resized to fit on the ring finger of your right hand."

I get up and hug him tightly. There are no words to be said, only emotions to be felt. This is the most beautiful gift my dad could've possibly given me.

"Thank you, Dad. I love you."

"I love you too, kiddo. Mom would've loved Acyn. You're in good hands and deeply loved." He squeezes me back.

After a moment, we let each other go. I sit next to Acyn, giving him a hug and kiss. "I love you."

"I love you too, Sunshine." He kisses me again. "May I?" he asks, motioning towards the box.

He takes it from my hand, gets down on one knee, and slides it on my finger. It fits me perfectly. I crash into him, hugging him so hard we both tumble to the floor. My dad laughs as I press a kiss to Acyn's lips before rolling on my back and holding my hand up to look at the ring again. It has a cushion cut diamond in the center with two smaller diamonds on the side and a gold band. I get up and give my dad another hug.

Grabbing my hand, he looks at the ring. "She would be so proud of you. I know it hasn't been easy with her not being here during this time, but know she's always with you." He kisses my hand before pulling me into another hug.

I wish I could say the loss of my mother hurts less with time, but there isn't a day I don't miss her. When major events happen in my life, her absence is only amplified. There are days the void is gaping, and I fear it'll swallow me whole. But I have my dad, Acyn, my supportive family and group of friends who hold me up and love me fiercely. I like to believe they were all handpicked by her and placed in my life exactly when I needed them. She may not be here, but her love for me transcends her death, and I feel it around me every day.

The next afternoon, my phone vibrates with a text from Marisa.

Marisa: On my way, babe! Can't wait for you to see everything.

Gloria insisted on me getting my rest instead of waking up early to help setup for the reception. With Ava in charge of the décor, I know she will bring what I wanted to life and make it better than I dreamt. Acyn and I had a lazy morning in bed, but we had to eventually get up to get him a new button down since I ruined his original one on our wedding night. I'll gladly take the blame and do it again. He's off to Greyson's house to get ready with the guys, and I'll be here at our house with the girls.

"What dress are you wearing today?" he asks with his tux bag slung over his shoulder before walking out the door.

"The one I wore for our wedding. I'm donating the other one to Brides for a Cause. Why?"

"Because I want to unwrap you again. There's something about that dress." He gives me a devilish grin.

Tugging on the collar of his shirt, I pull him towards me until his lips meet mine. "I look forward to it."

He kisses me again before pulling away and looking into my eyes, tucking a curl behind my ear. "I'll see you soon, Mrs. DeConto."

"That sounds so good coming from you and—" There's a knock at the door. It's probably for the best. We have a reception to get to. "I'll see you soon. Love you."

Opening the door, we're met by Marisa, Sevyn, and Quinn.

"Ladies and Sevyn." He nods as he steps around them.

"Excuse you, bro! Am I not a fucking lady?" Sevyn throws her hands up.

"You're lucky Zane married your crazy ass is all I'm gonna say." He smirks, dodging her punch.

"Alright, Harls! Let's get you glammed up," Marisa says, stepping inside and grabbing my hand.

A short while later, the girls have me feeling like a Queen. My kinky curls are in a simple half up, half down style with a floral gold accent barrette. Quinn has made it look effortless, with soft curls cascading down my back, even though we started the hairstyle last night. With kinky curls, sometimes they need to be stretched in order to achieve the desired look, and Quinn did just that. For my makeup, Marisa kept it natural with nude colors, a soft shimmer, and a hint of rose gold to give me a glowing, dewy look. Sevyn treated me earlier this week to getting my nails and toes done. My nails are almond-shaped with a nude base and rose gold foiling details.

Once I'm ready, the girls change into their dresses. It was hard for me to decide on a color scheme for the wedding. Instead, I decided I wanted rose gold accents. Their bridesmaid's dresses are rose gold satin with spaghetti straps and a cowl neck. All of them look stunning. It causes their warmly hued skin tones to look they're glowing. Raven arrives to take photos as we're gathering in the living room. I couldn't be surrounded by a better group of women. I'm not sure that I'd be where I'm standing without them. They've been there for and have helped me in countless ways. I'm grateful to be sharing this moment with them. It makes me teary-eyed, causing me to sniffle.

"No!" Quinn shouts, tipping her head back, fanning her face. "Do not start crying. My pregnancy hormones will have me bawling at the mere mention of tears."

"I'm sorry!" I laugh. "I can't help it." A tear rolls down my cheek.

"Cry away, babe! We didn't use waterproof makeup for nothing." Marisa says with tears in her eyes.

"You look gorgeous, and I know I've said it before, but I'm so happy you're my sister-in-law." Sevyn pulls me into a hug with tears in her eyes.

Raven is snapping pictures of us in our feelings, and it makes me laugh. I can't wait to see these pictures. I know without a doubt, one of them is getting framed. Someone's phone chimes. It turns out to be Sevyn's.

"Car service is here," she announces. "Are we ready?"

"Absolutely."

Sodo Park is a building with a rustic, elegant atmosphere. It's industrial, yet romantic. I felt it fit Acyn and me perfectly. The walls are brick with aged wood floors, and large wood columns line the length of the venue with white curtains hung whimsically between them. Wood beams criss cross the high ceiling, and natural light spills in from industrial style windows.

The soft warm glow of the halogen bulbs, hanging on string lights from the ceiling, give an enchanting look to the place. With Ava's touches, it looks like a scene from a fairy tale. While the venue provided most of the décor, Ava designed the accent pieces to make it unique for our reception. There's a floral arch, set up behind the bride and groom's table, made of sunflowers, champagne colored roses, white peonies, ranunculuses, and greenery. They made my waterfall style bouquet of the same mix.

They covered the guests' tables with white tablecloths and floral centerpieces. And of course, there's a designated space for our guests to take photos. It's decorated in the same floral mix as the arch behind our table. This is more beautiful than I imagined in my head. Seeing it with the unique details elevates this space even further. I didn't think that was possible, but I expect nothing less from Ava.

"Do you love it?" Sevyn asks. They all look at me expectantly.

Before I can answer, we're met by Gloria, Ava, and Acyn's two older sisters. All of them cry when they see me. I'm not sure what the point of wearing makeup today is.

"My dear, you are breathtaking," Gloria says, wrapping me in a hug.

"Thank you."

"We are so happy you're a part of our family now."

"Gloria, you're going to make me really cry."

"I truly am happy for you two." She kisses my cheek.

"Now that we live closer, hopefully we can get to know each other better." Annalise, Acyn's oldest sister, smiles at me.

"Yeah, welcome to the family," says Nora, his second oldest sister, giving me a tight hug.

His older sisters recently moved back to the area. They're connected at the hip, much like Acyn and Sevyn. It's interesting how that worked out. Maybe now that they're older, and the age gaps aren't as noticeable, the siblings will all become closer.

Ava is holding Mercy as she hugs me. I asked her to be a bridesmaid, too, and she looks stunning in her dress. Sevyn made Emery and Mercy's dresses so they could match the bridesmaid's dresses. The only difference is that they have cap sleeves with a square neck and a bow in the back.

"I know why Acyn wanted to marry you on the coast all by himself," she says low enough for only me to hear.

I toss my head back with laughter, but still feel the heat creep up my neck. "Ava!"

"What?" She shrugs with a smile. "I can't blame the man is all I'm saying."

I kiss Mercy on the cheek, and she lunges for me. Catching her, I pull her into my arms. "Mercy, you look like a princess." She giggles and pats her dress.

"Alright, little girl. Harlow has to go find her husband. You two are walking in together, right?" Ava takes Mercy from my arms.

"Yes." My heart skips a few beats. I saw him only a few hours ago, and you'd think it's been days with the way my body is buzzing with excitement.

"He should be on—"

Her sentence is cut short as he appears in the hallway with his entourage, and his eyes immediately find mine. He is so handsome it nearly hurts. Everyone else seems to fade away as he nears, wrapping his arm around my waist and pulling me towards him until our lips meet.

"Sunshine, you look more gorgeous with each passing day."

"I'm pretty damn lucky myself." I splay my hand across his chest and kiss him again.

Gloria embraces us both in a hug. "You two..." are the only words she can find as tears stream down her cheeks.

"Mom..." Acyn says, wiping them away.

"I'm just so happy for you both." She wipes her cheeks. "Okay." She takes a deep breath in an attempt to compose herself. "Felix will announce you two, and then you can come in."

"Sounds like a plan." I smile.

She leaves us alone again. I can hear the chatter and laughter of our nearest and dearest gathered in the reception area. I'm excited to spend the next few hours with them, celebrating our love. Acyn cups my face in his hand, holding me flush against his body as I look up into his eyes. He caresses my cheek, not saying a word as we look at each other. We stay like this until my dad saying our names pulls us from our moment.

"Ready, Mrs. DeConto?"

"Always, Mr. DeConto."

He interlaces his fingers with mine as we walk out to the cheers of our family and friends.

17
Ace

I was dreading the reception until I realized I get to be with the most gorgeous woman to walk this earth. I may be a little bias, but she's as close to heaven as I can get without dying. Everything about her is graceful from the way she walks, talks, and even how she snorts when she laughs. She makes everything near her glow a little brighter.

As I'm whispering something in Harlow's ear, I feel a tug on my suit jacket. I look down to see Emery, flower basket in tow, and her big brown eyes looking up at me.

"Uncle Ace, will you dance with me, please?"

Kneeling, I smile at her. "Of course, I'll dance with my favorite girl."

I've danced with her countless times tonight, but it's hard to say no to the twins. Yeah, I'm pretty much fucked when Harlow and I have kids. They'll want for nothing, and I can't wait to give them everything. I twirl Emery out onto the dance floor. She giggles as her dress spins out around her.

"Uncle Ace, will you bring me back a present when you leave on the airplane with Harlow?"

I chuckle. "What do you want?"

"A seashell. Like a mermaid."

"I think I can manage—"

"And pearls, too."

"Pearls?" I ask, raising a brow. "Did your mommy tell you to ask for those?"

She nods. "Mommy said go big or go home."

A chuckle resonates in my chest. "Figured. I will bring you back seashells." Looks like I can say no.

"Pinky promise?" She holds up her pinky.

Hooking mine with hers, I say, "Promise."

"Okay." She smiles, turning around and skipping off in the opposite direction.

And that's how you get finessed by a four-year-old. Harlow stands next to me as I watch Emery skip away.

"She looks happy."

"Yeah, once I promised to bring her back a gift, she was done with me. I'm pretty sure all those dances were to butter me up."

"Smart girl." She smirks.

I grab her hand, twirling her around, and pull her back into my arms. "Please tell me it's time to go."

She tosses her head back with laughter. "You've been a good sport. We can go. I'm sure they'll stay until the drinks run out."

"Thank fuck." I let out a sigh. I've reached my social quota for the next two weeks, maybe years. All I want is her.

We make our rounds, saying our goodbyes. My mom announces for everyone to gather outside for our farewell. Of course, we couldn't leave quietly. I've never seen my mom so proud of me in my life and it was something I needed to see after the choppy waters we were on. Minutes later, Harlow and I are walking through a tunnel of sparklers held out by our family and friends as they cheer us on, shouting well wishes.

A driver stands outside of the limo, holding the door open for us to slide in. She drapes her legs over mine as we settle into the seat, letting out a sigh.

"What's on your mind, Mrs. DeConto?"

"I don't know if I like Sunshine or Mrs. DeConto more." She simpers.

I chuckle. "Ready to have two uninterrupted weeks together?"

"I've been ready since you proposed," she says, giving me a look.

I already know what time it is. Without looking, my fingers find the button for the partition as she straddles me.

"You look like pure unadulterated sin in that suit."

I push her dress up, exposing her thighs as I caress them. "To match your energy, I've wanted to be inside you the moment I saw you in this dress."

Her lips crash into mine as she reaches down between us, unfastening my belt. Her hands are on a mission to get my dick out of my pants. Pulling it out, she strokes my length, causing my head to lull back. Her touch feels like ecstasy.

She raises her hips enough to pull her panties to the side. Her lips meet mine again as she slowly lowers herself onto me. She moans. It's one of my favorite sounds. I grip her ass cheeks as she bounces on my dick. This woman is everything. She leans back, giving me easier access to massage her clit. Her moans grow louder as she gets closer to the edge. I'm not sure if this partition is soundproof, but I don't care because the look on Harlow's face right now is one I aim to see daily. She bites her lip, and I can tell she's on the cusp of her release.

"Cum for me, Sunshine."

And she does. Her eyes lock onto mine as she unravels for me, crying out my name. One of her hands grabs the back of my neck and the other grasps my shoulder as she rides me to my release. I match her thrusts, gripping her hips and finding my release a few pumps later as I spill into her. Harlow doesn't stop riding me, though. She likes to make sure her pussy gets every drop.

Once she's satisfied, her hips stop moving, and she rests her forehead against mine.

"To think," she says breathlessly. "I get to be lost in you for a lifetime."

I rub my thumb along her bottom lip. "I've been lost in you since you gave me that first shitty cup of coffee."

She laughs. "This is how we're starting our honeymoon?"

"Nah, you started it by riding me like a professional jockey."

"Can you blame me, though?" She wraps her arms around my neck.

"Hell no." I kiss her. "You can ride me any time, any place."

We feel the limousine come to a stop. Greyson's gift to us is a private jet flight to and from the Seychelle islands, which is the only reason we're leaving immediately after the reception. Asher covered where we'll stay while there. I think it's safe to say we've got the best group of friends. I climb out of the limo first and hold my hand out to Harlow. She takes it, climbing out after me.

"Alright, Sunshine. Into forever."

It took us a day to recover from our travels. Flying privately was a luxury, but we were in the air for nearly two days. When we landed for the final time, I was tempted to kiss the earth. Even Harlow, who loves to travel, was happy to not have to board another plane. When we arrived, it was nighttime, and we didn't really see much. As soon as we got to the bungalow, we crashed.

Now that we've had an adequate amount of rest, we're walking the white sand beaches as the turquoise waves lap at our feet. The picturesque view and the smile on Harlow's face make the long trip worth it.

"Did you want to do something today?"

"No. This is all I wanted. To be here with you."

Our only plans are to rest, have sex, and be beach bums. I'd say we're doing a damn good job.

"Actually, maybe we can find a local place to eat... with proper food. I appreciate the butler, but foo foo fancy food doesn't really cut it for me."

"You don't like that shit either?" Being waited on hand and foot isn't all it's cracked up to be.

She bursts out laughing. "No! I was thinking it would be a more authentic Seychelles cuisine, but it's a little too fancy for my blood."

"I thought you liked it and I wasn't gonna spoil your enjoyment. But shit, let's go find some little hole in the wall, mom and pop place."

"Please, because I'm gonna starve between inadequate meals and marathon sex."

I scoop her up in my arms, and she squeals with laughter as I start toward the bungalow. "I can't have my wife starving."

After I got us lost, although I'll never admit that to Harlow, we pull up to the restaurant she found online. It's one of the highest rated and the trip gave us an opportunity to see the island in daylight. I'm not sure if it was me taking a wrong turn or Harlow having to stop to take pictures of everything along the way that took us so long to get here.

Regardless, we're here, and my stomach rumbles at the smell of the food coming from the restaurant. Although, it's not really a restaurant. There's only a window to order from and then there are various picnic areas near it. At this point, I think anything will be better than the food from where we're staying. We're only in the line for a few minutes before it's our turn.

"What can I get you?" the man asks.

"What do you recommend?" Harlow smiles, looking at the menu. "I want to fall in love with the food."

The guy smiles at her, and I don't miss the way his eyes take her in. "I think the food will fall in love with you."

Harlow tosses her head back with laughter. "A charmer."

"Let me know if it's working," he says. "I'll make you a plate of our best. How about that?"

"Sold." Harlow smiles as she steps to the side for me to order.

"What can I get you?" The man asks, all flirtatiousness gone.

"Mmm..." I say, pretending to study the menu. "I think I'll have... the same as my wife." I wrap my arm around Harlow's neck, pulling her toward me. The man is around our age and a little too fucking bold for my tastes.

Harlow leans into me as she giggles. "Calm down."

The man points the spoon at me, laughing. "I knew she was too pretty to be here alone. Let me guess, a honeymoon?"

"Yes!" Harlow says, holding her hand up to show him her ring.

"A very lucky man you are." He winks at me.

"I'm well aware." I kiss Harlow's temple

"The name is Michael, and you two are about to the eat the best food on this island." He smiles, resuming filling two Styrofoam containers with food.

A few minutes later, he hands us our containers. "What is it?" Harlow asks.

"Curry koko bernik, stir-fried squid, white rice, and papaya chutney."

"Squid?" Harlow asks, glancing down at that container with a look of uncertainty. I can't help but laugh at her.

"Try it." He reassures her. "You'll love it."

I pay him, and he tells us to visit again before we leave. I'm sure it's so he can see Harlow again. Flirty little fucker. If his food isn't good, I will let him know. But judging by the smell of it, it's going to be tasty.

"Not sure about the squid," she says, sitting down next to me at the picnic table.

"Live a little, Sunshine."

She pokes at what appears to be the squid with her plastic fork. I bite back a laugh. It takes her nearly a minute before she shovels some onto her fork and puts it into her mouth. She chews slowly before she lets out a moan.

"Ohhh my God!" she says with wide eyes. "Try it!"

Anytime she moans, I already know the food is going to be good. "I'm glad it is, because I would hate to have to fight your new friend."

She snorts with laughter. "So jealous for no reason."

I take a bite of food and want to shovel the rest of it into my mouth. "I have every reason to be with you."

Harlow smiles, resting her head on my shoulder, and then she digs into her food. When we finish, we order more to take back with us so we don't have to rely on the food the butler is trying to kill us with. We'll definitely have to figure something out with that, but this will do for now.

When we arrive back at our place, the sun is setting. Harlow grabs some blankets she somehow found on an island that is known for its perpetual summer.

"Let's watch the sunset."

I'm not gonna say no. I just follow her. Once on the beach, she settles between my legs, and I wrap my arms around her.

"Acyn..." she says after a few minutes of listening to the waves.

"Yeah, Sunshine?"

"You make me so fucking happy. I just needed you to know that."

I kiss the top of her head. "You've been lighting up my world since I met you with that brilliant smile and shitty cup of coffee."

"Fuck you." She laughs. "What if someone else told me I made shitty cups of coffee?"

"They would be forced to apologize and then suffer from burns because of the coffee I'd throw at them."

"But it's okay for you?" She snorts with laughter.

"Yes." I shrug. "Always has been. Always will be."

"You know... you're a jerk. But you're my jerk."

I let out a rumble of laughter before tipping her back and claiming her mouth. Her laughs quickly turn to moans.

"I'll be right back. My phone's ringing," I say to Harlow through the bathroom door.

Sevyn's name flashes across the screen. When I pick up, I'm met by Eli's little face.

"Uncle Ace..." he whispers.

"Eli." I chuckle. "Are you supposed to—"

"Hey! Who are you talking to, sir?" I hear Sevyn ask in the background. The phone clatters to the floor, followed by Eli's giggles and running feet.

Sevyn appears a few seconds later. "Oh, it's you." She smiles. "I'm surprised you answered and aren't balls deep in Harlow right now."

"For fuck's sake, Sevyn." I laugh.

"What? I've caught you two in the act before. I'm not new to this."

"Totally worth it. No regrets."

"So... why the fuck are you on the phone with your little sister?"

"Harlow's been sick today. I'm not sure what's going on."

"Did she drink the water?"

"Nope."

"It's probably something she ate. Maybe she got food poisoning."

"Nah." I shake my head. "I don't think it's that. We've had the same food. But she's been puking since she woke up."

She smiles. "Is she pregnant?"

"I—well... it's a possibility. She hasn't been on birth control and—fuckkkk, you're probably right."

"Is this a bad thing?" she asks.

"No. Hell, no. It would be the best thing. But Harlow thinks she has a bad case of food poisoning or something."

"Aw... bless her delusion." Sevyn snickers.

I hear the bathroom door open. "Aye, I gotta go. I'll talk to you when I get back."

"When you get back? I wanna know if she's pregnant now!"

"Gotta go, sis! Love ya." I hang up on her.

Harlow lays down on the bed, covering her eyes with her forearm. "Who was that?"

"Sevyn. Actually, it was Eli, but Sevyn caught him and took the phone."

She chuckles. "It was probably about their gifts."

"Yep..." My voice trails off as I stare at her.

She removes her arm from her eyes to peek at me. "What? Why are you looking at me like that? Do I have puke on me?"

"No... it's just that—do you think you could be pregnant... maybe?"

She stares up at the canopy draped over the bed. "Um..." she sits up, pressing her fingers to her mouth. For a moment I think she gonna puke again, but her eyes meet mine.

Her eyes widen as she gasps. "Acyn... I think I'm pregnant."

The look on her face is priceless. It's a mix of shock and wonder.

"Do you want to see if we can find a test? Or we can wait until after the honeymoon."

"Wait?" She slides off the bed. "Can you wait that long?"

"Fuck no, but I didn't want to sound pushy."

"Let's go find one then," she says with laughter. "I'm nervous now."

"Why? You'll be a great mom?"

"I don't know." She shrugs, slipping on her sandals. "I knew it would happen eventually with me not being on birth control anymore, but when it didn't happen the first few months... I kind of forgot about it. Well, until someone mentioned us having kids. I don't know. I wondered if we'd have kids or not. I put it out of mind instead of being hopeful, you know?"

I caress her cheek. "I didn't know you felt that way. You can always talk to me about anything, and I'll listen."

"I know." She kisses me. "And I'm grateful for that."

"Let's go see if you're knocked up or not."

"Knocked up?" She cackles. "Really?"

"Let's see if you're with child. Is that better?"

"No." She shakes her head as we walk out to the car. "That doesn't sound like you. Surprisingly, knocked up does, though."

"Of course, it does." I chuckle, shutting the door once she sits in the seat.

After a trip to the store, I'm sitting on the edge of the tub, waiting for her to pee on the pregnancy test.

"If it says I'm not pregnant, I'll probably cry. I thought of at least," she holds the stick between her legs, "fifty names. And," she pees, "I already have a vision of what their room would look like. The baby will be close in age with Kyrell and Quinn's baby, too."

"You thought of a hell of a lot in such a short time." I chuckle.

She places the cap on the end of the stick before washing her hands and flushing the toilet. "You're ready for a baby, right?"

"I'm ready for everything with you."

She kisses me. "And now we wait."

I realize my patience has its limits as we wait for the test to tell us if we're going to be parents or not.

"Check it." Harlow rests her chin on my shoulder as I reach for the test sitting on the edge of the sink. She looks away when I look at it.

"Sunshine," I put my arm around her shoulders, pulling her close to me, and hold it up in front of her face. "Look."

She looks at the test, then at me, and then back at the test. "I'm knocked up!" she squeals, grinning as she wraps her arms tightly around me.

When she pulls away, I pull her back to me and bring her lips to mine. This woman, wrapped up in my arms, has given me everything she possibly could. Her time, friendship, trust, love, soul, mind, heart...

every single thing she's willingly entrusted to me. I pick her up and she wraps her legs around me. My lips don't leave hers as I take her to the room. I need to feel her on me in every way. We're tangled as we crash onto the bed.

I reluctantly pull away from her to take off my jeans and t-shirt. She slides the straps of her sundress off her shoulders, pulling her arms out. I drag it down her body until it's sliding off her thighs, and she's fully exposed. I kiss her neck, grazing her skin with my teeth before sucking it into my mouth. Her hand grasps my length as she lines me up with her center. She gasps as I push into her. I watch as her eyes close and she bites down on her lip, taking every inch of me into her. My body shudders with the pleasure of her being wrapped around me.

"Harlow, look at me." I press a kiss to her lips as her eyes slowly open and look into mine. "You have my soul, Sunshine."

"Acyn..." she lets out a breathy moan as I move inside her.

She hooks one leg around my waist and the other she places over my shoulder, allowing me to plunge into her. I grip her ankle as I sit up, watching her breasts bounce and my dick slide in and out of her. She brings her hand down between us until her fingers are on her clit. I groan as I watch her massage herself. I love watching her. Heat pricks my skin as I feel the release I only find in her building in my core.

Harlow's breathing is ragged as she nears her climax. She's rubbing her clit faster, harder as she cries out with pleasure. Her eyes snap open, locking onto mine as her pussy tightens around my dick as she cums for me.

"Goddamn," I grunt. "You're so fucking tight."

She opens her legs wider for me. I grip her hips and thrust into her as she kneads her breasts and rubs her nipples. The sight of her beneath me, open for me, is my undoing. My release rips through me, causing my body to shake with pleasure as my hips stutter and breath hitches. I pump every drop into her, completely satisfied. She closes her eyes with a smile on her face, letting her body go limp. I collapse beside her and pull her into my arms.

"Can't believe you're knocked up." I chuckle and she bursts out laughing.

18
Sunshine

Later that day, we find ourselves on the beach, ready to watch another sunset. We spent the afternoon in a tangled mess of limbs. I'd still prefer to be naked and wrapped up in his arms, but we had to eat and to be honest, the sunsets are worth watching every day here. I relax on the blanket next to Acyn, resting my head on his shoulder, enjoying the warm breeze brushing past our skin and the sound of the ocean waves kissing the shore.

"Are we announcing this now or later?"

I sit up, getting a better look at him. "You want to announce it now?"

"Hell, yeah." he says, splaying his hand across my stomach. "Unless you don't want to."

"No, no. I do. You rarely willingly want to share personal things with people."

"Yeah, but I want everyone to know we're having a baby." He pulls me onto his lap.

"Your excitement is so damn cute." I kiss him. "Let's tell everyone then. But I think we should tell our parents first."

"Yeah." He nods. "My mom would kill me if she had to find out online.

I toss my head back with laughter. "She would."

The call back home to our parents is short, as it's much later there. I thought Gloria was going to faint from excitement. Our dads are much calmer, but there wasn't a dry eye. I realize we'll be lucky if we get to hold our own child after they're born.

When we hang up, I pull the tripod out of my bag and set it up in the sand. The vibrant turquoise ocean and setting sun will be our backdrop. I'm wearing a barely there, fluorescent yellow bikini and

Acyn, to my pleasure, is shirtless, wearing black swim trunks. He brushes the curls out of my face that were swept up by the wind.

"Ready?" I ask, straddling his lap.

He presses a kiss to my stomach before looking up at me, and I tangle my fingers in his curls. Sitting on his lap, I bring my lips to his, dipping my tongue into his mouth as we get lost in the bliss.

"Let me turn off the camera before we make a movie."

"I'm not opposed," he says, with his hands palming my ass.

"Of course not," I smirk. "You live for the thrill." I scroll through the pictures.

"Do you have—"

I press a finger to his lips. "Did you not just say you wanted to announce this with a picture?"

"Yes, I did," he says. "But—" I raise a brow "—take your time, Sunshine."

I snort with laughter as he swallows his words of protest. I hand him my phone. "Pick one or some. I can never decide."

Within seconds, he says, "this one."

I peer at the screen. "That's my favorite, too." He's kissing my stomach, my hands are in his hair, and I have the biggest smile on my face. The setting sun gives the illusion the water is glittering behind us.

"And these two," he adds, showing me. The second one is of him looking up at me, and there's a look of undeniable happiness on our faces. The final picture is of us in silhouette, kissing with the sun setting behind us.

"Perfect." I smile at him. His phone chimes a few seconds later and I hand it to him. "We'll upload at the same time. What should the caption be?"

I watch as he adds the caption 'knocked up'. He laughs as he does it, and I giggle as I type out the same.

"Alright, let's put it out there, Sunshine."

We hit the check at the same time. Not even thirty seconds later, our phones chime with notifications. I grab his phone, powering both of them off, and toss them to the side.

I wrap my arms around his neck. "It's out there. We'll talk about it with everyone else when we get back. Now, where were we?"

"Exactly where we want to be," he says, pulling me on top of him as my lips crash into his.

Our happy ending isn't really an ending, it's only the beginning of forever.

Keep in touch with me.
Scan the QR code above to sign up for my newsletter and follow me
on social media for regular updates.

6b738242-a921-47fd-a40a-0514709e73f2R01